Neptune's Fortune

ALSO BY JULIAN SANCTON

Madhouse at the End of the Earth

Neptune's Fortune

The Billion-Dollar Shipwreck and the Ghosts of the Spanish Empire

JULIAN SANCTON

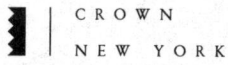

CROWN
NEW YORK

CROWN
An imprint of the Crown Publishing Group
A division of Penguin Random House LLC
1745 Broadway
New York, NY 10019
crownpublishing.com
penguinrandomhouse.com

Maps by David Lindroth Inc.
Border art on title and part opener pages by Shutterstock.com/Bemidji

Library of Congress Cataloging-in-Publication Data has been applied for.

ISBN 978-0-593-59417-9
Ebook ISBN 978-0-593-59418-6

Editor: Kevin Doughten
Editorial assistant: Jessica Jean Scott
Production editor: Chris Tanigawa
Text designer: Amani Shakrah
Production: Heather Williamson
Copy editor: Elisabeth Magnus
Proofreaders: Karen Ninnis, Lisa Lawley
Indexer: Stephen Callahan
Publicist: Gwyneth Stansfield
Marketer: Chantelle Walker

Manufactured in the United States of America

1st Printing

First Edition

The authorized representative in the EU for product safety and compliance is Penguin Random House Ireland, Morrison Chambers, 32 Nassau Street, Dublin D02 YH68, Ireland, https://eu-contact.penguin.ie.

For the seeker

Contents

Part III: A Brief History of Treasure Hunting

Part IV: The Search

Roger Dooley's Search Box Area

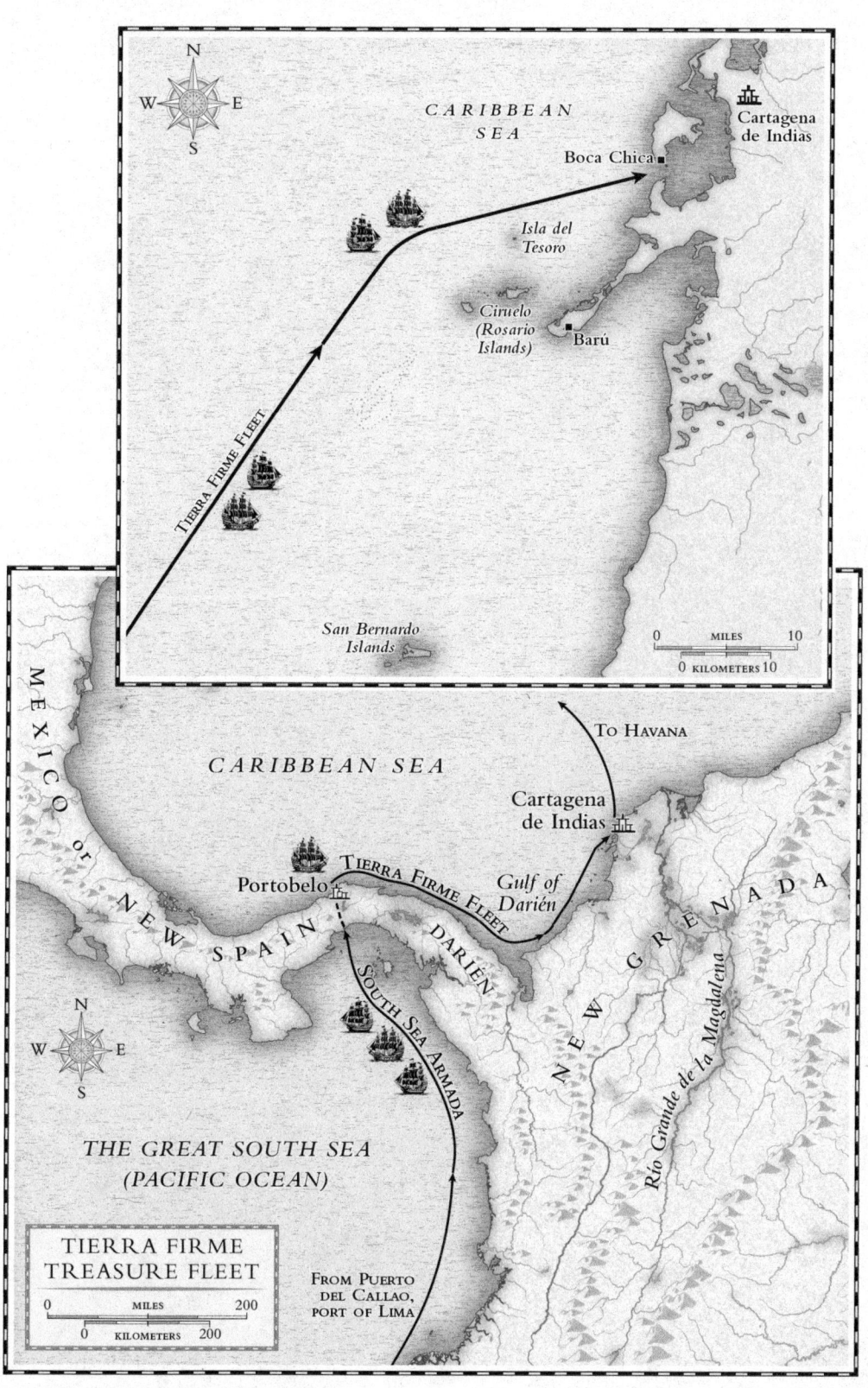

Neptune's
Fortune

Prologue

I first heard of Roger Dooley from his enemies. They told me he was a criminal, but no one could make clear the nature of his crime. That the self-described maritime archaeologist was, in fact, an avaricious treasure hunter went without saying for his detractors. Some tried to convince me that he was a grave robber. Others suggested he could be a drug trafficker, maybe even a human trafficker. "Roger Dooley," they said, was likely not even his real name. One rival claimed that he was a thief, that he had stolen the coordinates of his greatest discovery. I was told Dooley was "a crackpot," "a charlatan and a fake," a "bullshitter."

The tale of a supposed con man who had found a billion dollars in gold and silver on the seafloor sounded irresistible, but it didn't escape my notice that the sources of those epithets included his competitors in the pursuit of one of the most coveted archaeological sites in history, often called the Holy Grail of shipwrecks. The wreck was said to contain what officials in Colombia referred to as "the biggest treasure in the history of humanity," which would become the subject of a vicious custody battle between Spain, Colombia, titans of finance, and the Indigenous peoples from whose ancestral lands the ship's gold and silver had been taken centuries before.

Since Dooley had never explained how he'd done it—in part because he was bound by secrecy imposed from on high—the mystery around him only deepened. He had said almost nothing publicly in response to the barrage of criticism and conspiracy theories. Dooley was untraceable. A ghost. The special-purpose company founded by his mysterious English investor had long since taken down its website, and calls to its listed number went unanswered. Dooley had no academic affiliation. He was not on social media. Nobody who knew him would give me his contact information. After months of trying to track him down, I gave up.

One morning, I got a call from an unfamiliar number with a 305 area code. Miami.

"Hello?"

An ancient-sounding voice answered: "It's Roger Dooley."

I ran upstairs, put the phone on speaker, and started typing.

After all the outlandish claims I'd heard about Dooley, I had to ask myself whether I could trust what he was saying. But the more immediate challenge was to *understand* what he was saying. Dooley was born in New Jersey in 1944 and raised largely in Brooklyn before emigrating to Cuba as a teenager. He spoke imperfect English at a frenetic pace, with a thick accent and a slight stammer, in a desiccated rasp that sounded like a cross between Don Corleone and Ricky Ricardo played at double speed. Certain syllables bore faint traces of a Brooklyn inflection. Consonants for him were notional, in a manner typical of Cubans, who enunciate, as others in the Spanish-speaking world describe it, as if they have a hot potato in the mouth. At first, I could make out only a few scattered words. My notes from our initial conversations were nearly useless, littered with frantic question marks.

Adding to my confusion were his odd verbal tics. Many of his frequent, meandering asides, for example, began with "I said," regardless of who was speaking in the story, or whether he was even involved. (Those words could be hard to distinguish from the Spanish

o sea—roughly, "I mean"—which he liberally peppered into his
speech.) He often cut off sentences halfway through with "whatever"
or "anyhow," as if he were in a rush and details were unimportant. He
had a confounding habit of not using people's names, saying instead
"that guy you talked to" or "the Spanish guy." And when he cited a
number or a date or a dollar amount, he often tacked on numerous
alternatives: "Seventy, eighty, ninety million, a hundred million dollars
maybe." "In nineteen-eighty-two, three, five, something like that . . ."
The overall effect was an illusion of specificity that made it difficult to
pin him down on anything. I began to suspect that this was semi-
intentional, that it sprang from a second nature to muddy the truth.

I doubted whether I would ever learn the real story.

A few months later, I received an email from Dooley:

*You must plan a two-day visit to my house, to know me well if you
want to know how exactly I found one of the most important
shipwrecks in America.*

Thus began an exchange that would last several years, yielding
hundreds of hours of interviews, as Dooley unfolded his remarkable
story.

▪   ▪   ▪

Dooley's quest, the one that would come to consume him and indeed
to define his life, began in Seville, on a typically torrid day in July
1984. The thirty-nine-year-old archaeologist left his hotel after breakfast and made his way toward the Plaza del Triunfo, the city's central
square. He relished his morning walks through the Barrio Santa Cruz.
Shops were closed, tourists were sleeping in, and the sun had not yet
risen high enough to illuminate the narrow, labyrinthine streets. It
would soon become too hot to remain outdoors for long. He checked
his watch, a battered Rolex Sea-Dweller he never took off his wrist,
not even when showering or when exploring shipwreck-strewn

waters of the Caribbean. There was no time to dawdle: The doors of the archive would open soon.

Tall and wiry, with deep-set eyes and a conquistador beard, Dooley looked like a young Don Quixote and was imbued with a similar sense of purpose. He hurried through Seville's medieval maze and found himself at the foot of the cathedral, one of the largest in Europe, where the weight of Spanish history was as oppressive as the sun. Before him on the cobblestoned Plaza del Triunfo, past a minefield of horse droppings and a perimeter of palm trees, his destination: the General Archive of the Indies. A stately, two-story, seventeenth-century edifice, the archive stood as a temple to Spanish bureaucracy, containing four centuries' worth of records from the Americas—more than sixty million documents dating back to the time of Columbus, accounting for every conquest, every ounce of gold and silver stripped from the New World, every ship sent across the Atlantic, and every one that didn't return.

Dooley entered the palatial building, his footsteps echoing between the marble floor and the arcaded ceiling. He flashed his researcher's card to the guard on duty. Though he was born Roger Edward Dooley, in New Jersey, the document identified him under the more dashing alias of Roger Montañés Caballero, as he was known in Cuba. Caballero was his Cuban mother's surname, Montañés his stepfather's.

As it happened, Dooley was in Seville on Cuban government business. He was the chief archaeologist for a state entity called Carisub, newly formed on orders from President Fidel Castro in part to track down the many historic ships thought to have wrecked against the island's treacherous shores over the centuries and to pry out their riches. To many archaeologists around the world, the organization's emphasis on recovering treasure amounted to piracy, flouting international standards for the preservation of cultural heritage. Dooley himself had misgivings about the practice, which he feared would make him a pariah among legitimate archaeologists. But he felt he had little choice. He was raising two daughters in Cuba, where Castro ultimately controlled every sphere of human activity. The dictator had set his mind on claiming all the sunken treasure off his country's coast and would brook no competition. For Dooley, who had dedicated his professional life to finding shipwrecks, Carisub was the only game in town.

When he joined the company, in 1983, Dooley insisted to his colleagues that they should focus their efforts on finding a lost treasure galleon that was rumored to have wrecked in the shallows east of Havana in the late seventeenth century, in the clear waters just off the postcard-perfect white sands of Guanabo Beach. There were two ways to hunt for a colonial Spanish shipwreck in the Americas. You could start in the water, blindly towing a magnetometer or a side-scan sonar and investigating every hit, or you could start here, at the General Archive of the Indies, where many historic wrecks were thoroughly documented. In theory, the research approach was more efficient. In practice, though, it could be just as difficult to find clues in the Byzantine archive as it was to find treasure on the seabed, especially for the uninitiated. The classification system had hardly been updated since the 1700s. There was no comprehensive catalog, no index. "It's not like there's a shipwreck section," Dooley would later tell me. "You could spend twenty years there and not find what you're looking for."

For most of its existence, the archive had been a resource for scholars of Spanish colonialism. But recently, a more swashbuckling caste had begun to infiltrate its stacks. American treasure hunters—and Spanish researchers in their employ—had increasingly come seeking information that might lead to multimillion-dollar troves.

Dooley did not fit neatly into either camp. He had been tasked with locating a valuable wreck, but even if he found chests full of gold, he stood to gain nothing himself. All treasure would go to Carisub, and ultimately into state coffers. What Dooley dreamed of instead was the chance to excavate a galleon, a type of warship that for almost three centuries traversed the ocean, carrying men and merchandise to the New World and Asia and bringing unfathomable wealth back to Europe, forever altering the course of civilization on several continents. With their imposing bulk, elegant curves, colorfully painted sterns, and ornate decorations, the vessels were among the most distinctive and beautiful ships on the seas. Of the many galleons believed to have sunk in the Caribbean, only three had ever been found and identified, all of them ransacked by treasure hunters before they could be properly studied. Dooley had been calling himself a maritime archaeologist for more than a decade but had yet to conduct a by-the-book excavation of any kind. If he could lead the first thorough study of a Spanish galleon, it could help fill in an all-important missing chapter in world history. More importantly, it would make Dooley's name, a prize more precious to him than gold.

Dooley climbed the archive's grand staircase to the second floor and walked through a curtain to an area where desks were arranged under the high vaulted ceiling. He requested a file from the archivist and took his seat. Over the course of several years, the archaeologist had begun to understand the archive's chaotic ways. He was less intimidated by its befuddling organization and had grown accustomed to the antiquated spellings and the nearly illegible, unpunctuated scribblings of harried seventeenth-century officials. He came to recognize their various handwritings. "The king's scribe's was always beautiful, perfect," he said. "But most wrote like drunken doctors filling out prescriptions."

Since he'd begun delving into the archive the previous year, Dooley had confirmed that the galleon he was after was no fiction. Its name was *Nuestra Señora de las Mercedes,* the vice-flagship of the Caribbean treasure fleet, known as the Tierra Firme Armada. On the moonless night of March 13, 1698, its hold abounding with silver, the *Mercedes* struck a reef east of Havana and sank, according to records, "in four fathoms of water, a musket's shot from land."

The demise of the *Mercedes* and the investigations that followed generated reams of paperwork, which now told Dooley the rest of the story. He learned that all crew and passengers made it safely ashore, that much of the galleon's treasure was salvaged over several years, and that the unsubmerged top of the wreck was deliberately torched to prevent pirates from finding and looting it. Dooley believed there was little silver left. He also suspected that three centuries' worth of storms had fragmented the hull and dispersed its remaining contents over a large area.

He nevertheless resolved to learn everything he could about the ship, its history, and its afterlife in order to inform a possible excavation. To that end, he searched for references to the *Mercedes* stretching from ten years before its sinking to ten following the tragedy, beyond which point the collective memory of the event would have begun to fade.

The archivist handed him a heavy file—or *legajo*—labeled 377, from a section dealing with Caribbean affairs. Dooley untied the cord that held the bundle together like a Christmas present. He opened the hard, threadbare cover and was immediately transported to the early 1700s. Under the watchful eye of the archivist, he began to read.

The documents that Dooley was now handling were barely yellowed, their edges lightly frayed, the oak gall ink ranging from brown to black. With their high linen content, the sheets exuded no mustiness, only the faint sweet smell of aged paper. Summer temperatures in Andalusia routinely exceeded one hundred degrees, and though the underbudgeted archive lacked air conditioning, the dryness of the air in Seville had a preservative effect. ("It's why restaurants can leave a *pata negra* ham out in the open for days and it won't rot," Dooley hypothesized.)

For hours, in the suffocating heat, Dooley sifted through endless accounts of mundane colonial matters—church records, itemizations, legal disputes, petty complaints. His eyes strained to decipher the hurriedly ornate calligraphy, which often bled to the other side of the sheet, making the documents even harder to read.

Midway through the *legajo*, by which point the dullness of the pages would have discouraged all but the most obsessive of researchers, he discovered a packet of letters that would change his life. He noticed that they had been sewn together in a kind of booklet, an odd detail he would never forget. Reading through them, he understood that they had been sent to Havana from Santiago de Cuba, a city on the southeastern tip of the island. The missives dated back to 1708, the last year of Dooley's search. He expected to sort through it quickly, since little relevant information about the *Mercedes* was likely to have been withheld that long. But as he scanned the papers, words and phrases called out like siren song from the deep: "galleons," "battle," "English warships," "gold," "silver," "His Majesty's treasure," "everybody drowned" . . .

These letters were indeed about a shipwreck. But as he read deeper, he realized that it couldn't have been the *Mercedes*. The letters had been dispatched from Cartagena de Indias, the rich port city on the coast of what is now Colombia, just days after what appeared to have been a horrific tragedy. Dooley was perplexed: How, then, had the documents wound up in the records of Havana? At the risk of getting sidetracked, Dooley couldn't resist reading on. The story the letters told was more dramatic than any adventure novel he'd ever read. The reports, he learned, had been smuggled past an English blockade of Cartagena in a small, inconspicuous sloop with the instructions that the governor of Havana should immediately send them across the Atlantic ocean to Spain's Felipe V, to inform him of the loss of three of his ships and a literal king's ransom in gold and silver. Well versed in the period, as well as in the literature of treasure hunting, Dooley realized then that he had stumbled upon critical clues to the whereabouts of the most valuable shipwreck in history: the mythical *San José*.

Part I

The Last Days of the *San José*

I and my companions suffer from a disease of the
heart which can only be cured with gold.

—Hernan Cortés to Moctezuma's messenger

Chapter 1

The Graveyard of the Spanish

In surviving accounts, he is known only as the Frenchman. He was a prisoner aboard an English warship lurking off the coast of the Kingdom of New Granada—the imperial Spanish territory corresponding largely to today's Colombia—in search of vessels to plunder. For weeks the three-masted ship, part of a squadron of four, had been prowling the area, sailing far from shore to avoid detection. But in early May of 1708, the ship strayed close enough to land for the Frenchman to attempt an escape. When he sensed the opportunity, he climbed atop the bulwarks and threw himself overboard into the turbid, brackish waters where the Magdalena River spilled into the Caribbean Sea. It is unknown whether he jumped by daylight or under the cover of night. But had the English seen him, they would surely have done all they could to prevent him from reaching the shore alive.

Allowing his clothes little time to dry after the exhausting swim, he journeyed along the coast until he arrived at the port city of Cartagena de Indias and beheld its massive fortifications. Cartagena's defenses were among the most imposing in the Caribbean, designed to protect the formidable wealth within. Most of the riches taken from South America passed through Cartagena on their way back to Spain, and most of the African men and women forcibly shipped in to extract those riches passed through the city's slave market—one of the largest in the world.

The Frenchman walked beyond the ramparts into the city's bustling streets. Not long before, a French traveler wandering through Cartagena would have drawn sidelong looks, or worse. Decades of war between France and Spain had nurtured a profound mutual loathing. Just a decade earlier, the city had been ruthlessly sacked and set aflame by marauders under the orders of the French corsair Jean-Baptiste Ducasse. But in 1700, upon the death of Spain's heirless King Carlos II, France's Louis XIV installed his own grandson, Philippe, on the throne in Madrid, citing a circuitous line of succession. In the time it took for the news to spread across the oceans, the French and the Spanish had become allies in what would later be called the War of the Spanish Succession, perhaps the first truly global conflict. Bad blood was washed away. Once the butcher of Cartagena, Ducasse was suddenly recast as a heroic naval commander, entrusted to defend Spain's cities and ships against the English and the Dutch. The latter two countries were supporters of the Habsburg claimant to the throne, Charles of Austria. Having until then been allied with Spain, they were now the nation's enemies.

The English threat was precisely what the Frenchman was anxious to warn the Spanish authorities about. (One witness described him as a "deserter," which suggests he might have expected leniency in exchange for his information.) He was brought before Cartagena's governor-general, José de Zúñiga, who heard his declaration. "There are along these coasts four English ships," the Frenchman was reported to have said. "Two of seventy cannon, one of fifty, and one . . . which they call a fireship."

The escaped prisoner's report had a chilling effect on Governor Zúñiga. He had heard whispers of an English presence in the area, but none so specific. The danger could no longer be attributed to hearsay. The enemy ships' objective was all too obvious: to intercept the Spanish treasure fleet on its return from the fair in Portobelo, a harbor on the Isthmus of Darién (in what is now Panama), where galleons were currently filling their hulls with gold and silver.

For nearly a century and a half, the Tierra Firme fleet had sailed between Spain and the Caribbean every two years on average. The Spanish Crown relied on the regular influx of precious metals stripped from the New World to pay its troops and its many creditors, to sustain its empire, and to gild its palaces, churches, and wealthy men and women. Yet by 1708 it had been more than a decade since the last treasure fleet had come and gone. The convoy system had begun to collapse at the end of the seventeenth century as Spain's debts piled up, inflation spiraled, and the economy devolved into perpetual crisis. The war of succession delayed the dispatching of the galleons and merchant ships from Spain until 1706, and the constant threat of ambush in the Caribbean further prolonged their homeward voyage. Back in Madrid, Philippe, now King Felipe V, had grown desperate for the return of the galleons, which he expected would carry twelve years' worth of accumulated treasure. The English raiders, of course, would have had the same expectation.

It was clear to Zúñiga that the outcome of the war—the very survival of the Crown—could depend on the safe passage of the fleet. He ordered a scribe to make a copy of the Frenchman's declaration and entrusted it, along with corroborating accounts, to his thirty-year-old adjutant, Pedro de Fuentes, with instructions that he board a French sloop bound for Portobelo and hand the documents without delay to the captain general of the galleons, the Count of Casa Alegre.

Fuentes's westward journey took several days. While the bureaucrat did his best to avoid paying tribute to Neptune, sailors kept watch from the crow's nest, scanning the horizon for the English squadron. Only near the end of their voyage, in the Gulf of Darién, did they report anything unusual.

"Land!" bellowed a lookout, pointing off the port bow.

The sloop's captain, who knew the coast so well he could draw a map of it by memory, was taken aback. He was aware of no landmass at that latitude, at that bearing.

"Have a better look," he shouted, but the sailor could not make out the indistinct shapes in the distance. The captain sent another man to the top of the mast, yet the nature of the objects was no clearer to him—perhaps they were uncharted islands, perhaps they were foreign sails. The captain eyed the horizon. There was no time to investigate. Zúñiga's orders had been clear: The message he carried could not wait. They sailed on.

As the sloop approached Portobelo, Fuentes gazed at the crenellated bastions that guarded the town and still bore the scars of multiple raids over the previous century. The English buccaneer Bartholomew Sharp had attacked the town in 1680, when it was still recovering from the vicious assault led by his infamous compatriot the pirate Henry Morgan twelve years earlier. Somewhere in these waters, the body of Francis Drake lay in a lead-lined coffin, dressed in a full suit of armor.

For pirates and privateers, there was no more tempting target in all of Spanish America than Portobelo during the fair: It was here that galleons and merchant ships discharged goods from Europe (olive oil, wine, iron, textiles, clothing, books, armaments, etc.) and filled their emptied hulls with riches from all across the Viceroyalty of Peru, which covered most of South America.

Christopher Columbus had given this place its idyllic name: Porto Bello, beautiful harbor. This appellation would turn out to be grimly ironic. The picturesque setting that had so charmed the explorer from a distance—a placid haven nestled at the foot of misty emerald hills— turned out to be a pestilential swamp, known among colonists as "the graveyard of the Spanish," an inherently cursed place. "It destroys the vigour of nature, and often untimely cuts the thread of life," wrote one eighteenth-century traveler, the scientist Antonio de Ulloa. In his description, the town's infestations of jungle creatures rivaled the biblical plagues: "Serpents are here . . . numerous and deadly and toads innumerable, swarming not only in the damp and marshy places, as in other countries, but even in the streets, courts of great houses, and all open places in general."

The sloop weaved among the galleons and merchant ships that cluttered the bay and sidled up to the Tierra Firme fleet's magnificent flagship, the galleon *San José*. Fuentes was helped aboard the *San José* and led to the Count of Casa Alegre, Don José Fernández de Santillán. He delivered Zúñiga's message along with a report of the possible ships the sailors on his sloop had seen in the Gulf of Darién.

Casa Alegre's ornately appointed quarters occupied the stern of the vessel, their size and gilded splendor reflecting his rank. As captain general of the galleons, the count was at the top of the viceroyalty's hierarchy, superseding the viceroy of Peru himself. He was here not only as the commander of the fleet but as a proxy for the king.

No images of Don José are known to exist, but if he looked anything like his beloved older brother—a fellow high-ranking official whose portrait has survived—he might have had a sharp, aquiline nose; long, straight white hair; and calculating eyes.* At seventy-one, he had reached the culmination of a social ascent that had begun several generations earlier with his Sevillian ancestors, wealthy landowners and producers of wine, wheat, and olive oil in Andalusia since at least the fifteenth century. His own climb up Spain's aristocratic ladder had been secured with chests full of silver. Shrewd and stubborn, Don José had leveraged the family fortune to loan money to the chronically cash-strapped Crown, which rewarded his generosity with a succession of increasingly prestigious and lucrative colonial appointments.† And up until then, Don José had largely proven worthy of his

---

* As it happens, Casa Alegre's brother, Francisco de Santillán, bore an uncanny resemblance to an older Roger Dooley.

† While the granting of power in exchange for payment may strike modern ears as the very definition of corruption—as well as a recipe for incompetent leadership—it was typical of the transactional nature of Spanish politics at the time.

purchased positions. He had acquitted himself well as governor of the Maracaibo district, in modern-day Venezuela, and had earned the title of Count of Casa Alegre five years earlier in recognition of his heroic role in fending off an English assault on the vital Spanish port of Cádiz, from aboard the galleon *San José*.

Yet he had never before helmed Spain's all-important Tierra Firme treasure fleet, and he now felt the weight of an empire bearing down on his shoulders. Reading the Frenchman's warning as Fuentes looked on, he faced perhaps the most consequential decision of his life. The planned itinerary for the fleet's return, as it had been for Spanish treasure convoys for more than a century, was to sail from Portobelo to Cartagena, then to Havana, where it would unite with the New Spain treasure fleet sailing in from Mexico, then join forces with the French raider-turned-ally Ducasse, who would escort the ships on the dangerous homeward journey across the Atlantic to Cádiz, in southern Spain. It was not obvious to Casa Alegre how to react to the news that the English squadron was planning to ambush him somewhere between Portobelo and Cartagena. To set sail for Cartagena in hopes that the fleet could either evade, outmaneuver, or outgun the squadron was risky, but so was waiting out the threat in a disease-infested swamp, one that—history had shown—was not invulnerable to attack. And if he were to wait, then for how long? In a few months, hurricanes would begin ripping across the Caribbean. In the previous hundred years, such storms had destroyed far more ships, killed far more people, and taken far more treasure than had been lost to pirates and privateers.

Casa Alegre considered his duty to the king, who would have been growing more impatient for his treasure by the day, but also his own fate. At his age, death was a constant companion.

Despite Casa Alegre's absolute authority in Portobelo, this was not a decision he felt capable of making on his own. As with nearly every important matter, he sought the counsel of the fleet's intimidatingly self-confident second-in-command, Don Miguel Agustin de Villanueva. The sixty-one-year-old admiral was commander of the *San Joaquín*, the *San José*'s nearly identical sister galleon, completed the same year, 1698, by the same shipwright in the Basque country of Spain. Of noble origin, Villa-nueva held extraordinary sway over Casa Alegre. He had begun his military career as a soldier at fifteen and had steadily risen through the ranks of royal service. He had served in multiple Tierra Firme campaigns and had even fought in this very harbor when Spanish forces routed a French assault on Portobelo in 1684. If anyone knew how to respond to the English threat, it would be Villanueva.

The admiral largely dismissed Fuentes's report, saying it was "nothing to worry about." Was it truly news that raiders were intent on ambushing the Spanish fleet to steal its treasure? The possibility of attack was a perennial menace, and yet, over the previous two centuries, most Spanish treasure had safely arrived to the Royal Hacienda. Besides, with nearly four times as many ships, almost half of them armed, the Spanish convoy had little to fear from a four-ship squadron. The real danger, Villanueva argued, would be to postpone the galleons' departure and allow a greater English force to besiege the fleet in Portobelo, where its ships were sitting ducks.

Casa Alegre was reassured by his admiral's logic and his air of conviction. Yet, unwilling to have the consequences of the decision fall entirely on his and Villanueva's shoulders, he nonetheless convened a war council, a *junta* of naval and civil officials, who met at the Casa de la Contaduría, a grand building by the town's humble standards. Among them were colonial administrators, delegates from the merchant community, and the highest-ranking officers from the fleet's galleons and other warships. Once everyone had gathered in the room, Casa Alegre shared Zúñiga's letter and the Frenchman's alarming report.

IN THE SWELTERING STREETS OF PORTOBELO, meanwhile, the fair went on: Merchants, sailors, slaves, and soldiers engaged in a boisterous choreography of commerce that hadn't been seen there in twelve years. To anyone who had visited in the interim, Portobelo would now have been unrecognizable. During the *tiempo de galeones,* when the fleet was anchored in the bay, the sleepy, desolate jungle outpost was transformed as if by sorcery into one of the world's most vibrant marketplaces. Tents made of ships' sails were erected in the main square to house the exchange, where traders from Lima haggled with their European counterparts. The smells of Peruvian products like cacao, vicuña wool, fermented indigo, and Jesuit's bark swirled through the humid air, competing for attention with the grassy stench of manure. Droves of mules—convoys several miles long, containing hundreds of animals—had crossed over from Panama, on the Pacific side of the isthmus, carrying more than one hundred tons of gold and silver coins through tropical forests and mosquito-ridden marshlands. So much precious metal had been brought in that, as Ulloa notes of a typical fair, "the streets [were] encumbered with bales and chests of gold and silver of all kinds."

Before Casa Alegre had left Spain, in 1706, the king had sent him an unambiguous order: Once in Portobelo, Felipe had written, the captain general was to embark "all my gold and silver . . . without losing time" and "without allowing anyone to meddle." Corruption, smuggling, and tax evasion had become rampant within the colonies, threatening the health of the empire like a gangrenous limb. From an ocean away, the Crown struggled to stop their spread.

As the king's representative on the ground, Casa Alegre would ensure that his sovereign would receive every last peso he was owed in taxes and fees—and then some. In his zeal, the count had turned tyrannical. He was "inflexible in applying pressure," reported one observer at the fair, a prominent judge named Francisco de Medina, who had run afoul of Casa Alegre for having the temerity to confront him about his strict approach. In an effort to root out fraud, the captain general had "visited the merchants' houses and took from them, without discrimination, quantities of crates and [gold and silver] bars," Medina reported. Some traders stashed their wealth in the mountains and other hiding places to evade his grasp. When two Lima tax collectors failed to provide the money he expected, Casa Alegre had them locked up in dark, dank cells in the belly of one of the fortresses surrounding the town.

The captain general's strong-arm ways had helped him secure more than a million pesos for the royal coffers. Following a long-standing tradition, half of the king's treasure would be carried in the *capitana,* or flagship (in this case the *San José*), and half in the *almiranta,* or vice-flagship (the *San Joaquín*). This was a fraction of the merchants' earnings from the fair, most of which would likewise be entrusted in equal proportion to the two galleons, the largest and most heavily armed ships in the fleet. In addition, the two vessels had already embarked a substantial amount of treasure at an earlier fair in Cartagena. Along with the silver and gold were cases of pearls and uncut emeralds, as well as jewelry and luxury objects.

All of it was now at risk of ending up in English hands.

At the *junta,* Casa Alegre listened as the men proposed various plans. Some suggested that the fleet bypass Cartagena—and thus avoid the squadron that was awaiting them—by sailing straight to Havana. There was just one problem: After several years at sea, the storm-battered, worm-eaten hull of the *San José,* like that of several other ships, was beginning to leak and urgently needed to be careened in Cartagena before the long and dangerous journey to Cuba began. Others proposed that the fleet remain in place through the winter and that a heavy chain be drawn across the mouth of the harbor to prevent enemy ships from entering. But nobody was eager to spend more time in Portobelo, and the king could not afford to wait another year for his treasure.

A group led by Judge Medina, whom Casa Alegre considered an insufferable nuisance, floated the idea of sending a sloop—the same one that had brought Fuentes and Zúñiga's missive—ahead of the fleet to look out for English warships along the path from Portobelo to Cartagena. Of most pressing concern to the gathering were the shapes that the sloop's lookout had spotted in the Gulf of Darién. The small and nimble vessel could inspect the waters quickly, without attracting attention. If it found them to be clear, the fleet could set sail.

A consensus emerged and Casa Alegre appeared to agree to the plan. Yet several days passed and the sloop had still not left Portobelo, for reasons that have not been recorded. In the meantime, two French frigates had entered the harbor with more unnerving reports from Cartagena: English prisoners had confessed that squadrons of their nation's warships had been making regular trips between Jamaica—the seat of English power in the Caribbean—and the Gulf of Darién in order to keep watch on the comings and goings in Portobelo. The men of the fleet could practically hear the English shanties floating in from the east.

Casa Alegre convened a second *junta,* and once again the proposal to send a sloop ahead to reconnoiter the area was put to a vote. This time, however, there was one dissenter: Admiral Villanueva, who from the start had downplayed the English menace. His long, decorated career lent him an outsize charisma, which he now wielded to advocate once again for immediate departure.

The sooner the fleet could leave Portobelo, Villanueva argued, the higher its chances of safely reaching Cartagena. Every hour of delay brought greater risk of catastrophe. If indeed their movements were being watched, to send a scout would only warn the enemy of the fleet's intention to set sail and give the English squadron more time to prepare an assault.

The gathering struggled to understand Villanueva's reasoning: If the English were indeed around the corner, then they would be alerted to the fleet's movement no matter what. To leave Portobelo without first surveying the area would be lunacy.

But the admiral would not budge. "The force of four ships," he insisted, "[is] not sufficient to prevent the departure of the Armada."

Villanueva was overwhelmingly outnumbered. But though the matter had been voted on, the *junta* was not a democracy. Only one man needed to be convinced, and Casa Alegre, despite his higher position and greater age, deferred—as he had so often—to Villanueva's superior experience.

As it became clear that Casa Alegre was leaning toward Villanueva's position, Judge Medina, who had previously butted heads with the count over his draconian methods, could not contain his rage. His voice shaking with fury, he told the general that he was risking not just the ships and lives under his command but the very survival of the Spanish Empire.

"I was so upset that I warned him how that resolution of his departure would cause the loss of the army, and with it the total devastation of the monarchy," Medina wrote. "He was going to give himself up to the enemy."

Several men echoed Medina's outburst, including the captains of sea and war on each of the fleet's three galleons, who knew all too well the carnage that a confrontation with a well-armed enemy ship could wreak. Among the loudest voices was the fleet's third-in-command, Nicolás de la Rosa y Suárez, the captain of the *Santa Cruz,* known for his quick temper and propensity for dueling. But Villanueva and Casa Alegre were unmoved, believing it possible to chart a course to Cartagena that would elude the English.

Villanueva shut down the debate with a grandiose pronouncement: "The sea is broad and her paths are many."

The captain general's decision was final. "With no agreement other than his own," one member of the *junta* recalled, Casa Alegre "resolved to set the departure of said galleons for the day of May 28," without an advance sloop. Protestations died down in resignation and disbelief, and the council disbanded. While he convinced himself that he could lead the fleet to Cartagena without firing a shot, Casa Alegre returned to his quarters aboard the *San José* and drafted a battle plan in preparation for a clash with the English, should one become unavoidable.

If the Frenchman's report was to be believed, two of the four English ships had seventy cannons, eight more than the *San José* and *San Joaquín*'s sixty-two each. Casa Alegre knew well that battles at sea tended to be coldly arithmetical affairs: Enemy ships would glide slowly past each other in a dance of death, firing broadsides at close range, and whichever had the greater firepower usually won. But the captain general had confidence in the solidity of the twin galleons to withstand the barrage. Built a decade earlier in northern Spain, largely from lumber cut under the waning moon when it was believed the sap was closest to the root and the wood was sturdiest, the three-masted vessels, each around 135 feet long, with a capacity of about 1,070 metric tons, were the largest and strongest ever to lead the Tierra Firme fleet. And while some of the English ships might have had more guns, Casa Alegre reassured himself that he had more armed ships in total: In addition to the *San José* and the *San Joaquín* were the *Santa Cruz,* also known as the *gobierno,* with fifty guns; a French frigate named the *Sancti Espiritu,* with thirty-two; an *urca,* or hulk, known as "Nieto's ship," with thirty-four; and two smaller merchant ships with a dozen guns on each side. Casa Alegre believed the total firepower under his command gave him the advantage in the grim calculus of naval warfare.

On the nearly windless morning of May 28, sailors on all sixteen of the fleet's ships—including the eleven merchant vessels—scaled the rigging to vertiginous heights, resembling the monkeys that abounded in the trees around Portobelo, and lowered the sails for departure. Aboard his lavishly upholstered skiff, Casa Alegre was rowed from ship to ship, making his final inspections and rushing the proceedings along. When he passed by the *urca,* the captain of the infantry company aboard the ship, Don José Canis de Alzamora, called out to him and expressed his concern that he lacked munitions and that his gunners were in no condition to fight: Of the thirty-eight troops in his company, half were sick or convalescing. Casa Alegre responded coldly that he had no more men to spare. When Canis repeated his desperate plea for reinforcements, Casa Alegre, unmoving, told him to speed up the departure, unmoored his boat from the *urca,* and rowed away.

As he gained distance, Casa Alegre could hear Canis continuing to protest in anger and asking sailors to bear witness to his outrage. But if he had any doubts about his fleet's preparedness, the count kept them to himself. Now was not the time for indecision. As long as the winds were in his favor, he might have told himself, there would be no need to put his weakened men to the test.

At last, the ships sailed slowly out of the safety of the port in a long, majestic parade. After exiting the mouth of the harbor, the convoy tacked eastward toward the Gulf of Darién, keeping the coastline to starboard. After weeks of inhaling the stale vapors of Portobelo, the hundreds of voyagers—crew, soldiers, officials seeking passage to Cartagena and beyond—were glad at long last to be at sea. But the relief was tainted with fear. The beginning of the return trip to Spain should have been a cause for celebration. Instead, the likelihood of bloodshed gave the convoy the air of a funeral procession.

Chapter 2

Galleon Life

To anyone spying the fleet from afar, the two galleons would have been easy to distinguish by their size and defiant silhouettes. With their high stern castles, they were pitched ever so slightly forward, like charging bulls. They each had two gun decks, and ten gunports on the quarterdeck. The ships were square rigged, their sails stretched across horizontal spars that extended to each side of the ship. Each vessel had three masts, honed from the straight, soaring trunks of pine trees from eastern European forests. Each hull's planks were pine above the water-line and sturdier oak below, the lower portion sheathed in a thin layer of lead to guard against shipworms. A carving of a rampant lion served as the figurehead.

Like living beings, the *San José* and the *San Joaquín* had changed continually since their birth in the small Basque town of Mápil. Count-less adjustments, enhancements, and repairs made the twin ships look increasingly distinct over time. Both had reached their full splendor shortly before crossing the Atlantic. Their most intricate decorations were reserved for their sterns, bedecked with gilded balustrades fea-turing scenes from Greek mythology and three copper lanterns fram-ing colorfully painted carvings of each galleon's patron saint—Saint

Joseph cradling an infant Jesus in the case of the flagship *San José*. When the work was done, one observer marveled, "Such is the elegance and perfection of the new stern that it places the ship above those of other nations."

The *San José* and the *San Joaquín* were about twice the size of the average galleon in use from the late sixteenth century to the early seventeenth, the golden age of the Spanish Empire, when the traffic of treasure fleets across the Atlantic was at its apex, with some convoys containing more than one hundred ships. The archetypal oceanic war galleon originated in Spanish shipyards in the 1590s, having evolved from the carrack, a short-keeled, high-sided, and altogether unwieldy oceangoing craft of which Columbus's *Santa María* was a notable example. A lower forecastle reduced wind resistance, and a greater length-to-beam ratio (typically 3:1) improved maneuverability. Crucially, the stabler, less top-heavy galleon could support far more guns, which had become a necessity after Sir Francis Drake's surprise attack on Spanish America in 1578 proved that Europe's wars would not be contained to Europe. In the following decades, shipwrights across the Old World adopted the designs. None did so with more enthusiasm than the Spanish, whose economy had come to depend on regular infusions of treasure and raw material from across the Atlantic, and who needed ships with the capacity to carry it and the cannons to defend it.

Over time, shipbuilders in other seafaring nations, especially England and Holland, innovated further, developing the more hydrodynamic craft known as the ship of the line. The vessel, referred to in the Royal Navy as a man-of-war, was conceived for a new kind of naval warfare—broadside to broadside—in which speed, agility, and firepower made all the difference. Hulls were narrowed and cargo capacity was sacrificed to accommodate even more gunports. The seas had never seen more efficient engines of death.

Spain, meanwhile, remained committed to the obsolescent galleon, addicted as the nation had become to shipments of riches from the New World. As hulls elsewhere were being streamlined, Spanish galleons grew bulkier, more gluttonous, becoming the very embodiment of the empire's decadence. A dramatic rise in smuggling and tax evasion further stretched the dimensions of galleons as shipbuilders routinely flouted royally mandated proportions in order to accommodate more contraband. These changes had a direct effect on the ships' seaworthiness, compromising their ability to handle strong winds or agitated waters.

English and Spanish warships had diverged over the second half of the seventeenth century, the former evolving into nimble predators, the latter into lumbering prey.

THE SIX-HUNDRED-ODD PEOPLE aboard the *San José*—we'll never know exactly how many—were well aware of the deadly peril they faced. But the crew had little choice, and the passengers had decided it was worth the risk: The ships of the Tierra Firme fleet would be the first to return to Spain in twelve years, and with war raging on both sides of the ocean, there was no guessing when they would have another chance to go home with their newfound riches.

The poor and the wealthy aboard the ship shared a common destiny. The *San José* was a civilization at sea, a cross section of Spanish colonial society,* bringing together boys and men of every station, from twelve-year-old orphans brought on as apprentices, to bureaucrats and officers of noble birth, to sailors pressed into service against their will.

"It is an elongated town," wrote a royal official named Eugenio de Salazar, in a colorful letter about life on a galleon more than a hundred years before the *San José*. "It has its streets, squares, and apartments, walled in by bulwarks." He described a claustrophobic, distorted world "with doors in its floors."

---

* Of *male* Spanish colonial society, it should be noted, even if a few officers on the galleons may have traveled with their families.

Save for Casa Alegre, who lodged in an opulent and capacious cabin at the stern, and a scant few officers and dignitaries who likely had their own bed, nobody on board enjoyed anything so luxurious as personal space. Mariners, soldiers, musketeers, artillerymen, carpenters, caulkers, divers, gunners, and others ate and slept cheek by jowl in the dark wooden realm belowdecks, where anyone taller than five feet seven inches had to stoop and where lanterns bathed everything in a dim, flickering glow and the stench of tallow.

A blindfolded sailor, swaying with the motion of the waves, could orient himself on board the *San José* by smell alone. As soon as he descended through the topmost hatch, the briny caress of sea air would give way to the stagnant reek of hundreds of infrequently washed men. "There are rooms so closed, dark, and smelly," Salazar reported, "that they seem like vaults of the dead." A sulfurous top note hung in the atmosphere on the gun decks, in the powder magazine, and in the quarters of the artillery men, known as the Rancho de Santa Barbara, after their patron saint. The deeper a mariner sank into the bowels of the ship, the more the effluvia of the bilge overpowered other odors. Salazar described these putrid pools as "rivers . . . of especial filth, not filled with grains of gold . . . but with the all-too-common pearls that are lice, so big that some vomit out chunks of cabin-boy meat."

Even the drinking water aboard could be nauseating, becoming cloudy and rancid after a long time at sea. This sludge, Salazar wrote, "neither the tongue nor the palate would want to taste, nor the nose to smell, nor even the eyes to see, because it comes out foaming like hell and stinking like the devil."

Two spaces offered an olfactory reprieve. One was the tiny chapel at the base of the mizzenmast, in which incense burning in silver censers suffused the walls and fabrics of a space barely large enough to perform communion. Another was the galley—redolent of garlic, salt cod, salt pork, and olive oil—where cooks sweating over copper cauldrons slopped worm-ridden mush onto wooden plates.

On long journeys, livestock was brought aboard to provide eggs, milk, and fresh meat to high-ranking officers and sick crew members, contributing their own barnyard pungency. And as on any large vessel at the time, other creatures had made themselves at home, such as fleas, rats, cockroaches, scorpions, centipedes, and whatever other vermin had scuttled, crawled, or slithered aboard in Portobelo.

Mariners chanted to set a rhythm to their tasks. The *San José* added its own music: the snapping of halyards, the fluttering of banners in the wind, the deep moans and unnerving creaks of its weary timbers. Seabirds gliding above the convoy squawked along. With steady good weather, there was little to mark the days but the sequence of watches, morning prayers, and the rise and fall of the sun.

Most witnesses had nothing to report during the fleet's crossing of the Gulf of Darién, aside from calm seas and fair winds. Only one, Pedro García de Asarta, the captain of sea and war aboard the *San Joaquín,* mentioned a detail that would prove ominous in retrospect. As dawn broke on May 29, the second day of the journey to Cartagena, the fleet found itself two leagues—about seven miles—to the northwest of the Bastimentos Keys. A lookout on the wide circular platform of the crow's nest at midmast spotted "two small ships to windward, making full force of sail" before disappearing into the keys. They were too far off to identify, but even at that distance it was clear they were not warships.

Villanueva, the cocksure commander of the *San Joaquín,* remained untroubled: The sighting only vindicated his audacious plan to depart Portobelo without warning. Even if the spotted crafts had been English scouts, they were now receding in the wake of the Spanish fleet, as well as in the minds of its leaders. What threat they might have represented had been averted, and it suddenly seemed possible, even likely, that the galleons' treasure would reach safe harbor. But as long as the galleons held something men were willing to kill for, death would fly alongside the fleet. In fact, it had hovered over the treasure from the beginning.

Chapter 3

Tears of Dead Suns

The Inca, who populated the Andes before the arrival of the Spanish, believed that gold fell to earth as the tears of the sun god, and silver as tears of the moon goddess. It wasn't until the nineteenth century that astronomers discovered how close they had gotten to the truth: Spectroscopy revealed that our sun contains an abundance of gold in gaseous form, as well as silver and all of the heavier elements of the periodic table. And while these never escape the sun's core, the Inca were right about the celestial origins of the noble metals. The notion that gold and silver are born of grief—in the form of tears—is also remarkably apt. Astrophysicists have long hypothesized that heavy metals are the by-products of the death of massive stars, forged in the extreme heat and chaos of supernovas and blasted across the universe. More recently, it's been suggested that the conditions for the birth of the heaviest elements, including gold, are more likely to result from distinct but no less violent cosmic events: the collision of two neutron stars, the ultradense cores of collapsed supergiants, whose strong gravitational pulls draw them closer and closer in a swirling danse macabre until they crash into one another in a cataclysmic explosion releasing more energy in a few seconds than our sun has in its entire lifetime, as well as a smattering of gold.

However they were launched into space, the gold and silver atoms that would end up—billions of years later—constituting the coins and bars packed into the hold of the *San José* eventually found themselves suspended in a cloud of dust and gas circling the sun. Gold- and silver-flecked clumps began to form and accrete into pebbles, their increasing gravity attracting ever more matter until they condensed into a planet. Throughout the earth's infancy, meteors encrusted with gold and other precious metals—the tears of dead suns millions of light-years away—also rained down, splashing into oceans of fire.

The metals' heaviness caused them to sink toward Earth's molten core and settle into layers deep in the crust as it cooled. In periods of intense tectonic convulsion, such as the formation of mountain ranges, magma was forced through cracks in the crust. Different elements hardened at different temperatures, and gold and silver poured into fissures of subsurface rocks, becoming veins of ore. When the Andes burst into existence, about fourteen million years ago, gold and silver were thrust toward the surface in relatively high concentrations.

The Indigenous societies who exploited gold and silver in the Americas before the arrival of the conquistadors valued the precious metals for the same fundamental reasons that other people around the world had fallen under their spell. Too soft for many practical purposes, the elements derived their worth instead from their scarcity and their luster. Gold, especially, seemed impervious to the decay that affected all natural things and thus became associated with immortality. Neither air nor water nor the passage of time dimmed its sheen, which reflected the sun as if the metal were indeed a piece of it. It became, particularly for the Inca in Peru and the Aztec in Mexico, a means of communing with the gods. Gold and silver were not used as standard currency in the ancient Americas. Rather, they served decorative or ceremonial purposes, worked into beautiful and often spectacularly intricate objects that conferred not just status and prestige on the owner but something of the divine.

In Eurasia, where gold and silver coins had circulated for nearly two thousand years, the metals were venerated for their profane powers as stores of value and markers of wealth. Their pursuit drove the exploration and conquest of the Americas from the beginning. It was, in a sense, gold that called Columbus to the continent. In sailing west across the uncharted ocean, the Genovese explorer had hoped to reach the island of Japan, or Chipangu, which Marco Polo had fancifully described two hundred years earlier as a land where "gold is abundant beyond measure."*

Columbus believed he had discovered it upon reaching the coast of Cuba but was soon disillusioned when he failed to find the slightest glint of gold. His spirits rose when he arrived on the neighboring island he would call Hispaniola, where Taino chieftains adorned in golden jewelry greeted his ships on the shore. While there were no signs in the Caribbean of the rivers and palaces of gold promised in Marco Polo's travelogue, Columbus nevertheless returned from his first voyage with a few handfuls of golden objects, enough to avoid embarrassment. The modest amount he brought back to Spain's King Ferdinand and Queen Isabella—along with several hundred captured and enslaved Taino natives—whetted the rulers' appetites and set in motion a colonial mechanism that would lead to the death and subjugation of millions and upend the equilibrium of civilization.

"Get gold," Ferdinand would instruct a New World–bound Spanish master miner. "Humanely if possible, but at all costs get gold." In the centuries that followed, successive generations of Spanish colonists

---

* "I will tell you a wonderful thing about the Palace of the Lord of that Island," Polo recounted in one of his most beguiling—and embellished—evocations. "You must know that he hath a great Palace which is entirely roofed with fine gold, just as our churches are roofed with lead, insomuch that it would scarcely be possible to estimate its value. Moreover, all the pavement of the Palace, and the floors of its chambers, are entirely of gold, in plates like slabs of stone, a good two fingers thick; and the windows also are of gold, so that altogether the richness of this Palace is past all bounds and all belief."

followed the king's central command, conveniently ignoring its optional plea for restraint. The gold that flowed back to Spain was acquired at the expense of countless Indigenous lives. The sixteenth-century Spanish clergyman Bartolomé de Las Casas, a ferocious critic of Spain's treatment of America's Indigenous peoples, estimated that between twelve and fifteen million native people were killed in the decades following Columbus's arrival. While the true extent of the genocide is difficult to determine five centuries hence, it is certain that those slaughtered by the better-armed Spanish were greatly outnumbered by those who succumbed to infectious diseases imported from Europe, against which they were virtually defenseless.

Indigenous inhabitants were forced to extract the wealth of their own people's land on behalf of their oppressors, toiling in deadly gold and silver mines. Starting with Columbus in Hispaniola, governors throughout Spanish America had established a system of *encomienda,* which required Arawak natives to pay tribute to their Spanish conquerors in exchange for protection. Though Isabella had nominally outlawed slavery for natives, whom she declared subjects of the Crown in 1500, the tribute system effectively instituted a form of serfdom. The tax was initially to be paid in gold—at first a hawk bell full of gold dust every three months, per person—no matter how scarce the metal. Failure to deliver was punishable by death.

The Spanish obsession with precious metal reached an idolatrous intensity. "Gold is most excellent," Columbus wrote. "From gold treasure is made, and whosoever possesses it does all that he desires in the world, and is able to send souls into Paradise" (through the purchase of indulgences). It was not the golden calf the conquistadors worshipped—in fact, they melted down almost every shimmering object they encountered into bullion—but gold itself.

No amount of gold seemed to sate the Spaniards' hunger or temper their cruelty. The Aztec ruler Moctezuma's gifts of gold to conquistador Hernan Cortés were not sufficient to save his empire when the Spanish closed in on its glimmering capital city, Tenochtitlan, in 1519. Nor, fourteen years later in Peru, was the Inca emperor Atahualpa able to secure his own freedom, even after his people had delivered the riches that his captor, Francisco Pizarro, had required in exchange for the emperor's life: a small room filled with gold piled as high as Atahualpa could reach. Once Atahualpa's loyal subjects had hauled in the promised treasure, Pizarro went back on his word. He sentenced the Inca ruler to be executed for a variety of fabricated offenses, including idolatry. His execution triggered the rapid collapse of the Inca Empire, which at its height stretched as far as ancient Rome once had.

But if gold captured the conquistadors' imaginations like no other element, a chance discovery in 1545 turned Spain's attention to its more plentiful sister metal—and shaped the future of the empire.

There are many versions of the tale. They all begin the same way, with an Andean native, named Diego Gualpa in most tellings, trekking up a sharp reddish peak in the frigid highlands of southern Bolivia, almost sixteen thousand feet above sea level, known to the Indigenous Quechua people as Sumaq Urqu, or "Beautiful Mountain." According to one account, he was a simple hunter chasing a llama. Per another, attributed to Gualpa himself, he had climbed the slope with the intention of stealing from the gods. He had been sent by his European employer to a local shrine, where he snatched offerings—likely of gold or silver—that had been left to its resident spirit. On his descent, a sudden blast of wind knocked him off his feet, as if punishing him for his crime, and sent him tumbling down the scree. In one variant, Gualpa caught himself on a bush, tearing it out of the earth as he fell. When he arose and brushed himself off, he looked at his hands and found them scintillating. In the hole left by the uprooted bush he saw more of the silver dirt, along with several larger chunks of metal.*

To believe one version, Gualpa wrapped a few pounds of this pay dirt in a blanket and immediately showed it to his employer. In another, he at first kept his discovery a secret, mining it himself until

---

* In fact, the area of Potosí is largely barren of vegetation, one indication that the story of Gualpa's discovery owes as much to legend as to historical truth.

another native Andean noticed he was suddenly dressed in finer clothes and forced him to share his find. Perhaps because they were taken down by Spanish officials, all variants of the story have overtones of biblical revelation, the gust of wind either punishing the benighted Gualpa for his crime or guiding him to untold riches, as God led Moses to the burning bush.

All versions of the story end the same way too—the only way it could—with the Spanish taking possession of Gualpa's discovery and establishing a mine that would yield riches the early conquistadors had only dreamed of. The Beautiful Mountain was renamed Cerro Rico de Potosí, or the Rich Hill of Potosí.

By the close of the sixteenth century, the mountain's apparently inexhaustible deposits of ore had become the lifeblood of the Spanish Empire. The small mining outpost had burgeoned into a frenzied boomtown with a population larger than London's. European fortune seekers and Indigenous laborers—most of them forcibly drafted—flocked to the Imperial City of Potosí. Where the guanaco had roamed in peace and solitude not long before now sprawled the region's largest slave market. A poisonous cloud hovered over the valley. Dozens of refineries, churning out more than half the world's circulating silver, spewed toxic mercury—a key ingredient of the refinement process—into the once-crystalline Andean air and waterways.

In his million-word history of the city, written in the early eighteenth century, the creole chronicler and lifelong *potosino* Bartolomé Arzáns de Orsúa y Vela painted Potosí alternately as a mountaintop miracle and an alpine inferno rife with sin and misery. His darkest descriptions, rivaling Dante in their evocative power, were reserved for the depths of the mines themselves, in which native workers and African slaves fueled on coca leaves performed the deadliest tasks.

"Innumerable are those who have perished in its bowels: With each step they take in one of its mines they reach the threshold of death," Arzáns wrote. "Sometimes the light [they carry before them] goes out and there they perish; others are swallowed by the very ground where they step, because ignorant of the holes that pass below, they open up and bury them; others are buried from the loose debris that falls on them; others fall into those very deep wells and lagoons that are in there and drown. . . . Sometimes you will see them, by losing control of one foot, go down that ladder until they reach death. You will also see them sometimes resembling beasts walking on all fours with the load on their backs, and other times crawling like worms."

Arzáns was especially horrified by the mistreatment of Indigenous workers, whose land, he argued, had been "ill-acquired" by the Spanish. "But in the end," he wrote, "perhaps when they die they will be crowned with glory as a reward for their terrible labors, and many Spaniards who oppress them will be slaves in hell."

From the beginning, certain men of the cloth decried the moral cost of Potosí silver. As early as the 1550s, friar Domingo de Santo Tomás described the mine as "a hell-mouth that swallowed thousands of innocent and peaceful Indians each year." One Jesuit priest, Padre Pedro de Oñate, believed that the riches of the Indies were cursed, arguing that the use of forced labor, particularly of Indigenous miners, undermined the Christian faith that Spanish missionaries were attempting to teach.

Back in Spain, the discovery of America's seemingly endless supply of precious metals had indeed unleashed a kind of curse, not cosmic but economic: The overflowing amount of silver and gold that flooded into the country triggered two centuries of spiraling inflation that, in a vicious cycle, required the extraction of yet more treasure and made the empire yet more dependent on mining at the expense of other, more sustainable industries. Meanwhile, the cost of nearly constant warfare in Europe under the Habsburg kings had led to a series of debt crises that pushed the Crown into chronic bankruptcy. Little of the gold and silver that sailed across the Atlantic and up the Guadalquivir River to be disembarked in Seville remained in Spain. Most of it merely transited through the country as it flowed straight to the king's creditors across Europe. In the meantime, the Crown's debts kept growing and ever more gold and silver was needed to repay them.

More than a million silver coins—most of them pieces of eight, the basis of the modern dollar—are estimated to have been on board the San José on its journey to Cartagena, enough to fill a small room from floor to ceiling. Most of them had been cut and stamped in the Royal Mint of Potosí, brought by ship to Panama, and taken by mule from there through fifty miles of jungle to Portobelo, where they were loaded onto the galleons, packed in wooden boxes that contained about three thousand coins each and were nailed shut. In addition to the official cargo, a large but unknowable proportion of precious metal on the galleon was contraband, carried aboard in secret by private individuals seeking to avoid the royal fifth, the 20 percent tax that the king took from returning riches. Coins and finger-sized bars were hidden in trunks, stashed into false compartments, stuffed into boots, sewn into clothes, or worn as jewelry, which was not subject to taxation. A few Spain-bound travelers on other ships sometimes exploited this loophole by wrapping long gold or silver chains around their necks, some measuring more than ten feet.

As was the case throughout the history of the Spanish Empire, the silver in the San José's hull far outweighed the gold. But Casa Alegre's fleet sailed within a brief window in which the production of silver coins dipped and that of gold coins—from metal mined largely in what is now Chile—rose to unseen heights. There was perhaps as much as eight tons' worth of gold on board, more than had ever sailed in a single Spanish ship.

However brightly the gold and silver might have gleamed, every coin in the San José was stained with the blood of the people who had suffered or died to get it there, of the innumerable slaves and draftees who had disappeared into the depths of Potosí, of poisoned women and children. Critics like Arzáns and Oñate might have extended that tally even further to include all those who had been brutalized, exploited, or killed over the course of two centuries in the establishment of Spain's money machine, from the murdered Atahualpa to the hundreds of thousands of Indigenous soldiers felled during the early conquest of the continent, to the millions who were later put to death or died of smallpox in the wake of the *Niña,* the *Pinta,* and the *Santa María.*

The treasure of the *San José* was destined to finance yet more bloodshed in Europe, to send Spanish and French boys to slaughter and to pay for the guns and cannons that would tear English, Dutch, and German infantrymen apart. As history would have it, however, the treasure would never reach Cartagena—at least not for a few more centuries. But, cursed or not, it would nonetheless claim the lives of hundreds.

AS THE SUN SET on the mild evening of June 7 and a full moon took its place, Casa Alegre might have begun to feel that God was on the Spanish side—or at any rate on his. To have made it to age seventy-one in fine health was already a sign of Providence. To have done so in the disease-ridden tropics at the helm of a galleon in wartime was practically proof of divine grace. Since the beginning of the war his destiny and the *San José*'s had been intertwined. Both had been blessed with good fortune. It was aboard the galleon that Casa Alegre had led Spain's successful defense against an attempted Anglo-Dutch invasion of Cádiz in 1702. Two years later, he and his *capitana* had survived a brutal—if ultimately failed—campaign to reclaim Gibraltar from the English. Together they had crossed the Atlantic in 1706 without incident. And they had safely reached Portobelo despite the constant threat of storms, corsairs, and pirates. Now they had prevailed over the Cassandras and naysayers in the *junta* and had led the treasure fleet to the San Bernardo Islands, a day's sail from Cartagena, with nary a sighting of an English warship.

Yet two of the convoy's ships, the *gobierno* and a merchant vessel named the *Rey David,* were lagging behind, and Casa Alegre could not sail until all seventeen[*] ships were accounted for. By the time they

---

[*] A latecoming merchant vessel had joined the fleet en route.

caught up, clouds had veiled the moon and it had begun to rain. It was too late. Casa Alegre decided to remain for the night off the San Bernardo Islands, in hopes that God would watch over him and the *San José* for one more day.

The weather at dawn on June 8 was fair, and the air after the night's rainfall was crisp and clear, with no limits to visibility except the curvature of the Earth. The ships turned their prows to the northeast, a rare and welcome southeasterly breeze nudging the fleet gently along. Another sign of the Lord's benevolence, Casa Alegre must have thought. The plan was to pass the Rosario Islands, then round Isla del Tesoro (literally, Treasure Island),* and cut sharply to the northeast for a final ten miles to the natural gateway known as Boca Chica, the "little mouth" through which the fleet would enter the safety of Cartagena's bay. As long as conditions held, the convoy would arrive well before nightfall.

Sailing at three or four knots, with a light wind pushing it from behind, the *San José* appeared barely to be moving to those on board, contributing to an eerie and illusory serenity. Yet for several hours, the fleet advanced steadily toward the Rosario Islands.

The convoy stayed on this course until about three in the afternoon when the wind died down, then, sickeningly, reversed direction. It was now blowing from the north-northeast, straight onto the prows of the galleons and merchant ships, impeding their progress.

Right at that moment appeared the manifestation of the men's fears. A lookout in one of the crow's nests spied four sails along the northern horizon. Casa Alegre had prayed it wouldn't happen, but in retrospect, it had been inevitable. The general of galleons didn't need to look through his spyglass to know what flag the ships were flying. And he would have known all too well the formidable seaman who was leading them.

---

* The origin of this intriguing name has sadly been lost to history.

Chapter 4

Fire Above, Fire Below

Commodore Charles Wager, commanding the English squadron from aboard the seventy-four-gun *Expedition,* had been planning his attack for months. It was no accident that the Spanish treasure fleet had made it to Portobelo unmolested. Wager, commander of the Royal Navy's station in Jamaica, had allowed the galleons to gorge themselves on gold and silver before stalking them, the way a farmer fattens a pig for the slaughter.

Though thirty years Casa Alegre's junior, Wager already had the plump bearing and incipient jowls of an elder statesman. The towering periwig he wore in portraits, parted in the middle, with powdered gray curls cascading to his shoulders in the style of the time, helped complete the illusion.

He and Casa Alegre had followed strikingly different paths to this same swath of the Caribbean. Unlike the Spanish general, the noble-born heir of an agricultural fortune who had bought his way into naval command, Wager was a commoner with seawater in his veins. His paternal grandfather, a Royal Navy captain, had been killed when the vessel he commanded blew up during a battle with Spanish privateers, and his maternal grandfather had been a vice admiral who had helped take Jamaica from the Spanish in 1655 and had served there in the same position Wager now held, as commander of the English fleet in Port Royal. His father, a respected naval officer, had navigated the war-torn Mediterranean and London society with equal ease. "A brave, stout fellow this Captain is, and I think very honest," the naval administrator and notorious bon vivant Samuel Pepys remarked in his diary after dining with Charles Wager *père*.

Any English boy of Wager's nautical pedigree could have expected a nepotistic nudge into the Royal Navy, with an apprenticeship at an early age and a quick rise along the officer track. Yet Wager's father died the year he was born, and his mother chose a more tranquil life for her young son, entrusting him to the care of a Quaker merchant captain named John Hull, who made regular transatlantic crossings between England and Massachusetts. But the fire within Wager—whether inherited from the men in his family or inspired by their example—would not long be suppressed.

A devout pacifist, Hull refused to carry a single cannon aboard his ship. Full of merchandise and free of guns, Hull's vessel one day proved an irresistible quarry for a French corsair, who chased the merchant ship down. As the attackers closed in and prepared to send their grappling hooks, Hull abandoned the fight and descended belowdecks to await his fate. Out of religious conviction, he would sooner lose his cargo, his livelihood, even his life than take up arms against another man. Wager, then a cabin boy, had no such compunction, and no urge to be captured, killed, or humiliated. Despite his young age and his lowly position, he gathered the crew on the deck and claimed to speak for the captain.

"If you will place yourselves under my command, and stand by me," he cried in his manliest voice, "I have conceived a plan by which the ship may be rescued, and we in turn become the conquerors." Wager outlined an action so foolhardy perhaps only an adolescent could have come up with it. Won over by the boy's ardor, his older and more experienced shipmates went along with it. Were the gambit to fail, as it by all rights should have, every man aboard would likely have been executed. Instead, it went off exactly as Wager had intended.

As the assailants vaulted aboard, Wager and the merchant crew made themselves scarce on the deck. Once the marauders were belowdecks sizing up their booty, Wager gave the signal and led a charge onto the nearly empty French vessel, where he and his followers grabbed guns and blades foolishly left behind. One party returned aboard their ship and encircled the raiders, while another took command of the corsair's frigate and slashed the grapplings connecting the two craft. Armed with nothing but wit and courage, Wager had not just fended off an attack but claimed his first prize.

Or so the story goes. Whether or not it is entirely true, it became part of both Quaker and British naval lore, told and retold with the embellishments that sailors are prone to, and in later hagiographies of Wager would be cited as an early indication of future greatness. Soon after the events are said to have occurred, the Royal Navy, having perhaps heard of the cabin boy's exploit, offered him a post as second lieutenant aboard a fifty-gun ship. He earned his first captaincy at twenty-six and served for the next decade and a half with competency and honor, but with few chances to prove his mettle in combat. Throughout the war of succession with Spain and France, he had seen action in the Mediterranean, but mostly from afar.

His (possibly apocryphal) youthful triumph against the corsair notwithstanding, he had not so far lived up to the memory of his illustrious forebears, mainly because he had not been given the opportunity. As the newly appointed commander of Jamaica Station, in Port Royal, Wager saw an attack on the galleons as his chance to distinguish himself at last—to accomplish the crucial war aim of intercepting Spain's treasure in hopes of turning the tide of the conflict in Europe, toppling the House of Bourbon, and precipitating the fall of the Spanish Empire, England's greatest rival in its quest for global hegemony. The hunt was for Wager a matter of honor: "A man who does not fight for a galleon," he would later say, "will not fight for anything."

In the process, he stood to become richer than his father and grandfathers could ever have imagined. English Admiralty law allowed Royal Navy captains in wartime to keep the majority of whatever treasure they seized from enemy ships. There was enough gold and silver in the *San José* and the *San Joaquín,* Wager estimated, to make him the wealthiest man in Europe twice over.

Though he sailed under the banner of the Royal Navy, his tactics were those of a privateer. At the helm of the *Expedition,* the commodore had been cruising the waters between Cartagena and Portobelo since December, alongside the three other ships in his squadron, the *Portland,* the *Kingston,* and the fireship *Vulture,* designed to be set aflame and, once the crew had escaped into rowboats, sent crashing into the hull of an enemy vessel.

His spies had informed him that the galleons had arrived in Portobelo in April, months after they were expected. By then, Wager had been on the hunt for nearly half a year with just one brief provisioning stop in Jamaica, an exhausting and dangerous length of time to be at sea. After just three months without fresh food, symptoms of scurvy—waxy skin, swelling limbs, loosening teeth, putrid breath—would begin to appear. Losing patience, the commodore considered raiding the galleons right in Portobelo Harbor, as Henry Morgan had decades earlier, but feared being overpowered by Spain's more numerous forces. He resolved instead to intercept the fleet in open waters, where his faster ships would stand a better chance.

An ambush at sea is a far trickier operation than on land. There are few places to hide on a flat and limitless battlefield. If you can see the enemy, the enemy can surely see you. The success of Wager's offensive would depend on his being able to surprise the Spanish, which in turn depended on an imbalance of information—he would have to know of the treasure fleet's whereabouts without Casa Alegre's men knowing of his.

Wager had a crucial advantage: He knew where the galleons would be sailing from and where they were likely to head, since the route of the Tierra Firme fleet hadn't changed in more than one hundred years.

He just didn't know when they would depart. By late May, the galleons had still not sailed. Wager kept his spyglass pointed to the southwest, expecting Spanish sails to breach the horizon any day.

In the early afternoon of June 3, a single ship finally appeared from the direction of Portobelo. Enemy or ally? As the vessel closed in on the *Expedition* its contours became clearer: not a galleon, as he had hoped, but a far smaller sloop, a merchant ship, which hoisted an English flag to the masthead, signaling a desire to speak with the commodore.

The merchant captain said that he had been sent by Captain Pudner of the English warship *Severn,* who had been lurking among the Bastimentos Keys to keep watch on Spanish movements in and out of Portobelo. The messenger handed Wager a letter from Pudner, revealing the news that a lookout had seen the Spanish fleet set sail from Portobelo four days earlier. Racing to alert the commodore, the sprightly sloop—likely the same vessel that García de Asarta had spied from aboard the *San Joaquín*—had outpaced the heavily burdened treasure fleet, which could sail only as fast as its slowest ship, by more than a day. At last Wager had the final piece of information his plan required: the *when* of it.

Now it was up to him to choose where. The sea was indeed broad, as Villanueva had hubristically proclaimed, but Wager believed there was in effect just one path the Spanish convoy could take to Cartagena. Coming from Portobelo, to the southwest, and hugging the mangrove-lined coastline of New Granada to starboard, the fleet would find its way to Cartagena barred by the peninsula of Barú, and by the archipelago that extended past its tip, known today as the Rosario Islands.

Wager reasoned that the large galleons would not risk sailing through the narrow passage between the islands, where they were likely to run aground on shifting sandbars, and that they would instead have to tack west around the archipelago and cut back east to Cartagena's Boca Chica. The commodore led the squadron to a position somewhere off Isla del Tesoro, where the English ships would linger like highway robbers awaiting wealthy travelers around the bend on the only road to town. It was only a matter of time, he believed, before the Spanish fell into his trap.

A day passed, then two, then three, with no sign of the fleet. Though he had been careful to maintain his distance from Spanish shores, Wager began to fear that the enemy had learned of his presence. His suspicions would surely have focused on the French prisoner who had daringly escaped one of his ships the previous month by jumping overboard. The commodore was now convinced that the general of galleons had outsmarted him by heading straight to Havana from Portobelo.

But having waited six months, he could wait a few days longer. On the clear, calm afternoon of June 8, two barely perceptible white specks peeked over the horizon, about ten miles away. Their topmasts were unadorned and their forms indistinct. But as fifteen more sails joined them over the course of the day, Wager had no doubt that this was the convoy he'd been after.

WHAT HAD SEEMED TO CASA ALEGRE like providential assistance from nature had turned into betrayal. As soon as the wind changed, around three in the afternoon, the four English warships turned in his direction and came bearing down on the fleet like wolves charging a flock of sheep, the fickle gust now at their backs.

There was still a chance to avoid calamity, Casa Alegre thought. Since the way to Cartagena was blocked, and he couldn't veer east through the perilous reefs between the islands, he would ride the wind westwards, where he could either confront his enemy from a more advantageous position, or, with any luck, evade him long enough to escape into the night.

LOOKING THROUGH HIS SPYGLASS, Wager could by now clearly distinguish the unmistakable profiles of two Spanish galleons. The flagship may have looked familiar: He and the *San José* had nearly crossed paths at the Siege of Gibraltar, years before and an ocean away.

"I had been informed," Wager wrote in his journal, "that the three

Admirals"—meaning the three galleons—"now had all the money, therefore thought if we could get these 3 it would be the best service."

Having failed to pass Ciruelo, the westernmost of the Rosario Islands, the galleons and several armed ships turned toward his squadron and attempted to arrange themselves in a file that Wager, observing their struggle, derisively called "a kind of line of battle." The galleons hoisted the white royal Spanish pennant to their topmasts, signaling their intention to engage.

His senses quickened, Wager raised the red flag of battle to his own mast. He called to the *Kingston,* which was within hailing distance, and ordered its captain to attack the *San Joaquín.* He then sent a message by boat to the *Portland,* directing its captain to chase the *Santa Cruz.* The fireship *Vulture* would stay behind for now: The last thing Wager wanted was to incinerate the treasure ships and send his prize to the bottom of the Caribbean.

CASA ALEGRE WAS BOUND BY conflicting duties. He was both the captain general of the fleet and the commander of its flagship. He was the protector of the merchant vessels but also the guardian of the king's treasure. He had determined one thing from the outset: Even if he couldn't guarantee that the treasure would reach Spain, he would die before allowing the English to seize it.

Everything Casa Alegre had done in the two years since he had arrived from Spain was leading to this. All would be for naught if he were to fail now. Yet from the moment Casa Alegre decided to confront the English ships head-on, the fastidiously orchestrated battle plan he had devised in Portobelo began to fall apart. He turned the *San José*'s prow to the northwest but in his haste, perhaps in panic, neglected to fly the royal banner from the sternpost or to fire a lone cannon shot, which were the signals the fleet's other captains had agreed upon to initiate battle formation.

The Spanish warships, each about a mile apart, were left to figure out from the *San José*'s sudden change in bearing that the battle had begun and scrambled to take their places. Per Casa Alegre's preestablished strategy, the *gobierno* (the *Santa Cruz*) was to occupy the vanguard of the line—the tip of the spear—followed by the French frigate *Sancti Espiritu,* then the *urca,* transporting Canis's half-infirm infantry. Fourth in line—dead center—was the *San José,* and in its wake three other armed ships, with the mighty *San Joaquín* in the rear guard. The warships would provide cover for the unarmed merchant vessels downwind to make their way to Cartagena. Under ideal conditions, the cumulative firepower of a tightly formed Spanish line would prevail over the three English men-of-war. But the wind threw Casa Alegre's plans into disarray.

The *gobierno* endeavored for an excruciatingly long while to reach the frontmost position. Its captain was the headstrong Nicolás de la Rosa, who in Portobelo had urged Casa Alegre to postpone departure or at least to send a sloop ahead to scout the seas. As leader of the first ship to face the squadron, the thirty-five-year-old captain was now expected to bear the brunt of the general's decision. But despite his fury at Casa Alegre, he was a man of honor and would do as ordered. Or rather attempt to: Before squaring off with Wager's ships, he had first to fight the wind, and he was losing.

The *gobierno*'s difficulties cascaded down the line, and in the end the Spanish formation was less a spear than a broken arrow. As it flew on its slow and wobbly path toward the English warships, the dread of inevitable carnage knotted the stomachs of the men and boys on board the galleons. The sluggishness of their progress against the wind only allowed more time for the terror to build among sailors, officers, gunners, and musketeers as they collected weapons and prepared the ships for battle. Some surely spread sand on the deck to provide grip and prevent the wood from becoming dangerously slick with blood. Others may have scribbled makeshift wills or goodbye letters to loved ones back in Spain. The surgeons readied their tourniquets and bone saws and cleared their tables for the wounded, knowing that they would soon be drenched in gore. Intended to bolster the men's courage, the drummers' martial beat sped the pounding of their hearts.

Though outnumbered, the English ships of the line were built for just this kind of fight. Benefiting from their superior speed and agility, as well as the advantage of the wind, they had the luxury of picking their partners. The mêlée that ensued off the Rosario Islands was far more chaotic than the orderly dance outlined in Casa Alegre's plan, or, for that matter, in the *Fighting Instructions* issued by English generals-at-sea in 1653, the foundational text of modern naval warfare, which Wager would have known by heart.

ON WAGER'S ORDERS, THE *KINGSTON* raced past the entire Spanish line to catch the gold- and silver-filled *San Joaquín* off guard with a volley of cannon fire.

But the wily, war-tested Villanueva was prepared for just that, and almost simultaneously, thirty-one elaborately decorated, unnecessarily beautiful ten- and sixteen-pounder bronze cannons protruding from two rows of gun ports on the *San Joaquín's* side launched balls of cast iron back at the *Kingston* with deafening blasts.

"Our Almiranta," reported one Spanish observer, "was so quick and ready that when the enemy fired the first piece, the riposte was already on its way, with such equal speed that the cannonballs might have collided in the air."

Those who heard the cannonballs shriek past them thanked God for his mercy. The sound meant they were still alive. Much of the fire had flown above the men's heads. The English gunners had tilted their cannons high, not to sink the ship, but to cripple it, so that they could climb aboard and rip out its precious entrails. The English salvo had broken off the *San Joaquín's* main topsail yard, the wooden arm perpendicular to the mainmast that had held the all-important topsail aloft. The fractured yard and limp canvas now dangled uselessly from the mast. In addition to regular ammunition, the *Kingston's* cannons fired chains, crowbars, nails, shrapnel, and split shot—twin iron bars linked together with weights at each end—that were designed to shred sails and shatter masts and could do the same to flesh and bone. The smell of saltpeter hung over both ships as gunners rolled the scorching cannons back to the gunports, and sailors turned the vessels around for another exchange.

SEVERAL MILES AWAY, WAGER'S *EXPEDITION* charged at full sail toward the *San José*. In his hurry, the commodore cruised right past the thirty-four-gun *urca* without paying it the honor of a cannon shot—all that mattered was the treasure aboard the galleon. Not content to have been spared, the hulk's captain, José Canis, ordered his gunners to pursue the far-larger *Expedition*.

"Let us not lose this chance!" he bellowed.

Considering that Casa Alegre had coldly rebuffed Canis's plea for more men back in Portobelo, it was an act of profound courage and chivalry to now come to the captain general's rescue. Before the *Expedition* sailed out of range, the *urca* turned its side toward the English and fired its guns at the man-of-war's prow. Though they did little damage, they had at least caught Wager's attention, forcing the commodore to turn around and engage. The two vessels now sailed side by side, close enough for the Spanish to hear the English cries and see the fear and bloodthirstiness on their faces.

Before the *urca* could get off another broadside, the mighty *Expedition* unleashed the full force of its artillery at the valiant smaller ship. In the few seconds that it took the English guns to fire, the *urca* was utterly incapacitated—its sails punctured and rent, several of its masts cut down like trees. Canis, in a report, described the devastation caused by a single cannonball: "The *urca* received a shot of twenty-four pounds, which destroyed a cannon from the lower gun deck, damaged the launch and the ladder to the castle, and blew off the arm of a man, the ball remaining inside the ship."

The cannonball was just one of dozens that the *Expedition* fired. The cast-iron balls shattered the *urca's* thick planks like rocks hurled through glass. To those inside, each new puncture was an open window revealing the smoking cannons of the aggressor. In addition to sailors and a company of troops, the *urca* carried a number of passengers, who huddled belowdecks on the side farthest from Wager's guns, cringing in terror as the ship shuddered with every shot fired and received. Among them was Judge Medina, who had shouted at Casa Alegre before the men of the *junta,* urging him not to sail. The insubordinate outburst had led Casa Alegre to kick Medina and his belongings off the *San José,* where the judge had a berth, and to place them instead on the *urca.* As the English assault wore on, Medina felt sure that with this banishment, the captain general had effectively condemned him to death.

But the blasts suddenly stopped, giving way to a haunting, muffled silence, pierced only by the ringing in Medina's ears. When it was clear no English riposte was coming, the judge rushed to the gun deck to provide succor and refreshment to the gunners, and through the ports saw the *Expedition,* none worse for the attack, leave the *urca* in its wake. With their masts disabled and their sails in tatters, the men watched powerlessly as Wager bore down on the Spanish *capitana,* the galleon *San José.*

IT WAS SUNSET WHEN THE TWO SHIPS MET, and a fiery light washed across their sails. With loaded muskets in their hands, cutlasses and daggers in their scabbards, soldiers on both vessels steeled themselves for the terrifying prospect of man-to-man combat. Infantrymen climbed the rigging in order to snipe down at the enemy's deck. Even the septuagenarian Casa Alegre would have armed himself in preparation for an English boarding.

As soon as the *Expedition* and the *San José* were abreast of one another, half a musket's shot away, more than fifty cannons went off from both sides in rapid succession, seeming to tear the very fabric of the air apart.

Men aboard ships hundreds of yards away could do nothing but observe the hellish spectacle. Luis de Arauz, a witness on a Spanish auxiliary vessel called the *Nuestra Señora del Carmen,* described "incessant fire during the battle, horrible the roar of the artillery . . . especially that of our *capitana,* which from all sides looked like a volcano."

There are few Spanish accounts of the battle from the *San José's* perspective, for reasons that will become clear. English logs, meanwhile, are frustratingly concise, providing ample detail about wind direction and relative firepower but little insight about the experience of the men on board. A more forthcoming English officer present at the Battle of Trafalgar close to a century later gives us a visceral description of what it is like to endure the hell of a battle at sea: "It bewilders the senses of sight and hearing. There was the fire from above, the fire from below, besides the fire from the deck I was upon. The guns recoiling with violence, reports louder than thunder, the decks heaving and the sides straining. I fancied myself in the infernal regions, where every man appeared a devil. Lips might move, but orders and hearing were out of the question. Everything was done with signs."

Aboard both ships, the combatants followed nearly identical rituals between each round of cannon fire. The dead and wounded were carried off. As musket shot whistled around them, sailors braced the yards while younger mariners—either immune to vertigo or with little choice in the matter—clambered high up the rigging and ventured along the yards to take in sail so the ship could be slowed and turned around for another assault. Deckhands quickly and gingerly carried charges of gunpowder from the magazine up to the gun decks, stuffing them down the smoking, scalding mouths of the cannons followed by whatever projectile they meant to send hurtling at the enemy. Several strong men would then wheel each gun back into place, ready to wreak more destruction.

The ships were in constant motion, and their cannons could fire anew only when they were once again aligned with their target. Naval battles consisted of long stretches of recovery and reloading interspersed with short bursts of apocalyptic chaos, in which, for less than a minute, cast-iron balls and musket shot flew in both directions at twice the speed of sound.

It was an uneven fight from the beginning. Not only did Wager have more guns and a more agile vessel, but he also had the weather gauge—the wind in his corner—allowing the *Expedition* to lead the dance. Casa Alegre's gunners, meanwhile, struggled to keep up with the cannonade, managing to get off only two broadsides in the time it took the English to unleash six. Spanish troops, firing muskets across the narrow waterway that separated the ships, also had poor aim, at least according to one English officer's mocking account: "We received all their shot, they being such ill marksmen that though we were within musket shot and sometimes much nearer yet, we had not so much as a man killed or wounded for the first [few] hours."

A more likely reason the Spanish musketeers struggled to hit their targets was that they couldn't see what they were shooting at. The battle had begun when the sun went down, and as the sky darkened, smoke engulfed both ships. Cannonballs and other projectiles came flying from nowhere, cutting trails through the haze, pulverizing wood and bone, and sending splinters of both in all directions, the hurtling shards even deadlier than the shot itself.

A fire broke out on the ravaged *San José,* sending the Spaniards into disarray. Their surrender was all but guaranteed. Wager could taste victory. He would soon be hauling his prize, the richest vessel in the seas, back to Jamaica.

Then a powerful explosion came from deep within the galleon, according to English witnesses, shaking the ship and sending a shock wave across the water. Wager and his men claimed they were nearly scorched themselves. The galleon "blew up," the commodore wrote, and "the heat of the blast came very hot upon us and several splinters of plank and timber came aboard us afire." As English sailors hurled the burning fragments of the *San José* overboard, they could hear Spanish screams from beyond the smoke.

PEERING OUT FROM THE *URCA*'S GUN DECK, where he was tending to the ship's wounded gunners, Judge Medina strained to make out the *San José* through the night and the shroud of smoke. "I saw from the distance of three ship's lengths, that aboard the *capitana* could be discerned a clarity brighter than that of gunfire," he wrote. "And observing how unusual it was that the light did not cease, I inquired about the reason, which no one could determine."

The source of the strange light soon became horrifyingly evident. "In the brief interval it took to recite a prayer, there rose a blaze on the ship toward the prow." Tongues of fire flicked from the gunports. Flares and grenades shot out into the sea. The flames took little time to spread across the wooden deck and slither up the masts and the rigging, reaching higher than the top of the mainmast, sending sparks high into the night sky. Soon the *San José* was encased in what Medina described as a "balloon of smoke." The judge couldn't be sure, but he thought he heard a series of blasts, "as if from three barrels of powder."

In addition to a hollowing pang of grief and pity, Medina must have felt a sense of relief and perhaps a perverse gratitude toward Casa Alegre. If it weren't for his confrontation with the general, the judge would have been on the *San José*.

FAR CLOSER TO THE ACTION, Wager and his men could see the glow of the blaze diffused through the smoke, but little else. In a matter of minutes, the Spanish side went dark and silent. When the smoke cleared, the *San José* had vanished. A floating city, gone in an instant. Where the galleon had been was now a field of flotsam. Of her six hundred souls, fewer than twenty men were left,* clinging to the *San José*'s singed remains.

"She immediately sunk with all her riches, which must be very

---

* Because of the chaos of battle and the multiplicity of accounts, it's unclear how many survivors there were. Spanish and English records differ, but the number was probably between seven and seventeen.

great," Wager wrote in his journal, with a brevity that belied his profound disappointment. The sinking of the Spanish fleet's flagship was not a triumph but a devastating failure. The treasure that he had been seeking for months was now plummeting to unknowable depths, alongside the bodies of Casa Alegre and his men.

The commodore was left to wonder how it had happened. He had been careful to aim the *Expedition*'s guns at the masts and rigging. If, as he believed, there had been an explosion in the bowels of the *San José*, what had caused the detonation? Any seasoned seaman's first guess would have been that several barrels of powder had blown up and set off a chain reaction. But explosives were stored in a room well below the waterline specifically to avoid the kind of conflagration that had just doomed the *San José*. So how could Wager's cannons have sparked the blast? Could the galleon's own guns have somehow set off the barrels? Had an explosion caused the fire or had it been the other way around?

Wager had to consider the possibility that the loss of the *San José* had not been an accident—that he had, in a sense, been bested. If he had put himself in Casa Alegre's shoes, he would have understood that losing the gold and silver upon which his king and country depended was dishonorable enough, but allowing the English to claim it was intolerable. The elderly Casa Alegre might have sooner ordered the detonation of the powder magazine and committed his own body to the deep than live out his remaining years in disgrace. It was common, after all, to scuttle or burn ships rather than let them fall into enemy hands. It would have been a far grander gesture to do so while hundreds were still on board. The general might well have calculated that the gold—and his honor—were more valuable than his life and the lives of his men.

Wager didn't linger on the question. Two galleons remained afloat, and he believed he could still salvage a prize from the battle. He lit a lantern on the mizzen peak to identify himself in the dark to the other English ships and then set a new course, leaving the refugees of the

San José to tread water among the wreckage and the floating bodies, well beyond sight of any coastline.

AS THEY WATCHED THE LANTERNS of the *Expedition* recede, the survivors had little hope of making it through the night. Yet they were the lucky ones. They were all young sailors and soldiers who had been perched in the rigging when the fire broke out, the sole reason they were spared. The most senior among them was the *San José*'s boatswain, who would later testify that he had not heard an explosion. In fact, he and other surviving sailors and infantrymen had been so high above the action, some possibly farther away than Wager himself, that they could say little about the circumstances of the ship's demise. Looking down below, all they could see was confusion, "people rolling over each other." Then "all of a sudden" the men found themselves in the water. They would remain there for more than twelve hours, clinging to the floating foremast of the *San José,* before they were picked up by one of the English ships. When questioned by Spanish authorities afterwards, they could report only that they had been gripping the yards amid the flames one second, and in the blackness of the Caribbean Sea the next.

The *San José* sank too quickly for anyone on deck—let alone below—to escape. The few who managed to jump into the water were pulled down by an irresistible current, sucked into the void behind the foundering ship.

Chapter 5

"To the Last Drop of Blood"

A few miles away, the other treasure-laden galleon, the *San Joaquín,* had managed under Villanueva's able command to slip away from the *Kingston.* The merchant ships, meanwhile, had taken advantage of the battle to sneak behind the Spanish line and would soon enter Cartagena's harbor. Left with no ship to fight, his man-of-war battered but navigable, Capt. Timothy Bridges turned the *Kingston* to the west and witnessed a burst of fire in the distance. He feared the worst. "Saw a ship blow up ahead of me," he wrote in his log, "some of my men at the same time calling out that Commodore Wager was blown up."

Bridges immediately made sail to come to Wager's aid and pick up what survivors he could. As he approached, "the smoke blew away and I discovered the commodore to my great satisfaction and finding the *Expedition* fore tack [ahead]."

The sinking of the *San José,* the narrow escape of the *San Joaquín*—wherever it was—and the crippling of the *urca* had left a single Spanish warship stranded, the *Santa Cruz.* The *gobierno,* as the Spanish called it, was now on its own, and the three English men-of-war were converging upon it.

The ship's thirty-five-year-old commander, Nicolás de la Rosa—the Count of Vega Florida—had earlier in the night shaken off the *Portland*. But now it was one against three.

Vega Florida was well aware that, with his ship's 50 guns against the English squadron's combined 180, his defeat was mathematically predetermined. But he was not the surrendering type—as attested by the scar on his arm from a grave wound he had sustained in a swordfight with an infantry captain who had insulted him years earlier in Cartagena.

Squinting into the night from the deck of the *Santa Cruz,* Vega Florida could see the lights of the three English men-of-war close in on him. There was gold and silver in the hold of the *gobierno,* most of it belonging to private individuals, yet nowhere near the amount aboard the *San José* and the *San Joaquín.* It was not this treasure for which Vega Florida was prepared to die but his honor and that of Spain. More prosaically, he would also fight to keep the ship itself, of which he was the principal owner.

Around one o'clock in the morning, the *Expedition* arrived abreast of the *gobierno,* along its starboard side, close enough for Vega Florida to hear the voice of Wager himself calling out in accented Spanish: "Strike your sails for Queen Anne!"

The obvious hopelessness of Vega Florida's position was his strength: Confident in the overwhelming superiority of their firepower, the English had let down their guard and offered the Spanish commander a clear shot at close range, the best chance he would surely get to inflict maximal damage on the squadron's flagship. Knowing it could well lead to his death, Vega Florida unleashed the full power of his battery and infantry against the *Expedition*'s flank, wreaking more destruction in a single broadside than the *San José* had in two hours of battle.

The *Expedition* reciprocated immediately and with greater force, firing its shot into the *gobierno*'s stern and smashing the rudder to bits, "which seemed," Wager wrote, "to have disabled him from making sail." Amid the screams of the wounded, the Spanish had little time to recover before the *Portland* and the *Kingston* filed past the *gobierno*'s starboard side in quick succession and fired their own artillery, each broadside chipping off more critical pieces of the vessel.

With their superior maneuverability, the English ships of the line circled the *Santa Cruz* like sharks and fired their guns relentlessly: Wood flew to splinters, lines and sails went limp, bodies too. But even as the men-of-war riddled the *gobierno*'s hull with holes, they couldn't silence its guns. More Englishmen died in the confrontation with the *Santa Cruz* than at any other phase in the battle. At one point, either struck by a cannonball or ignited by accident, a keg of powder blew up aboard the *Portland,* killing six men.

From the quarterdeck, Vega Florida raged at the English, but also at his countrymen, who he felt had left him to fight the entire squadron alone. He battled on for more than an hour "without hope of rescue, since nobody was seen nor came to our aid at the beginning nor at the end of this endless defense."

Around two o'clock, the rising moon cast a bluish light across the *Santa Cruz* and revealed the extent of the devastation. The deck was a mess of shattered wood, tangled rope, corpses, blood, and viscera. Belowdecks, the surgeon triaged among more than sixty gravely wounded men, sawing at mangled limbs with nothing but liquor to dull the pain. A crew member rushed up to inform Vega Florida that water was rapidly rising in the hold, now five palms deep, gushing in through twenty-three punctures below the waterline.

The English assault had left the *gobierno* without "masts, yards, mizzen, sails, or rigging that weren't destroyed," as Vega Florida described his predicament. Without a rudder or working sails, his ship had been reduced to "a buoy in the sea." Several guns had been blown out of commission. Dozens of his men had been killed. Still Vega Florida did not concede. Instead he delivered a fiery speech, ordering his officers and crew and soldiers to "fight to the last drop of blood in defense of our holy Catholic faith [and] the glory of our king and lord, Felipe the Fifth (may God watch over his soul)."

Escape was unlikely, but not out of the question. Though the *gobierno* was incapacitated—"lying so like a log in the water," as Wager put it—the squadron was hardly better off, "our ships being pretty much disabled in sails and rigging," per Wager. Yet whatever hope Vega Florida had of making quick repairs and getting away vanished as soon as he saw the approach of the squadron's fourth vessel: the fireship *Vulture*.

In a world of wood and canvas, fireships were weapons of mass destruction. Mountains of combustibles and explosives were set alight atop a latticed deck, through which a continual flow of air fed the inferno as the unmanned ship, its sails fixed by the departing crew, charged in the general direction of the target. Grappling hooks affixed to yardarms snagged in the enemy's rigging and held the victim close as the fire spread from ship to ship. Fireships were designed less to torch opposing vessels—though they could do that with horrifying efficiency—than to strike terror.

With the arrival of the *Vulture* came Wager's ultimatum.

"Surrender or burn!"

Vega Florida could not be certain that the commodore wasn't bluffing. The ship, after all, was worth more to the English commander as a prize than as a charred wreck on the ocean floor. Vega Florida scanned the horizon in all directions one last time, but by the light of the moon he could see no sign of the other ships in the Spanish fleet. He was alone. Faced with the prospect of total annihilation, the Spanish leader nevertheless stood firm.

"He told them many times that he would rather die," recalled a witness. The same could not be said of the *gobierno*'s moneyed passengers. As water continued to rise in the hold, they begged the commander to surrender. At last Vega Florida relented, but only after having everyone aboard testify before a notary that he had done everything he could to save the ship, a requirement under Spanish law and a salve to his wounded honor.

Having done so, he lowered the foretop sail in submission, indicating to the English that the ship was now theirs. Vega Florida asked for quarter, or honorable terms, which Wager, acknowledging the Spaniard's tenacity, felt obliged to grant.

Wager sent several boats full of his men to take command of the *gobierno* and begin stanching the incursion of water. In its hold, among crates of cacao, they would find thirteen chests of pieces of eight and fourteen bars of silver. Wager's share of the haul would be enough to make him a very wealthy man and catapult him to the upper echelons of British society. His exploit against the galleons—known forever onward as "Wager's Action"—would help earn him the office of the First Lord of the Admiralty, the head of the Royal Navy. A bas-relief of what came to be called the Battle of Barú, complete with a flaming *San José,* would be carved onto his marble tomb in Westminster Abbey. Yet in this moment he was crushed. "It was a great disappointment to take a Rear Admiral of Galleons and have such an account," he confided to his journal. The amount was indeed a mere fraction of what was believed to be aboard the *San José* and the *San Joaquín.*

The former galleon was lost, but the latter could still be taken. The *Expedition* being in no condition to make sail, Wager ordered the *Kingston* and the *Portland* to chase down the *almiranta* before it reached safe harbor. They patrolled the seas around Cartagena throughout the next day and night. It wasn't until the following morning, Sunday, June 10, that the English ships spied the *San Joaquín,* ensconced among the Salmedina Shoals, a treacherous reef to the north of Boca Chica, the entrance to the Bay of Cartagena.

Immediately the English captains recognized the brilliant seamanship and tactical acumen of the *almiranta*'s commander, Don Miguel de Villanueva. With their superior knowledge of the area, the Spanish had successfully navigated past the barrier of reefs and sandbars to seek refuge from the squadron. As the wind blew from the direction of Cartagena, to the east, the *Kingston* and the *Portland* could not sail upwind of the *San Joaquín* and interpose themselves between the galleon and its destination lest they be driven into the shoals. They could do little more than fire their stern guns from a cautious distance, killing a Spanish sailor and blasting away the galleon's flag, but posing no real threat to the *almiranta,* which fired back with its full artillery.

After standing off in this manner for several hours, the English ships sailed away, leaving Villanueva to cruise freely into Boca Chica with half of the Spanish treasure on board. Wager was furious upon learning of their defeat, and would later send the captains of the *Portland* and the *Kingston* before a court-martial. Word of Villanueva's triumph spread across the Caribbean. "[English] traders . . . say that the Spaniards laugh at them," reported Thomas Handasyd, the governor of Jamaica and Wager's superior. "This talk is enough to concern any true English man."

WHEN VILLANUEVA ARRIVED IN CARTAGENA, he had still not heard of the *San José*'s fate, or of the *gobierno*'s. Once he did discover what had become of them, he couldn't escape the irony that it was he who had urged the fleet to sail urgently from Portobelo despite the warnings of an English ambush, and yet he had made it safely to port, having done little to protect his fellow galleons. If he felt any guilt, he acknowledged none in the official record. He would not have to: With Casa Alegre's death, he was now the highest-ranking official on the Spanish Main.

The *San Joaquín* and its treasure wouldn't set out for Spain for another three years. With Villanueva once again at its helm, the galleon joined the fleet that left Cartagena in August 1711, led by Jean-Baptiste Ducasse, the French former corsair and onetime scourge of Cartagena. But Villanueva and the *San Joaquín* never reached Spain. Shortly after setting sail, the galleon was caught in a storm and separated from the rest of the convoy. Before long, Villanueva spied six English sails to windward. History was repeating itself. Villanueva fought no less valiantly to save his ship, but this time he was hit with a musket shot. Surrounded and gravely wounded, his shirt soaking with blood, he had no choice but to strike his colors.

The triumphant English took their prize galleon back to Jamaica, the ailing admiral still on board. Villanueva died of his wound in Port Royal, satisfied that he had played one last trick on the English: As they would soon discover, the *San Joaquín*'s hold had been emptied of its treasure, which was now on its way to Europe aboard Ducasse's frigate.

BY THE TIME THE GOLD AND SILVER reached Madrid, the royal share of the treasure had been significantly depleted to pay for repairs and provisioning for the Spanish fleet in Cartagena. Fifteen years after the last shipment of precious metals from the Americas, the Spanish Crown was left with less than a quarter of the more than 1 million pesos loaded into the *San José* and the *San Joaquín* in Portobelo and set aside for royal coffers.

The amount of private treasure that went down with the *San José* remained a mystery; no complete manifest was written and much of the gold and silver brought on board was undeclared, and thus never counted. But it was certain to far surpass the king's cut. Villanueva estimated that between 9 and 10 million pesos had been packed into the *San Joaquín,* and it is likely even more would have been on the *San José.*

As the historian Carla Rahn Phillips has written, "The legend of the *San José* had begun even before she sank." In April 1708, almost two months prior to the battle, Wager reported hearing that there were 11 million pesos on the ship. After the conflict, Handasyd, the governor of Jamaica, wrote to London that the true sum was likely closer to 14 or 15 million. Inflated by speculation and rumor, estimates of the total size of the lost treasure would grow steadily over the centuries. The amount is believed by many to be worth several billion dollars in today's money, taking into account not just the meltdown value of the gold and silver but the historical value of the coins.

The legend of the *San José* took especially deep root in Colombia, where generations would dream of finding the inestimable hoard of gold and silver lying on the ocean floor just off Cartagena, fantasies made sweeter by the notion of reaching back in time to reclaim riches taken by the colonial oppressor. Such reveries play a key role in *Love in the Time of Cholera,* by the Nobel Prize–winning Colombian novelist

Gabriel García Márquez. The book's lovelorn protagonist, Florentino Ariza, is stricken with "an overwhelming desire to salvage the sunken treasure so that Fermina Daza"—his beloved—"could bathe in showers of gold." (Márquez valued the treasure at "five hundred billion pesos in the currency of the day," a magic realist embellishment compounded by a translator's error in the English version.)

"That treasure lying in its bed of coral, and the corpse of the commander floating sideways on the bridge, were evoked by historians as an emblem of the city drowned in memories," wrote García Márquez in his characteristic way of blurring reality and fantasy. Later in the novel, a duplicitous character claims to have dived to the wreck and offers an even more phantasmagorical description: "He said he had seen an octopus inside, more than three centuries old, whose tentacles emerged through the openings in the cannon and who had grown to such a size in the dining room that one would have to destroy the ship to free him. He said he had seen the body of the commander, dressed for battle and floating sideways inside the aquarium of the forecastle."

Science offers a more plausible image of the *San José*'s afterlife. From the moment the wreck crashed into the seabed, it became a draw for marine life. Fish, crustaceans, mollusks, and microorganisms became its new inhabitants, infiltrating every chamber, every crevice, the barrel of every cannon. Beyond the reach of light, they began gnawing at all organic matter on the ship, from the oak and pine planks of the hull and deck to the bodies of Casa Alegre and his men trapped within. Over days, months, years, decades, the sea soaked through the timbers, gradually replacing the fresh water in the wood's molecules with brine and turning the ship's mighty beams to mush, causing the structure of the ship eventually to collapse and flatten. Masts that hadn't been blown away or burned down were felled at last. Various metals fared differently under the assault of the sea. Exposed iron nails and cannonballs disintegrated almost entirely while those nestled in the mud were well protected. Seawater oxidized silver coins, corroding their outer layers and mortaring them together in a concretion of sand, shell fragments, and crumbled iron. The bronze of the guns resisted the electrochemical onslaught far better. Meanwhile, the destructive power of the sea would have virtually no effect on the tears of the sun. Gold's imperviousness to oxidation, its stubborn refusal to relinquish its electrons, is at the source of its mystical aura. After centuries on the ocean floor, the gold escudos would remain as resplendent as the day they were minted.

The metal lay undisturbed as everything transformed and decayed around it, yet gold never sits idly in the human imagination. Even from the bottom of the ocean, the gold of the *San José* cried out for an owner.

Part II

Rapture of the Deep

There comes a time in every rightly-constructed
boy's life when he has a raging desire to go
somewhere and dig for hidden treasure.

—Mark Twain, *The Adventures of Tom Sawyer*

Chapter 6

The Dooley Boys

Poring over accounts of the battle nearly three centuries later, under the vaulted ceiling of the General Archive of the Indies in the summer of 1984, Roger Dooley was transported into the fiery fray, englobed by smoke as cannonballs screamed past him. He forgot for a moment about the other sunken galleon, the reason he had come to Seville in the first place. The *San José* had eclipsed the *Mercedes* in his eyes.

"That's when I fell in love," he told me. "What a story!"

Even more enticing, the letters sitting on his desk at the archive, which Governor Zúñiga had sent in haste to inform King Felipe of the tragedy off Cartagena, contained numerous clues to the final resting place of the *San José*. It was unlikely that any researcher or treasure hunter pursuing the lost *capitana* had seen them before, since they would have had no reason to consult that obscure *legajo*, number 377. The galleons had squared off "six leagues from this port," one missive reported, while another claimed that "explosions had been heard at sea eight leagues from the San Bernardo Islands." Yet another placed the battle "within sight of the Isles of Barú," referring to the Rosario Islands. "Where it burned it is not possible to dive in any way." That observation only further enticed Dooley. The ship might have lain too deep for salvage divers of the eighteenth century to reach either by free diving or by the use of diving bells, which allowed salvors to descend in a bubble of trapped air. But in the second half of the twentieth century, marine technology had developed at a furious pace. Deep-sea wrecks that had been unreachable before were now accessible, or soon would be.

A notion began to form in his mind, as in that of García Márquez's lovesick hero, that he could one day reach the *San José*. Like Florentino Ariza, he had fallen in love at first sight, and his unrequited passion would only grow over the decades. But the ship, for him, was not a means to an end. The object of his obsession was the galleon itself. It would become his Fermina Daza, the Dulcinea to his Don Quixote.

For Dooley, the treasure of the *San José* was not limited to the gold and silver aboard; it was the wreck itself and everything within. "I was always dreaming, someday I'll find a *capitana*," said Dooley. The *San José* was not just any *capitana*. The vessel and its sister ship, the *San Joaquín*, were the most spectacular galleons ever built for the Indies fleet, and the last. Over the course of the eighteenth century, Spanish craft started to look more like the frigates and ships of the line of other seafaring nations: slimmer, quicker, less grandiosely anachronistic. The *San José* also stood apart because of the circumstances of its demise.

Of all the New World–bound galleons that disappeared, most were dashed against shallow reefs during hurricanes, their contents often spilling out over miles. Their worm-ravaged timbers were reduced to scattered fragments by three centuries of waves, tides, and storms, and their remaining structures concealed beneath mounds of sand and coral. The vast majority of colonial-era wooden shipwrecks no longer looked anything like ships. Aside from fragments of treasure and cargo buried in the sand over a wide area, all that was left of most vessels was their ballast rocks—large, river-smoothed stones loaded in a ship's hull to keep her stable. Once all the timbers and sails and papers and clothing and crates and bodies had washed or rotted away, only these rocks remained on the seafloor, like so many gravestones, to indicate where the ship had lain. The *San José,* by contrast, was one of precious few galleons to have been lost in battle. Because the ship likely sank in deep waters, relatively far from shore, there was a strong chance, Dooley reasoned, that its wreck had remained relatively cohesive, offering a rare archaeological opportunity to study a Spanish galleon, shedding precious light on a period at the foundation of our globalized system of commerce. If Dooley could follow the archival clues all the way to the galleon, if he could excavate the wreck containing the greatest sunken treasure in history and publish his findings, his colleagues could no longer dismiss him. The world would learn his name.

Dooley may have been a romantic, but the rational side of him knew well how unrealistic a prospect it was for him to find the galleon and to secure permission to excavate it. For one thing, it was likely— though far from certain—that the wreck lay in Colombian waters. If so, he would need permission from Bogotá to undertake a search. He had no connections in the country, and there was little chance the Colombian government would entrust a project of such national importance to an unknown archaeologist from Castro's Cuba, especially one who had never before led a rigorous excavation. For another, Dooley was still an employee of Carisub, Cuba's pseudoarchaeological treasure-hunting outfit, and the higher-ups in the Communist Party would surely not allow him to freelance for another nation. Unless his life were to take an unexpected turn, the *San José* would remain a distant dream. Its ghostly sails had appeared on the horizon. To reach them, he would have to wait for favorable winds.

■　■　■

What predisposes a man to spend a lifetime chasing an impossible dream?

In Roger Edward Dooley's case, one might start to answer that question with his older brother, Michael. Born just thirteen months apart, the siblings had only each other to lean on through the abandonment of their father, their mother's remarriage, and a move to a foreign country. But though the two boys shared certain predilections and passions, the trajectories of their lives would be vastly different. Michael—impulsive, brash, all roguish charisma—would blaze a trail that led him to heights of heroism in his adopted country, and ultimately disgrace. He would be a man with a name. Roger, gentler, sweeter, more studious and contemplative, idolized him from the shadows, even as he occasionally resented him. In some ways, Roger would follow a path Michael had indicated, would walk through doors that his connections opened. Tracing it to its earliest roots, one might see Roger's obsession as the result of a young man seeking to find a spotlight of his own.

The boys were born in New Jersey to a Cuban mother, Isabel Caballero, whose mastery of languages, shorthand, and typing had earned her a job as a secretary at IBM, among other companies, and an Irish American father, Edward Michael Dooley, who worked at the Brooklyn Navy Yard during World War II. Isabel gave birth to Michael in Orange in late 1943, and to Roger in Newark on December 21, 1944. A surviving photo of Edward and Isabel shows him holding her close, both smiling and exuding marital bliss. It is among the few images Roger has ever seen of his father, who left the house when Roger was about three.

"My mother complained that he was always drunk," Roger recalled. "He used to bet on horses. One day, he took all the money we had for food and gambled it on horses. She had enough and they separated."

Isabel took Roger and Michael back to Cuba to stay with her mother. A few years later she met, fell in love with, and married a former baseball player named Armando Montañés, who worked in the hotel business. A honeymoon in Miami reminded Isabel how much she preferred life in the United States, and she convinced Armando, despite his hatred of the cold, to move with her to New York, a one-hundred-mile ferry ride and a three-day drive from Havana. After a stint in the Bronx, the family settled in a fourth-floor walkup in Brooklyn, on the west side of Prospect Park.

The differences between the two Dooley brothers would become steadily more apparent, especially as they entered their teens. A year older, Michael was short and stocky, while Roger was tall and skinny. Michael was a scrapper, Roger a daydreamer. When Michael went to the park to play football, Roger sold cold Kool-Aid by the sidelines. Michael picked fights and Roger ran away. Roger sought thrills at the movies, Michael on the streets. Roger tried to join the church choir (but couldn't hold a tune). Michael joined a gang, the Crewcuts.

Roger seemed to direct inward the intensity that Michael radiated out into the world. His were adventures of the mind. Their cousin Sandra Caballero, who visited them frequently, described Roger at the time as "the kindest, most loving, funny cousin ever. Very curious, very hyper, highly intelligent. Would not let go of a thought once it was in his head." Caballero recalled that he "always had a project that he wanted to do, find, write, research, draw. He just held on to it. It was like a dog with a bone. He did not know how to let go."

Michael was his brother's opposite, she said. "Tough. Hard. Judgmental. Not kind. Bullying." Caballero claimed that Michael would rough up Roger at times, which Roger did not remember. "He was a little out of control," Caballero said. "My aunt had her hands full with him. . . . Everybody thought he was off. . . . He was always very good to me, Michael, but he wasn't very good to many people."

Despite his aggressive nature, Michael loved and protected his little brother. He took lickings for Roger and inflicted more on local kids who harassed him. Seven decades later, and nearly twenty years after his death, Michael continued to cast a shadow over Roger. "I don't like talking about my brother," Dooley told me several times. But inevitably he would return to the subject, alluding in unspecific terms to a dark history. "He always wanted to be a mercenary," Dooley said. "He would only think about killing."

Back in Brooklyn Roger engaged in a less violent, more poetic form of delinquency. He played hooky from his Catholic school with his friend Edward, a skilled thief. Together they would go to Pops' drugstore on Eighth Street and ask Pops for items on the top shelf behind him. As the old man climbed the ladder to reach them, Edward opened the cash register and scooped out wads of bills. The two boys then crossed the street into Prospect Park and spent their ill-gotten wealth on horses—not betting on them, as Dooley's father did, but riding them through the park. Dooley's favorite was a former circus horse named Dancing Ball. "When he heard music, he would dance."

Dooley's parents discouraged his sensitive side. He loved the piano and wanted to learn to play, but his mother refused to buy him lessons, considering it an effeminate pursuit. His stepfather, meanwhile, pushed him toward baseball, telling him he had the long fingers of a pitcher, and taking him often to nearby Ebbets Field to see Jackie Robinson and the Brooklyn Dodgers. But Dooley had little interest in the game. When Armando took him to the 1956 World Series, a historic matchup in which the Dodgers defeated the seemingly indomitable Yankees, Dooley could think only of how much he'd prefer to be outside the stadium scrambling for home run balls with the other local scamps. Already he was thinking of treasure.

For all his extraordinary diligence later in life, turning page after brittle page at archives around the world in hopes of finding the slightest crumb of information about a long-gone ship, the young Dooley proved ill-suited to drudgery. He abandoned almost every professional commitment he made, from shining shoes ("It was horrible") to delivering the paper ("You had to climb three, four, five stories—they paid me nothing"). If there was one sign of the perseverance he would later become known for, it was his dedication to swimming and diving, a passion he shared with Michael. He spent hours a day at the YMCA pool, challenging himself to hold his breath underwater for longer and longer.

One glacial winter day, he exited the club in a light jacket, still wet from the pool, and caught pneumonia. He spent several days in bed, and as soon as he was well enough to leave the house, Dooley went straight back to the pool and caught a second, more serious pneumonia.

Dooley's brush with death hardened his stepfather's resolve to leave the frigid city for the warmth of Havana and seek work in the Cuban capital's booming hotel industry.

Armando's fateful decision would alter the course of Dooley's life. In the fall of 1957, Dooley took the ferry from Florida to Cuba for the last time. As he watched Key West recede, side by side with his brother, the blond, blue-eyed, thirteen-year-old Brooklyn boy who spoke bad Spanish thought little about how much everything was about to change.

The Caballero-Montañés family moved to an apartment in the Vedado neighborhood, a few blocks from the Malecón, the iconic thoroughfare that wound along Havana's rocky coastline. When Dooley arrived, the Malecón was a pastel parade of finned, chromed, oversized American cars befitting Havana's emergence as a Caribbean rival to Las Vegas, poised to overtake Sin City as the North American capital of vice. From the same stretch of coast three centuries before, Dooley would have seen the galleons sail into port, past the ramparts of El Morro, the castle that stood at the mouth of Havana's harbor as it had since 1589.

Their new home was a short walk from the glamorous Hotel Nacional, where Isabel got a job in the accounting department. A grandiose, multitiered water fountain marked its entrance. Beyond its doors, the best musicians in town played *son* and rumbas for gamblers and well-heeled, rum-drenched American tourists. By helping to manage the hotel's books, Isabel was unwittingly contributing to an operation with close ties to the American Mob, particularly to the notorious kingpin Meyer Lansky, who ran the Nacional's casino and presided over Havana's underworld, with a hand in everything from the city's high-end resorts to its proliferation of brothels.

A few blocks away stood the Havana Hilton, the brand-new jewel of the chain's empire, where Armando Montañés was hired as night manager. Opened in March 1958, the hotel was the tallest in the city, a 660-room totem to the devil's bargain struck between the corrupt, murderous military dictatorship of President Fulgencio Batista and the American gangsters—men like Lansky and Santo Trafficante—who effectively ran the town. (These Mob bosses didn't own the Hilton outright, as they did a number of other hotels, but they controlled the investment bank with the biggest stake in it.)

Dooley spent endless hours at the Hilton and often stayed the night. If the hotel was to Havana what the Plaza was to New York, Dooley was its Eloise, playing in its halls, gallivanting in the casino, splashing in the pool, spraying movie stars and mobsters.

For the most part, visitors to Havana—the kind who frequented its swankiest hotels at any rate—were blissfully oblivious to the bloody rebellion brewing on the eastern end of the island nation. For several years, guerrillas in the thickets of the Sierra Maestra mountains, led by a charismatic young firebrand named Fidel Castro, had been wearing down Batista's far more numerous and better-equipped forces. Castro's stated aims to overthrow Batista and rid the country of the corruption that underpinned his regime, to nationalize lucrative Yankee-owned industries and plantations, to institute land reform, to restore democracy, and to share Cuba's wealth with its poor had made him a Robin Hood figure in the countryside.

In the cities, however, the government succeeded in maintaining an illusion of peace and business as usual. For a while, it was possible for the Dooley brothers to live as if they were still in the United States. They weren't listening to Radio Rebelde—the clandestine station launched by Castro's right-hand man and chief strategist, the swaggering Argentinian Che Guevara—but to Paul Anka and Frank Sinatra. Their mother would speak to them only in English, which Roger found embarrassing in public.

Michael was a poor student and was repeatedly held back, but he flourished in the streets. He imported his Marlon-Brando-in-*The Wild One* persona wholesale to Havana. When he found there were no local gangs to join, he started one with another rebellious American teen. The boys prowled through sunny Havana in heavy black leather jackets emblazoned with "The Devils," itching for any pretext to swing their fists or pull out a knife. "He would go to school just to fight," Roger recalled.

Roger, by contrast, dutifully attended their American school, a grade ahead of his older brother. At home he would watch American movies and TV shows. His favorite was the new hit series *Sea Hunt,* starring Lloyd Bridges as a former navy frogman who solves undersea crimes, explores shipwrecks, evades sharks, and—in one early episode—confronts perfidious treasure hunters seeking sunken gold. The show's dazzling underwater sequences introduced millions to the concept of scuba diving, a discipline then in its infancy. *Sea Hunt* triggered a yearning for underwater adventure in Dooley. When he dove to the bottom of the Hilton's pool, he imagined himself side by side with Bridges, speargun in hand, dappled by refracted sunlight.

As they grew accustomed to life in Havana, and as their Spanish improved, Michael and Roger began hanging out with the older boys and young men in their neighborhood. The group's uncontested leader was a champion spearfisherman known as El Rubio, or the Blond One, who rode a motorcycle and regaled his followers with the tale of how he had won a spearfishing competition in Miami by killing a shark, whose size got bigger with every telling. One day, El Rubio invited them to go spearfishing with him and his crew. Roger and Michael didn't have masks or fins or spearguns, or the money to buy any, but the two Brooklyn hustlers devised a solution: They dove beneath the piers where old fishermen cast their lines, and collected hundreds of lead sinkers that were strewn among the rocks. With the money they made from selling the lead in downtown Havana to be melted down, they could buy equipment from the only dive shop in the city.

Over time, the Dooley boys proved to be among the most capable members of El Rubio's team and would regularly take part in competitions. They often trained just off the Malecón, in view of the cruising cars, and explored a mesmerizing alien realm with rolling hills of coral and Edenic aquatic gardens. Roger and Michael became intoxicated by this bejeweled dream, an underwater world more sublime and colorful than anything above sea level. Better still, they had it to themselves, swimming among schools of fish of all sizes that no land- or boat-bound fisherman had access to. They let the current carry them as they chased grouper and red snapper. "I used to swim twenty, thirty blocks along the street," said Dooley. The party would sell much of their bountiful catch to a French woman who lived by the water and would buy everything, even octopus, which Cubans—not knowing how to properly cook it—eyed with disgust.

Not far from the rocks that bordered the Malecón was an abrupt, sixty-foot drop-off that Michael and Roger plumbed with increasing ease, daring each other to stay longer underwater and dive deeper on a single breath. Their sibling rivalry contended with their survival instinct. They learned to equalize the pressure in their ears, to streamline their bodies, their heads pointed straight down as they calmly descended, finning with a minimum of effort to keep their heart rates low. With each dive their lung capacity increased and they made more efficient use of their air, allowing them to reach sixty, seventy, eighty feet, depths to which only the short wavelengths of the light spectrum can penetrate, washing the seabed in violet, blue, and green.

In the silence beneath the waves, Roger and Michael were more or less equals. As it had been in Brooklyn, water was their sanctuary. The sea was where the siblings' increasingly diverging worlds overlapped. When Roger wasn't studying or roaming through the Hilton, and when Michael wasn't causing mayhem in the streets, they were in the beatific waters off Havana, swimming alongside El Rubio and his apostles. As soon as they ducked their heads below the water, the sounds of modernity fell away and they found peace—a place cut off from the inexorable drama of human events. But above sea level a geopolitical hurricane was about to change the world forever, and they would be right in the middle of it.

Chapter 7

Patria o Muerte

Dooley's grandest ambition—the wild notion that he could one day find the galleon *San José*—was in some sense the product of his unique upbringing, torn as he was between the optimistic swagger of postwar America and the delirious fervor of revolutionary Cuba.

The Dooley brothers awoke on the morning of January 1, 1959, to a riotous clamor in the streets of Havana. Roger saw jubilant crowds, many wearing the red-and-black armbands or waving the red-and-black flag of Castro's movement, their cheering and singing syncopated by honking horns, festive drumming, and bursts of gunfire. The previous evening, Che Guevara had announced on Radio Rebelde that government forces in the strategically key city of Santa Clara had surrendered to his guerrillas, who had been outnumbered ten to one, after a bloody battle. With Guevara's troops closing in on Havana, President Fulgencio Batista fled minutes after midnight on New Year's Eve to a military airstrip and boarded a plane bound for the Dominican Republic with a coterie of loyalists and their families. (Lansky and his associates would flee shortly afterwards.) It took little time for news of Batista's escape to flood across the capital, for members of the urban underground to come out of hiding, and for masses of civilians to take to the streets.

The fourteen-year-old Dooley let himself get swept up in the crowd. By late morning, exultation at the ouster of a dictator whose government had murdered thousands curdled into mayhem as people directed decades of pent-up anger at symbols of the oppressive regime, crony capitalism, and the American gangsters. Mobs set fire to Shell Oil service stations and to the headquarters of the newspaper *El Tiempo* (whose owner was a steadfast Batista supporter). Dooley watched as citizens broke into bars and casinos and dragged slot machines into the street, beating them like piñatas until centavos cascaded out. As troubled as he might have been by the violence, Dooley followed in their wake and picked up handfuls of coins.

Castro's top commanders, Guevara and the twenty-six-year-old Camilo Cienfuegos, entered the capital the following day. Cigar-chomping guerrillas in their mismatched uniforms and wide variety of headwear—berets, cowboy hats, baseball caps, kepis, stiff-brimmed captain's hats—took over the ballrooms of the city's finest hotels. More than six hundred rebel fighters bivouacked on the new tiled floors of the Havana Hilton.

Dooley was enthralled by the so-called *barbudos,* or "bearded ones"—a racially diverse assortment of young soldiers that despite the moniker included many women—whose stink after months of battle filled the Hilton's marble-walled lobby, striking a discordant note with the hotel's air of luxury. He was impressed most of all by the amount of weaponry and ammunition on display in the hotel and beyond. "Everybody had a gun," he recalled. His stepfather carried a Thompson submachine gun and gave him a 22-caliber pistol. Michael got a .38 revolver. Dooley circulated among the rebel troops, asking for bullets. Before this excitable, towheaded skinny kid whose American accent was fast dissipating, the guerrillas were happy to oblige, giving out rounds as if they were bubble gum. He met Guevara and got an autograph from the equally dashing Cienfuegos.

Hundreds of thousands massed along the avenues of Havana on January 8 to witness the triumphant arrival of Fidel Castro, who paraded through the capital in a cortege of armored vehicles, basking in the adoration of the crowd amid a rain of confetti, parting a sea of red-and-black banners. Dooley, who watched from the terrace of the Hilton, recalled seeing El Comandante riding atop a tank.

That night, after Castro had addressed the nation on TV and a dove had alighted on his shoulder, further buffing his messianic aura, he and his entourage commandeered the top floor of the Havana Hilton, with the rebel leader claiming a $250-a-night penthouse suite for himself. In the weeks that followed, Dooley's stomping grounds turned into the de facto headquarters of the Revolution and the lobby became a bedlam of guerrillas, journalists, and thrill-seeking celebrities, including Erroll Flynn, who had fought alongside Castro. The decadent glamour of daiquiris and showgirls had given way to the rugged, idealistic romance of revolution, but the Hilton was still the place to be.

Castro complained that he could not get to the business of organizing the revolutionary government because he was constantly swarmed by crowds and reporters. The solitude he craved could be found only at night, when Armando Montañés was on duty at the hotel. "Several times, he called my stepfather and said, 'Hey, I'm here,'" said Dooley. "My stepfather would go down the service elevator to the basement, open the door, and take him directly to the kitchen."

Dooley was present on multiple such occasions when the rebel leader hankered for a late-night snack. "He likes to cook," recalled Dooley, using the present tense long after Castro's death. "He goes, 'Okay, . . . ' and starts making food" for all in attendance, including young Roger Dooley, who chewed quietly as Castro conversed with his closest confidants.

Even if he was too young—still too American—to understand the forces convulsing Cuba, Dooley was enamored with the panache of the *barbudos* and yearned to don fatigues himself. The guerrillas at the Hilton developed a fondness for him and welcomed him into their fold. His stepfather asked him to stand sentry at a door of the hotel. Soon he joined the youth brigade known as the Commando Juvenil. He carried his gun with him wherever he went. The only place he would enter unarmed was the water, in which he sought refuge from the revolutionary tumult at every chance he got.

Over the next few months Dooley did come to appreciate the sweep of Castro's movement. Among other ways, he learned it as he and his Brooklyn friends had learned about baseball: by collecting trading cards. In 1959, the Cuban government published a collection of colorful cards to teach the country's youth about the major events and heroes of the Revolution. For the new government, these cards were a powerful propaganda strategy. For Dooley, they were a business opportunity. Just as he had hawked Kool-Aid in Prospect Park and his daily catch on the Malecón, he now resold revolutionary cards at a bus stop near the cemetery to kids seeking to complete their albums.

Already then, Dooley had a knack for being at the right place at the right time, for insinuating himself into world affairs. Within the year, he would come within a dozen yards of one of the twentieth century's most iconic events. On the quiet afternoon of March 4, 1960, stevedores at the Havana docks were unloading the cargo from a 4,300-ton French vessel called *La Coubre,* which included several tons of munitions from Belgium, when two thunderous blasts ripped the ship apart and shook the surrounding buildings. Nearly a hundred people were killed and about three times that many injured. The cause of the conflagration was never clearly determined, but for Castro and his vast propaganda operation, there was no doubt: The explosion was not an accident but an act of sabotage, likely directed by the Eisenhower administration, which was growing increasingly alarmed by Cuba's expropriation of American-owned assets including banks, sugar mills, and oil refineries.

The next day, Castro led a procession for the dead along the Malecón and through the heart of the city. On a platform at the corner of Twenty-Third Avenue and Twelfth Street, in front of the

Christopher Columbus Cemetery, the leader gave an hours-long eulogy that turned into a saber-rattling tirade: "If they"—meaning the Americans—"think of landing troops, let them go ahead. . . . We are a people capable, even, of marching forward against the mushroom cloud of nuclear explosion. . . . Cuba will never be intimidated, will never retreat."

Dooley was among the crowd, close enough to the stage to see the spittle fly. He recognized Guevara and other top brass from having seen them at the Hilton (and from his card collection) but not Jean-Paul Sartre and Simone de Beauvoir, the leftist French philosophers who had been invited to attend. Nor did he make much of Alberto Korda, the bearded photographer on assignment for the newspaper *Revolución* who was snapping pictures of the speakers, including one of Che in his black beret looking heroically into the distance, that would years later count among the most famous photographs in history.

Castro closed his speech with words that would become a revolutionary battle cry: *"Patria o muerte!"*—The fatherland or death. For all his previous nonchalance about the Revolution, Dooley now felt a patriotic stirring as he listened to Castro's atomic-age St. Crispin's Day speech. It had been just over a year since he'd left his quintessentially American existence in Brooklyn—ball games at Ebbets Field, outings with his mother to Times Square movie houses, his beloved YMCA pool—but these memories now felt distant, like someone else's life.

IN THE WAKE OF *LA COUBRE,* Michael and Roger were pulled toward different destinies, the former in the highest levels of the military, the latter in the trenches. In preparation for an amphibious American invasion he believed was inevitable, Castro, known by then as the country's Líder Máximo, decided to establish a detachment of elite military frogmen analogous to U.S. Navy SEALs, trained in land, air, and marine combat. An avid spearfisherman, Castro was adamant that the new unit of *tropas especiales* be trained in the latest scuba techniques.*

To compose his frogman unit, Castro resolved to recruit Havana's finest divers. He assembled this crack team from the ragtag group of spearfishermen, divers, and wayward youths who spent half their lives in the waters off the capital's shores. The most gifted among them was Juan Álvarez Forteza, a poor, Black lobsterman and spearfisherman who before the Revolution had delighted tourists in passing boats by diving for the coins they threw to him and returning to the surface with the coins in his mouth. The government's call eventually reached El Rubio's crew. At fifteen, Dooley was a year too young to join, but his older brother fit the ideal profile: an accomplished spearfisherman and a natural leader, powerfully built, ruthless, eager to see action. Michael—who by then went by the easier-to-pronounce nickname of Maico—would go on to lead missions targeting CIA operatives, according to Roger.

Michael's position in the unit would bring him into proximity with the most powerful men in the country. Castro employed the special forces as his security detail while traveling abroad. When at home, he often asked Michael and members of the *tropas especiales* to take him spearfishing off Cayo Piedra, his private island in the south of Cuba.

More than sixty years later, Roger still told stories of Michael's feats with barely suppressed awe. He recounted the time Michael and Álvarez took a Russian-made torpedo boat at night to waters fifty meters off Cayo Sal, an uninhabited island between Florida and Cuba, where they had heard that a small band of counterinsurgents had assembled in preparation for an attack on Cuba's northern beaches. After blackening

---

* Castro would go on to become a scuba-diving fanatic. Knowing of his fondness for diving, the CIA would later devise a plan to have an intermediary gift him a diving suit with a breathing apparatus dusted with foot fungus and tuberculosis. That assassination attempt ended in failure, as did other cartoonish CIA plots, like the exploding seashells placed in Castro's favorite diving spots, and the exploding cigar.

his face, Michael snorkeled silently to the island, snuck up on a stray fighter who was holding a walkie-talkie, grabbed him from behind with his hand over the man's mouth, thrust a grenade in his face, and told him either they would both die then and there, or the man would come with him back to Cuba. The fighter chose the latter option.

Envious of his brother's sudden transformation from juvenile delinquent into an elite paratrooper, Dooley sought another way to distinguish himself in service to the Revolution. An opportunity for advancement came in late 1960 when the Cuban government recruited volunteers among the *milicianos* and youth brigades to form several new battalions. Those who were selected would be allowed to exchange their black berets for more prestigious olive-green ones, a critical selling point for Dooley. Though here too the minimum age was sixteen, Dooley snuck through and was immediately sent on a grueling two-day, sixty-two-kilometer march across the countryside. This fitness test was followed by a two-week training program—marching, shooting, crawling with a rifle under low-slung barbed wire—held at Batista's lavish former country estate. "When we got there, they were still taking out furniture," Dooley recalled. "He had a solid-gold telephone."

Dooley completed his training, joined the 116th Battalion, and received his green beret. His company was stationed in a house in Miramar and was regularly mobilized in anticipation of an invasion Castro was convinced would come at any moment.

Dooley's irrepressible imagination bucked against the drab conformism of military life. Seeking to add flair to his uniform while awaiting a landing by counterrevolutionary forces, he left his trench and bought two bandoliers, which he filled with cartridges and wore in a cross over his chest in the flamboyant style of Pancho Villa.

"Take that shit off," his superior said when he returned. "Where do you think you are? Mexico?"

Castro had warned of an assault for so long that when the moment actually arrived, it came as no surprise. Before dawn on April 16, eight B-26 bombers flew over Cuba and unleashed bombs, missiles, and

machine-gun fire on airfields outside of Havana and Santiago in a si-
multaneous attack designed to neutralize Cuban air defenses. Seven
men were killed. It was obvious to all observers that the operation had
been hatched in America and that the action was prelude to an imminent invasion.

As he had following the explosion of *La Coubre,* Castro gave a eulogy for the victims of the attack that doubled as an ardent call to arms.
On a dais erected once again in front of the Christopher Columbus
necropolis, the leader delivered his most impassioned speech yet. His
voice strained and cracked above the roar of the crowd, at the front of
which stood Dooley's battalion. Like a virtuoso conductor exerting
absolute control over his orchestra, Castro built to a frenzied cre-
scendo, in which he made a seemingly off-the-cuff declaration that
would alter the global balance of power: "What they cannot forgive us
for," he exclaimed, "is that we made a socialist revolution under the
very noses of the United States!"

Up until that point, Castro had been deliberately vague about the
ideology behind his movement. But now, with American-financed
troops preparing to land on Cuba's shores, he had nothing to lose—
rather, he had little choice but to ally himself with the United States'
Cold War rival, the Soviet Union.

Dooley, who had joined the militia not out of any political conviction but because he sought the cachet that a gun and a uniform im-
parted, was now brandishing his rifle and chanting as loud as any of his
comrades, eager for the chance to fight and perhaps die protecting his
newly socialist homeland against the capitalist forces dispatched by the
country of his birth. In the span of a year and a half, the American boy
had become a Cuban man.

EARLY THE NEXT MORNING, Dooley and his comrades were loudly
roused from their bunks at their barracks in Miramar. They were ordered to dress for battle and assemble outside, where a fleet of military
trucks awaited. Amid the chaos and confusion, they were told that the

predicted invasion had begun. Dooley felt as if he were being swept up by history.

Several hours earlier, a group of *milicianos* driving a jeep on a deserted road along Cuba's southern shore had seen movement off the Bay of Pigs. The jeep drove onto the beach known as Playa Girón and swung around to catch a group of black-clad frogmen in its headlights, waist deep in the water and making their way toward land. The frogmen immediately aimed their automatic rifles at the car and opened fire. Bullets whistled around the vehicle and riddled its doors and windows as the driver slammed on the accelerator and the tires spun in the sand. The jeep's lights went out and the militiamen escaped into the darkness. Within minutes, a militia truck arrived with reinforcements, cornering the frogmen on the beach. A bloody firefight broke out, casings flying, rounds streaking through the night. The frogmen were merely the first wave, the vanguard of an onslaught that included 1,500 CIA-backed Cuban exiles seeking to topple the new Cuban government.

His rifle in hand, Dooley got into a truck without knowing where it was headed. His comrades from the battalion's light combat company got into others. It would be the last time he saw many of them. They were sent straight to the Bay of Pigs to confront the invading forces head-on after just two weeks of training. Among them were teenagers and sixty-year-olds, with nothing but automatic rifles to defend against tanks, rocket launchers, and machine guns.

Dooley, meanwhile, had been sent to Jaimanita, a small fishing town on the outskirts of Havana, to help Castro's dreaded secret security force, the G2, round up citizens deemed insufficiently loyal to the Revolution and temporarily detain them lest they rise up in support of the invasion. Dooley was then sent to stand guard in front of the Biltmore, Havana's most exclusive private country club and home to its only golf course, on which Castro was to establish his permanent residence. He had lucked into perhaps the cushiest deployment of the Bay of Pigs.

Two days later, he learned the fate that had befallen his comrades who had been sent to the front lines. Though their heroic efforts had contributed to the ultimate defeat of the invaders at Playa Girón, they suffered more casualties, proportionally, than any other unit involved in the fighting. When he heard the news, Dooley was left to contemplate the arbitrariness of his good fortune. He realized that it could just as easily have been him in the back of that truck. "I should have died out there," he said, still haunted by the memory. The close call had a sobering effect, taking some of the edge off his patriotic zeal. If he was to remain in the military—and there were few other jobs open to him at sixteen in postrevolutionary Cuba—it would not be as cannon fodder.

He coveted his brother's stature. If Roger was no different from the nameless grunts sent to die on the beach, Michael was one of an elite few. His frogman unit was sent to the Bay of Pigs after the fighting was over to recover weaponry left on the seafloor by fallen members of Brigade 2506, the CIA-backed group of Cuban exiles. Once his battalion was demobilized, Dooley sought to join Michael's *tropas especiales* now that he was of age. After all, he spent most of his free waking hours in the water. While off duty Michael went diving with Roger using the unit's scuba equipment. "He didn't exactly teach me," Dooley said. "He just gave me a tank, a regulator, and a weight belt, and threw me in the water."

Dooley might not have had Michael's natural toughness or brawny build, but there was no question that he was as skilled a diver as his brother. He was a good sharpshooter, too, having won several competitions. One day, he gathered the courage to ask his brother about becoming an elite navy diver.

"You can't do it, Yoyi," Michael said, using an affectionate nickname for Roger. "They won't let you because they can't have two brothers in the same unit." He must have known he was breaking his brother's heart.

Roger would later wonder whether Michael had told him the truth.

He yearned to prove that he had the makings of a hero, that he could be more than Maico Montañés's bookish little brother. He learned of a new school in Havana that would prepare recruits to be among the first fighter pilots in Cuba. If he couldn't dive his way to glory, he would fly. He showed up at the recruitment center downtown and found nearly a thousand young men with the same idea. An IQ test weeded out about half of them. A thorough physical examination further winnowed the group. Of those that remained, many were shunted off to a mechanic track. In the end, Dooley was one of just forty or so selected to participate in the program, which would teach him to fly Soviet-made MiG jets.

The school enforced strict discipline. He lived, studied, and trained in Ciudad Libertad (formerly Camp Columbia), Havana's only airbase, from which Batista had fled, and where the dove had landed on Castro's shoulder.

In October 1962, Dooley's superiors would place him in the crosshairs of the American military machine on the brink of a third world war. That month, a U.S. spy plane flying high over Cuba had photographed several Soviet-made nuclear surface-to-air missiles that could reach nearly every city on the U.S. mainland. Demanding the immediate removal of the missiles, President Kennedy imposed a naval blockade around Cuba, which Russian ships proceeded to breach. On Saturday, October 27, an American U-2 reconnaissance plane was shot down over the island. That same day, Russian leader Nikita Khrushchev received a letter from Castro urging him to respond to an American invasion of Cuba by "eliminat[ing] such danger forever through an act of clear legitimate defense, however harsh and terrible the solution would be." The Cold War thus threatened by the inexorable logic of escalation to boil over into thermonuclear Armageddon. Such a conflict, Kennedy had been warned, would likely wipe out a third of humanity. And Dooley feared he'd be the first one to go.

That night, as Kennedy's and Khrushchev's fingers hovered over nuclear buttons and the world held its breath, Dooley was in a hole.

A half-dozen Soviet-built MiG 15 fighter jets had just arrived at the airstrip. The planes were lined up on one end of the short runway, prepared for takeoff, their pilots awaiting orders in the cockpits. All support personnel had gone back to the barracks—all except Dooley, who'd been left on his own on the tarmac at the wheel of a jeep.

Dooley was ordered to remain on the strip to shuttle the pilots back to the base in case tensions were suddenly defused. And judging from the increasingly alarmed headlines over the previous week, the bellicose rhetoric on all sides, there was no reason to imagine they would be. Seeking a semblance of shelter from American bombs, Dooley dug out a shallow foxhole among the rocks that lined the runway and lay down in it with his rifle by his side. To throw off the bombers, the lights had been shut off in every building on the air base. Dooley looked up at a sky illuminated only by the stars and the thinnest sliver of moonlight.

He thought of the short distance that separated the United States from Cuba. He had made the crossing between Key West and Havana many times. It had taken him half a day by ferry. It would take bombers a few minutes. As he stared at the sky, all he could think was, "The first bomb is going to hit me."

Dooley did not sleep that night. He kept his eyes fixed on the stars, alert to the slightest movement, hoping he could distinguish the black of a bomber's underbelly from the black of the night, telling himself that if he saw a shadow approach, he would bolt.

The sun rose on Sunday morning. Later that day, Khrushchev and Kennedy reached a last-minute accord whereby the Russian missiles would be dismantled and removed from Cuba, with the tacit understanding that the United States would eventually withdraw its missiles from Russia's doorstep, in Turkey. Castro was enraged at what he considered a betrayal by Khrushchev, but Dooley was not displeased.

He graduated from the school in mid-1963. The next and final step of his training would be to get into the cockpit of an actual MiG jet. To his surprise, his instructors told him that this last phase would take place in Russia and that it could well lead to a permanent appointment as a pilot in the Cuban air force.

When he announced to Michael that he was leaving for Moscow, he felt for once like his brother's equal.

"You can be a frogman and I'll become a pilot," he said with pride. Dooley preferred the sea to the sky, but there was no disputing the prestige of the job. He expected Michael to congratulate him. Dooley was instead stunned by his brother's cold indifference. "Nothing," he recalled of Michael's reaction. It was as if Dooley had failed him by charting his own path.

In preparation for his new life, Dooley gave away his warm-weather clothes and managed to find the closest approximation available in Havana of a Moscow-appropriate wardrobe—parka, boots, fur hat. He began taking Russian lessons. But when he handed in his paperwork for his travel documents, the officer in charge furrowed his brow.

"You were born in New Jersey?" he asked.

Dooley's American origins had not raised any red flags when he had first moved back to Cuba with his family, before the Revolution. After all, Havana had been practically run by Yanks. But now that the United States had emerged as the greatest threat to the Castro regime, and Dooley was about to be sent to a Soviet air base, where he would be privy to sensitive military secrets, his U.S. citizenship by birthright had suddenly become a major liability.

"Bring me his whole file," the officer called out.

Dooley was sent home, assured that it would all be sorted out. Weeks passed with no news. When an officer called at last, it was to say that the rest of the group had already left. It was too late.

Dooley had hoped that by becoming a fighter pilot he might shape his own destiny, separate from his domineering brother. After his ambitions were dashed, he became despondent and turned to Michael for guidance. The latter was all too happy to welcome Roger back under his fraternal authority. The desire to escape his brother's shadow had been a driving force of Roger's young life, but it was ironically by following Michael into the ocean that he would find the recognition he sought, and the source of his own obsession.

Chapter 8

Depths of Obsession

The 1960s were a period of unbridled exploration comparable to the first wave of conquistadors' traversing the globe. The new frontiers were not beyond the horizon but above and below, in the black expanses of space and of the ocean's abyssal depths. And by many measures, the well-mapped cosmos was better understood than the uncharted, lightless oceanic underworld, teeming with monsters large and microscopic.

The rush to explore the ocean's depths and understand its mysteries became an earthly analogue to the space race that was then pitting the United States against the Soviet Union. Several public and private entities around the world had launched ambitious, science fiction–influenced projects to study the possibility of living and working underwater. As the Soviet bloc's island outpost in the Caribbean, Cuba was well positioned to serve as a base of operations.

Michael Dooley wanted in. Shortly after getting married—Fidel Castro's brother Raúl was the best man—Michael left the special forces to work for the Havana aquarium but continued to put his diving skills to use in the service of the nation. The country's subaquatic capabilities might have been negligible, but Michael believed he and his brother could be the ones to lead them into the future. The first step would be to study the history of humanity's forays below the ocean's surface, a task that fell primarily to Roger, the more academically inclined of the two brothers. He had long been searching for a way to distinguish himself from Michael, to wriggle out from under his shadow. With his self-guided dive into the research of the deep, he discovered where his gifts truly lay. In the process, an obsession was born.

Dooley learned that the feat of breathing underwater had been first achieved thousands of years ago, and on multiple continents. Sponge farmers in Crete would breathe through hollow reeds while swimming over shallow reefs. Upon arriving to the New World, Columbus observed native hunters doing much the same, using reeds as snorkels as they swam below the surface on their backs to sneak up on waterfowl. Attempts to go deeper than the length of a reed, requiring more sophisticated methods, date back to antiquity. Aristotle wrote of men descending to the seabed with inverted cauldrons over their heads to retain air. His student Alexander the Great was said to have surveyed the depths of his empire from within a glass enclosure tethered to a ship and dropped to the seafloor, a surely apocryphal story. Leonardo da Vinci, in one of his codices, sketched an underwater breathing contraption that, while ingenious in theory, was never put into practice.

Edmond Halley, of comet fame, perfected the design of the diving bell in 1691. An elaboration of the simple principle described by Aristotle, the device consisted of a large, weighted chamber—essentially a barrel with heavy weights along its open bottom and in some instances a glass window to let in light—that trapped a pocket of air as it was lowered from a ship, allowing the divers within to breathe before swimming out from the bottom and coming back to gulp more air.

The early nineteenth century brought the first functional, watertight diving suits, permitting helmeted divers to breathe air pumped down from the surface. In 1865, French inventors Benoît Rouquayrol and Auguste Denayrouze developed the first demand regulator, which, as a diver inhaled, automatically equalized the pressure of the air to that of the surrounding water. A prototype of their diving suit so dazzled the novelist Jules Verne that he outfitted Captain Nemo with one in *Twenty Thousand Leagues Under the Sea.* Nonfictional divers, however, found the design unwieldy, and it was not widely adopted.

The most transformative advance in diving technology came courtesy of the French naval lieutenant and spearfishing enthusiast Jacques-Yves Cousteau, who, during the German occupation of France in the early 1940s, partnered with the automotive engineer Émile Gagnan to develop a system that paired a simplified demand regulator with portable tanks of compressed air, allowing divers in masks and fins to swim freely at various depths. The innovation had effectively turned humans into amphibians, as radical an extension of mankind's reach as the invention of the airplane.

Just as impressive as Cousteau's engineering instincts was his marketing acumen. His self-contained breathing apparatus (scuba), patented in English-speaking countries as the Aqua-Lung, began selling worldwide in the late forties and became a phenomenal commercial success, turning Cousteau into a sage of the oceans and a very rich man. The Dooley brothers, whose introduction to the Aqua-Lung came from watching *Sea Hunt,* were among the first to use the system in Cuban waters, in the early '60s, after Michael joined the *tropas especiales* and gave Roger access to the equipment.

Cousteau's invention, Roger Dooley would write in one of several articles he contributed in this period to Cuba's *Mar y Pesca* magazine, "cut the umbilical cord that retained man to his native soil; it didn't liberate him, however, from his eternal physiological servitude: narcosis and decompression." Indeed, the deeper scuba divers went, the more they were subjected to narcosis, the altered mental state that results from breathing gases—namely oxygen, nitrogen, and carbon dioxide—at high pressures. It was a euphoric sensation to which Dooley would grow addicted. He never drank to excess and had no interest in drugs. Narcosis was his stimulant of choice, and he dove deeper and deeper to chase the thrill. "When you go down fifty meters, it's like you've had one drink," he told me. "Sixty meters, you've had a couple. You feel great, perfect. The blue is more blue. You want to follow the fish." Some divers, in their daze, forget their surroundings, lose track of time, and run out of air. Others have felt tempted to share their regulator with passing fish.

Dooley, in pursuit of an ever more intense fix, and seeking to prove his abilities, once set out to descend with tanks down to one hundred meters, thought to be about the limit of human tolerance when breathing bottled air. His diving partner, who would accompany him by boat when the day came, told him he was crazy. It was the equivalent of driving a hundred miles per hour through a city: as exhilarating as it was reckless. Only a small handful of divers around the world had done it before, and Michael was not one of them, which was surely part of the appeal for Roger. His goal was to reach the bottom of a precipitous drop-off near Havana, where he had once seen bioluminescent coral glow in the indigo depths beneath him. He sank slowly to the lulling rhythm of his own breath, the regulator marking each intake of cold, dry air with a sharp, hissing *khaaa* sound, and a flow of bubbles accompanying each exhalation. With every extra meter, every extra second, he grew more ensorcelled by this alien world and risked never leaving its embrace. By the time he touched the sandy bottom, he was completely dazed. "I looked at my watch and I couldn't read it," he recalled. At one hundred meters—where the pressure is eleven times that of the earth's atmosphere at sea level—air was entering his lungs at a concentration he'd never breathed before. According to the calculations he'd made before his dive, he could spend only about one minute at the bottom before slowly ascending back to the surface, lest he run out of air. He had no desire to leave, yet he shook free of his trance and forced himself to follow the plan he'd established. "I knew I had to head back up or I'd do something stupid." His stunning accomplishment would never be recorded, known only to his friends and brother.

The other form of physiological servitude Dooley described was the requirement of decompression. The longer divers spent at depth, the slower their ascent to the surface had to be to allow pressurized gases to gradually dissolve in their tissues and lungs. Should they rise too quickly, the gases would form bubbles that expanded within the body, causing serious, sometimes fatal afflictions collectively known as the bends. Such considerations limited the amount of time divers with limited air supply could spend below, as well as how deep they could descend.

Thus was born the concept of the underwater habitat, which would in theory allow aquanauts—as undersea explorers came to be called—to spend indefinite periods of time at depth. Flush with postwar optimism and the futuristic spirit of the space age, several visionaries decided to test the viability of the concept by building semiautonomous living quarters–cum–laboratories on the seabed. Cousteau and his team oversaw some of the first such experiments: Conshelf I, which housed two aquanauts for a week at a depth of ten meters off of Marseille in 1962; Conshelf II, a starfish-shaped underwater "village" in the Red Sea built the following year; and 1965's Conshelf III, a structure one hundred meters deep off of Nice, France.

Cousteau's project inspired others around the world to follow suit. Among them were Michael and Roger Dooley, who pushed the Castro government and Cuba's Academy of Sciences to fund the first such structure in Latin America.

Roger's research electrified his imagination and filled him with utopian fervor. "Three-quarters of our planet is submerged," he wrote, again in *Mar y Pesca*. "Oceanographers have calculated that the sea can cultivate vegetation nine times more efficiently than on land. In general, our marine world contains enough food, minerals, and fuels to sustain double the current global population. Humanity rightly aspires to exploit in the near future the resources that the ocean provides to satisfy its needs, which will be possible once the conquest of the continental shelf begins."

Their efforts would lead to a Cuban-Czechoslovak collaboration called Caribe I, designed as an answer to Cousteau's Conshelf project. On July 18, 1966, Michael Dooley and a Czech aquanaut (an unusual job in a landlocked country) named Josef Mergl entered the bright orange tank, which rested fifteen meters below sea level off the country's northern coast, eighteen miles east of Havana. They remained there—eating, sleeping, reading, working, resting—for three days. There was no room to stand in the submerged habitat. Roger made regular dives from the surface to deliver supplies and food. The descents were especially dazzling at night, when bioluminescent life pierced the darkness of the sea.

"Inside was all quiet and happy," Michael wrote in his journal at the end of day 2. "Outside I had seen the most beautiful colors that I can remember." Day 3: "I am tired by the reporters' questions and would like to be left alone."

It hardly compared to the three weeks that the inhabitants of Conshelf III had spent at one hundred meters the year before, but it was a start. The Dooleys had planted a stake for Cuba in the conquest of the deep, all the more impressive given the country's limited resources.

Fresh off this success, the brothers were once again called upon to do their country proud on the aquatic stage. In 1967, Cuba hosted the eleventh international spearfishing tournament, and Castro was determined to turn what had in previous years been a relatively obscure, small-scale competition into a major showcase of his increasingly isolated regime, directing the world's eyes to the splendor of Cuba's seas. More than thirty nations participated—triple the previous year's number—their teams parading in a lavish opening ceremony in Havana that rivaled the kickoff to the Olympic Games.

Michael and Roger were tapped to train Cuba's national team, their most high-profile assignment yet. Juan Álvarez Forteza, the former leader of the *tropas especiales,* whom the Dooley brothers had known since their days free diving with El Rubio's crew, would be the team's captain.

In the lead-up to the three-day competition, Roger helped the divers build up their stamina and breath control to go deeper and last longer on a lungful of air. Grouper, red snapper, and hogfish were the most common targets for the competition. Sharks, stingrays, and barracuda were forbidden since they tended to fight back. Cuba enjoyed a clear home-field advantage. Not only were its divers more familiar with the territory, but it was also understood that Castro expected a victory. A French Polynesian diver won the individual event, but the Cuban delegation's first-place finish in the team event was hailed as a triumph for the country and further cemented the Dooley brothers' roles as Castro's foremost envoys to Neptune's kingdom.

Roger Dooley was invited by the coast guard to lead classes in swimming, diving, and self-defense (he had become a black belt in judo). Dooley grew close with several members of the division's top brass and often socialized with them. At one coast guard party in 1967, he and a musician friend were messing around on the piano when a beautiful dark-eyed girl caught his attention. Dooley was twenty-two, and Zulema, the daughter of a coast guard secretary, was fifteen. They had little in common beyond a physical attraction, which was sufficient for a chaste, years-long courtship to begin, under her mother's close supervision. Dooley didn't mind the slow beginning. He was already involved in an all-consuming love affair with the sea, a passion he increasingly shared with his brother.

The siblings were becoming true partners, yet Michael always led the way. Having earned the president's favor with the Caribe I project and the spearfishing triumph, Michael was given a top position at the Institute of Oceanology, part of the Academy of Sciences. That he had been a poor student and claimed no expertise in the field posed no problem; Castro's good graces were all the qualifications required for virtually any job in Cuba. That Michael had recently married the daughter of the Academy's president evidently did not hurt either. He eventually hired his brother and closest collaborator, and together the Dooleys founded the Department of Underwater Investigations, with a mission to explore Cuba's largely uncharted continental shelf. Michael ran the group, while Roger was designated as head of underwater archaeology. He had no formal training in the discipline, but then, neither did anyone else in Cuba.

Unlike Michael, Roger discovered that he had an undeniable gift for research and a seemingly inexhaustible curiosity about the sunken remains of the past, be they from the pre-Columbian era, the golden centuries of the treasure fleets, or the twentieth century. He found it as thrilling to explore libraries and archives—sparse as they were in revolutionary Cuba—as it was to scour the seabed with a mask and fins. Just as he had experienced the intoxication of narcosis when he'd descended to one hundred meters, he was enraptured by the mysteries of the deep, entangled in a siren's embrace from which he would never escape.

Michael, Roger, and Juan Álvarez, perhaps the most accomplished diver in the country at the time, formed the core of the department. Their secretary was Che Guevara's soon-to-be widow, Aleida March. Rounding out the unlikely band of aquatic researchers with no academic background was an underwater photographer who turned out to be an incompetent diver. Shortly after forming the group, Michael contacted Alberto Korda, the photojournalist who had taken the world-famous snapshot of Guevara at the funeral for the victims of the *La Coubre* explosion. Cuba's most celebrated photographer, Korda had been at Castro's side since his days in the jungle and had gone on to travel the world with the caudillo, until he committed three blunders in rapid succession. First, while accompanying Castro on a state visit to the Kremlin, Korda made a crack about Nikita Khrushchev's bald head that made Castro laugh but did not go over well with the Soviet premier. Second, without Castro's permission, he sold a photograph to an Italian magazine showing the supreme leader in shorts, revealing the pale legs about which Castro was cripplingly self-conscious. But his most egregious faux pas was to submit a bill for all the expenses he had incurred on the road. For Castro, who was allergic to questions of money and, as legend had it, so unaccustomed to paying for anything as head of state that he didn't even have a bank account, Korda's invoice was an unforgivable affront to his authority. After being stripped of his official function, Korda—who had previously documented the Dooley brothers' Caribe I project—looked to restart his career from below sea level.

Korda was not a strong swimmer, and he was afraid of deep water. But his vivid color photos masterfully captured the stunning biodiversity of Cuba's waters and its beguiling wrecks. It fell on Dooley to train him, as he did all of the divers who worked for the Department of Underwater Investigations.

Dooley's favored training location was the wreck of a steam- and sail-powered three-mast ship called the *Sánchez Barcáiztegui,* which lay eighty feet deep inside Havana Harbor. The Spanish cruiser had been patrolling the bay to guard against an expected landing by Cuban rebels on September 18, 1895, when, in the darkness shortly before midnight, a steamship crashed into its bow, puncturing its hull below the waterline. The *Sánchez Barcáiztegui* soon flooded, pitched forward, and sank, taking more than thirty crew with it.

Years later, its remains were dynamited to clear the passage for other ships, leaving behind "just a jumbled mass of plates and beams partially covered by mud," as described by an American reporter whom Dooley guided through the wreck site in the late '60s. Mangled as it was, there were still spaces to enter, oddly shaped remnants of cabins and passageways and staterooms. A Cubist rendition of a ship, the wreck proved ideal, with its odd protrusions and angles, for Dooley to teach young recruits the intricacies of wreck diving. It also served as a de facto school of maritime archaeology for him, where he essentially taught himself the discipline, putting into practice as best he could the scientific techniques he had been reading about: studying the distance between objects, drawing conclusions about how they got there, conserving artifacts. The *Sánchez Barcáiztegui* was the first wreck partially salvaged by the Department of Underwater Investigations. Dooley returned to the site constantly, addicted as he had become to the discovery of archaeological details, no matter how small, that gradually filled in a picture of the past. Over the course of many dives, he and his team identified an area corresponding to what they believed had been the officers' quarters based on the concentration of valuable objects they found buried there, including a finely crafted candleholder, a teapot, perfume bottles that still seemed to bear traces of their fragrance if you concentrated hard enough, and golden medals that had once been pinned to the uniform of the commander. Though he had gone down with the ship, nothing remained of his body. Amid the wreckage, Dooley and his divers had also discovered corroded silver coins, as well as about a dozen perfectly round twenty-five-peseta gold coins that gleamed flawlessly even in the feeble light that reached those depths.

Many of the objects were displayed alongside Korda's photographs on the ground floor of the headquarters of the Department of Underwater Investigations, a seaside mansion once owned by a well-known baseball player. But most of the gold coins had been placed in a vault at the National Bank of Cuba. (Michael would later call Roger: "Remember the president of the bank? He was thrown out. They came to see me and asked if I'd gotten a receipt for those coins. Because when they opened the safe box, the coins were gone.")

From his earliest dives, Dooley had been fascinated by the vestiges of history concealed beneath the ever-shifting surface of the sea, that veil in perpetual motion, billions of years old yet at each instant new, with no memory of its own. Though he had been barred from becoming a pilot, diving was for him another way to fly, to soar and plunge, to travel not just through space but through time. Finding objects on the seafloor—the bottles, the coins, the captain's medals— connected Dooley directly to the last humans who had touched them, a melding more visceral than any museum display could offer. He could practically taste the tea in the teapot that had held nothing but seawater for decades. The entanglement seemed to defy the laws of physics. The countless ships that had foundered on Cuba's treacherous coastline since the days of Columbus were portals to the past. And Dooley wanted to pass through them all.

He considered it shameful that scholars on an island so pivotal to the trade routes of the Spanish Empire knew so little about the historic wrecks that littered its waters. So he set out to formally catalog them. In his office at the department's headquarters, Dooley hung a large map of Cuba. Each time he learned about a wreck, he placed a colored pushpin on the map to indicate its location. To establish this landscape of loss, he turned to the men who knew the sea best. He spent months driving along the island's coast to meet with state-run fishermen's cooperatives, asking members to tell him about any unusual forms they might have spied in clear shallow waters off the sides of their boats, but also to share local legends, myths, and rumors about lost ships, passed down through the generations. In the absence of a written record, this was how history survived, however distorted. These stories not only led Dooley to numerous wrecks but also imbued them with life.

Dooley came to be known across Cuba as the man to call when strange objects were found on the seafloor. One day in the late '60s, a lobster fisherman on the north of the island saw something shine through the glass-bottom bucket he used to search the shallows. The lobsterman, named Cuní, dove down and picked it up, at first mistaking the finger-sized metal bar for brass or copper. But when a rival fisherman and notorious scrap metal hustler in a nearby village offered him a thousand pesos for it, Cuní figured it must be worth far more. He took it to the local bank, which identified it as gold and alerted authorities in Havana. When government agents asked Cuní where he had discovered it, he claimed not to remember exactly and offered contradictory details, leading the agents to believe he had found a larger sunken treasure and was attempting to keep it to himself. They sent photos of it to Dooley and asked for his help in elucidating the mystery of its origins. He analyzed the images in detail, unsure what exactly he was looking for. He could not see any markings of any kind on the bar's smooth, unblemished surface, nothing to indicate its origins. Perhaps the absence of markings was itself a clue, he wondered. He had begun to assemble a small personal library on Spain's Caribbean fleets, and in consulting his volumes he learned that all officially registered gold bullion bore the mark of an assayer, attesting to its weight and noting that the royal tax had been paid. Dooley concluded that Cuní's unmarked gold bar had to have been contraband, the kind that was typically squirreled away in every nook and cranny of Spain-bound galleons, sewn into clothes or stuffed into bags of grain. But in that case, what could explain the presence of the solitary gold bar on the seabed? Where was the galleon from which it came? Dooley and his team searched the seabed in that area "inch by inch" and found nothing. Cuban secret police, meanwhile, tailed Cuní for years hoping he might lead them to a stash of gold. He never did.

Each artifact he examined, each shipwreck he dove to, deepened Dooley's practical education. In this haphazard, incremental manner, he was gradually becoming the archaeologist he had pretended to be. To his frustration, however, the Cuban government of the 1960s and '70s did not have the budget to properly excavate the wrecks he encountered, or to care for the objects his team was able to salvage. He had ordered three specialized tubs in which to conserve historical pieces; only two were built, and since no thorough excavation was ever authorized, they ended up being used to cool beers. Even if he had been granted the necessary resources, he had to realize that he was not qualified, in his midtwenties, to lead the kind of ambitious excavation he was reading about in the books and journals he pored over, the kind that was just starting to be undertaken by the first generation of serious maritime archaeologists on wrecks from antiquity in the Mediterranean. His love of history was not yet backed by expertise. Entranced as he was by the artifacts he and his divers found, Dooley—being an archaeological autodidact—didn't always know what to make of them. Not that he let his inexperience diminish his confidence, as he demonstrated when he spoke with the American journalist Richard Fagen, one of the few stateside reporters allowed to operate in Cuba in the late '60s. In an article for *Skin Diver* magazine, Fagen described photographs Korda had taken of a colonial Spanish wreck that Underwater Investigations had discovered off the tip of Varadero Peninsula: "The most tantalizing aspect of the photographs shown to me were two coral-encrusted cannons resting exactly parallel and very close to each other. Roger Montanes [*sic*] explained that these two barrels had been a single piece of ordnance joined together like Siamese twins, with a common touch hole designed to fire two balls linked by a long chain—a fearsome demasting device. He said that he had read that such twin cannons were manufactured at one time but that to the best of his knowledge none had ever been recovered from the sea."

Dooley would later admit that he had gotten this entirely wrong, that no such weapon had ever existed. What he had "read" he had more likely imagined. Dooley was so starved for genuine scholarship that he asked friends and acquaintances who managed to gain permission to travel abroad if they could return with whatever books on shipwreck salvage, Caribbean history, maritime archaeology, and treasure hunting they could get their hands on. He assembled much of his library thanks to his mother's brother, a Cuban-born, decorated World War II veteran who still lived in the United States and would regularly mail Dooley books and articles about diving, archaeology, and treasure hunting. The volumes kept flowing in until Cuban authorities caught on. After intercepting several packages, they interrogated Dooley about why he was receiving materials from an enemy state without permission. How were they to know that these texts about galleons and underwater discoveries did not contain coded messages?

He would have to make do with what few books he could find in Cuba. It was clear that there would never be enough for him to fulfill his archaeological ambitions. Meager resources and the trade embargo Kennedy imposed on the island had left its bookstores and libraries understocked. The Academy of Sciences' budget, Dooley said, allowed him to order all of one book a year from abroad. Like every social science, archaeology depended on informed conjecture—the ability to form hypotheses—but without proper information, all that was left was imagination, of which Dooley had no shortage.

Chapter 9

Sea Change

By the late 1960s, the large map of Cuba in Dooley's office at the Department of Underwater Investigations was studded with dozens of colored pushpins, each one representing a shipwreck that he and his team had catalogued and inspected, many of them previously undiscovered. The project to document all of the island's wrecks consumed his life. To his dismay, most were unremarkable modern vessels that had been scuttled after falling into disrepair. There was nothing exciting about them, no drama to their demise. The *Sánchez Barcáiztegui* remained the most historically noteworthy wreck he'd explored, and he knew every inch of it by heart. Dooley longed to track down some of the elusive shipwrecks he'd read about, such as the Spanish warships sunk by the U.S. Navy off Santiago de Cuba in the Spanish-American War of 1895 or a German U-boat that had disappeared in Cuban waters during World War II. But above all he yearned to find and excavate one of the majestic galleons thought to have wrecked along the island's shores at the height of the Spanish Empire. There was no greater prize in his eyes.

In 1968, the year he finally received a decent salary thanks to his job at the Academy of Sciences, Dooley proposed to Zulema to, as he put it, "get beyond the kissing and holding hands stage." The two were married shortly after. Dooley's mother had arranged for them to spend their honeymoon at the glamorous Hotel Nacional, where she still worked. It was there, on one of their first nights alone, that the young newlyweds had their first screaming match. This was normal, Dooley tried to convince himself. All couples fight. But a fault line had been established between her needs and his ambitions, and it would only expand over time.

Even as life at home grew tense, he was beginning to find professional fulfillment as currents brought him ever closer to the world he wished to join. In September 1970, the World Confederation of Underwater Activities—a global organization founded by Jacques-Yves Cousteau and known by its French acronym CMAS—held its first international scientific symposium, in Havana. It had been Michael Dooley's idea. He had risen to the group's attention following Cuba's victory in the spearfishing tournament and his participation in the Caribe I underwater habitat project. Invited to attend a CMAS gathering in Paris shortly after, Michael won over the organization's leadership, which made him its vice president of science. In that capacity, he convinced Cousteau and his colleagues to host the symposium in the Cuban capital.

The event drew some of the most respected maritime archaeologists in the nascent field, including one of Roger's heroes, the Israeli scholar Avner Raban. That Michael asked Roger to head Cuba's archaeological delegation was the honor of the younger man's life. That there was nobody more qualified to do so, however, testified to the nonexistence of underwater archaeology as an academic discipline in the country. Dooley's keynote presentation at the symposium, delivered nervously before Raban and other international eminences, made no secret of the country's shortcomings in this area and noted that this was particularly ironic given Cuba's centuries-long reputation as a graveyard of ships. "For more than a century our seafloor has been invaded by smugglers and subaquatic thieves who pillaged the historical riches of this country left and right," he argued.* "It was not until 1969"—the year he and his brother founded the Department of Underwater Investigations—"that we began to undertake a methodical and analytical study of what constituted the principles of subaquatic archaeology in Cuba."

Dooley's talk was a call to arms, drawing attention to Cuba's role as the "key of the New World," and to the unmatched potential of its innumerable shipwrecks, if properly studied, to enrich our understanding of history. He imagined that he would be the one to lead this study. But his experience at the symposium, where top archaeologists including Raban overloaded him with books and journals and wisdom gleaned from years of fieldwork, made it clear to him just how much he had to learn about the profession—the modern techniques of observation, excavation, conservation, and analysis—and how much he had been faking it up to that point.

In 1971, following a change in the leadership of the Academy of Sciences, the Department of Underwater Investigations was forced to disband. Michael returned to the military, where he would quickly rise up the special forces' chain of command. Time and again, Michael had been singled out by Cuba's ruling class and afforded increasingly more power and prestige. Roger's path, by comparison, was a constant struggle for recognition. His years in the department had been perhaps the happiest and most fulfilling in his life. But with the breakup of their team, he was at last free to pursue a life on his own terms, out of his brother's shadow.

Dooley was now a father—Zulema had given birth to a daughter, Liliam, in 1971—and with a family to take care of, he resolved to obtain a degree in maritime archaeology at the Academy of Sciences,

---

* This quote is taken from a *Mar y Pesca* article largely based on Dooley's presentation to the symposium.

becoming in earnest what he had claimed to be for several years. Since no such degree was on offer, he had to cobble together the course of study himself, pursuing a three-year degree in oceanology, which he would follow with a master's in traditional archaeology.

The study of ocean physics taught Dooley about all the forces that can affect a ship before it sinks and afterwards: winds, currents, temperature, pressure, marine life, and the chemical action of the sea. The Academy's archaeology program, by contrast, was strictly landbound, focused on Cuba's pre-Columbian settlements—and with a government-imposed underpinning of Marxist theory. He participated in two excavations, including one of a two-thousand-year-old site, which taught him the essential concepts of the discipline—the biochemical interplay between object and environment, the emphasis on minimal interference and on studying the spatial relation between objects. These would be the same considerations whether the site in question was submerged or buried. Dooley continued throughout this period to dive and set records, as if he were still competing with Michael. He was the first to explore the two deepest underwater caves in the country, one at sea and one inland, filled with fresh water down to seventy-two meters, at the bottom of which his flashlight sliced through perfect blackness and found fish with no eyes. He ventured through a previously unexplored network of narrow underwater tunnels, wandering a once-dry landscape that had long since been drowned by rising seas, and found his way to what he called a "saloon," an air-filled chamber with a sandy floor and prehistoric pictograms on the ceiling.

All the while he added to his growing database of Cuban shipwrecks. It was in this period that Dooley made his two most historically important discoveries to date. He was leading a class on archaeology for divers in Santiago de Cuba, on the eastern tip of the island, where a major naval battle had taken place on July 3, 1898, turning the tide of the Spanish-American War in favor of the United States. The confrontation, in which several Spanish warships were sunk, definitively severed Cuba's colonial ties to Spain. Maps drawn by the defeated Spanish had placed one of the ships, the destroyer *Furor*, just off the coast, but it had never been found. Dooley decided to search for it and invited his students and local divers to conduct a methodical survey of the area. Assuming that the metal hull would have remained largely intact and would be visible to the naked eye, they didn't use any survey equipment other than fins, masks, and bottles, but merely fanned out to ensure that no stretch of the seafloor would be overlooked. They found the *Furor* lying in twenty meters of water.

Searching for the wreck of the cruiser *Cristobal Colón,* the last ship to fall in the Battle of Santiago, was more difficult. That was by design. It was known that the *Colón's* captain had scuttled the 366-foot cruiser by a deserted beach at the mouth of the fast-moving Turquino River to keep it out of American hands and avoid further bloodshed. Local fishermen had a general sense of where the wreck was, but no one had dared to explore the turbulent, shark-infested waters until Dooley picked a spot and dove down. What he would remember most clearly about the dive, one of the most challenging he'd attempted due to the treacherous currents and low visibility, was the roar of boulders and smooth river rocks rolling underwater. Struggling to keep his movements controlled and efficient in order to conserve air, he descended slowly, unable to see more than a few feet in front of him. All of a sudden, at about twenty feet of depth, the waters turned crystal clear, and the "monster" of a wreck jumped out at him. The vessel lay against a craggy slope, ninety feet down at its deepest point. Every surface of the battered cruiser had been colonized by algae and coral. Dooley pursued fish into the corridors, past guns, down stairwells, and through what structures remained intact, the first human being to traverse the ship in seventy years.

IN THE ACADEMY OF SCIENCES, as in every institution in Cuba, loyalty to the Communist Party was valued more highly than any professional credential. Having registered with the Youth Communist Party in order to join the militia as a teenager, Dooley was granted authority over nonparty members in his department regardless of their age or qualifications, earning him little more than their suspicion and resentment. But as he settled into family life, Dooley was feeling increasingly disenchanted by the party. He no longer felt the revolutionary fire that had launched him into the streets of Havana in his teens, especially now that Castro's regime was proving itself, in the eyes of many, to be just as corrupt and authoritarian as Batista's.

As his thirtieth birthday approached—by this point his blond hair had darkened and he had grown a beard to conceal his weak chin—Dooley was informed that he would soon age out of the Youth Communist Party. To continue benefiting from preferential treatment, he would have to join the party proper, which required he devote several years of service to the country. The Communist Party secretary for the Academy of Sciences had taken the liberty of signing Dooley up for a job harvesting sugarcane in the provinces, a coveted opportunity to prove his devotion to a government that claimed above all to serve the peasantry (and was desperate to increase its production of sugar, which it bartered for Russian oil). Dooley, who believed he had finally found his calling in maritime archaeology, was crestfallen. He turned down the assignment, claiming that he was writing his thesis and that he needed to take care of his aging grandmother. Shocked by Dooley's audacity, the representative brought him before the party secretary for all of Havana, who urged him to reconsider, warning that the consequences of refusal would be grave—including permanent suspension from the party, which controlled all the levers of power in Cuba. Dooley expressed his regret but still declined. On one hand, he knew it wasn't advisable to defy the party. On the other, every day he spent hacking away at sugarcane was one spent away from the water.

Dooley's single-minded dedication to his passion put him at odds not only with the party but with Zulema, who was growing ever more fanatical about the precepts of the Revolution and unquestioning of its propaganda. There remained affection between them, but the ideological rift had grown too wide to bridge. Their daughter Lili recalled her parents' frequent loud spats: "My mother and father were very different," she said. "The mix between a faithful communist, humble mother and a free, idealistic, dreamer, American father was not a good mix in the '70s in Cuba."

Dooley earned his master's in archaeology in 1975, two years after receiving his oceanology degree. He had officially become Cuba's first maritime archaeologist. But the pride he felt quickly gave way to the realization that there simply wasn't much for a maritime archaeologist to do in Cuba. There was no budget to commission a proper excavation of any of the wrecks he'd found, especially not during a global economic crisis that left the country with a dire shortage of hard currency and threatened to undermine the very foundations of Castro's government. And his meager academic stipend was barely sufficient to put food on the table.

Despite his tight finances, Dooley gave his daughter a happy childhood. They lived in a small apartment on the corner of a quiet, tree-lined street in the Vedado. Lili's first memory of her father was of sitting on the floor while he read in his study, surrounded by maps, old books, and piles of *National Geographic* magazines. She recalled thumbing through "historical catalogs of weapons, shipbuilding, anchors, etc. that had very nice pictures. I liked them a lot." At bedtime, he would tell her "the real stories of pirates in Cuba, of the buried treasures in the sand." The most prized object in the house was a large amphora that Michael had taken from an ancient wreck while diving in France. (It had fallen and cracked several times, and Dooley had fixed it with glue.) But Lili's favorite part was the entrance hall, which Dooley, in an imaginative flourish that made the most of his limited resources, had covered from floor to ceiling with colorful images of fish and coral cut out from magazines, "like a giant printed fish tank."

From behind his wooden desk, Dooley watched Lili's eyes widen as she flipped through his books. Seeing her share his passion, he felt his love for her grow every day and couldn't bear the idea that she would want for anything. His obsessions would have to wait. In his early thirties, he was ready to make significant contributions to maritime archaeology, but Cuba wasn't. In the meantime, he needed money.

He approached the Ministry of Tourism and proposed to turn Cuba into a prime diving destination. Nobody was more familiar with the country's dazzling coral reefs, caves, and shipwrecks than he, and now he sought a chance to profit off his knowledge. All he would need, he said, was a small budget and a boat. The ministry agreed, but the budget he received was even smaller than he'd requested, and the boat was made of cement and floated with difficulty. It was nevertheless sufficient for him to locate the most sublime diving spot in Cuba, a paradise off the Isle of Pines, near Castro's private island. Dooley and a team of scientists spent three months in the area's crystalline waters, bathed in a resplendent spectrum of blues, documenting every canyon, every cavern, every species of sea life, every anchor, every wreck.

The need to provide for his family drove Dooley to loosen some of the archaeological rigor he'd long espoused. Not content to let these underwater splendors speak for themselves, he felt compelled to dress them up to give divers a frisson of adventure: He dropped a centuries-old iron cannon onto the seabed, letting foreign visitors imagine that it had come from a lost Spanish treasure galleon. The gun had in fact been salvaged on the other side of the island, but nobody knew what ship it was from, and, as he told himself, it wasn't being conserved any better above sea level. Here, at least, it was more likely to make people dream. Archaeology and tourism followed different rules, but they were both fundamentally about telling stories.

Roger Dooley's life seems in retrospect to be a great tangle of choice and fate. He was a relentless hustler, a quality that served him well in a mercurial environment like Castro's Cuba, where staying afloat required guile and gumption and constant adaptation. And yet these qualities would eventually mark him out for suspicion in circles where sober judgment, deep experience, and academic discipline made one's reputation. He had the makings of a great researcher, and an interest in prioritizing historical preservation over a quick cash grab, and yet to survive and attempt to thrive, he took risks that could have huge consequences.

Perhaps the most profound of these came in 1978, when a far more profitable—if more politically fraught—opportunity came his way, once again via his brother. Michael had reconnected with a shady Cuban American figure named Fernando Coba, who in the 1950s had lived in Brooklyn two doors down from the Dooleys' apartment. Though he and their mother were friendly, Isabel had warned her sons to "be careful with that guy." Coba was then known as, among other things, a smuggler of people and merchandise, particularly skilled at forging birth certificates to allow Cubans, Puerto Ricans, and Russians to enter the United States. He returned to Cuba after the Revolution and became a top official of its secret police force, the widely feared G2. But in 1963, according to U.S. intelligence sources, he fled aboard the S.S. *Shirley Lykes,* blending in with more than a thousand refugees—mostly families of exiles and Bay of Pigs invaders—who made the trip from Havana to Port Everglades, Florida. Some claimed Coba had turned against Castro after the latter's turn toward socialism, others that he had been discharged from the police force for reasons related to drug trafficking. The CIA didn't buy either explanation: A declassified report on Coba from 1964 described him as a likely "Castro agent."

The Castro regime, it turns out, was just as suspicious of him. In the late 1970s, based in Miami, Coba ran a medical air-transport service permitted to operate flights between Cuba and the United States. After President Jimmy Carter relaxed restrictions prohibiting Americans from traveling to Cuba, Coba thought to expand his operations to facilitate flights to Havana and back for Cuban American exiles. The government-approved Panamanian company that had previously operated such flights—Havanatur—had just been expelled from the United States, which considered the outfit to be an illegal Cuban agent. Desperate for the dollars that American travelers would bring, the Castro regime authorized the creation of American Airways Charter, with Coba at its head, to take over Havanatur's U.S. business. But unsure what game Coba was playing—the operation would, after all, be the perfect cover for a double agent—the Cuban government would need its own trusted man on the ground in Miami to keep a close eye on him. Michael, being of American birth and unquestionably loyal to Havana, would have been perfect for the job. The idea was quickly dismissed, however, as Michael's membership in the Communist Party and his high-ranking position in the military would surely have put him on the radar of U.S. intelligence.

The state turned to his brother, Roger, who was also born in the United States, and whose rejection of the party now seemed fortuitous. That he had experience in tourism and had trained to become a pilot provided further justification. For once Dooley was offered a chance that had been denied to his brother. He gladly accepted. In 1979, he moved to Florida and became vice president of American Airways Charter. In the United States, he stopped using the surname Montañés and was once again Roger Dooley. From $17 a month, his salary jumped to $1,500 a week. And from the humility of life in communist Cuba, he was thrown headlong into the hypercapitalist, cocaine-fueled, neon-tinted decadence of Miami. Dooley was never tempted by the ubiquitous white powder, but with his natural exuberance and chaotic, mile-a-minute patter, he fit right in.

According to an investigative report on American Airways Charter in the Spanish-language edition of the *Miami Herald,* "The once-unknown company now handles the $70,000,000 annual business generated by the trips of Cuban exiles." For the first time, Dooley was living large and made regular trips to Havana to visit his family, lavish gifts in hand. It was on one of those visits that his second daughter, Betty, was conceived.

He would also bring home books on archaeology, diving, and nautical history that were unavailable in Cuba, gradually building out his personal library. While he welcomed the higher salary, access to such books was to him perhaps the most valuable perk of his assignment. But it was unclear when he would ever return to the work he loved. Just a few years before, Dooley had been on a seemingly straightforward path to his goal of becoming a world-class maritime archaeologist, a gifted diver and dutiful student rubbing shoulders with luminaries in the field. Yet his life's detour through Florida had taken him far astray from those ambitions, and now his association with Coba and his suspicious network threatened to put them forever out of reach. Throughout his time in Miami, various voices among the city's community of Cuban exiles accused the employees of American Airways Charter of being agents of Castro's government. Before long, Dooley received a visit from the FBI at the company's Hialeah offices.

"Do I need to get a lawyer?" he asked.

The G-man told Dooley it was not him they were interested in but his brother, which didn't particularly surprise Dooley, given Michael's ties to Castro's inner circle. After asking him a series of questions, the agent assured Dooley that he had nothing to fear from the FBI. But that didn't mean he had nothing to fear.

One night, about a year into the job, Dooley was working late at the office and hankering for a sandwich. He stepped out the back door to the stairwell. There, in a corner, was a black Samsonite case that clearly did not belong to the old janitor, the only other person in the building at that hour. Dooley walked over to it, crouched down, and inspected the suitcase but made sure not to touch it. His heart pounding, he warned the janitor to stay back. All too aware of the spate of attacks that had targeted Cuban interests in the United States since the late sixties, he called the police, who arrived with a bomb-sniffing dog. The dog trotted over to the corner, sniffed, and signaled that the case was packed with explosives. Dooley believed that the suitcase, which was promptly disposed of, had been planted by Alpha 66, one of several anti-Castro terrorist organizations operating in Miami. Shortly after the incident, which was covered by the local papers, a member of another such outfit, Omega 7, hurled an unlit Molotov cocktail through the window of a different Cuban-affiliated charter company, operated by Coba's wife. "The next time, if they continue the trips to Cuba, we'll burn it down," the group warned the *Miami Herald*. From then on, Dooley looked over his shoulder wherever he went and never kept the same car for long. The gnawing sense of persecution he felt in the streets of Miami exceeded anything he'd felt in totalitarian Cuba.

The threat of assassination was the only exciting part of the job. Dooley's responsibilities at American Airways Charter consisted primarily of cosigning checks to make sure Coba wasn't skimming. The sinecure was well paid, but it was an unstimulating bore and an obvious dead end in his pursuit of maritime glory. Dooley sought a way back out to sea. The minimal requirements of the position left him plenty of time to start his own side hustle, called Scuba Cuba, organizing trips to Cuba for wealthy Americans. For the diving-obsessed in America, Cuba was the ultimate destination and Dooley its sole gatekeeper. "Due to political circumstances over the past 20 years, Cuban waters have experienced virtually no divers," a Scuba Cuba brochure read. "The net result being virgin reefs, walls and wrecks."

Scuba Cuba allowed Dooley to take advantage of the growing craze for scuba diving and wreck hunting. In the late 1970s and early '80s, American pop culture was suddenly replete with subaquatic spectacles. Headlines announced several multimillion-dollar troves of silver and gold found in sunken ships. *The Deep,* based on *Jaws* author Peter Benchley's novel about treasure hunters in Bermuda, was the second-highest grossing movie of 1977 after *Star Wars,* only partly because of Jacqueline Bisset's permanently wet T-shirt. The underwater thrillers of Clive Cussler topped the bestseller list year after year.

In late 1981, Cussler and Al Giddings, the swaggering diver and cinematographer who'd shot the underwater scenes in *The Deep* as well as in that year's James Bond movie *For Your Eyes Only* (and who would go on to shoot *The Abyss* and *Titanic* for James Cameron), planned a scouting trip for a movie about Cuba's forbidden, wreck-ridden depths and engaged Dooley to organize it for them. Cussler backed out at the last minute, but Giddings went ahead, joined by the esteemed Stanford professor and journalist Richard Fagen, who had befriended Dooley years before while writing the article about the Department of Underwater Investigations. Fagen—a Cuba specialist who had interviewed Fidel Castro several times—described Dooley as "Cuba's foremost underwater archaeologist and explorer." His detailed diary of the trip makes it clear he and Giddings had fallen totally under Dooley's charm, taken in by his contagious sense of adventure.

They all met up in Miami. "We get the gear out of storage, and head in Roger's Cadillac (he changes cars every month or so for safety) . . . for the back of the airport where the private planes are," Fagen wrote in his diary. "For sure, the CIA has at least half a dozen planes there, and the drug runners at least 200." They took off in a Cessna 420 propeller plane, motored over the Keys, and landed in Havana an hour and a half later. From there, they flew to Santiago, where Dooley was eager to show off the cruiser *Cristobal Colón,* the Spanish-American War wreck he'd discovered a few years before.

The trio traveled the next day to the mouth of the Turquino River, where the Spanish vessel was located, but Dooley and his old friend Juan Álvarez had trouble finding their way back to it through the roiling, muddy waters. The divers could not see more than twenty feet ahead. But eventually, the *Colón's* imposing silhouette emerged, a shadow at first, revealing its coral-covered contours only up close. "The wreck is still impressive. Roger and I swim the circumference," Fagen wrote. "I begin to see the shapes beneath the encrustations. There are the two engine telegraphs, the compass, the steering pedestal, a vast ring of speaking tubes. All are intact. I take my knife and scratch through to the edge of one engine telegraph. It is solid brass."

Dooley and Fagen watched in disbelief as Giddings brought up object after object from the wreck: bottles, platters, the ship's nameplate and binnacle. "Back on deck, we examine the loot," wrote Fagen. "It is clear that the *Colón* is a treasure trove of lovely artifacts if the Cubans will do the work necessary and take the care. The bridge, for example, could be reconstructed in a museum in all of its glory. It all would be very nice. Roger—always the capitalist—says he is going to sell this stuff to the Spaniards!"

That night, over a dinner of plantains and meat, the men toasted to their finds with beer and Portuguese wine. Dooley—who has trouble winding down after he has begun talking—entertained his American friends with yarn after yarn. He joked about the heavy, unwieldy Soviet equipment Cuban divers were forced to rely on, including a knife that could supposedly cut through rock. And he mentioned the sunken Nazi U-boat off the coast of Cuba that he vowed one day to find. Perhaps, he suggested, *that* could be the film. "We begin discussions of what kind of movie could help Roger," noted Fagen. That Dooley was dreaming of Hollywood despite his close association with the Castro regime is a testament to his irrepressible optimism, his expansive sense of the possible.

On the third night of the trip, after a visit to another wreck from the same momentous battle, Fagen and Dooley roomed together, affording the journalist an intimate look at Dooley's personal quirks: "He has a touch of vanity. Uses sprays, powders, and a hairdryer," Fagen noted with amusement. Fagen continued to closely observe Dooley at dinner the following night: "People are talked out except for Roger. He goes on at 1,000 words a minute in both languages." And the next day, when Dooley was unable to secure the charter flight back to Havana that he had promised for his friends, Fagen identified an enduring quality of Dooley's, which would come to bear in his later quest for the *San José:* "I think Roger acts entirely in good faith, but he wants *so* much to pull these things off that he brushes over details."

The visit impressed upon Fagen and Giddings the necessity of helping Cuba to properly care for its invaluable wrecks—many of them hundreds of years old—and emboldened them to arrange a meeting with Castro to discuss the topic, knowing of his fondness for diving. "Without a commitment of funds on the part of the Cuban Government, and some kind of counterpart funds on the U.S. side, it will be impossible ever to do the kind of salvage and museum work which the *Colón* needs," Fagen wrote in a report. But all hope for such U.S.-Cuba collaborations would soon come to a crashing end, and with it Dooley's good standing.

In February 1982, Dooley, Coba, and five other people affiliated with American Airways Charter were charged with violating the trade

Roger Dooley visiting the Torre del Oro (tower of gold) in Seville,
which overlooks the Guadalquivir River, in 1984.

Roger Dooley collection

The General Archive of the Indies in Seville contains more than sixty million documents dating back to the time of Columbus.

Archivo General de Indias

The research hall of the General Archive of the Indies, where Dooley searched for clues to the final resting place of the galleon *San José*.

Archivo General de Indias

A painting of the *San José*, commissioned by Dooley and based on his obsessive research.

Roger Dooley collection

Wager's Action off Cartagena (circa 1747), by Samuel Scott, offers a dramatic depiction of the Battle of Cartagena on June 8, 1708, drawing from English reports that the *San José* "blew up."

National Maritime Museum, Royal Museums Greenwich

An engraving of the hellish silver mines of Potosí, where most of the *San José*'s silver came from, circa 1750.

The Portobelo fair, where riches from the viceroyalty of Peru were loaded onto galleons to be shipped to Spain.

No portrait of the Count of Casa Alegre, captain general of the *San José* and the Spanish treasure fleet, is known to exist, but this painting of his brother and fellow high-ranking official, Francisco, may bear a resemblance.

Courtesy of Javier de Solis

Commodore Charles Wager, commander of the English squadron that intercepted the Spanish treasure fleet on June 8, 1708. Portrait by Godfrey Kneller.

National Maritime Museum, Royal Museums Greenwich

Roger and Michael Dooley with (back row from left) their stepfather, Armando Montañés; their mother, Isabel; and a friend in Brooklyn's Prospect Park, circa 1958. Though younger by a year, Roger was the taller of the two brothers.

Roger Dooley collection

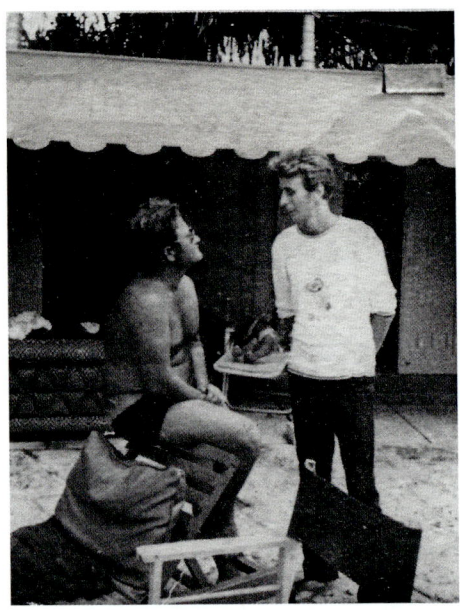

Roger (right) and Michael in
Varadero, Cuba, 1967.

Roger Dooley collection

Cuban guerrillas at
the Havana Hilton
in January 1959.
Lois Herman/Corbis

Cuban rebel leader Fidel Castro
at his temporary headquarters in
the Havana Hilton, with his son
Fidelito, in February 1959.
Bettmann/Getty Images

Dooley (far left) with the victorious
Cuban team at the World
Spearfishing Competition in 1967.
Roger Dooley collection

Dooley in Havana, 1963.
Roger Dooley collection

El equipo Cuba que nos representará en el VII Campeonato Mundial de Caza Submarina.

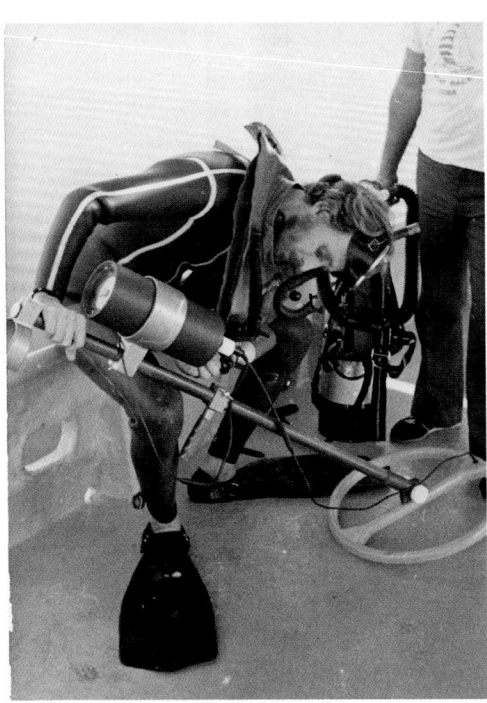

Dooley preparing to use an underwater metal detector.

Roger Dooley collection

Dooley addressing fellow underwater researchers at the first scientific symposium of the World Confederation of Underwater Activities, or CMAS, in Cuba, 1970.

Roger Dooley collection

The *Trinidad*, the cement diving boat on which Dooley conducted his surveys of the Cuban coastline in the late 1970s.

Roger Dooley collection

Dooley with shipwrecked artifacts
confiscated from Cuban fishermen, 1976.

Roger Dooley collection

Dooley (left) and a colleague promoting
his diving charter company Scuba Cuba
in Las Vegas, 1981.

Roger Dooley collection

Along with journalist Richard Fagen, Dooley (in yellow) heaves at the anchor of the
Spanish–American War wreck *Cristobal Colón*, near Santiago de Cuba, 1981.

Courtesy of Al Giddings

Cuban diver Juan Álvarez Forteza, Dooley, and Fagen examine artifacts from the Spanish–American War wreck *Cristobal Colón*.
Courtesy of Al Giddings

Dooley (center) with French diving pioneer Jacques-Yves Cousteau (in gray shirt) and members of his research team in Havana, 1985.
Archivo General de Indias

embargo by bringing contraband into Cuba, as part of Ronald Reagan's crackdown on the island nation. Among the items transported, according to court documents, were "four Pepsi-Cola dispensing machines, communications equipment, office equipment and supplies, numerous quantities of foodstuffs, United States currency, perfume, scuba equipment, mail, auto parts and tires and aircraft parts. Testimony at the trial also revealed that computer equipment had been obtained in the United States and sent to Cuba."

Both Dooley and Coba had fled the United States before they could be sentenced to prison. Following a grand jury investigation of American Airways Charter, they knew that charges would be imminent. Dooley was in Mexico when the news broke. Days earlier, he had intentionally spilled coffee on his soon-to-expire U.S. passport so that he could request a replacement from the American embassy in Mexico City before the axe fell. Since he had never become a Cuban citizen, this would ensure that he could continue to travel internationally for another ten years—as long as he didn't set foot in the United States.

His American idyll was over. "At least I got to live well for two years," he said. The long-term repercussions were more severe. Though Dooley managed to avoid jail time, his name—and various aliases—would wind up alongside those of international criminals, terrorists, and spies on a list of blocked persons, established by the U.S. Treasury Department's Office of Foreign Assets Control. The designation technically forbade him from doing business in the United States or with American citizens. Dooley did not immediately grasp how devastating the implications would be. He would be marked as an international pariah, eradicating any hope he still harbored of returning to academia and working alongside his archaeological heroes on shipwrecks of global historical importance. The Miami job was supposed to be merely a way station on the road to that dream, a means by which to afford it. Instead, the bright, respectable future he imagined would become a casualty of his compromise.

The fallout from the American Airways Charter affair deposited

Dooley back in Havana, where despite being able to afford material comforts out of reach for most Cubans thanks to his American savings, he was back in the same archaeological backwater he had left, with its limited opportunities for someone desperate to do serious underwater work—only now limited in his ability to travel and marked as a criminal in the eyes of his home country.

And yet, in another of those swings of luck that seemed to define Dooley's life, another door was about to crack open in Cuba.

Chapter 10

Nuestra Señora de las Mercedes

While Dooley had been in Miami, Castro's close friend Max Marambio, a Chilean businessman who had served as a bodyguard to President Salvador Allende before Augusto Pinochet's coup, had founded a state company called Carisub, whose mission was to extract wealth from Cuba's waters in an effort to shore up the nation's disastrous finances.

The organization had no scholarly pretension, and its activities were shrouded in intrigue. "From the creation of Carisub . . . the localization and extraction of values were veiled by a thick, impassable curtain of mystery and secrecy," wrote the Cuban archaeologist Carlos Hernández Oliva, "and it's no exaggeration to compare it to something like a military secret."

Whereas state-owned ocean exploration entities elsewhere in the world might seek offshore oil or mineral deposits, Carisub's divers were after rather more exotic resources, such as black coral—a deepwater species used for jewelry—and rare tropical fish for collectors' aquariums. Perhaps swayed by his meeting with Fagen and Giddings, Castro was particularly intrigued by Cuba's many shipwrecks. But whereas Fagen had emphasized their cultural value, Castro was more interested in prying off the metal they contained—everything from the bronze propellers of modern wrecks to sunken Spanish treasure.

Either way, the wrecks would have to be located first, so Marambio called on the preeminent—essentially the only—maritime archaeologist in Cuba at the time. And Roger Dooley, his options as limited as ever, had no choice but to accept.

Dooley told himself that he would make the best of it; he would take advantage of the government backing to conduct serious science within the strictures of Carisub's acquisitive mission. In 1983, he became the scientific vice president of Carisub. "The director of the company had to be someone from the Party," Dooley said. "But I basically ran it."

For many of Dooley's colleagues, it was easy living, being paid to hunt for treasure in turquoise waters by day, dining on Caribbean lobster and freshly speared fish by night, and sipping whiskey at all hours. But Dooley began to suspect that Carisub's director, a bon vivant named Vicente de la Guardia, was in no rush to actually find anything, so keen was he to perpetuate the good life and bask in one perfect sunset after another. Several people who knew de la Guardia say they rarely saw him sober.

Dooley was determined to bend Carisub's mission toward his own more reputable ends. In early 1983, he insisted that the company focus its attention and resources on locating and excavating one specific, historically important shipwreck. Castro could not be expected to fund the organization forever without seeing results, he argued. In truth, Dooley was the impatient one. He had been cataloguing Cuban shipwrecks for more than a decade but had yet to properly study one. His career had taken a number of detours, but as he approached forty he was at last in a position to prove his worth as an archaeologist, to earn the respect of his peers around the world, and to give his young daughters a reason to be proud of him.

His Carisub colleagues agreed with Dooley's plan to search for a single significant wreck, as long as it was believed to hold enough treasure to justify their efforts. But which one? The most authoritative source on shipwrecks in Cuban waters was the list that Dooley himself had compiled, and it was far from exhaustive. None of the hundreds of vessels in the catalog was thought to contain much of value. Dooley's library, assembled over many years including during his Miami stint, contained books about American treasure hunters plying the Caribbean for Spanish ships, a self-mythologizing subculture that had flourished since its birth in the mid-twentieth century. Their books were defiantly unscientific, filled with embellishments, rumor, half-truths, and outright fabrications. Yet in the absence of anything more reliable, they were Dooley's best leads. One of them made passing mention of an *almiranta* from the Tierra Firme fleet that had run aground on Cuba's northern shore in the 1690s but offered no further details.

Dooley thought back to the day, about a decade earlier, when he had paid a friendly visit to the Cuban historian Francisco Pérez de la Riva at his house on Guanabo Beach, an hour or so east of Havana. In a room filled with nautical objects and books, the elderly scholar had brought out two silver artifacts to show to Dooley. One was a finely wrought crucifix, the other a distorted and heavily oxidized coin. The silver piece of eight was blackened and bubbly, as if it had survived a fire. Pérez de la Riva had found the objects in the sand while walking along the beach after winter storms. Suspecting that they were of Spanish origin, he had sent images of them to an expert at the Smithsonian Institution in Washington, who confirmed his hunch and estimated that they dated back to the late seventeenth century. Pérez de la Riva entrusted the coin to Dooley, in hopes that he might one day investigate the matter further.

Dooley had kept the blackened piece of silver, and as he contemplated it now, he was mesmerized by the magnitude of the story this humble, misshapen piece of silver seemed to tell.

His mind turned to a yarn told by one of the treasure hunters he had read about, Kip Wagner, who had found Spanish coins in the 1950s in the sands of Vero Beach, Florida, after storms. Convinced they came from a shipwreck off the shore, Wagner dedicated his life to finding it.

His efforts eventually paid off—even if he would never become rich himself—when he and his associates discovered several Spanish wrecks, remnants of a treasure fleet destroyed in a 1715 hurricane.

Dooley wondered whether Pérez de la Riva's find might similarly have migrated from a centuries-old Spanish wreck just off the coast. Finding this ship, if it existed, would become Carisub's primary objective.

Under his direction, the company began conducting a survey of the reef along Guanabo Beach, towing an aging proton magnetometer behind a dilapidated boat and keeping an eye on an indicator on board that would reveal the presence of an iron deposit. Since gold and silver are not magnetic, the treasure itself would not be detected by the finned, oblong device. Nor would the cannons, which on an *almiranta* would have been made of nonmagnetic bronze. Instead, Dooley was searching for ferrous vestiges of a more prosaic nature—anchors, nails, bolts, and other ship's fittings—that would indicate the final resting place of the galleon.

Each time the magnetometer registered a hit, Dooley's team dropped a buoy to mark the spot and continued on. With every chirp of the device, and every corresponding squiggle etched onto a roll of paper on board, Dooley's hopes jumped as well. It was difficult to resist the temptation to strap on bottles then and there, to dive down and rummage through the sand. But as he knew too well from his archaeological studies and readings, it is crucial in any rigorous search to proceed systematically, to execute long, straight back-and-forths across an area in a process known colloquially as "mowing the lawn." Only once the search box has been fully covered can each individual hit be investigated. With the help of geographers armed with theodolites, Dooley established a precise map of the magnetic anomalies along the reef.

He and his divers then methodically examined each one. After several weeks, the team had identified concentrations that indicated two possible wreck sites. Carisub's divers descended to the first site and scoured the bottom. Dooley had instilled in them one of the fundamental tenets of archaeology: "There are no straight lines in nature." Such a man-made form appeared almost immediately before them, a 4.5-meter-long anchor, lying on a reef as if it had just fallen, save for centuries' worth of corrosion and a coating of seaweed and coral. Soon after, another, nearly identical anchor was found, both of them matching late seventeenth-century designs.

The anchors marked the spot where the mighty vessel had sunk, but the timbers were gone, and the cannons, coins, jewels, and other remains were buried deep under sand. A snorkeler looking at the seabed from above would never have suspected that a shipwreck lay beneath.

Without documentary support, without a story to breathe life into this inert scattering of iron, there was no way of knowing what ship the anchors had once been connected to. A Cuban scholar had provided Carisub with a packet of archival documents. But they did not provide an answer. Dooley decided to travel to the General Archive of the Indies in Seville, that temple sacred to historians and treasure hunters alike, as he had on several previous occasions.

It was there, sweltering in the Andalusian heat among piles of centuries-old papers in the summer of 1984, that Dooley determined that the galleon he and his team had been searching for was *Nuestra Señora de las Mercedes*—Our Lady of the Mercies—the treasure-laden *almiranta* of the Tierra Firme fleet, which had run aground on the shallow reef off Guanabo Beach on March 13, 1698, shortly after leaving Havana on its return voyage for Spain.*

As with each time he visited the archive, it took him several days of

---

* In the course of his research, Dooley would run across several names that he did not yet recognize but that would in time become profoundly important to him. Among them were the future captain general of the *San José*, Don José Fernández de Santillán, yet to be dubbed the Count of Casa Alegre, who had on a previous voyage helmed the *Mercedes*. Another was the *Mercedes*'s captain of sea and war, Don Nicolás de la Rosa—later to be known as the Count of Vega Florida—who would wage such an honorable fight against Wager's squadron ten years later as the leader of the *Santa Cruz*.

trudging effort to familiarize himself anew with the nearly illegible scrawling and antiquated, inconsistent shorthand of seventeenth-century accounts. Sentences were *encadenada*—chained together—in such a way that they had no obvious beginning or ending. Punctuation was virtually nonexistent. L's, R's, Y's, V's, and F's were indistinguishable, depending on the writer. But over time Dooley grew accustomed to such idiosyncrasies. Archival research was to him a form of time travel: After a while he stopped deciphering and was merely reading, as if he had been the document's intended recipient. Gradually, hundreds of scattered pages combined in his mind to form a riveting narrative.

The voices of sailors quoted in these firsthand accounts began echoing among the walls of the archive's reading room.

"Captain, we are very close to a shoal where I fished four months ago, and there is very little water," warned a gunner named Jandro to the pilot of the *Mercedes,* Juan Días Lezcano, as the galleon approached the coastline.

Días shot back, telling Jandro it was obvious "he was drunk." The pilot continued on his stubborn course until the *Mercedes* struck bottom in four fathoms of water, "a musket's shot from land."

Every measure was taken to lighten the load in hopes that the galleon could extricate itself, including by cutting the masts. All were in vain—the *Mercedes* would never sail again. The men built rafts from the wreckage and rowed ashore. Soon after, they erected a makeshift fort, pointing cannons out to sea to ward off any passing pirates who might be drawn to the wreck like vultures to fresh carrion.

To further throw off the pillagers and keep the remains in one place, officials decided to torch the portion of the ship that projected above the water. Dooley imagined how the flames might have licked the night sky and cast a glow across the shore, how its castaways along the beach might have felt the heat of the blaze as they watched their former home burn.

Salvage efforts in the months that followed the sinking rescued several million pesos from the wreck, which lay about thirty feet deep. But much more remained of the abundant treasure, and scavengers were secretly diving down to it, as evidenced by the wide circulation of coins from the *almiranta* throughout Havana.

"Many people with little fear of God and to the detriment of their consciences have hidden a large quantity of gold, silver, both minted and in bars and carved, gemstones and jewelry, etc., etc. of great value," decried a bishop named Compostela. Treasure hunters—then already a reviled breed—were threatened with excommunication: "Cursed be those excommunicated, by God and his blessed mother Amen. Orphans be their children and their wives widows, amen. May the sun darken them by day and the moon by night."

But the pillaging continued. As a last resort, Spanish officials decided to give salvaging rights to one of the treasure hunters, a Havana resident named Joseph Clemente Fernández, on the condition that he give a quarter of his findings to the king.

Recovery efforts at the turn of the eighteenth century took more than a year. According to official accounting that Dooley reviewed, 5,787,833 pesos were salvaged out of the 6,319,775 pesos officially embarked on the *Mercedes*—which meant there were likely more than 500,000 pesos left on the reef.

The amount—none of which he could hope to benefit from—was of little concern to Dooley. The more valuable treasure for him was the critical information he gleaned about the wreck site: along Guanabo Beach, four fathoms deep, a musket's shot from the shore—or about four hundred yards. Armed with this knowledge, Dooley returned to Cuba and revisited the site of the two anchors he and his divers had found. The location closely matched the descriptions in the archival record.

"That is when we knew we had found the *Mercedes*," Dooley recalled.

It was an electrifying triumph. Roger Dooley, whose education in marine archaeology had been loosely cobbled together, had located the only galleon ever discovered along the Cuban coast, and an *almiranta* to boot. Had it been found by a more established team, or in the waters of another country, the news would surely have jolted international academia. But Cuba was increasingly isolated from the ivory towers of the West, and—Dooley's efforts notwithstanding—had yet to demonstrate serious archaeological expertise.

The *Mercedes,* Dooley believed, could change everything, not just for him but for Cuba's standing in the social sciences. Finding the ship was just the beginning. At last he had the opportunity he had long hoped for to conduct a rigorous excavation, and on a ship of undeniable historical significance. He couldn't imagine more ideal circumstances to prove himself and capture the field's attention.

Eager as Dooley was to begin planning the excavation, his services were suddenly requested elsewhere, and refusal was not an option. Castro had decided to commission a lavish documentary to showcase Cuba's underwater marvels—from its shipwrecks to its diverse marine life—and, as usual with such whims, he wanted it immediately. He gave Carisub an effectively unlimited budget to film it, and Dooley was appointed as producer and director. In the fall of 1984, just after discovering the *Mercedes,* Dooley decamped to the island's southern coast to begin filming. He could think of no better location to show off Cuba's underwater landscapes than the sublime reefs he had discovered off the Isle of Pines. He would call the film *Blue Treasure Island.*

Shooting and editing took several long months, during which his mind frequently strayed back to the galleon that he and his team had discovered, and that was awaiting his intervention. He began to daydream about founding a naval museum in Havana Harbor to showcase artifacts from the *Mercedes* and others. In 1986, after finishing work on the film, Dooley returned to Carisub's headquarters in Havana, ready to present a detailed plan to properly excavate the *Mercedes* that summer. He had just parked his Toyota truck in the Carisub lot when he saw Vicente de la Guardia, the company's director, stagger toward him.

De la Guardia made no effort to hide his frustration about Dooley's expensive plan. The matter had already been decided. According to Dooley, the director said Carisub's team would prioritize the finding of coins above all archaeological concerns and would use destructive techniques designed for that purpose. Among them was the propwash, a tool designed by an American treasure hunter to redirect the strong current created by a ship's propeller straight down to the seafloor, blowing large craters into the site. Also referred to as a blaster, it was in Dooley's estimation the underwater equivalent of taking a bulldozer to Pompei. Nor did De la Guardia rule out the use of explosives to break through coral incrustations, as Carisub had done on other sites. There was even talk of blasting cannons apart to find contraband coins that the Spanish were known to stuff down barrels to avoid paying the king his due on imported treasure.

Dooley's jaw dropped as he listened to the future he had in mind being unceremoniously ripped away from under him. His shock spiraled into rage. De la Guardia's plan, he said at the risk of insubordination, would forever contaminate a site of world-historical importance for the sake of a few coins.

In his fury, Dooley shouted at De la Guardia: "I don't want anything to do with you! I don't want anything to do with Carisub, or with the government!" He threw the keys of his company-issued truck at his boss, an incautious outburst given De la Guardia's high standing in the Communist Party. "I'm finished. I quit," he said, before storming off on foot.

Most contemporaries from Dooley's time at Carisub have either died or kept their silence. One exception was Alejandro Mirabal, who joined Carisub shortly after Dooley's departure in 1985 and acknowledged Dooley's key role in the organization's early years. A diver and professed archaeologist who holds the Guinness World Record for exploring the greatest number of historical shipwrecks—more than 240 around the planet—Mirabal made no secret of the company's focus on treasure hunting. Carisub's official mission, he said, was "the rescue of noncirculating values"—"You could try and find a more fancy name for treasure hunting, but you may not be as creative," Mirabal said. "Our job was to find treasure and we had the exclusivity for the entire country, in the water *and* inland. We investigated every myth and urban legend about buried treasures in land as well. It was fun. With time and the effort of some workers (mostly intuitively), we slowly turned the company into an archaeological institution, with an archaeological approach, although the need to find 'treasure' for the survival of the company never disappeared."

The vast majority of academic archaeologists today consider treasure hunting to be a sin against the practice. In such circles, the pursuit of riches is seen as incompatible with diligent scientific study. Yet Mirabal took issue with the notion that the eventual excavation of the *Mercedes*—which didn't begin until 1991—was in any way improper. He pointed to an unpublished report he wrote about the effort many years later, documenting what he claimed was an unimpeachable process. "Despite the fact it was realized about twenty years ago, the excavation was executed with great scientific rigor by a professional team that applied experience gained in other countries, under the supervision of the Academy of Sciences of Cuba, the office of the city historian, the Department of Cultural Heritage . . . and the Faculty of Geography of the University of Havana."

Mirabal's report, reflecting the conclusions of Carisub, suggested that the *Mercedes*'s pilot, Días, had grounded the *almiranta* intentionally, having perhaps been bribed by Havana officials who hoped the local economy, and thus they, would benefit from an ambitious salvage effort.

"In our opinion," Mirabal wrote, "the motivation may be due to the taste of Havanans for salvaging shipwrecks. Since the beginning of the seventeenth century, true specialists in the field have lived in the city."

Dooley found the hypothesis of an intentional scuttling preposterous, driven by conjecture and wholly unsupported by the archaeological evidence. Not that he had a chance to closely examine it, since it had never appeared in a peer-reviewed publication.* In the late '90s, Cuba granted search rights to the area to a Canadian treasure-hunting company. The company would later claim to have found baskets full of seventeenth-century nails and spikes buried in the sand, suggesting that Carisub had carelessly collected and cast aside all "unimportant" iron objects so as not to throw off metal detectors seeking gold and silver.

Dooley said he quit because the lack of archaeological rigor in De la Guardia's plan would waste his and Cuba's best chance for a serious, diligent excavation of a historical ship. De la Guardia is not around to give his side of the 1986 altercation with Dooley, having died a few years later. But what is clear is that the two could not stand one another and that egos were as much at stake as archaeological ethics.

De la Guardia "was stubborn as a mule, but a very straight and honest person," Mirabal claims. Mirabal preferred not to comment on Dooley's departure, since he was not privy to the discussion. "Roger is a nice guy," Mirabal said. "He might embellish one thing or the other because he's that way. But he wouldn't lie to you outright. That's not the Roger I knew."

Abandoning the *Mercedes* was one of the biggest regrets of Dooley's life. He slept poorly for months. "I hate myself that I never finished that," he told me. He spoke of the galleon as he might a fiancée he'd left at the altar, but it's just as fair to say that she left him when Carisub took the excavation out of his hands. At age forty, he wondered whether he would ever find that passion again.

Discovering the galleon with his team at Carisub had validated everything he'd worked for in his life so far—all the hustle, all the dives, all the flailing in the dark. Despite a lamentable lack of resources,

---

* The only official record of the excavation of the most historically important colonial era shipwreck in Cuban waters is a collection of artifacts found at the site, exhibited at a small museum in Havana.

despite being professionally confined to what was increasingly seen as a failed state, Roger Dooley could lay claim to a major discovery, a rare accomplishment in marine archaeology. The glory, for once, was his alone. He had achieved it without Michael's help or influence. But he was suddenly powerless to capitalize on that success, having impetuously cut himself off from the only organization in Cuba that allowed him to pursue the work he loved.

For all his heartache over the *Mercedes,* he was left with one thing: In the course of his research at the Seville archive during that summer of 1984, he had chanced on clues to the location of the greatest shipwreck of all time. And it would soon become his life's goal to find it.

Part III

A Brief History of Treasure Hunting

I think it's a very good joke—a good
one played on us and on the bandits by the
Lord or by fate or by nature, whichever you
prefer. And whoever or whatever played it
certainly had a good sense of humor. The gold
has gone back to where we got it.

—B. Traven, *The Treasure of the Sierra Madre*

Chapter 11

In the Wake of Captain Phips

I met Roger Dooley nearly forty years after he first set out to find the *San José.*

After receiving his initial email early in my reporting on the galleon, I took him up on his invitation and booked a ticket to Miami. The seventy-six-year-old man who came to pick me up at my hotel in a GMC truck looked just as I imagined a man who seeks shipwrecks for a living would, with flowing gray hair, a thick white beard, a crooked nose, and, on his right hand, a scar from the bite of a moray eel.

On our drive to his apartment building in Aventura, I kept in mind the words of a Spanish maritime lawyer who worked on cases of salvaged Spanish gold: "Beware the siren song of the treasure hunter," he'd warned me before my trip.

"I'm not a treasure hunter," Dooley assured me when we got to his airy twenty-first-floor condo overlooking Miami Beach and the extravagant properties below, including Lionel Messi's. He insisted that his interest in the *San José* was strictly archaeological. He told me he'd never found a single gold coin in a shipwreck, though he would later tell me about the gold coins his team had found on the *Sánchez Barcáiztegui* in Havana Harbor. The only silver coin in his possession, he said, was the misshapen one from the *Mercedes* that the historian Pérez de la Riva had given him decades earlier. Treasure hunters were "horrible," he said, describing them as modern-day pirates driven by greed and a heedless sense of adventure, who ransacked important historical sites and rendered them worthless to proper archaeologists like him.

Yet visitors to his apartment would be forgiven for mistaking him for one. Yellowed maps of the Caribbean and paintings of galleons lined the walls; his shelves were overstuffed with books on Spanish galleons and treasure hunting, accumulated over more than half a century; on his glass coffee table was a special edition of *National Geographic* all about pirates; elsewhere was a miniature treasure chest, just beneath a wood carving of a white-bearded sea dog that looked remarkably like Roger Dooley.

Despite his condemnation of treasure hunting, Dooley kept pulling out books about its most notorious practitioners, speaking of them with an odd mix of opprobrium and admiration. It seemed important for him that I know their stories in order to understand the magnitude of his work. As he piled the volumes onto the kitchen counter for me to consult, it became clear that he believed these fortune seekers had set the stage for him. They may have been rapacious, greedy, and reckless, but Dooley identified with their sheer doggedness, their refusal to abandon pursuit. These were the qualities that led them, and not the righteous academics, to find the richest Spanish wrecks in the Caribbean. What, I wondered, was Roger telling me about his own motivations?

TREASURE-LADEN SPANISH SHIPS embarking on the journey home during the colonial period faced a daunting dilemma: Leave too early, in the clement spring months, and risk encountering pirates, privateers, or enemy squadrons; leave too late and risk encountering hurricanes. To avoid the fate that befell the *San José,* many commanders delayed departure as long as possible, abandoning their galleons to the wrath of the sea. This was not an irrational decision. Captains who lost their money to a raider could hardly hope to recover any of it. Nature, however, has little use for treasure. Thus, riches could perhaps be clawed back from the seafloor—provided they had not sunk too deep. Few shipwrecks were ever truly lost.

It was not the wind alone that doomed ships caught in the dreaded hurricanes of summer but a deadly alliance between wind, water, and earth. The gusts and waves hurled ships toward land, where they were dragged across shallow reefs and eviscerated. Such events were not desired, but they were planned for. If there were any survivors—and proximity to land meant there often were—they could mark the location of the sinking and return the following season to begin salvage. While diving bells were occasionally employed to retrieve lost weaponry and treasure, Spanish officials preferred using native or enslaved African divers, who were both cheaper and more effective. They often jumped in the water carrying a heavy rock to speed their descent and sifted through sands and wreckage for sea-blurred riches. Indigenous divers, in particular, tended to be more physically suited to the task than Spanish sailors, who often couldn't swim at all. Salvors found it easier to push them beyond the limits of human endurance—just as officials had thought little of sending native and enslaved miners into the deadly bowels of Potosí.

"It is solely because of the Spaniards' greed for gold that they force the Indians to lead such a life, often a brief life, for it is impossible to continue for long diving into the water and holding the breath for minutes at a time, repeating this for hour after hour, day after day," wrote the sixteenth-century friar Bartolomé de Las Casas in *A Short History of the Destruction of the Indies,* his harrowing account of Spain's mistreatment of America's Indigenous populations. "The continual cold penetrates them, constricts the chest, and they die spitting blood, or weakened by diarrhea."

The recovery of treasure was no less important to the mission of the Carrera de Indias than the acquisition of it. Throughout the colonial period, the Spanish salvaged every peso that divers could reach from the wrecks that could be located, leaving little for anyone else to scavenge. Yet there remained a handful of treasure galleons that were known to have foundered in shallow waters but that salvors could not find their way back to. As word spread of fortunes lying on the seabed waiting to be collected, these wrecks entered into legend.

Among the most famous disasters of the golden age of galleons was that of *Nuestra Señora de la Pura y Limpia Concepción,* vice-flagship of a treasure fleet returning to Spain from Havana in September 1641. Like the *San José* on its final voyage, it had not been careened in months and the caulking between planks had rotted away in several areas, causing dangerous leaks. It floated deeply and awkwardly, overloaded with crew, cargo, and silver—the official tally of 4 million pesos dwarfed by the unusually high amount of contraband hidden throughout the ship and secreted into personal affairs. In all, it is believed there were one hundred tons of precious metals aboard. A week after leaving Havana, the *Concepción* encountered a storm so powerful the men chopped down the mainmast and threw it overboard, along with much of the deck cargo and eight bronze cannons, to keep the ship from capsizing. Water gushed into the hold through leaky planks and rose to more than ten feet. When a gigantic wave crashed over the poop deck and tore away the carving of Our Lady of the Conception, the ship's patroness, the men saw it as a sign that they could not count on divine protection.

The storm passed and the *Concepción* somehow stayed afloat. The commander, Don Juan de Villavicencio, decided to put into San Juan, in Puerto Rico, for repairs. Yet the pilots grossly misjudged their position and the galleon became ensnared in a labyrinth of shallow reefs off the island of Hispaniola, known as the Bajo de los Abrojos—or the "keep your eyes open" shoals. Towers of coral smashed its rudder, sliced open its underbelly, and put an end to its journey. The ship sank bow first, forcing the hundreds of men aboard to scramble up the steeply sloped deck to the small portion of the stern that jutted out above the water. As they struggled to build makeshift rafts from whatever wood they could salvage, another violent storm bore down on them. Rafts and boats were so overcrowded that additional survivors attempting to climb aboard were kept away at the point of a knife.

It may have been their blood that drew the sharks. The predators did not wait for men to fall overboard but lunged onto the overloaded rafts and yanked their screaming prey off, dyeing the sea red. Over the course of several days, the rafts drifted apart. Nearly half of the sixty-four men on the largest one succumbed to sharks, thirst, or starvation. A few threw themselves overboard to put a quick end to their ordeal, each death lightening the raft and increasing the chances of survival for those who remained. Another raft was luckier: Its men were picked up by English pirates who found the story of the pilot's error uproariously amusing, robbed the survivors of all their silver and gold, and deposited them on a deserted shore. Of the 150 men who stayed behind on the wreck for want of a raft or wood to build one, only one survived, a native Mexican slave named Andrés de la Cruz, who drifted on a plank for many miles to Puerto Plata, where he was granted his freedom.

In the decades that followed, Spanish authorities made several attempts to locate and salvage the wreck, but neither Villavicencio nor any of the survivors could recall its location, having been profoundly lost when they ran aground. In time the Spanish stopped searching, but a new generation of adventurers who had heard tales, distorted by translation and time and drunken embellishment, of a lost silver-filled galleon set out to claim its sunken treasure.

By the 1680s, when whispers of a wreck replete with unimaginable riches reached the ears of a young Boston ship captain called William Phips, even the *Concepción*'s name had been forgotten. Phips's own life story would sound like the stuff of sailors' yarns if so much of it weren't supported by a detailed accounting. Phips, who had begun his professional life as apprentice to a ship's carpenter, was described by his famous biographer, Cotton Mather, as a character out of a folktale: "Tall, beyond the common set of men, and thick as well as tall, and strong as well as thick." He had made a name—and a tidy sum—for himself by finding and salvaging a small Bahamian wreck containing a modest amount of silver. The money allowed him to purchase passage to England, where he charmed several venturesome aristocrats to back his plan to find what he assured them was the most valuable of all shipwrecks, by which he meant the *Concepción,* even if he did not know to call it that. Phips even gained an audience with King Charles II, who, amused by his audacity, agreed to lend the American an eighteen-gun frigate in exchange for a quarter of any treasure recovered.

The expedition was in almost every way a failure. Most of Phips's crew turned out to be unruly brutes, drunks, and cutthroats, causing mayhem wherever they stopped. When they arrived at the wreck site of the *Maravillas,* another all-too-well-known treasure ship, and found it had been picked clean, several of them lost patience and led a mutiny against Phips. They "approach'd him on the quarterdeck with drawn swords in their hands, and required him to join with them in running away with the ship, to drive a trade or piracy in the South Seas," wrote Mather. Cornered and unarmed, Phips "rush'd in upon them and with the blows of his bare hands fell'd many of them and quell'd all the rest."

After months of searching for the *Concepción* off Hispaniola, Phips returned to England empty-handed. Yet when he met with his wealthy investors, he told them a story that made them forget the thousands of pounds they'd already sunk into his escapade and whetted their appetite for more vicarious adventure. At a tavern in Puerto Plata, he said, he had drunk with an old Spaniard who knew of the lost galleon— though, strangely, not its name—and offered key information no one else had about where it had sunk, almost fifty years earlier. With two ships and a more reliable crew, Phips said, he was all but certain to find the treasure of the *Concepción.* Phips didn't explain how the Spaniard had come across the information. His account nevertheless delighted his financiers and convinced them to invest still more.

He returned to the West Indies in the fall of 1686 aboard the twenty-two-gun frigate *James and Mary,* accompanied by his trusted former second mate, Francis Rogers, who now captained a sloop called the *Henry of London*. In Puerto Plata, Phips pretended to be a mere trader to avoid alerting the Spanish to his true mission. He remained in port while Rogers discreetly took several native divers with him aboard the *Henry of London* to the Ambrosia Bank, where the old Spaniard had said the treasure lay. A month later, Rogers returned. He put on a somber face upon entering Phips's cabin, leading Phips to believe that he had come up empty yet again and that his good name was now surely ruined. But while Rogers was delivering what appeared to be bad news, one of his men snuck a large silver bar under the table. The captain stubbed his toe against it.

"Why? What is this? Whence comes this?" Phips asked, utterly confused.

Rogers immediately dropped the act and, now beaming, revealed that after just one day of searching they had found the wreck, as well as its silver, gold, pearls, and jewels. Rogers led Phips back to the site, where, over the following weeks, divers working seven hours a day brought thirty-two tons of silver to the surface aboard the English ships.

Phips was hailed as a hero upon his return to London. His financiers, who had been mocked in aristocratic circles for entrusting their money to the smooth-talking American captain, made a fifty-two-fold return on their investment. Charles's brother and successor, James II, received one-tenth of the haul, which was valued at £210,000,* and knighted Phips "in consideration of the service done by him, in bringing such a treasure into the nation." With his one-sixteenth share of the treasure, Phips would return to Boston a wealthy man and go on to become the first governor of Massachusetts Bay Colony.

Phips's extraordinary discovery, and the ease with which he appeared to make it, kicked off what the historian Peter Earle has called

---

* The equivalent of about $40 million today.

"the great treasure hunting boom."* The following year, the once-desolate wreck site of the *Concepción* swarmed with ships of various nations as divers fought for Phips's scraps. London was now teeming with promoters who promised to replicate Phips's feat, claiming exclusive knowledge of rich undiscovered wrecks. Following the demonstration of Edmond Halley's diving bell in 1691, charlatans professing to have developed methods to dive deeper and longer than ever before preyed on credulous financiers. A feverish market developed for shares in treasure-hunting expeditions and patents for newfangled salvage contraptions. Stockjobbers boosted the trading, sending share prices soaring and contributing to London's first stock bubble.

The English Crown granted exclusive rights to search for treasure across vast swaths of the Caribbean that didn't belong to it (including the waters in which the *San José* would sink), counting on its royal share of the findings. But few expeditions ever left, and fewer still discovered anything worth reporting. Investors lost fortunes, yet promoters and stockjobbers thrived. They had discovered a perennial principle of treasure hunting: It was generally far more profitable to sell the dream of treasure than to try and find the riches themselves.

In his classic 1953 book *The Silent World: A Story of Undersea Discovery and Adventure,* Cousteau described the dynamic succinctly: "Legends of undersea treasure are ninety-nine per cent hoaxes or swindles, in which the only wealth uncovered is that which passes from the investor to the promoter. The get-rich-quick aberration that resides in

---

* Phips's exploit had launched, if not a thousand ships, then a thousand *plans* to launch ships. In time, it would become all too clear how big a part luck had played in his discovery. The writer Daniel Defoe, whose interest in maritime adventure would later lead him to publish *Robinson Crusoe,* phrased it thus: "Witness Sir William Phips's voyage to the wreck; it was a mere project; a lottery of a hundred thousand to one odds; a hazard which, if it had failed, everybody would have been ashamed to have owned themselves concerned in; a voyage that would have been as much ridiculed as Don Quixote's adventure upon the windmill."

most of us is never more successfully exploited than by treasure promoters with faded maps of sunken galleons."

Ironically, it was Cousteau's invention of the Aqua–Lung that, in
the second half of the twentieth century, opened up the seas to a new
caste of adventurers who would discover Spanish gold and silver to
rival Phips's fabled hoard. Thus was born the second golden age of
treasure hunting.

Chapter 12

The Big Five

Back at his apartment, as night was falling over Miami Beach, Dooley brought out more books from his bedroom and dropped them heavily on the white kitchen counter. These new volumes, thoroughly highlighted and annotated, were about the men he called the "Big Five" of treasure hunting's postwar golden age—Art McKee, Kip Wagner, Robert Marx, Mel Fisher, and Burt Webber—all of whom operated largely, like him, out of Florida, birthplace of so many misbegotten dreams. In discussing the stories of these men with me, Dooley wanted to show how different their techniques and motivations were from his. Yet I couldn't help but remark on clear similarities, if not in their archaeological diligence, then in their undeterrable optimism.

DOOLEY NEVER MET ART MCKEE BUT recognized him as the "grandfather of treasure hunting." McKee, born in 1910, had earned this title not just because he was older than the rest but because his first finds predated the invention of modern scuba gear. He began his career as a hard-hat diver in New Jersey, working on underwater salvage and repair operations in a cumbersome full-body suit, with globular helmet and weighted boots, breathing through a long hose connected to a support vessel. In his early twenties, McKee moved to Florida, where the weather allowed him to swim year-round, on the orders of an osteopath who tended to his bum knee. He settled in Homestead and got a job as chief diver on a pipeline project in the Keys. Once the project was done, he found work as a pool boy but continued to dive on his own, trudging along the sandy bottom in his forty-pound boots, not knowing quite what he was looking for, merely reveling in having the seafloor to himself.

In 1938, a commercial fisherman friend invited McKee out to sea to investigate a site in shallow water off Tavernier Island, where he had spotted a large pile of smooth, round rocks that seemed out of place among the jagged coral. McKee donned his boots, screwed his helmet to his breastplate, climbed over the side of the boat and sank to the seabed, less than thirty feet below. The dim aquamarine light filtered through the small circular window of his helmet. Scrambling slowly among the piles of rock, he found several iron cannons, as well as other coral-encrusted nautical artifacts: knee-pins, nails, and deadeyes. There was little doubt: Here lay a shipwreck, likely centuries old. Returning to the site shortly after, McKee uncovered a handful of blackened silver coins that, once stripped of their sulfide patina, revealed themselves to be Spanish in origin.

With this stunning discovery, McKee was suddenly cast as the hero in a real-life version of the swashbuckling B movies proliferating in movie houses across the country. He wrote to the Archivo General de Indias in Seville, requesting information on any ships that may have been lost in the area. Having written in English, he expected no reply, so he was stunned weeks later to receive a thick packet containing copies of historical documents and a chart pinpointing his wreck, as well as eighteen other ships that had foundered during a 1733 hurricane off Plantation Key. The wreck he and his companion had located, he learned, was the *capitana* of that year's treasure fleet. McKee notified the Florida government, which granted him the first permit from a

U.S. state to salvage a historical wreck site, in exchange for 25 percent of his findings. To his disappointment, Spanish salvors had thoroughly cleaned out his *capitana* two centuries earlier. Little of value remained, yet the discovery left him wondering what other ancient riches might be lying offshore, waiting to be claimed.

"I detested history as such," McKee later admitted, articulating the sentiment that would most clearly distinguish him from Dooley. He was interested not in what could be learned from a wreck site but in what could be gained from it. History, to him, was just a means to an end. Among his primary inspirations in deciding to devote his life to salvaging wrecks after finding the 1733 *capitana* was a 1942 book called *I Dive for Treasure*. The author, a diver named Lt. Harry Rieseberg, recounted his sensational discoveries of Spanish treasure and fantastical undersea adventures involving deep-diving robots, ravenous sharks, gun battles, and, in one instance, a knife fight with an octopus the size of a building (perhaps a cousin of the giant octopus Gabriel García Márquez would later place inside the *San José*). The book's subtitle was *A True Saga of the Sea*. There was no acknowledgment that the first-person work was pure fiction, to put it charitably—a hoax, more accurately—or that its spectacular underwater photographs were achieved through trickery, shot in a fishtank with small figurines and a normal-sized octopus. McKee, like many others at the time, took Rieseberg at face value, and the book went on to become a seminal text of modern treasure hunting, setting the tone for a profession rife with exaggeration and deceit.

McKee cultivated the image of a pirate, wearing a captain's hat and embracing the nickname "Silver Bars," which he earned after an expedition he led discovered three bread loaf–shaped chunks of silver off of Gorda Cay in the Bahamas. He named his salvage ship the *Jolly Roger* and delighted in fending off rival treasure hunters who encroached on his sites, leading to several armed confrontations.

"Art was cunning and clever," recalled the treasure hunter Burt D. Webber, Jr., who apprenticed with McKee as a young man in the '60s. "He was the reincarnation of Long John Silver"—at least as played by the English character actor Robert Newton in the 1950 film adaptation of *Treasure Island,* the role that popularized the image of pirates as peg-legged, tricorn-hatted, parrot-befriending chewers of scenery. "That's who he reminded me of," said Webber. "He had that smile and that gleam in his eye."

McKee built a museum on Plantation Key to showcase his discoveries, a crude pastiche of a colonial fortress flying the skull-and-crossbones flag. It was an instant success, making the cover of *LIFE* magazine. McKee realized early on—as had the promoters and con men of Phips's age—that the real money lay not in treasure itself but in the dream of treasure.

He and the museum staff took tourists out to the site of the *capitana* in a glass-bottomed boat where, for $10 a pop, they could dive down, sift through the sand, move ballast stones around, and take home a certificate saying they had dived on an authentic Spanish galleon. (Never mind that the *capitana,* built well after the demise of the *San José,* was not technically a galleon but a ship of the line—McKee didn't sweat the historical details.) The excursions were a hit, but McKee wondered whether they might not better trigger the imagination, and thus be even more profitable, if the site looked more like the popular conception of a shipwreck. So, with the help of his friend Mickey Spillane, the bestselling crime novelist, McKee, in his own words, "dressed it up" (much as Dooley had in Cuba when he threw the iron cannon of unknown origin back into the water to give tourists something mysterious to look at on their dives). Together they turned a historically important vestige into an underwater attraction, staging the cannons and many of the other artifacts McKee had removed— some of them from other vessels—and planting rows of thick timbers to resemble the ribs of a ship.

If such stunts would today be considered archaeological malpractice, they were nowhere near as destructive as the techniques McKee used to find artifacts in the first place. What he desired most was to discover a virgin wreck, one that Spanish salvors had never found. For decades, he pursued a lost treasure frigate nicknamed *La Genovesa,* and he would not let preservationist compunctions get in his way. His preferred search method was dynamite. When he found a promising site on Jamaica's Banner Reef, he stuck numerous one-pound sticks throughout the ballast pile and, once safely back on his boat thirty feet above, connected the wire ends to a battery to detonate the charges. He instantly felt the blast beneath his feet. From an archaeological perspective, this was like setting off a bomb in an ancient Egyptian tomb. Delicate remains that might have shed light on the ship and its period, from glassware to ceramic crockery to wooden crates, were blown to bits. The explosion had killed nearly all life within its range, and the waters were soon cloudy with sand, detritus, and fish parts. Then, predictably, came the sharks. The swarming predators at first prevented McKee's crew from working what was left of the site. When the men finally descended, they encountered a few bronze medallions and ivory lice combs but not a single piece of eight or ounce of gold. The ship was not the *Genovesa,* yet amid the rubble there was now no way to identify it. Before the blast, the site had held artifacts of colonial life that would each have told stories of the past. Now it was all but silent. McKee had erased a page of history, and for nothing.

His search for the frigate would last decades more. McKee's final expedition left for the Pedro Shoals, fifty miles southwest of Jamaica, on September 18, 1979, when McKee was sixty-eight years old and withering away from kidney disease. A few weeks later, the crew located a ballast pile at the exact depth described by the documents. With adrenaline masking his pain, McKee donned his old diving helmet for the last time. Sucking away sand from the ballast pile with the use of an airlift—a kind of underwater vacuum cleaner that fed onto a surface vessel—McKee uncovered a small silver bar. This was indeed the *Genovesa,* but as he and his crew would soon learn, she was no virgin. Eighteenth-century English salvors had left virtually nothing behind.

McKee died a few weeks later. "It's a constant greed, you know," he had said of his lifelong pursuit of treasure. "But it's a hell of a lot of fun."

Dooley had begrudging respect for McKee as a treasure trailblazer. Yet he found his approach fundamentally misguided, both ethically ("a constant greed") and methodologically ("it's a hell of a lot of fun"). Though Dooley had known his share of adventure, fun wasn't what drove him. He coveted knowledge, not gold; glory, not thrills. It may have been more diverting to spend one's days diving among coral reefs in search of treasure than at a library, but the latter strategy was both more successful and more cost-effective, Dooley believed. "It's better to spend a few thousand dollars in the archives than millions in the ocean," he said. If McKee had followed that dictum, Dooley added, he might have found the *Genovesa* more quickly, or learned that it wasn't worth the effort.

THE SECOND OF THE BIG FIVE was Kip Wagner, whose experience had inspired Dooley to find the *Mercedes*. Wagner was an Ohio contractor who in the mid-1940s had come to Florida to build a motel and, seduced by the state's weather and sultry mystique, decided to plant roots there. He settled in Wabasso, a town midway up Florida's Atlantic coast, not far from where Spanish fleets would catch the Gulf Stream back to Europe.

One afternoon, Wagner and a building partner of his, an old sailor named Capt. Steadman Parker, waited out a rainstorm in a nearby bar.

Parker looked out the window. "This would be a good time to go look for some coins on the beach," he said.

"What coins?" Wagner asked.

"Hasn't anyone told you about the old Spanish coins that wash up on the beach here?"

It was the kind of local secret a few midday beers could pry loose. For generations, people in the area had found silver pieces of eight along the beach. One man who collected a cigar box full of gold and silver coins had supposedly been murdered for his treasure decades earlier. More recently, an elderly beachgoer claimed to have encountered about two thousand of the blackened discs since he was a boy and, mistaking them for flat skipping stones, hurled them all back into the ocean.

"The best hunting is always after a storm or a good hard rain squall like we've got today," Parker said.

Intrigued by the tale, Wagner scoured the shoreline with his World War II–era mine detector, hoping to find one of the coins himself. He became a familiar early-morning sight on the beach, with his white pants, white hair, and, when he wasn't wearing a white T-shirt, white tufts on his chest, back, and shoulders. When nothing turned up, he took a bulldozer to the palmetto-strewn dunes and at last dug up dozens of coins. At first, he melted the silver down and made jewelry out of it, giving many trinkets away to local children. Then it dawned on him that they might have more value as historical artifacts.

"I began to notice something peculiar about them," he wrote. "Not one of the coins that carried dates was minted after the year 1715." In his research at the local library, he had read about a notorious 1715 hurricane that had claimed ten of the Spanish treasure fleet's eleven ships and more than a thousand of its men, one of the deadliest maritime disasters in history. In all, the fleet was thought to have transported 14 million pesos. Historians were confident that the fleet had disappeared off the Keys, two hundred miles away, but Wagner suspected they were wrong, that the pieces of eight he'd found had to have come from one of those wrecks. A fortunate encounter with a long-forgotten, nearly two-century-old book by a Dutch navigator named Bernard Romans lent credence to his hunch: Directly opposite the mouth of the St. Sebastians River—just up the coast from Wabasso— "happened the shipwreck of the Spanish admiral," Romans wrote in 1775. To Wagner's delight, the crumbling book even contained a detailed, cartographically accurate foldout map pinpointing the location of several of the wrecks. "This was almost too much," Wagner would later write. "Like having your cake and eating it too."

Armed with Romans's text, and documents that a friend had obtained from the General Archive of the Indies in Seville, Wagner searched for the vestiges of the site where the survivors of the 1715 fleet had camped, the spot from which they organized a massive salvage expedition and fought off English pirates who circled the ships' sunken carcasses. His endless beachcombing yielded little but junk: bedsprings, tin cans, bobby pins, old chains, "even half a pair of patented divining rods."

It was Wagner's dog who found it. On a morning walk along Sebastian Inlet in 1959, as Wagner inspected a bluff in the wild palmetto scrub that matched Spanish survivors' description of the campsite's topography, his dog began lapping water from a deep hole. Wagner scooped some of it in his mouth and tasted no salt: It was evidently a freshwater well, dug by man's hands long before. Returning with his bulldozer, Wagner unearthed bricks, cannonballs, and gun mounts, as well as a gold ring encrusted with six small diamonds. That confirmed it: Here was the survivors' encampment.

Wagner looked out at the ocean. It stood to reason that the castaways would establish their camp as close as possible to one of the wrecks they were salvaging, within cannon shot of the English raiders preying on them. He could practically see their ghostly outline against the horizon. One day, he floated out toward these visions atop a surfboard. After powering past the row of giant breakers, he scanned the ocean floor through a small glass window he'd fitted into one end of the board. "Suddenly I spied something on the bottom," he wrote. "I dived down for a closer look, and sure enough, there, uncovered, lay four or five ship's cannon."

On his very first attempt, he had located the remains of a ship from the 1715 fleet. Together with a band of eight *Treasure Island*–obsessed friends—one of whom wore an actual black eyepatch at one point because of an operation—he invested in scuba gear and a diving boat and set out to find the other ships of the fleet.

Doing business as the Real Eight Company, Wagner and his men made their first big strike in January 1961. One of the divers, fighting against the current and the washing-machine action of a restless, bone-chilling winter sea, was inspecting a sparse scattering of pieces of eight when he glimpsed two blackish-green rocklike clumps about a foot and a half across. Unsure what they were, he heaved each nearly 150-pound object off the seafloor and fought gravity as he finned breathlessly back up to the salvage boat, his regulator spewing a reverse cascade of air bubbles toward the surface. The clumps turned out to be a cluster of silver coins and still held the shape of the wooden chests that had contained them before teredo worms reduced them to pulp.

Slack-jawed at the day's haul lying on the deck, one of Wagner's men danced a jig and sang, "We're rich, we're rich," adding, "There must be at least $80,000 worth of coins here."

A few months later, on the beach near one of the wreck sites, Wagner's nephew discovered something that made the pieces of eight seem like loose change: a finely wrought gold chain, eleven feet and four and a half inches long—the kind wealthy Spaniards would coil around their necks to cheat the royal tax collector—thought to have belonged to the captain general of the fleet, one of the successors of the Count of Casa Alegre. It looped through an intricate two-inch-long golden pendant in the shape of a dragon, which functioned as a whistle. The pendant opened up to reveal a solid gold toothpick and a golden earwax spoon. The splendidly wrought object, the only one of its kind ever found and perhaps ever made, is among the most spectacular and valuable pieces of Spanish treasure discovered on the ocean floor. Real Eight sold it at auction several years later to a Pennsylvania couple for $50,000, or almost half a million dollars today.

By 1966, Wagner estimated that he and his associates had salvaged approximately $3 million worth of gold and silver from several wrecks of the 1715 fleet. "We are convinced that our total find now exceeds even the fabled riches of Sir William Phips . . . recovered in 1687," wrote Wagner. Many of the coins and artifacts were sold at auction. After Florida scooped out its 25 percent cut and Real Eight took enough to cover its growing operational costs, the remainder was divided among all the partners. Nobody got phenomenally rich. But breathless national news coverage of the eye-popping sums found on the seafloor nevertheless sparked boyish dreams of finding chests of gold among readers across the country.

Around that time, *National Geographic* published a cover story on Real Eight's treasure-hunting operation and sponsored a successful exhibit of its finds. "What followed the next few weeks would have made the California gold rush almost seem tame by comparison," Wagner wrote in his memoir, *Pieces of Eight*. Practically overnight, the beaches that Wagner had once ambled down alone with his metal detector were now teeming with hopeful hobbyists, as amateur scuba divers thronged to the long-undisturbed seabed. Treasure madness had broken out, and opportunists and con men emerged along the coast to take advantage of it, promising to guide would-be adventurers to ancient wreck sites, selling gold-finding machines and pendulums and other contraptions. Dive shops sold out of equipment, and demand for John Potter's recently published *Treasure Diver's Guide* was so high that local libraries took it out of circulation.

First published in 1960, Potter's haphazardly researched, five-hundred-page compendium (of which Dooley had a battered, dog-eared, and extensively highlighted early edition) contained histories of hundreds of wrecks around the world, most of them undiscovered or— if they'd been located—only partially salvaged. The book proved as unreliable as it was exhaustive, yet it soon became an indispensable resource for the treasure hunters who flocked to the Caribbean and the Florida coast in the wake of McKee and Wagner. "It should have been named *The Treasure Diver's Bible*," Wagner wrote, "as it is one of the most essential tools a treasure hunter needs if he wants to be successful."

Among its most tantalizing entries was the one devoted to the *San José*: "By an eyewitness report she went down 'off Barú Island,' between the Isla del Tesoro (Treasure Island) and Barú peninsula. The seafloor in this area is jagged and irregular, varying greatly in depth but nearly all within SCUBA range. A closer fix on the *San José*'s position has already been determined through researches in England and can probably be further narrowed down with patient and well-guided digging in Cartagena and Seville. The wreckage of this *Capitana* can be counted on for at least $5,000,000 [pesos]—mostly in gold. It is one of the most attractive treasure salvage prospects in the world."

The entry was grossly inaccurate, claiming, for example, that the Spanish fleet had been ambushed upon leaving Cartagena rather than on the journey *to* the port city. Nevertheless, the estimated size of the bounty, and Potter's assurance that it would be relatively straightforward to find, helped turn the *San José* into what treasure seekers would come to call the Holy Grail of shipwrecks.

ROBERT MARX AND BURT WEBBER—the two youngest of the Big Five—each seriously contemplated mounting expeditions to locate the *San José* before turning their sights to other ships. They were among the second generation of twentieth-century treasure hunters: Marx, a former marine, got his start working the 1715 wrecks with Wagner's Real Eight Company, and Webber was a protégé of Art McKee and became his chief diver on the 1733 wrecks. Frequent competitors—today we might call them frenemies—both men fully embraced the romance and swagger of treasure hunting. They understood that, in order to lure investors, they had to look the part. Marx was burly, frequently shirtless, with a bushy mustache and an offputtingly small swimsuit. Webber, by contrast, was wiry and bug-eyed, and rarely without a black beret. Both were fond of posing with machine guns, which they kept for protection from rival crews, but also perhaps to fulfill fantasies of the pirate life.

Marx was, as the *Los Angeles Times* put it, "a born showman." In 1962, when he was twenty-six, he reenacted Columbus's first transatlantic journey at the helm of a faithful replica of the *Niña,* a feat that earned him a knighthood in Spain. He later attempted a similar crossing in replicas of Viking ships to help prove his theory that Norsemen reached Central America centuries before Columbus and in fact created the Mayan civilization, a postulation that drew scorn and ridicule from serious scholars. A self-trained maritime archaeologist, he committed numerous sins against the profession. He referred to sunken coins, bullion, gems, and jewelry as "goodies" and prioritized finding them over other, more historically significant artifacts. To throw other treasure hunters off the scent of one valuable wreck, he dragged its large iron anchor several hundred yards so it would lure their magnetometers away from his find, thereby destroying the integrity of the site.

In 1972, after searching for a decade, he at last discovered part of the wreck of the treasure galleon *Maravillas,* an *almiranta* of the Spanish treasure fleet that had crashed into another galleon in 1656 and sunk off the Bahamas with untold amounts of silver. Or rather, he *rediscovered* it: Spanish salvors had taken all that was readily accessible shortly after the accident; by the time William Phips encountered it, in the 1680s, the wreck had been thoroughly worked over. But scuba technology and modern excavation methods allowed Marx to uncover heaps of treasure that had remained buried: silver bars, gold bars, emeralds, and thousands of pieces of eight. It is said he and his crew brought up 2 million dollars' worth in just ten days; their total haul was likely several times that. But keeping treasure is often just as challenging as finding it. Almost as soon as it came aboard, the treasure of the *Maravillas* began disappearing. A thief among the crew made off with two sacks of coins containing more than six hundred pieces of eight—about $30,000 at the time. What was left was eventually lost in a bitter custody fight with the Bahamian government, as a result of which Marx was forbidden from coming anywhere close to the *Maravillas,* the object of his obsession.

"It's like *The Treasure of the Sierra Madre,*" Marx later said. "Treasure destroys people's minds. It destroys friendships. And that's why I say, Treasure is trouble, and the more the treasure, the more the trouble." Not that he would ever quit the treasure business.

Like most successful men of his profession, Marx was primarily not a purveyor of treasure itself. What he offered were fantasies of treasure. He was a prolific author, eventually publishing almost sixty books and hundreds of articles about his adventures, which were filled with unbelievable—and unverifiable—accounts of encounters with pirates, great white sharks, and countless other dangers. He was brilliant at keeping his investors on the hook. Aboard the *Maravillas* when it went down, he told them, was the single most valuable artifact to ever sink:

a solid gold statue of the Madonna and Child, intended as a gift from Spanish colonists to the king of Spain. Marx never cited his sources, and no historian has been able to corroborate the tale. Nevertheless, this story kept funds flowing to Marx's crew for years. As he and Webber would later joke, "The treasure's in the checkbook."

Marx died in 2019 at age eighty-five. Dooley called him "the worst of the treasure hunters" and also "a friend."

BURT WEBBER, BY CONTRAST, was long known as the unluckiest of treasure hunters. Born in Pennsylvania in 1942, he was determined early on to pursue a life of oceangoing adventure. He learned to dive in frigid quarry lakes, where he found his first underwater treasure, a discarded slot machine. He had wanted to become a navy diver but was rejected because of his asthma and allergies. Instead, he moved to Florida to join Art McKee's diving crew, which he would come to lead. After several years of working the 1733 wrecks with McKee, he broke out in search of a treasure wreck of his own.

Webber understood the technical aspects of the job better than perhaps any other treasure hunter. He showed a particular affinity for magnetometry and helped develop several advanced tools, such as a handheld cesium magnetometer that could register small ferromagnetic objects—like musket balls—that earlier devices would have missed. But despite his mastery of cutting-edge technology and his methodically planned, well-funded expeditions to find famous lost ships, Webber was perennially star-crossed, enjoying little of the serendipity that had guided McKee, Wagner, and Marx to wealthy wrecks. He had come close a few times. In the early 1970s, he had set his hopes on the *Maravillas* and believed he had pinpointed its location, only to find a rival salvage boat anchored above the site when he got there. It was Marx, who had discovered the wreck that very morning.

Webber was about to give up wreck hunting for good when a friend, a fellow treasure enthusiast named Jack "Blackjack" Haskins, suggested he go after the ship that had kicked off the first great treasure-hunting boom: the *Concepción,* which had made William Phips's fortune in 1686 but had since been lost again. It was second only to the *San José* in prestige, and since it was known to have sunk in shallow—albeit treacherous—waters off the Dominican Republic, it had previously tempted many treasure hunters who assumed Phips's divers must have left plenty behind. Even Cousteau and his crew of undersea explorers had gone looking for it in 1968. But when he dove down to the shoals among which he believed the *Concepción* had sunk, documentary cameras rolling, the only artifacts the Frenchman found beside iron cannons consisted of diving weights dropped by a modern treasure hunter who had been there before. It was evident that, whatever they had found, it wasn't the *Concepción.*

"I knew that everybody had looked for it and failed," Webber would later say. Still, the thought would not leave him alone. The only way to put it to rest was to go after the ship. His first expedition—called Operation Phips I—proved yet another expensive failure. Webber surveyed nearly all of the Silver Shoals, where Phips was known to have discovered his famous treasure, and found nothing but a maze of coral that had grown only more intricate since Phips's day.

It didn't surprise Webber that Phips had not left enough clues to find the treasure of the *Concepción*—it was, as he knew well, in a treasure hunter's nature to cover his tracks. But soon after, Haskins made a discovery that would reverse Webber's infamous bad luck: the log of Phips's salvage ship, the *Henry of London,* which had survived in a provincial English archive. It was enough to justify a second bid at the *Concepción.* The coordinates the log contained were so precise that Webber located his target on the fifth day of the search, in November 1978.

What was left of the *Concepción* looked nothing like a ship. It didn't look like much at all, in fact. The site was composed of concentrations of treasure and cargo scattered among towers and canyons of coral. Webber's team took jackhammers and dynamite to the coral, dismissing archaeological or ecological concerns. One underwater photograph shows Webber breaking a stick of indigo that had been among the galleon's valuable cargo. As the precious pigment dissipated into the sea, it looked in the black-and-white photograph like blood, an apt metaphor for the damage being done to the site.

Webber's efforts revealed that the treasure Phips had left on the seabed was likely as large as what he had removed from it. An account of the discovery in *The New York Times* in 1979 described the find as "one of the richest in modern times," estimating its worth to be between $40 million and $900 million. After all, a single gold chain from the *Concepción* was sold at auction for $500,000. The Dominican Republic's assessors, however, offered the far lower estimate of $14 million, from which Webber's cut was determined. Webber wouldn't reveal how much his personal take was, except to say he had converted much of it to real estate in the Dominican Republic and had lived comfortably off it since.

In the *Times* report, Webber's chief financier, a Chicago-based investor and former Proctor & Gamble product manager named Warren Stearns, teased their next target. He "would reveal neither the name of the Spanish galleon sought nor the estimated worth of the booty. But he said that the treasure ship must have a potential recovery of at least $50 million, 'otherwise it is not worth the risks.'" What Stearns didn't tell the reporter was that the ship in question was the galleon *San José*.

WHATEVER WEBBER'S HAUL FROM THE *CONCEPCIÓN* ended up amounting to, it was surely less than the gold and silver discovered by Mel Fisher, the most successful of Dooley's Big Five, a shipwreck salvor of such renown that he became a celebrity among the general public. He was the treasure hunter par excellence, defining the profession with his extravagance and eccentricity as Long John Silver had defined the stereotypical pirate.

Fisher, who was born in Gary, Indiana, in 1922, built his first diving helmet as a boy from a five-gallon paint can that he flipped on his head, much like the ancient divers described by Aristotle. He led a peripatetic youth, fighting the Germans in Europe, diving and spearfishing in Tampa, and eventually settling in Torrance, California, where he established the country's first and likely last chicken farm–cum–dive shop, selling both feed and scuba equipment. Fisher became monomaniacal about finding sunken riches.* He pursued gold and silver with an evangelical fervor exceeding even that of his treasure-hunting peers, which he traced, as they did, back to a boyhood love of *Treasure Island*. "It's been estimated that one third of all the gold that has ever been mined in the world has gone down in the sea," Fisher once said, without citing a source for the dubious claim. "That's a hell of a lot of gold."

He and his wife, Dolores, a pioneering scuba diver with several records to her name, were equal partners, a treasure-hunting power couple. They began by diving for gold in California's rivers in the late 1950s, hoping to find deposits the 1849ers might have overlooked. But they soon decided they'd have more luck scouring Florida's reefs for shipwrecks. They formed a company called Treasure Salvors Inc. By then, it was well known that Kip Wagner and Real Eight had dibs on the 1715 fleet. Undeterred, Fisher managed to get in on the action by making Wagner an irresistible offer: Treasure Salvors would work the 1715 wreck sites for free for one year and split its findings with Wagner's band, which had neither the time nor the resources to cover the entire area.

The partnership was fruitful, uncovering several new sites, but Mel and Dolores had no desire to remain at Wagner's service. To make real money, they'd have to find a Caribbean wreck of their own.

After trying and failing to find the *Concepción* near the Dominican Republic (it was Fisher's weights Cousteau had discovered on the seabed), the couple searched for wrecks closer to home, off the Florida coast. The most enticing such wreck, as described in Potter's *Treasure*

---

* His first major find was one of Al Capone's gambling ships, which a rival gangster had blown up off Long Beach.

Diver's Guide, was that of *Nuestra Señora de Atocha,* which had sunk in shallow waters off the Keys in a 1622 hurricane. "There should be at least $1,000,000 in gold and silver today in the ballast of the *Atocha,*" Potter promised.

Beginning in the mid-1960s, the Fishers dedicated their lives to locating and salvaging the *Atocha,* as well as the *Santa Margarita,* which had gone down in the same storm. "Today's the Day" became Mel Fisher's optimistic mantra, printed on T-shirts for his crew and repeated ad nauseam to his investors to keep funds flowing even during the long stretches when his expeditions came up empty. A magnetic self-promoter of Barnumesque audacity, Fisher built a full-size replica of a Spanish galleon, the 160-foot *Golden Doubloon,* to serve as Treasure Salvors' headquarters and as a floating museum in which he displayed artifacts salvaged from the 1715 wrecks. He inspired a cultish devotion among young aspiring treasure hunters. His salvage boats were crewed by a rotating cast of dreamers, drinkers, and drifters, many of whom worked for free, partly in hopes of striking it rich, but really for the chance to bask in his bacchanalian aura. Fisher passed rum around liberally aboard his expeditions and nurtured a festive atmosphere with team-building traditions like dancing the hokeypokey and singing maudlin choruses of "Home on the Range."

Fisher was more mystic than scientist. He relied on intuition to guide his search operations. "We would start digging in a specific area and get on a little trail of material, which was always exciting," recalled Jim Sinclair, who worked as a diver on Fisher's crew before becoming an archaeologist, "and then you'd get a call in the morning from Mel, who would say, 'Hey guys, I had this dream last night . . . ,' and he'd send us twenty miles in a different direction." No search technique was too esoteric for Fisher, who wouldn't hesitate to invite dowsing-rod-wielding crackpots on board just in case. He'd consulted with mediums who claimed to be able to communicate with dolphins, or with the souls of the *Atocha's* victims. Among Fisher's unorthodox beliefs was that sea turtles liked to rub themselves against bronze cannons and that they could home in on shipwrecks the way pigs sniff out truffles. "Mel would say, 'I just saw a turtle, let's follow it that way,'" Sinclair recalled.

Though he was prone to magical thinking, Fisher could also be clear-eyed and pragmatic. He invented a device, which he called a mailbox, that fit over a ship's propeller and redirected its force downward, sending clear, fast-moving water from the surface to the murky seabed, where it blew away sediment and overburden in seconds. One of the first times he used the mailbox, on the site of one of the 1715 wrecks, its powerful jets revealed the ocean to be, in his words, "paved with gold." In the ensuing years, Fisher's technique would come to be widely adopted by treasure hunters and widely lamented by archaeologists.

He also made sure to surround himself with more scientifically minded collaborators. Among them was the historian Eugene Lyon, who was deeply familiar with the Seville archives. In 1970, Lyon discovered that, because of a gross misinterpretation of historical documents, Fisher's group had been searching for the *Atocha* in the wrong place. The galleon, he told Fisher, was likely to be found off Key West, one hundred miles to the south of where Treasure Salvors' operation had been looking aimlessly for years. Another critical hire was the Dartmouth-educated archaeologist Duncan Mathewson, who despite having no experience with the sea—he'd done his fieldwork in Ghana—and never finishing his PhD, brought an element of rigor to Fisher's project. He strove to convince Fisher's skeptical band of pirates that adopting proper archaeological methods, such as plotting all artifacts on a grid to examine their spatial relationships before scooping them up, could greatly enhance the value of their finds: A random gold coin hoovered up from the seabed would be worth far less to collectors than one with a proven connection to history. Good archaeology, he argued, could establish provenance, which in turn made for a higher return on investment.

"My job as an archaeologist was to try to get everybody to see that the whole assemblage was greater than the sum of its parts," Mathewson said, adding that his entreaties didn't always resonate with Fisher's investors. "There were some real hardcore private venture folks who just really wanted to get the gold and actually melt it down."

The *Atocha* was at heart a family business, with the Fishers' adult children and their spouses eventually joining the crew. On July 14, 1975, Fisher's eldest son, Dirk, then twenty-two years old, emerged from the water shouting; he had found five bronze cannons in thirty-nine feet of water. Thanks to Mathewson's archaeological study, the team had picked up the wreckage trail of the *Atocha*. The hull couldn't have been far away.

Three days later, the joy turned to horror. Dirk organized a twenty-eighth birthday party for his wife, Angel, aboard the search vessel *Northwind*. They anchored off the Marquesas Keys on a still summer evening and celebrated late into the night, drunk on champagne and the elation of discovery. After everyone went to sleep, the 60-foot converted tugboat—which had a leaky bulkhead and a quick-filling bilge—suddenly capsized. Six people were caught inside when it turned turtle. Two crew members squeezed out of the pitch-black ship through a porthole. Another, breathing from a quickly shrinking pocket of air as the water rose to the floor—now the ceiling—found a flashlight floating by him in his overturned cabin, switched it on, took a deep breath, forced open the engine room door, and followed the beam of light through the dark water to safety. But Dirk, Angel, and a third crew member, Rick Gage, were unable to escape and went to the bottom along with the *Northwind*. In all, four lives would be sacrificed at the altar of the *Atocha*.[*]

People who knew Fisher said he was destroyed, but the death of his son and daughter-in-law did nothing to dent his resolve. "It's a powerful ocean," Fisher told the *Key West Citizen* after the tragedy. "It takes people and ships."

---

[*] Two years earlier, a twelve-year-old boy named Nikki Littlehales, son of a *National Geographic* photographer, was sucked into the mailbox and hacked up by the propeller blades, later dying of his wounds.

The search for the hull of the *Atocha* and the mother lode of the treasure would take sixteen years. Throughout that time, Fisher fantasized about finding other Spanish wrecks. He was particularly tempted to search along the coasts of Cuba, which for centuries had been the point of convergence for treasure fleets returning to Spain. But as long as Castro was in power, American salvors had little chance to gain access to them. There was just one possible way in.

By the 1970s and early '80s—when he was splitting his time between Havana and Florida—Dooley had earned a reputation as Castro's man underwater and a valuable backchannel. When they first met, in Key West, Fisher asked Dooley to broker a meeting with Castro. He handed the archaeologist a copy of his latest book to give to the president, with an inscription that read, "Let's play ping pong!" Fisher believed that shipwreck salvage could be an area of cooperation and possibly a vector of détente between Americans and Cubans, just as table tennis had been for the United States and China. Along with the book, he gave Dooley a few reels of film he thought would help entice the Cuban dictator. Dooley decided to screen it for several officials back in Cuba before passing it along. They were watching in the dark, to the whirr of a spinning projector, when footage of shipwreck excavation suddenly cut to an underwater orgy.

"Mel, you can't show a film of people fucking to Castro!'" Dooley told Fisher when the two met again.

"I've gotta keep him interested!" Mel replied.

Dooley didn't pass the film along.

Around the same time, Fisher became interested in going after Casa Alegre's *capitana* off the coast of Cartagena, but the wreck was thought to be too deep to access with methods of the day. "Everybody throughout that time was very interested in the *San José,*" said Sinclair, Fisher's former collaborator. But "while Mel might have had dreams about it," he added, "technology had to catch up with the dreams that people had."

On the rainy morning of July 20, 1985—exactly ten years after the drowning of Dirk and Angel Fisher and Rick Gage—Mel Fisher's son

Kane directed the salvage vessel *Dauntless* to a position off the Marquesas Keys, along the trail of wreckage established by Lyon and Mathewson. A twenty-six-year-old diver named Greg Wareham suited up, splashed into the water, and began his slow descent. The squalls and dark clouds above the surface made it difficult to see beneath it. It was only toward the bottom, fifty-four feet down, that visibility improved. Out of the murk appeared an enormous mound of oblong objects. As Wareham approached, his metal detector went off. The thirty-foot-long heap before him consisted of hundreds of silver bars.

He hurried up to the surface to share the news with Kane, who immediately radioed home base to send a triumphant message to his father: "Throw away the charts—put the charts away—we've got it! Silver bars—we've got it!"

Mel Fisher motored out to meet the *Dauntless* and its fellow salvage boats the next day, with thirty-two bottles of champagne and a box of plastic cups. He found that a gaggle of reporters had beaten him to the spot, hoping for a glimpse of treasure.

"When those aboard the ragtag fleet saw Mel about to board [the *Dauntless*]," Eugene Lyon observed, "he was welcomed with shouts and cheers such as few victorious Admirals have ever received from their assembled ships."

The search for the *Atocha*'s mother lode had come to a glorious end. Mel Fisher is considered the most successful treasure hunter of all time, not just because he found the treasure, which he claimed was worth $400 million, but because he and his investors got to keep it. He had been close to losing it all. Reneging on a longstanding agreement with Fisher that it would take a 25 percent cut of findings, the state of Florida began confiscating all recovered treasure in the mid-'70s. In 1982, Fisher's lead attorney successfully argued before the US Supreme Court that the *Atocha*'s wreckage was outside of Florida's waters, and that Admiralty Law was thus in effect. The court awarded Fisher's camp total ownership of the galleon, and the state had to return all artifacts. ("That guy, what a lawyer," Dooley said in awe.)

The excavation of the wreck began in 1985. Mel Fisher had become a star, appearing on Johnny Carson's *Tonight Show.* To aspiring treasure hunters, he was a demigod. In Key West, he became an attraction in his own right, walking around town with a nine-foot gold chain from the *Atocha* draped around his neck. The Fishers built a museum to showcase their discoveries and, crucially, earn tax-exempt status.*

His company sold the *Atocha's* coins (which were predominantly silver) at specialized stores in Key West and elsewhere, making sure to dole out the treasure gradually so as not to flood the market. Fisher surely became a millionaire several times over, but the oft-cited figure of $400 million, which he claimed to have extracted from the *Atocha,* is by most accounts a gross exaggeration—classic Fisher bluster. Whatever the true figure was, he wanted more. In 1998, police raided his Key West office and the seventy-six-year-old Fisher was arrested for selling counterfeit coins at $2,500 to $10,000 apiece at his gift shop. He was spared jail time only because he was dying of cancer.

Of all the major galleons of the Carrera de Indias—meaning *almirantas* and *capitanas*—that had ever been sought, only four had been found and identified: the *Maravillas* (1656), the *Atocha* (1622), the *Concepción* (1641), and the *Mercedes* (1698). All of them were *almirantas,* or vice-flagships, and all of their delicate wrecks were ransacked for their treasure before a proper archaeological excavation could tease out all the precious historical data they held. Once they were salvaged, the sites couldn't be put back together. This, and not the galleon's legendary treasure, was what made the *San José* so important to Dooley: Not only was it a *capitana,* but it presented the first and perhaps last

---

* One of the museum's main attractions was a glass case containing a large gold bar salvaged from the *Santa Margarita;* a small hole was cut in the glass enclosure, allowing visitors to slip their hand in and hold the bar to feel its weight, but preventing them from pulling the large bar out. Industrious thieves nevertheless found a way to make off with it in 2010.

opportunity to conduct a rigorous interrogation of a Spanish galleon, to deepen our understanding of a vessel that had altered the course of history yet about which we knew remarkably little. And, more personally, such a study—if he could somehow pull it off—would allow Dooley to make up for the biggest regret of his life: leaving the *Mercedes* behind.

Chapter 13

The Green Light

On one level, treasure hunting is a story of grit and greed, of ingenuity and dumb luck, of unwavering perseverance and delusional optimism. Which is to say it is the story of American enterprise. Dive deeper, though, and you'll find that what motivates treasure hunters and their investors is not necessarily profit. On average, it's more profitable to throw suitcases full of cash into the ocean. Pioneering maritime archaeologist Peter Throckmorton memorably described treasure hunting as "the worst investment in the world." A single day at sea, with expensive survey equipment and a crew to run it, can cost tens of thousands of dollars or more. Searches can take decades, and many are unsuccessful. The Big Five are the Big Five because they are the exceptions. Salvors who do find a significant amount of treasure are unlikely to keep it. Legal challenges inevitably arise and can drag on for years, leading many treasure hunters to bankruptcy and despair.

Most of the treasure hunters who have earned a living from it didn't make money directly from the treasure itself. They sold stories and fantasies to their investors, who funded their expeditions in the unlikely prospect of a massive payday, and to the general public, in the form of books, museum tickets, or guided tours to wreck sites.

The smartest ones preyed on other treasure hunters by leasing out search areas and taking a cut of whatever they found, or by selling information that might or might not lead to a pile of gold, as Dooley said Marx routinely did.

The history of treasure hunting is best understood as a series of legends—legends passed down from the age of the conquistadors and legends treasure hunters tell about themselves in the press and in their memoirs, more or less grounded in truth. At its heart, treasure hunting is a romantic, practically literary endeavor. All of the Big Five cited Robert Louis Stevenson's *Treasure Island* as a key influence. Webber, the last living member of the pantheon, told me he was brainwashed by "too many Erroll Flynn movies."

Ask treasure hunters why they do what they do and you're likely to get an unsatisfying or tautological answer. "I was always fascinated with the Spanish colonial period," Webber said, plainly. "Why? I don't know." In general, they are no more capable of articulating what drives them to seek sunken riches than English mountaineer George Mallory was of explaining why he wanted to climb Mt. Everest. The answer might as well be the same: "Because it's there." Reading between the platitudes, one comes to understand that for those afflicted with treasure fever, centuries of submersion make gold shine brighter in the imagination.

By the 2000s, decades after the heyday of the Big Five, Florida's shores teemed with weekend wreck divers who dreamed of replicating Kip Wagner's and Mel Fisher's feats, the way hapless day traders imagine they're just one lucky bet away from being the next Warren Buffett. They were concentrated in the Keys, where *Atocha* lore loomed large, and along the stretch of the state's Atlantic coast off of which Wagner, Fisher, Marx, and their followers had discovered the remnants of the 1715 fleet. The bulk of all the accessible treasure at those sites had been raised over more than half a century. For the dozens of low-budget teams diving for scraps, the seabed was like an underwater slot machine. The odds of finding a significant amount of treasure were low, and the house always won—the house, in this case, being the companies that acquired or inherited Wagner's and Fisher's leases to the search areas, and who took a sizeable share of what little amount of gold and silver subcontractors found (usually 50 percent), after the state took its own 20 percent cut.

For these hobbyist salvors, many of them humble retirees who spent their meager savings on diving equipment and gasoline, treasure hunting was more about the hunt than the treasure. They would consider themselves lucky to find a dozen silver coins and a handful of ceramic shards over a decade. The salvor community shared tips, leads, and finds online, mainly on a forum called TreasureNet. When it convened in person, skulls and crossbones abounded. Some wore pirate hats. Live parrots were not uncommon.

The largest recent gathering of this subculture took place in Key West in the fall of 2022. Mel Fisher's descendants organized the three-day event to celebrate the quadricentennial anniversary of the sinking of the *Atocha*. With a mix of salvors, investors, Fisher fans, and general enthusiasts in attendance, it was in effect a treasure hunters' convention. Despite his avowed contempt for the vocation, Dooley was planning to go. He insisted I accompany him to research my book, saying there would likely never again be so many figures from treasure hunting's twentieth-century golden age in one place. He drove me down from Miami Airport and we shared a room at the Marriott, where many of the weekend's lectures and events would take place. (As soon as we got to our room, Dooley looked for a spot to hide his laptop, which contained nearly forty years' worth of research on the *San José*. He ended up stuffing it behind the plumbing under the bathroom sink.)

Free-roaming chickens slalomed between drinkers' legs during the meet and greet at a bar on the marina, where white-haired, paunchy men swapped Mel Fisher stories and whispered the latest scuttlebutt on the possible location of undiscovered troves. The accessory de rigueur was a necklace with a silver piece of eight or a gold escudo for a pendant, from either the *Atocha* or one of the 1715 wrecks. A half-dozen men flashed an even more prestigious status symbol: a large class ring with the words "*Atocha*—Golden Crew" engraved around a bejeweled center that resembled a red-and-white dive flag, signifying that they were among those who had discovered the galleon's mother lode in the 1980s. As the liberally flowing beer and rum began kicking in, Fisher's daughter, Taffi, took the mic to announce that a salvage crew was at sea that very moment and that it was likely that they would encounter the *Atocha*'s still-missing stern castle before the weekend was over—exuding the kind of cultish optimism that her father was known for, which kept crews working and investors investing even during meager harvests of gold. She led the crowd in a raucous cheer: "1, 2, 3, *Today's the day!*"

THE GLORY DAYS OF TREASURE HUNTING arguably peaked in the late 1970s and early '80s, when Fisher and Webber made international headlines for their sensational discoveries. In the twenty-first century, as the world's top museums began to condemn the historical pilfering that had helped them build their collections and to repatriate ill-acquired relics—Cambodian sculptures, Benin bronzes, and so forth—back to their countries of origin, the treasure hunter was increasingly seen as tantamount to a looter or a grave robber. Yet the men and women at the Key West bar on this day proudly embraced the term, defiantly out of step with a modern world that in their eyes had grown too cautious, overly sensitive to claims of cultural spoliation, and a lot less fun as a result.

Dooley was generous with his knowledge and rarely withheld his expertise, even if it was in the service of a cause he objected to, like treasure hunting. For decades, Fisher and his team called on Dooley for help in analyzing artifacts and wrecks. "He's usually the first person I call because he's got one of the greatest libraries on all of the lost ships," said Gary Randolph, a member of Fisher's Golden Crew who would come to oversee the company's operations. "He's a wicked good researcher." Thanks to his unusual persistence, his profound understanding of the historical period, and his familiarity with the most arcane recesses of the Sevillian archive, Dooley had identified objects from the *Atocha* and other wrecks that had mystified scholars. "The last one we called him about was a papal seal that they used to stamp into the wax," said Randolph, who wore a piece of eight from the 1715 fleet on a necklace. "He came up with some family history on whose it was, who they were, what the markings meant, even dug down deep on what the colors should have been."

Dooley claimed he refused payment or credit in such cases, lest he be accused of profiting from treasure himself. He realized that his association with men like Fisher, Marx, and Webber, as well as his history with Carisub—to say nothing of his obsession with the *San José*—opened him up to criticism. He understood the allure of treasure hunting and suspected he might easily have fallen prey to it if he had come of age in America rather than in a communist country where personal enrichment was inherently suspicious and where all boats coming and going were inspected by the coast guard. "If I was not living in Cuba," he told me, "I would be one of those treasure hunters."

Throughout the weekend, I got the impression that Dooley was floating between realms. Never a big drinker, he mingled with unease among the cosplaying pirates, even though he knew many members of the Fisher entourage by name, and most seemed to know—or know of—him. Perhaps, as a product of Castro's Cuba, he fit in awkwardly with the boastful, backslapping, beer-swilling, gold-besotted, all-American crowd. Or perhaps he wanted to make it clear that he was not one of them and that he disapproved of their motives and methods.

As speaker after speaker recounted the history of Mel Fisher's operations and the salvaging of the *Atocha* in the grand ballroom of the Marriott the following day, Dooley was slumped in his chair, scrolling on his phone, frequently shaking his head at mentions of treasure and at what he considered offenses to archaeology. "What happened to the *Atocha*'s timbers, huh?" he whispered to me at one point. "Some were left to rot in a warehouse. They apparently threw them back in the water. No one knows where they are. It's a disaster."*

Only once on the Key West trip did I see Dooley fully in his element. We were sipping mojitos from plastic cups in the late afternoon on the terrace of a Cuban bar, where a band was playing *són* music. Moved by the rhythm and the rare cocktail, Dooley got up and danced, displaying an agility that belied his age. He managed to tie even this moment of whimsy to his passion for Spanish shipbuilding. Shouting over the band, he explained that the *clave,* the rhythm at the foundation of so much Cuban music, originated in the shipyards of Havana in the colonial era. It is named, he told me, after the hardwood pegs used to fasten planks together, which slaves turned into a particularly resonant percussion instrument, banging two together to recreate beats born in Africa.

In a moment of elation, Dooley said, "Let's go to the waterfront for the sunset. Maybe we can catch the green light!" When I seemed quizzical, he explained, "When the sun sets, if the conditions are perfect and there's nothing in the way, the last ray of light you see before it disappears behind the horizon is bright green, but only for a second and then it's gone."

I'd heard of this uncanny flash of light but had always taken it for a myth, more of a metaphor than a verified physical occurrence. Jules Verne had written a novel about it, *Le Rayon Vert,* or "the green ray," in which the principal characters seek to observe the titular phenomenon off the coast of Scotland. Verne's 1882 story had described the light as being of "a green which no artist could ever obtain on his palette. . . . If there be green in Paradise, it cannot but be of this shade, which most surely is the true green of Hope!" In Verne's telling, the

---

* This, it turned out, was not quite true. Duncan Mathewson later told me where the centuries-old planks from the *Atocha* and the *Santa Margarita* ended up: at the bottom of the College of the Florida Keys Dive Training Lagoon, "where they still are today available for study."

light was the very essence of truth: "At its apparition all deceit and falsehood are done away."

We walked to an area by the water where dozens of people had gathered to catch what was shaping up to be a perfect sunset. But what made it so photogenic, what refracted the sun's reddening glow so beautifully, were the low-hanging clouds that threatened to get in the way of the light Dooley so longed to glimpse. He dragged me away to get a view unobstructed by people, boats, or distant islets. The orb approached the horizon at an angle. Dooley sped along the waterfront to align our vantage point perfectly, so the sun would set cleanly on the horizon. When he found the ideal spot, we watched it sink, slowly at first, then quickly into the sea. As it dwindled to nearly nothing a scrim of haze masked the final seconds of its descent and robbed us of the green light.

Dooley kept his eyes on where the sun had been. "Maybe we'll see it tomorrow."

Part IV

The Search

The pessimist complains about the wind;
the optimist expects it to change;
the realist adjusts the sails.

—William Arthur Ward

Chapter 14

"The Luckiest Damned Man on Earth"

W hen Roger Dooley left Carisub, in 1985, he was already half a
decade behind in the race for the *San José*.

By then, millions had already been spent in pursuit of the *capitana*
by an altogether new cast of treasure hunters, better equipped and better financed, more comfortable in a coat and tie than a diving suit.
Such had long been the pattern of fortune seeking: First the trail is
blazed by the lone eccentrics, free spirits, and roguish obsessives, then
comes the investor class. Just as the gold diggers, prospectors, and
wildcatters of the American West had given way to industrialists over
the previous century, the shipwreck-strewn waters of the Caribbean
that had long been the playground of dreamers like the Big Five and
Roger Dooley were suddenly being eyed by the establishment.

Jim Banigan was a moderately successful Wall Street stockbroker
who seemed to embody the late '70s idea of the American Dream:
tall, good-looking, well liked, with a house in the suburbs of New Jersey, a wife, and four young children. Beneath the surface, however, he
was suffering—from persistent pain in his stomach, but more importantly from stifling boredom. Seeking a diversion from the drudgery of
securities trading, he was drawn in by the treasure madness that was

gripping the country. He and a friend, a fellow broker named Jim Maloney, sank an undisclosed amount into Burt Webber's search for the
Concepción. Banigan hedged risk for a living. He was good enough at
his job to know it was a foolish bet, but to his surprise it had paid off
when Webber found the multimillion-dollar wreck in 1978. More to
the point, he had found a thrilling escape.

The following year, at the age of thirty-eight, Banigan doubled
down. He and Maloney founded the Cayman Islands–based Glocca
Morra Company—a nod to their Irish roots—for the purpose of going
after the galleon of galleons, the *San José*.

"It was every kid's dream to find a treasure, to do something different," Banigan's wife, Marie, would later tell the *San José Mercury News
West Magazine*. "Jim was very adventuresome. But he wasn't frivolous.
He thought [the *San José*] was definitely there, and there was no reason
he couldn't make millions."

THERE WASN'T A TREASURE HUNTER worthy of the name who
hadn't fantasized of finding the *San José*. Several efforts had even gotten beyond the daydream stage and attracted investments. Robert
Marx had perhaps gotten closest, acquiring a permit to survey the
depths off Cartagena in 1972. Nothing had come of it, however, and
Colombia's maritime authority—Dimar—had since jealously protected the general area in which the *capitana* was thought to lie. No
American, it appeared, would ever again be granted permission to
seek the *San José*'s tantalizing treasure. But Maloney had a friend on
the inside, a smooth-talking Bogotá businessman named Fernando
Leyva Durán, whose brother Álvaro was a congressman at the time
and whose cousin was a high-ranking defense official. Leyva had
grown up partly in the United States and had gone to college with
Maloney in New Jersey. He claimed that he had been so enamored
with the *San José* story as a child that his schoolmates teased him about
it. Banigan and Maloney cut him into Glocca Morra, and Leyva,
working his government connections, secured the search permit that

had eluded so many other treasure-hunting outfits. With this autho-rization in place, the team brought on more backers, including a co-terie of investors from Bank of America and actor Michael Landon of *Little House on the Prairie,* each of whom put in a reported $150,000. Should the project be successful, the returns promised by Glocca Morra based on what they claimed was historical evidence, were 37 to 1—meaning that their $150,000 would turn into $5.5 million.

"I would suggest that anybody who has an ounce of red blood in their veins would not find it difficult to get interested in this project," one of the investors, a management consultant named Joseph Patter-son of Orange County, told *West.* Another investor, an elderly Pasa-dena real estate entrepreneur named Wayne McAllister, said, "I guess there's one word for it all, and that's greed, isn't it."

As the search got under way, one Glocca Morra official warned another: "Treasure hunting is not particularly good for one's soul. It brings out the worst in people."

To establish a search area, Glocca Morra called on some of the biggest names in the treasure business, including Dr. Eugene Lyon, the historian who had helped guide Mel Fisher to the *Atocha,* and Jack "Blackjack" Haskins, whose archival research had proved invalu-able to both Art McKee and Burt Webber. Drawing from Spanish and English records, these experts blocked out an approximately 330-nautical-square-mile search box to the west of the Rosario Islands.

Once the area was established, Banigan and Maloney needed someone to search it. They approached Webber, the most successful treasure hunter to date, known for his command of advanced survey technology. Webber was eager to follow up his triumphant discovery of the *Concepción* with an attempt at the *San José.* Before accepting, though, he sought the counsel of his main backer on the *Concepción,* the shrewd Chicago venture capitalist Warren Stearns. All it took for Stearns to sour on the project was a meeting in Bogotá with Maloney, Leyva, and Colombian officials. What began optimistically turned confrontational after Leyva demanded what Stearns considered far too high a percentage of the treasure for his services. Stearns was further put off when the discussion veered off track and the participants began negotiating the possibility of seeking treasure in nearby Lake Guatavita, the lagoon twenty miles outside Bogotá into which—legend had it—the people of the Muisca civilization had ritually thrown golden objects and emeralds in sacrifice to the gods. As part of the ritual, the Muisca chief himself was said to cover himself in gold dust and walk into the lake, giving birth to the myth of El Dorado, the Golden One. It was apparent to Stearns that gold fever had clouded the thinking of the men around the table, just as it had the conquistadors of yore. Stearns warned Webber to forget about the *San José.*

With Webber out, Glocca Morra entrusted the project to a stolid navy veteran named Bob Smith, who quit his job at an offshore engineering firm in California in the hopes of discovering the wreck (and, like the rest of the crew, reaping a small percentage of whatever treasure was found). The search took place in three phases. The first called for a survey of the seafloor by side-scan sonar, a technology that had become commercially available not long before. Starting in June 1980, Smith and his team cruised back and forth across the search area defined by archival researchers Lyons and Haskins as well as Commander John Cryer, aboard a 110-foot yacht called the *Morning Watch,* hauling a "towfish," a torpedo-shaped object mounted with a side-scan sonar. As it flew above the seabed, the device's transducer sent regular high-frequency acoustic pulses—narrow beams of sound waves—that fanned out to port and starboard, covering a range of several hundred meters. After bouncing off objects, the sound waves returned to the fish. It was not depth or distance the sonar system measured, but the time it took an echo to return and the direction from which it came. On the basis of that data, depth and distance could be calculated. The device's transducer relayed this information to a plotter on board the *Morning Watch,* which represented the data visually onto scrolling rolls of wet paper, gradually scratching out an image of the seafloor in ink. Bursts of sound behaved in many ways like beams of light, only slower, allowing the search team to "see" through the darkness of the ocean.

Like light, sonar reflected differently off different surfaces, causing some to appear brighter than others in the resulting image, depending on their texture and angle. And as with light, the absence of a returning signal appeared as a shadow. While the image drawn by the plotter was in no way a photograph, it could be mistaken for one.

After "mowing the lawn" across the search area for several weeks, the Glocca Morra team had gone through "rolls and rolls and rolls" of paper, Smith said. The side-scan survey results were sent to Texas A&M, whose respected maritime archaeology department identified eighty-four targets that warranted further investigation. But, Smith said, "nothing stuck out as realistic. Nothing jumped out as a wreck to them."

This was unwelcome news for Banigan, who had left his Wall Street job to devote himself entirely to the *San José* search. What had started as a lark, an amusing distraction from the day-to-day, was fast turning into monomania. He was now spending much of his time in Cartagena, away from his family. Since he had no technical expertise, there was little for him to do there but inquire about the search and fret about the slowness of its progress. If anything, he got in the way. But Smith and his collaborators didn't mind. It was hard not to be charmed by Banigan's enthusiasm. Making him happy became as powerful a motivation as getting rich.

"Jim was a very popular guy," recalled one member of the team. "He was very outgoing. Somewhat volatile, but he was very likable. He was almost childlike in his love of a good adventure like this. I don't think he'd experienced anything like it."

In the second phase of the search, Bob Smith's crew returned to the area and attempted to find their way back to each of the anomalies that Texas A&M's archaeologists had found, in order to take a closer look.

Glocca Morra's search for the *San José* was different in nature from the quests of the Big Five. It seemed less improvisatory, less dependent on the whims and ego of a single charismatic leader. At least on the surface, Glocca Morra was made up not of Peter Pans and lost boys but of respectable investors and professional surveyors, with more established backgrounds. Another difference was that the *San José* was thought to lie at a depth of more than one hundred meters, well beyond the physiological limits of scuba diving. Wherever the galleon was, it would be enshrouded in cold, inky darkness. There would be no glint of gold to catch a diver's eye. The wreck would not be happened upon or spied, as Wagner had first perceived remains of the 1715 fleet through a window in his surfboard, just a few feet beneath where people swam every day. Finding the *San José* would instead require the intermediary of marine robotics, which had advanced by leaps in the previous decade. It would be a triumph of technology, rather than a gloriously human melding of detective work and physical prowess.

In addition to a side-scan sonar, the surveyors now came with the most advanced search technology on the market, including an ultrasensitive magnetometer and a video-enabled remotely operated vehicle (ROV). Since GPS, developed by the U.S. military, was not yet approved for commercial use, the surveyors relied on a radio navigation system, triangulating the signals from three transponders.

Glocca Morra's archaeologist, Roy Doty, sent the ROV to take video of every anomaly. Most turned out to be exactly what Texas A&M had predicted: nothing. Geological formations. Endless hours of black-and-white video from the ROV show the robot's light sweeping across sand and coral, catching the occasional fish. If the vast majority of the footage was enough to put even the most passionate surveyor to sleep, the few exceptions woke them from their stupor. Among them was a single cannon, apparently made of iron, its muzzle pointing into the void. More than forty years later, filtered through fading memories, the crew's accounts of the event vary. Doty and several of his colleagues occasionally allude to there having been several cannons. Smith, meanwhile, recalled there having been only one, and surviving video appears to back him up. Attempts to return to the exact site of the cannon were unsuccessful, Smith adds. "We could never find the cannon again."

In addition, Doty said, the ROV found numerous woodpiles. Manipulating its robotic arm from aboard the surface vessel—a task made especially difficult by the action of the waves on the ship, which transferred down the cable to the ROV, causing the arm to bob up and down hundreds of feet below—the crew carefully picked up several pieces of wood. Doty and Banigan had them sent to labs at the University of Florida and the University of Georgia for carbon dating. "Analysis showed that the wood was within the timeline of the *San José*," said Doty, who added that the samples were found to be European in origin. From the cannon and the wood, Jack Haskins considered it likely that Glocca Morra had discovered, if not the *San José* itself, then at least the debris field of the Battle of Barú. It wasn't proof, but evidence was mounting that the team was closing in on the galleon. It was enough to keep Banigan happy.

Over the course of 1980, word got around Cartagena that well-funded Americans were fishing for the legendary treasure of the *San José*, attracting unwanted attention. "We were boarded by pirates one night," recalled Garry Kozak, who worked for Klein, the company that made the side-scan sonar, and helped train Smith's team. "They took everything off the boat that wasn't bolted down, the outboard engine, anything on deck that they could get they took. The cabins were locked, so they couldn't get inside. Probably a good thing for us."

"Banditos," as Smith called them, began harassing Glocca Morra's yachts, circling them in speedboats and firing potshots in their direction. The attackers presumably thought the treasure had already been found and figured it would be easier to steal the gold than to raise it from the seabed. As bullets whistled past him, Smith feared the worst, but the brigands left eventually. "I think they were playing games with us," he said.

So, it appeared, was the weather. For several months, the sea was too choppy to search with any accuracy, as the waves would cause the surface vessel to yank violently on the cables of the underwater survey robots, rendering their data virtually useless. Throughout that time, the expedition was spending tens of thousands of dollars on food, fuel, salaries, and maintenance. By July 1981, a year into the project, Glocca Morra was approaching bankruptcy.

The money had vanished and the search permit was about to expire. In little more than a year, the surveyors had found "nothing concrete" to prove they had discovered the *San José,* Smith said.

"We were in the process of losing everything," said Smith, whose dreams of treasure had been shattered by the harsh realities of personal finance. "I had to go back home and feed my kids."

If Jim Banigan had remained the keen, sober-minded analyst he had been before getting involved with the *San José,* he would have surely done the same. He had run through his savings and left his wife and children largely to fend for themselves. But instead of cutting his losses, he had come to believe that pursuing the galleon's riches was the surest way to ensure his family's future. He was proof that treasure fever was not merely an affliction of oddballs like Robert Marx and Mel Fisher. Investment savvy and suburban respectability provided no immunity.

Having already sunk so much cash into the project, Banigan was unwilling to abandon it. He and Maloney decided to report good news to the Colombian authorities: They had a position on a cannon that appeared to be from the right period, in an area defined by historian Eugene Lyon as the likely location of the galleon. (They didn't mention that they had been unable to find the cannon again.) Shortly after, the permit was extended.

In a desperate bid to replenish Glocca Morra's coffers, Banigan flew to Chicago to meet once again with Warren Stearns, who had previously turned down an offer to invest in the *San José* campaign. This time, rather than try to sell the financier on the project itself, Banigan practically got on his knees. The search, he said, was all he had left to live for.

Stearns was not the sentimental type. But for all his focus on cold facts and the bottom line, he was softened by Banigan's display, "It was very easy to like him, very easy to feel protective towards him," Stearns told *West* magazine. "What he was telling me was that he was basically on his last legs. He had devoted his career, his contacts, what money he had—to this. If new life was not breathed into this, he was just done. He was a very emotional guy and it was sort of like the end of the world."

To Banigan's relief, Stearns agreed to invest his own funds and offered to raise even more, but on one condition: He would take over management of the project. Fernando Leyva, with whom he had previously butted heads, would no longer have a say in the operation. From that point on, it became Stearns's show.

The main factor that convinced Stearns to join the effort—aside from pity for Banigan—was Banigan and Maloney's idea of returning to the search area with a submarine, the *Auguste Piccard*. Built in Switzerland to take tourists to the bottom of Lake Geneva during the Expo 64 world's fair, the mesoscaphe was then the largest civilian submarine in existence, ninety-four feet in length, twenty-two feet in beam, with a submerged displacement of 178 tons, and able to dive to a depth of nearly five thousand feet in theory, deeper than many military subs at the time. It was designed by the famed Swiss hydrographer Jacques Piccard and was named after his even more famous father, the physicist and balloonist Auguste Piccard (an inspiration for Tintin's Professor Calculus and, later, *Star Trek*'s Jean-Luc Picard). Jacques had intended to use the vessel after Expo 64 to conduct advanced oceanographic research, but the ever-practical government of Switzerland, failing to see the advantage this would bring to the landlocked country, had other plans. The *Auguste Piccard* was auctioned off to a businessman based in Mobile, Alabama. He offered to lease the craft to Glocca Morra for a bargain since it required significant repairs: It was in poor condition, having been left in Mobile for a number of years under the charge of a motorcycle gang.

The plan to use the *Auguste Piccard* struck some of the experienced surveyors on the team as extravagantly expensive. For Stearns, who was no marine tech expert but a fine psychologist and an investment savant, extravagance was precisely the point. It was the perfect sales tool: He could tell potential investors that no submarine had previously been used in a treasure hunt but that the billions of dollars in gold and silver presumed to have gone down with the *San José* were worth every cent. Grand ends justified grand means. And even if it didn't succeed, financing a submarine to search for sunken Spanish gold would be the ultimate cocktail-party boast, lending a swashbuckling sheen to even the most conformist of investors.

Flamboyance aside, the use of the *Auguste Piccard* did offer some technical advantages over hitching sonar and magnetometers to a boat, a search method Burt Webber once compared to "towing a parachute through a pine forest." Unlike surface vessels, which pitched, rolled, heaved, and yawed on the waves, submarines could remain perfectly steady below a certain depth, even in the roughest waters. Any measurements taken from tools mounted on the vessel would be considerably more accurate than those connected by cable to the surface.

Presuming, of course, that a competent crew could be found to man the sub. To conduct this third phase of the search, Stearns didn't tap his friend Webber, who had never undertaken a search at that depth. (Webber nevertheless took Stearns's decision as something of a betrayal, since the two had long discussed going after the *San José* together.) Instead, Glocca Morra hired Helmut Lanziner, a widely respected Canadian surveyor and engineer who had extensive experience on deepwater offshore projects in the Arctic.

Finding a captain was more delicate. The first man picked for the job turned out to be, according to Lanziner, a belligerent drunk, who on the trip from Alabama to Cartagena broke into Lanziner's cabin and stole all but two bottles of scotch from a case that had been intended as a gift to Colombian customs officers. ("I was told . . . that it was customary to give a case of scotch and a case of red wine," Lanziner recalled. "It was obviously a bribe.") Lanziner called him out on it, and after the captain openly insulted him in front of Colombian officials, Lanziner fired him on the spot. The replacement captain was no better. He claimed to have worked primarily on Canadian ships in the Arctic, and when Lanziner—who knew that world well—pressed him further on it, the man said, "Well, you know, they have this stupid law about drinking, and I got caught."

As a last resort, Lanziner called a friend in Vancouver, an English merchant marine captain named John Swann. Trim, bald, and bearded, the straight-shooting Yorkshireman had many of the qualities that the previous captains lacked, not least that he could be trusted around a case of liquor. He had come from a seafaring family in the English port town of Kingston-upon-Hull, had worked on ships since he was a boy, and had helmed massive tankers through every ocean in the world. There was just one problem: He had never helmed a submarine before. "I spent most of my life desperately trying to stay on top of the waves," said Swann, a consummate, unhurried raconteur whose nautical tales could hold an entire pub rapt. But as a licensed Master Foreign-Going, an unrestricted UK captain's designation, Swann was qualified to operate any kind of vessel on the seas. He figured he could learn on the job. After all, above or below the waves, weren't the principles of navigation the same? "I had ample experience in ballast systems and pumps and that sort of thing, which of course is 90 percent of the job," Swann said of his thinking at the time. But above all, he was enticed by the promise of another good story to tell: "Scratch an Englishman," he was fond of saying, "and you'll find a pirate"— a motto worthy of Commodore Wager himself.

Beginning in October 1981, with Swann at its helm, the *Auguste Piccard* began strafing the narrowed-down search area with a side-scan sonar mounted on its hull, which had been painted bright orange. Swann was surprised by how steady the ride felt compared to the ships he was used to. "I was never a very good sailor, I hate to admit," he said. "I had the Nelson touch: I was always a little seasick or queasy whenever I went back to sea after leave. But I found it quite comfortable in the submarine because once it gets to sixty feet or so [below sea level], there's nothing—no movement at all."

Anyone suffering from claustrophobia would not have found the experience so soothing. Walking down the *Piccard*'s single, central passageway required crew members to squeeze between equipment, sleeping quarters, and operation stations to port and starboard. Between seven and twelve men shared the dark, constricted space most days: Swann, Lanziner, several crew to operate the side-scan sonar and the sub itself, and a Colombian naval officer sent on board as an observer, who never quite took to the submarine life. When he wasn't needling the Glocca Morra team with questions, he was asleep, waiting for the dive to be over. Despite his nosiness, he was widely liked.

Once the *Piccard* was fully submerged and all stations had checked in, Swann gave his dive orders. "Take her down to thirty meters, zero bubble," he said, instructing his crew to keep an even keel. As the mesoscaphe descended, the men occupied their stations in absolute silence, listening closely for any unusual sound, making sure that no water was seeping in as surrounding pressure squeezed the hull and tested its integrity. Who knew the extent of the damage the neglect of the biker gang had wrought, and how reliable the repairs had been?

"Rig for deep dive," said Swann once the *Piccard* had reached thirty meters and established communication with the surface support vessel. With the diesel engine switched off, the submarine's one-hundred-horsepower motor ran on batteries. All that could be heard as the *Piccard* sank ever deeper was the low hum of the electronic equipment—until suddenly, somewhere below one hundred meters, the pressure would cause the viewing ports to contract with a sharp snap that made every man aboard jump, no matter how many times they'd heard it.

The only viewing ports that remained unobstructed were the two at the nose of the *Piccard,* which for most of the descent showed nothing but blue-black darkness. Unable to see outside, the men built a three-dimensional image of their surroundings in their minds. Deep in a dive, Swann often stood with his eyes closed, his brain projecting a film of the submarine cruising through its environs. He was not sure why, but it helped.

When they'd entered the sub, the men were usually in sweatbands, shorts, and T-shirts, or just as often shirtless. The deeper they went, the colder it got, thanks to the overactive A/C system. Most of the crew put on sweaters. As the hours went by the air became stale with carbon dioxide from the men's exhalations, compounded by the lingering smell of diesel and the aft toilet.

The *Piccard* proceeded with its search at an average speed of three knots. Swann attempted to maintain a constant height between twenty and thirty feet above the hilly bottom as the submarine progressed in straight, overlapping rows from one end of the box to the other and back. Throughout this time, the vessel received frequent pings from two Colombian navy submarines—the *Pijao* and the *Tayrona*—seeking to get a bearing on the search team. Swann and his men, unwilling to lead the Colombians straight to the treasure, rarely responded. "One of the advantages of the *Auguste Piccard* was that she was so quiet that they couldn't track us," said Swann, who took additional comfort in the knowledge that the *Piccard* could dive far deeper.

There seemed, however, to be little risk of leading the Colombians to the treasure, since the search was turning up nothing. Banigan and Stearns grew impatient with the slowness of Lanziner's methodical mowing-the-lawn approach. The financiers urged the crew to instead inspect one specific anomaly after another. "They were a hindrance in doing a proper job," Lanziner recalled. "It was typical of people who had never done a search before."

On December 10, 1981, just as the submarine was making a hard turn to starboard at the end of one of these tracks, the plotter connected to the side-scan sonar began outlining a shape unlike any the crew had yet seen on this expedition, with bright patches and straight lines, a likely sign of a man-made object. The team's oceanographer, Mike Costin, recalled peering through the tiny viewports at the bow: "I could look out with the lights turned out to reduce back-scatter for sixty or eighty feet and see a whole lot of the target." It wasn't clear what he was looking at. It certainly didn't look like a Spanish galleon, but he didn't expect it to after so many years of decay and sedimentation.

Several men aboard insisted on stopping the *Piccard* then and there to examine the anomaly, which lay at a depth of about two hundred meters, but Lanziner refused: To interrupt the submarine's methodical back-and-forth pattern would distort the data gathered and compromise the entire operation. Among the best surveyors in the field, the even-tempered Canadian did not share Banigan's sense of urgency and desperation. He had not blown his savings on the search. He had been hired to do a job and he was going to do it right.

At each successive pass, the image on the plotter became more defined. It was only once the *Piccard* surfaced and the rolls of paper were assembled aboard the support vessel, the *State Wave,* that the full picture came into view. Unable to contain his excitement, Stearns had joined them on the ship to go over the readings. The object they had encountered was the only large target in the area, pointed on one end and square on the other. At about 140 feet, it was approximately the same length as the galleon *San José.* And its position was where Glocca Morra's historians had predicted it would be, apparently buried under coral at a depth of more than two hundred feet. Magnetometer readings, meanwhile, showed a steep spike immediately over the anomaly, indicating a high concentration of ferrous material that archaeologist Roy Doty assumed to be iron cannons. "The only thing that it could represent would have been the *San José,*" said Swann. "We didn't see the name painted on the stern or on the bow, but by process of elimination it couldn't have been anything else."

Stearns felt, he would later say, like "the luckiest damned man on Earth." He rushed back to Cartagena, woke up Banigan, and told him the news. Banigan called his wife, Marie, back in the United States.

"We found it!" he shouted with manic glee. "It was where we said it was!"

Chapter 15

Target A

Over the following days, Capt. John Swann said, "We went back many times to try and get into the wreck, keeping in mind now that it had been down there virtually three hundred years and was nothing more than a small reef covered in crustaceans, et cetera, that was of an approximate size—with a higher end and a lower end—that would represent the typical Spanish galleon of those days." The crew made several attempts to break the carapace of encrustation that, they believed, kept them from billions of dollars in gold and silver. Swann sat the *Piccard* on top of it and ballasted down in an unsuccessful effort to crack it open under the submarine's weight. The men tried dragging anchors across the outcrop using the surface support vessel and even considered planting a small explosive charge to blast it apart. A member of the security team that Stearns had hired—apparently ex–Navy SEALS—was an explosives expert, claiming to have worked on the navy's secret program in San Diego to train dolphins to deliver bombs. But when Lanziner and Swann asked him to assist them, he refused to enter the submarine, evidently afraid. Swann began to doubt that the man and his team were SEALs at all, especially after one of them was robbed of his $7,000 monthly salary in the streets of Cartagena and demanded more money. "They were, frankly, a pain in the arse," Swann said. "They created more problems for me than you can imagine."

Having failed to get to the wreck they were convinced lay within this shell, Lanziner and Swann resolved to film the target from every angle. Careful not to disturb the muddy seabed—which would have clouded the water—Swann laid the *Piccard* gently down beside the outcrop as an engineer sent two ROVs to take what would, over the course of several dives, amount to many hours of video. Much of that footage has since disappeared. Swann maintains that a copy ended up in the hands of a former Colombian navy official, but the original Glocca Morra crew has not seen it since the early 1980s. I asked Lanziner whether, in his recollection, the video showed the ship itself.

"No, no," said Lanziner.

So what could be seen?

"Projections that came out," he recalled forty years later. "They were probably masts or broken-off masts. Some of them were cut off. I think you could see a nice circular pattern on the cut section."

After a long day of filming, Swann prepared to return to the surface. To his alarm, the *Piccard* didn't respond to his crew's commands. Even with the motors at full throttle it would not lift off the bottom. Swann realized only then that the submarine had been slowly sinking into the mud over several hours. He attempted to deballast to lighten the vessel, but even after he had shed all the ballast he could afford to lose, there was no movement. They were stuck fast.

Swann asked the chief engineer, CJ, to have a look through the observation port in the forward hemisphere.

"I can't see a damn thing!" CJ reported.

It was worse than Swann had thought. The *Piccard* was submerged in mud up to the viewing ports. It had been a long day of work, and the submarine's air reserves would soon begin to run out. Already the atmosphere was growing thick, the men's breathing heavier. They began to fear that the *Piccard* was itself about to become another shipwreck and that its crew would suffocate and die just feet away from the bodies of Casa Alegre and his men—if indeed anything remained of them after nearly three hundred years.

Refusing to panic until every option had been exhausted, Swann strove to wriggle free. He had the motors go hard to port, then hard to starboard, over and over. To accentuate this attempt to rock the submarine, Swann ordered the dozen men aboard to line up in the narrow center line and swing their bodies to the left, then to the right in a coordinated fashion. Still the *Piccard* refused to budge. The floor felt hard and unyielding. The action seemed futile—worse than pointless, in fact, since the effort demanded additional oxygen, depleting reserves yet more rapidly. The men were dancing in their own grave.

About fifteen interminable minutes into this exercise, however, they began to sense the ground shift beneath their feet. Barely perceptible at first, the seesawing motion increased steadily as momentum built. Suddenly, the mud relinquished the submarine and the 178-ton vessel—emptied of ballast—shot up, as Swann described it, "like a bloody torpedo."

The crew had no time to celebrate their liberation. Rocketing toward the surface, the *Piccard* could easily crash into the keel of the *State Wave,* the support vessel floating immediately above it. At the speeds the mesoscaphe was reaching, such a collision would surely sink both craft.

Once again demonstrating the nautical wherewithal that qualified him for the captaincy despite his inexperience with submarines, Swann managed to regain control of the *Piccard*'s ascent just before it surfaced and moored it against the *State Wave.*

After examining the submarine's propeller shaft and cleaning out the mud, a technician found a piece of barnacle-dotted wood wedged inside the void space. He brought it to the *State Wave,* where archaeologist Roy Doty examined it. "There's actually indentations showing that the wood was worked and drilled," Doty said. Samples were sent to Beta Analytic, a private lab in Coral Gables, Florida, for radiocarbon dating and analysis. "Their average value would be 365 B.P.

[before present], or the date 1585 A.D.," read the report, which noted an error term of fifty years.

For Banigan, the lab report was the ultimate vindication. All the money he'd invested, all the time spent away from his family, all the heartache would pay off in the end. "If it were not for dreamers like Banigan," Stearns later said, "who against absolutely all odds are willing to chase something like this, I happen to think the world would be a little worse off. Maybe a lot worse off."

The evidence gathered up to that point—the cannon sighting, the woodpiles, the side-scan sonar results and magnetometer readings, the hours of video, and the piece of wood wedged in the *Piccard*—was enough for Stearns to formally declare to Colombian authorities that the Glocca Morra team had found the galleon *San José*—and to demand their cut.

As part of Glocca Morra's agreement with Colombia, Stearns was required to provide the location of the target, along with supporting evidence. In early 1982, he and Swann traveled to Bogotá to meet with a government delegation. The wily Chicago financier did not trust the Colombians and feared they might attempt to take the treasure out from under him once he divulged the coordinates. Stearns, "who was very suspicious of the people he was dealing with, wasn't about to give the exact location" and cede his only advantage, said a source in whom Stearns had confided. Another knowledgeable source said that Glocca Morra's high-priced Colombian lawyer told them they "would be fools to give them the exact location" and thereby allow the government, which had all the power to dictate terms, to renege on its agreement on some technicality.

Accompanied by Swann, who cleaned up his pirate look and bought a new suit adapted to the formality of the situation and the cold and wet weather of Colombia's mountain capital, Stearns met with a government committee. According to people affiliated with Glocca Morra, initial conversations with the Colombians had led the treasure hunters to believe that they would be entitled to 75 percent of whatever treasure was found at the site, the generous share reflecting the risk and money that the North Americans were putting up. The committee greeted Stearns and Swann with smiles and hearty congratulations. But as soon as Stearns shared the (intentionally inexact) location of the target, the committee stipulated that the treasure would be divided evenly between the discoverer and the state, 50-50, as suggested by the Colombian civil code, itself based on ancient Roman law. His options limited, Stearns bit his tongue and shook on the amended deal.

A few days later, as storm clouds darkened the city, Stearns and Swann met with the committee again to sign the contract. When Stearns reviewed the fine print, he saw that Colombia's lawyers had further adjusted the terms. Glocca Morra's cut was now down to one-quarter of the treasure. Stearns protested, which the committee appeared to have anticipated.

"Come on, Mr. Stearns," said one of the officials according to an attendee's recollection. "Twenty-five percent of billions of dollars is still a healthy amount of money."

Stearns decided to play the only card he had left. "By the way," he said, "that position we've given you . . . It's been found to be an error."

At that moment, "you could have heard a pin drop," recalled Swann. "The smiles disappeared. It was an icy reception." The atmosphere had suddenly turned threatening.

Swann and Stearns exited the room without signing the contract. It was night when they left the building under a downpour. Stearns hailed a cab. "I'm getting on a plane to the U.S.," he told Swann over the sound of the rain. "I suggest you get out of here as soon as possible. Demobilize and get the hell out of here." He shut the car door and the taxi drove off.

Swann left immediately for Cartagena and began to dismantle the search operation, a process requiring, among other things, that the *Auguste Piccard* recover sonar transponders dropped to the seabed. The captain ordered his crew to move quickly. After what had happened in Bogotá, Swann sensed that he and his men would not be welcome in Colombia much longer. The more time they spent in the nation's territorial waters, the greater the risk of a serious confrontation.

They weren't fast enough. Upon surfacing from a dive in the late afternoon, the crew of the *Piccard* found a Colombian gunboat waiting for them. It was operated by DAS, the country's ruthless security force, which has been accused over the decades of torture and extra-judicial killing. Calling down to the *Piccard* from the bridge of the gunboat, the DAS agents informed Swann and his team that they were under arrest for operating a submarine in Colombian waters without a license—a curious accusation given that the maritime authority had long sanctioned the *Piccard*'s operations and a navy observer had been on board at all times. Swann had every reason to fear that he and his men would be jailed and prevented from leaving the country.

"I immediately advised them that all my papers had been entered correctly, the submarine had been entered properly, had been cleared properly, and that we had a legal representative and the ship's agent, and that we'd been operating there for many, many, many months without [a problem]," Swann recalled. "But that was to no avail because this was clearly a trumped-up thing." To resist the order would be to invite the Colombians to attack the submarine. Swann obeyed the most important rule of seafaring: The safety of the crew had to come first. He had no choice but to capitulate.

As Swann cruised alongside the patrol vessel, one of the Colombian navy officers assigned to observe operations aboard the *Piccard* turned to him and said, "Captain, we don't like DAS. We don't even allow them into the navy yard."

Swann might have found the comment unhelpful in these circumstances. But then he realized what the Colombian was subtly telling him. Though the officer could not explicitly recommend that the crew defy DAS's orders, Swann took his statement to mean that if the *Auguste Piccard* were to make a dash for the navy yard in Cartagena, the gunboat would not follow. As soon as the submarine was level with the Colombian navy site, Swann veered hard aport into the yard. Once the DAS agents realized what had happened, the gunboat made the turn and accelerated to catch up, but it was too late: The *Piccard* had managed to sidle into a pen alongside one of the navy's submarines.

"They stopped dead," Swann said. "They didn't come in."

The naval officer who had served as a liaison for the Glocca Morra team, Lázaro del Castillo, made a few phone calls and managed to place Swann and the crew under house arrest in the navy yard under his jurisdiction—a relief to all, as it kept them out of the hands of the dreaded DAS.

FROM THAT MOMENT ON, relations between Glocca Morra and Colombia would remain contentious. In March of 1982, just a few days before its search rights were set to expire, the company filed a confidential report to Dimar, Colombia's maritime authority, declaring that the anomaly it had identified, "Target A," the report claimed, lay "in the immediate vicinity of the coordinates 76°00'20"W 10°10'19"N."

"Although the target appears to be a natural rocky formation, it has several features indicating it is not natural to the seabed," read the report. "A defined magnetic anomaly . . . was recorded during passes over and across the target. Portions of the target have shapes covered by sediment and forms that are difficult to discern or explain in terms of natural phenomena.

"A few pieces of wood lodged in the hull during submarine operations in the area. Since the submarine was primarily descended in the downhill region of the target, it was believed that the samples came from the seabed area within 5 to 100 meters west and north of the target. The wood samples were analyzed and declared to be over 300 years old." The report never explicitly stated that Target A was thought to be the *San José,* but it was widely understood.

Quickly, doubts began to emerge about the nature of the anomaly Glocca Morra had found. Treasure hunter Burt Webber—who was admittedly not impartial, having been denied the chance to search for the *San José*—said he was told by multiple firsthand sources about a meeting of Glocca Morra's principal partners at a hotel in Key Biscayne, Florida, following the discovery of what was assumed to be the wreck of the *capitana*. In attendance were the researchers Eugene Lyon and Jack Haskins, who had helped establish the search box and who had recently been taken down in the *Auguste Piccard* to view the target. Stearns spread out a large chart of the waters off Cartagena and threw a pack of Marlboros to the west of the Rosario Islands to mark the spot where Lanziner and his team had supposedly found the *San José*.

"That's a very large area that pack of Marlboros represents," Haskins said, by Webber's account. "But I can tell you this, when I went down on that dive, what I saw was no representation of a shipwreck. It looked like natural geology."

Stearns turned pale. "Warren was furious," said Webber. "He needed Haskins's support, but Jack couldn't because that's not what he saw."

It's impossible to verify this story, since Webber wasn't in the room, and everyone who was has since died. Stearns, for his part, was quoted at the time as saying that there was a "million-to-one" chance Glocca Morra had not found the *San José*. But another member of the team has questioned the discovery. Oceanographer Mike Costin, who participated in the *Auguste Piccard* expedition, later told the Associated Press, "We found something, but I don't think it was the *San José*." *National Geographic* photographer Emory Kristof, who had been invited to visit the site, later said, "It was my feeling that they had a nice little coral island, and that they did not have a ship."

Banigan, who believed he had been close to claiming his share of a treasure that would allow him never to work again, felt that future slipping away. In the summer of 1983, the Colombian government at last allowed the treasure hunters to return to the area to verify their claim. By that point, Glocca Morra had combined with other investment groups to form a new company called Sea Search Armada.[*] The 1983 search effort was described as an "attempt to relocate and identify the shipwreck as that of the *San José*." This time, inspectors from

---

[*] The names Glocca Morra and Sea Search Armada have been used interchangeably from this period on.

Colombia's maritime authority, Dimar, would be on board the search vessels. The *Auguste Piccard* had removed its transponders from the sea-floor the previous year, preventing Glocca Morra from following their signal back to the anomaly known as Target A. All parties understood that the coordinates originally reported in 1982 were incorrect. Instead of searching at that position, the expedition searched for markers placed by the *Auguste Piccard*. In two expeditions, the surveyors that Sea Search Armada contracted did find their way back to the rocky outcropping, but they did not conclusively identify a shipwreck, let alone the *San José*. The only man-made object they discovered at the site was a metal basket believed to have been left behind by the *Auguste Piccard*'s crew, designed to hold small artifacts. Bizarrely, the two expeditions reported widely different positions for the same object, but both sets of coordinates were more than 1.5 nautical miles away from the 1982 coordinates. Rather than bring clarity, the expeditions only added more confusion.

Banigan, for his part, remained convinced that the galleon had been found. But he began to fear that its legendary treasure would elude him in the end. Just as Zeus punished Tantalus for his hubris by keeping food and water eternally just out of his reach, it seemed that the gods—or at least geology and the Colombian government—would forever get between him and the gold he so coveted. He returned to Wall Street, working at a job he hated as he dealt with worsening pain in his gut, the *San José* dream having morphed into a nightmare from which he struggled to wake up.

Decision makers in Colombia, whatever doubts they might have harbored, proceeded as if the spot identified as Target A was indeed the *San José*. But even as it continued to negotiate with Sea Search Armada (SSA), the government—having evidently found Stearns to be untrustworthy and questioning whether SSA had sufficient funds to recover the treasure—began secretly holding discussions with other well-funded private parties to salvage the wreck.

The most determined among them was the Texas oilman John McMillian, of Northwest Energy, who hosted a lavish dinner with several senior ministers in Bogotá in a bid to take over SSA's claim to the *San José*. One can imagine the memorable impression he left on his dining companions. "With steely eyes and a clipper mustache, McMillian . . . looks something like the man who comes to foreclose on orphans," read a colorful profile in *The Washington Post* in 1979. "He speaks in an ominously quiet voice. In the movies, he would play the smoothie who corrupted Joan Crawford." McMillian's exploits "are near-legendary in some energy circles, and he is widely referred to as one tough SOB."

Having gotten wind of McMillian's effort, Stearns launched a countercampaign, dismissing McMillian in the press as "an opportunistic interloper with no background, no legal rights, making statements that he's a serious bidder." Stearns was confident that "Colombian law and legal opinions give us exclusive rights to enter into a salvage contract with Colombia."

But the more time went by without a contract, the less solid Sea Search Armada's prospects became. There being no particular urgency to salvage a galleon that had lain in place nearly three centuries, negotiations dragged on for years. SSA estimated it had spent $9 million by that point, and without the expected gold and silver, debts were piling up fast.

In 1984, as investors grew increasingly concerned, Fernando Leyva—who had been pushed out when Stearns took over the project—sensed an opportunity to return to the fold. He assured his partners that he could speed up the process and secure a contract for at least 50 percent of the treasure but that it would cost them, several SSA investors told *West*. "He talked openly and often of the need for payoffs," the article reported, citing the investors. "To do it discreetly he wanted to renegotiate a higher percentage of the project so that he could offer a stake to the Colombians the firm needed to have in its pocket."

Stearns, who called Leyva "the greediest son of a bitch I ever met," insisted that SSA never ended up bribing anyone. Nevertheless, in the summer of 1984, the Colombian government at last drafted a new contract granting SSA a 35 percent share of the treasure found at or immediately around the reported coordinates. Believing this was the best offer they would get, the North American investors signed the agreement on September 21.

Around this period the Sea Search Armada team sorted out permits to return by ship above the anomaly they had identified as the *San José*. This time they brought heavy-duty equipment—akin to an underwater crane—designed to crack apart the encrustation of coral that had resisted all their previous efforts to break through. They showed the work they were doing to members of the government's newly formed commission on shipwrecked antiquities, who worried that SSA was destroying a culturally important site. According to the commission's cofounder, Rodolfo Segovia, SSA even applied for the authorization to use explosives. "So we stopped them," recalled Segovia, who also served as president of the giant state-run offshore company Ecopetrol, which had effectively laid claim to the riches in Colombia's seabed. "We stopped them and we began really making it difficult for them to continue."

The Colombians never countersigned the agreement with SSA. By the end of 1984, the administration of President Belisario Betancur decreed that all shipwrecks within Colombian waters were national patrimony and reduced the share of any private company reporting the discovery of a wreck to a 5 percent finder's fee, taxable at 45 percent, and—particularly devastating to SSA—applicable retroactively.

As furious as Warren Stearns was about seeing SSA's cut gradually shrink from an expected 75 percent to an insulting 5 percent, his backers were even more enraged—murderously so. According to Burt Webber—who heard the story secondhand from a close associate of Stearns's—one Chicago investor "who was responsible for bringing in a lot of the money that Warren is credited to have raised . . . reached the conclusion that Warren profited very well from this whole thing, and was [so] upset he was going to put out a contract on him."

Jim Banigan, who had been at the origin of the *San José* endeavor and who had begged Stearns to get involved in the first place, would not have been among the suspects. Though he remained an investor, he had long since grown disillusioned with the project and regretted the toll it had taken on him and his family.

He would never have a chance to make up for the lost time. The pain in his gut turned out to be terminal cancer, of which he died in 1986. Shortly before, he had spoken with his wife about the galleon. "He thought maybe if we'd gotten the money, we would have lost our soul," Marie Banigan said. "He thought maybe we weren't meant to have it."

OVER THE NEXT FEW YEARS, as it became the subject of increasingly bitter legal and political maneuvering, the *San José* receded still further from the grasp of modern civilization, sinking deeper and deeper into history as if into quicksand. President Betancur's term ended in 1986 with no resolution on the matter. His successor, Virgilio Barco, was determined to turn to foreign governments to collaborate on the salvaging of the galleon that they believed SSA might have found— regardless of the accuracy of the reported coordinates. It would set a lofty new standard for international collaboration in the sphere of cultural preservation.

A proposal from Sweden, whose king Carl XVI Gustaf visited Cartagena and lobbied Colombian leaders to push his country's effort, was selected after a supposedly open bidding process that critics dismissed as a sham. Press reports revealed that the Barco government had held secret negotiations with a consortium of Swedish companies claiming to represent the kingdom, well before opening up the bidding to other nations as required by law. The discovery of irregularities in these discussions, including promised payoffs and undeclared commissions, led to a major corruption investigation by Colombia's congress that would ultimately sink the Swedish bid.

The failure of the Swedish proposal gave Sea Search Armada's remaining investors renewed hope that their claim on the galleon's treasure could be salvaged. Banigan had died, and both Maloney and Stearns had abandoned the project, convinced it was going nowhere. But the recently restructured company now began to fight back under its newly elected leader, Jack Harbeston, a combative, buttoned-up, Seattle-based consultant in his early fifties who had previously invested about $40,000 in the search for the *San José*.

Harbeston had intended to write off his *San José* investment as a loss, but his tax accountant wouldn't let him do so because Harbeston could not prove that the endeavor had in fact been a failure. As far as he could determine, the galleon remained in limbo: found but untouchable, there and not there. Harbeston hadn't closely followed the quarrelsome exchanges between SSA and Colombia, but upon reviewing the matter now determined that the company could win in court what it had failed to achieve underwater.

"I thought we could win because the laws were clearly being broken by the government of Colombia, and in particular the trade agreement between Colombia and the U.S.," he told me.

Under his direction, SSA waged a legal assault on multiple fronts. In January 1989, it engaged an ace Colombian lawyer named Danilo Devis—promising him a cut of the treasure if his efforts were to succeed—to sue the Colombian government in civil court, asserting SSA's rights over the *San José* wreck, which the company considered its property per earlier agreements. Harbeston even raised the matter with Washington. He enlisted SSA investor and former Nixon collaborator John Ehrlichman to work his contacts and place a lengthy complaint into the *Congressional Record* in 1988, decrying the "expropriation" of an American company by an allied government. "There's no doubt that [the Colombians] are trying to steal the treasure," Harbeston told the press. "The value of what's down there could double [Colombia's] foreign reserves."

SSA had long been a nuisance for the Colombian government. But Harbeston's efforts to turn the dispute into a diplomatic scandal had made an enemy of it. "Sea Search Armada is a commercial company of

pirates," said Segovia, of the country's commission on shipwrecked antiquities. "They are a nest of piranhas."

Colombia was determined to cut treasure hunters out of the process once and for all. It was decided that the most effective way to do
that, ironically, was to engage the services of another treasure hunter.
In 1993, as SSA's civil suit was working its way through the court system, the nation's government hired the brilliant forty-one-year-old
American ocean engineer Tommy Thompson to conduct a search of
the coordinates at which SSA had reported finding Target A. With
limpid blue eyes and a raffish black beard, Thompson had made headlines for his discovery in 1988 of the S.S. *Central America,* a sidewheel
steamer that sank in a hurricane off the Carolinas in 1857 along with
425 souls and fifteen tons of California gold in coins and bullion.
Using custom-built robots, Thompson's company, Columbus-America
Discovery Group, would recover an estimated $100 million worth of
gold from a depth of more than seven thousand feet. It was for Thompson's advanced tech and his prowess as a surveyor, rather than his nose
for gold, that Colombia paid his company nearly a million dollars to
see whether the *San José* lay where SSA had claimed it did.

After combing the seabed for nineteen days at and around SSA's
coordinates, Thompson and his crew returned to Cartagena on July 3,
1994. Asked if they'd found any evidence of a wreck, Thompson said,
"None." The area, he told a Colombian magazine, was "as desolate as
the surface of the moon." There was no sign of the rugged terrain or
the hillock of coral seen in SSA's videos, let alone of a galleon. Nor
did the depths Thompson encountered match those SSA had described. Sea Search Armada had long acknowledged an error in the
coordinates but had attributed it to the inaccuracy of pre-GPS survey
technology, rather than the likelier explanation that Stearns had intentionally misled authorities. Thompson unequivocally rejected that
notion.

"It's not a simple error," he said. "The technology to navigate with
precision, with errors of about five meters, has existed for ten years.

The possibilities are that they found the galleon and kept it secret, or that they didn't find it and kept it secret. The important thing is that whatever they knew, they didn't report it to the government." Alongside Thompson's effort to verify SSA's claims, a piece of wood that Glocca Morra had found at the site was taken out of the vault in which Colombia kept all evidence of historical shipwrecks and was reanalyzed. "The wood sample presented in the Hypothesis does not correspond to a species used in the construction of ships: It is not oak, pine tree, beech tree or fir tree," a government report would later affirm. "The most probable thing is that it is a root." The same report claimed furthermore that it was physically impossible for the wood to have been part of the galleon, as it bore traces of radioactive contamination. "The wood sample was alive and grew up subsequently at the beginning of the atmospheric tests with atomic bombs dating to the 1950s. It corresponds to the modern age."

To Harbeston, it was obvious that Thompson was conspiring with the Colombian government to strip SSA of its claim and maneuver to take the treasure for himself. Thompson admitted that he was interested in the *San José* but said he was motivated only by "scientific curiosity about the galleon." By the mid-'90s, as standards of cultural preservation were strengthening around the world, it had become common for treasure hunters to deny that they were treasure hunters and instead to brandish the fig leaf of science. But it would later be revealed that Thompson had long had the *San José*'s precious cargo in his sights. Before deciding on the gold-laden *Central America* in the early '80s, Thompson had considered going after several other notorious deepwater shipwrecks, including the *Andrea Doria,* the *Titanic,* and the *San José.* He was "convinced that the *San José* had carried more than a billion dollars in treasure to the bottom," wrote Gary Kinder, who interviewed Thompson extensively for his bestselling book *Ship of Gold.* Thompson had ultimately decided against pursuing the galleon because of the difficulty of negotiating with a foreign government for permission. But now that Colombia had invited him into its waters, those regulatory hurdles had collapsed. The treasure of the *San José* was his for the taking.*

Just three days after Thompson returned from his expedition to the supposed site of the *San José,* the civil court of Barranquilla issued a long-awaited ruling in Sea Search Armada's suit against the government of Colombia. It was determined that, according to the civil code in force at the time the discovery was announced, the company was entitled to 50 percent of "assets of economic, historic, cultural and scientific value . . . which might be found . . . within the coordinates and adjacent areas" and which "have the quality of treasure." The court also sequestered the site, forbidding the removal of any man-made objects found there. The vagueness of the ruling only raised more questions: What was the radius of the "adjacent areas" around the coordinates? If, as Thompson reported, the region was barren, what exactly was SSA claiming 50 percent *of*?

And if the galleon wasn't there, then where was it? The answer would come from the unlikeliest of sources.

---

* The ensuing years would provide more reason to question Thompson's motives. Having made millions off the sale at auction of gold and artifacts from the *Central America,* Thompson was sued by investors—as well as descendants of those to whom the gold was originally destined before it sank in 1857— who claimed he had cut them out of profits. In 2012, Thompson skipped his scheduled court date in Ohio and went on the lam. U.S. marshals caught up with him three years later at a hotel in Boca Raton, Florida. Though he was never convicted, Thompson has been in federal prison since 2015, held on contempt of court for refusing to divulge the location of five hundred gold coins that went missing. He claimed not to know where the coins were, telling prosecutors that he had consigned them to a trust in Belize.

Chapter 16

Adrift

In the mid-1980s, as Sea Search Armada pressed its problematic claim to the *San José,* Roger Dooley was left to rue the tragic irony of what he had done by quitting Carisub in a righteous fury. In refusing to take part in the state-sponsored pillaging of the *Mercedes,* he had cut himself off from the sole opportunity available to a maritime archaeologist in Cuba, the country to which he was now confined due to the vagaries of fate and the U.S. government. He had crushed the very dream he was trying desperately to hold on to. And if he could thank Michael for helping to get him as far as he'd gotten toward that dream, he could blame only himself for throwing it away.

In truth, Dooley had faced an impossible dilemma. If he'd participated in Carisub's despoliation of the *Mercedes,* he might have been able to keep working on shipwrecks in Cuba but would have sacrificed any such ambition he had outside the country, presuming he could ever leave. He had been swept up in geopolitical currents that left him adrift in midlife doldrums, suddenly bereft of purpose, powerless to pursue the course he'd charted.

And yet he couldn't stop thinking about Casa Alegre's galleon. "Since I was a child, I remember his mention of the *San José,*" his daughter Liliam told me. "All my life he has been gathering data about that shipwreck." Ever since he had found Governor Zúñiga's letters about the *capitana* in the Seville archives, he had fantasized about finding and excavating it. He knew then how unrealistic the dream was. He had no backing, academic or otherwise, and was unknown outside a small group of people in Cuba and the scant few foreign specialists he had crossed paths with over the years. Reports trickling out of Colombia, about North American treasure hunters who claimed to have located the wreck, made the prospect seem even more unlikely. But as the years went by, increasing doubt over Sea Search Armada's discovery gave Dooley reason to hope.

Dooley could see no direct path to his destination. Like a sailor confronted with headwinds, he would have to approach his goal obliquely, turning one flank to the gale and then the next. In the first and most dramatic of these turns, Dooley reinvented himself as an underwater filmmaker, a profession that allowed him to maintain a connection to the sea. *Blue Treasure Island,* the documentary he had codirected at Castro's behest, had been a moderate success, winning the second prize at the International Underwater Film Festival in San Sebastian, Spain. Shot with a high-performance camera that his friend Al Giddings had passed down to him, custom-built for the diving scenes in the 1977 blockbuster *The Deep,* the film had a technicolor gloss, showcasing the Caribbean's splendors as well as Dooley's keen aesthetic sense—informed by filmmaking books and the original storyboards for *The Deep,* which Giddings had given him to use as inspiration. It also demonstrated his flair for the dramatic. Watching the movie next to me decades later, Dooley sang gleefully along with the synth-heavy score he had commissioned and laughed as he confessed that the way he was able to get such a good extended close-up of a spiny lobster was by mortally wounding it before rolling the camera.

He soon put his newly acquired cinematic skills to use, on a 1988 film called *The Summer of Miss Forbes.* The movie was part of a series written by Gabriel García Márquez, a close friend of Castro's, and produced by Carisub founder Max Marambio, who evidently bore no grudge against Dooley despite his resignation from the organization. As coordinator of underwater photography, Dooley choreographed a climactic phantasmagorical sequence in which the heroine, played by acclaimed German actress Hanna Schygulla, is stabbed to death by her lover in a bedroom at the bottom of the sea, among the coral reefs. Dooley followed this effort up with work on *Tesoro,* a Spanish-language answer to *The Goonies* in which a group of kids go after pirate treasure, by the Puerto Rican director Diego de la Texera. Carisub, which controlled all underwater activity in Cuba, let de la Texera use actual Spanish coins salvaged from the seafloor.

When Jacques-Yves Cousteau, the father of modern diving who had become a practically mythical figure in his own lifetime thanks in part to his TV series, traveled to Cuba in the mid-'80s to film a feature documentary titled *Forbidden Waters,* it was Dooley who showed him and his team the subaquatic sites.

"He wanted to dive in Matanzas," Dooley recalled of his conversations with Cousteau. "I told him, 'That's bullshit, there's nothing there. I suggest you go to Oriente,'" where Dooley had discovered the wrecks of the *Furor* and the *Cristobal Colón.* From aboard Cousteau's famed research vessel *Calypso,* a decommissioned British minesweeper outfitted with an onboard laboratory, Dooley guided the red-hatted oceanographer's team to marvels he knew better than anyone: reefs, caves, and shipwrecks, including the *Sánchez Barcáiztegui,* and the most visually stunning landmark he'd found, which he called "the Wall of Anchors." An underwater ledge in the port of Havana on which innumerable anchors large and small had gotten snagged over four hundred years, littered with bottles spanning the centuries, the surreal graveyard of iron seemed to have sprung from García Márquez's imagination.

Dooley's adventures in filmmaking nurtured dreams of Hollywood glory that few in Cuba would have dared entertain. The repressive policies of the Castro government could not contain Dooley's optimism. In the early '90s, he worked on several feature film scripts about aquatic adventures and managed, somehow, to attract interest from studios. He met in Havana with Al Giddings and Sony Pictures CEO Peter Guber to discuss his idea of turning the story of the lost Nazi U-boat into a movie. Guber, a diving enthusiast who had produced *The Deep*, was sold. Put into development at Columbia Studios, the idea went the way of most ideas in Hollywood—nowhere. But the momentary hope redoubled Dooley's resolve to leave Cuba for good.

The country was mired in an ever-worsening economic crisis due in part to the drying up of subsidies from a democratizing Russia. What kept Dooley in Havana, aside from his presence on the U.S. Treasury's watch list of banned nationals, were his beloved daughters, Lili and Betty. Dooley had grown increasingly estranged from their mother, Zulema, as her deepening devotion to communism and the principles of the Revolution despite widespread evidence of their failure clashed with Dooley's Western fantasies. "They were always fighting about politics," said Betty. "[I] never saw love between them, like hugs or kisses, they would scream to each other." In the mid-1990s, citing irreconcilable differences, they would divorce.

Dooley became ever more cynical about the Revolution as he saw what was happening to his brother. Since rejoining the special forces in the '70s, Michael Montañes had fought in communist rebellions around the world, risen to the rank of lieutenant colonel, and enjoyed privileges unavailable to most Cubans, even to top-ranking officials: frequent foreign travel and access to hard currency and luxury goods, including the ultimate status symbol in Cuba, Rolex watches. (Castro famously wore two on one arm.) While in Spain in the '70s, Michael had bought several Rolexes and had given one to his struggling little brother.

He soared to the top of Cuba's military-political establishment. His closest allies and protectors in the government were his special forces leader, Col. Tony de la Guardia, and his identical twin brother, Brig. Gen. Patricio de la Guardia. (They happened to be related to Roger Dooley's former boss at Carisub, Vicente de la Guardia.) Tony was one of Castro's most trusted subordinates, to whom the Líder Máximo

assigned the most delicate covert operations. A playboy sometimes referred to as Cuba's James Bond, he had doubled as a state-sponsored
arms dealer in Cold War proxy conflicts around the world, often in
defiance of international law. Tony was tasked with bringing in desperately needed foreign cash by any means necessary. Under his command, the Cuban Interior Ministry's MC Department—which also
oversaw Carisub—effectively became a massive smuggling operation,
involved in the traffic of Cuban cigars, guns from Russia, and ivory
and diamonds and fighting cocks from Angola, among other merchandise. In 1988, Tony began helping Colombian and Panamanian drug
barons bring cocaine to the United States via Cuba. When international authorities caught on, Castro denied any knowledge of the
scheme and pinned the blame on Tony de la Guardia. For good measure, he roped in the country's most popular general, Arnaldo Ochoa,
a close friend of Patricio de la Guardia whose increased defiance of the
Castros was seen as a mortal threat to the regime.

On June 12, 1989, Michael Dooley invited the De la Guardia
brothers to his house to toast the twins' fifty-first birthday. He had
prepared lobsters and enchiladas. But by eight o'clock, only Patricio's
wife had shown up. Tony de la Guardia and Ochoa had been arrested
that afternoon. Patricio had said he'd be late for dinner; he had been
summoned to the Ministry of the Interior. As soon as he arrived, he
was locked up.

Men soon came for Michael as well, threw him in jail, and interrogated him about the activities of his superiors. Ochoa and the De la
Guardias were accused of treason and subjected to a show trial whose
outcome was no less predetermined than those of Stalinist Russia.
Castro addressed the nation for several hours. Less than six weeks after
their arrest, Tony de la Guardia and Ochoa were executed by firing
squad.

Authorities could never clearly establish Michael's involvement in
what Castro called "the De la Guardia gang," and he was released after
a week. He avoided the most severe punishment but was nevertheless
a victim of the subsequent purge, forced into early retirement, stripped

of honors and perquisites, of his expensive car and his house, and condemned to disgrace and ignominy. The government to which he had dedicated his life, which had given him everything, had taken everything away.

Michael's sudden reversal of fortune shocked Dooley. Not only could he no longer count on his brother's protection and connections, but if the state could so coldly turn on such a devoted servant, what kind of future could Dooley look forward to in Cuba?

By the early '90s, money had become a serious problem for Dooley. He had long since burned through the savings he'd accumulated in his manic Miami days. And though he landed occasional film work, such as when Al Giddings hired him to consult on a Discovery Channel documentary about diving in Cuba, these opportunities were few and unpredictable. He continued to work mostly in tourism, establishing a diving charter company in Panama—through which Cuba ran much of its foreign-facing business—called Caribbean Treasure. (The "treasure," Dooley was quick to specify, referred to the natural wonders of the sea.) But mere subsistence continued to be a struggle.

He felt he had no choice but to offer up his skills as the foremost connoisseur of Cuba's wrecks, and consulted with various foreign treasure hunters from around the world interested in exploiting them, including "this guy from France, this guy from Africa," he said, with characteristic vagueness. Asked how he justified working for commercial salvage operations, Dooley insisted that, far from selling out Cuba's cultural heritage, he was in fact *protecting* the shipwrecks by undermining the foreign pirates.

"I'd say [to the investors], 'Tell me what you're after, and I'll look at your project,'" Dooley said. "They'd say, 'I found this book that says there's a ship in this or that area,' and I'd say, 'Forget it, there's nothing there.' I'd warn them that they'd have to pay for a license, for a driver and a boat and gasoline, and that contractors would take advantage of them, charging them thousands of dollars a day. It was actually good business for them *not* to find anything."

Among the treasure hunters he claimed to have dissuaded from working in Cuba was the notorious Robert Marx, who called Dooley from Havana one day asking about shipwrecks he was hoping to explore. Dooley said he reminded Marx that his escapades had already gotten him essentially banned from the Bahamas, Jamaica, and Brazil and warned him that the same was likely to happen in Cuba.

Dooley's consulting work had one upside: It allowed him to pursue his own decades-long project of cataloguing and charting all of the island's wrecks. It also provided him with the funds and opportunity to make numerous trips to Spain, to visit the General Archives of the Indies in Seville as well as the kingdom's domestic archives in Simancas, housed in a drafty fortress that had left archivists and researchers shivering since the fifteenth century. Each time he went, Dooley would systematically tack on extra time to further investigate the *San José,* combing through hundreds of *legajos* and eventually compiling what he believed to be the largest trove of archives on the galleon and its cargo that any historian had assembled.

From fragmentary information, long-dead figures involved in the *San José's* birth would find new life in his mind. Among them were Pedro de Aróstegui, the Basque contractor who in 1696 received the commission from the Crown to build the *San José* and the *San Joaquín,* and brothers Miguel, Juan, and Geronimo de Echebeste, the master builders who directed the construction of the vessels. Dooley pictured the hundreds of laborers and craftsmen in the shipyards of Mapil who'd clambered onto the hulking, skeletal forms of the twin galleons, colossal wooden beasts coming into existence rib by rib, plank by plank.

He came to know Francisco Antonio Garrote, who ran the shipyard in which major modifications on the *San José* were made at the turn of the eighteenth century, including its ornate stern design with a carving of Saint Joseph carrying the infant Jesus. He read the words of the powerful vice admiral Antonio de Gaztañeta, a seminal ship designer whom Dooley calls "the forerunner of modern Spanish naval engineers," after sailing the *San José* and *San Joaquín* from their birthplace in the Basque country to the Atlantic port of Cádiz: "Throughout the voyage, I was able to experience and verify [the] seagoing performance of both ships and can therefore conclude that, for ships of this quality, they are the best that have ever been built."

The information contained in these *legajos* would probably not help him find the ship, he thought, but it would allow him to identify and interpret the wreck if ever he did locate it. But by the mid-'90s, that dream seemed more elusive than ever. His trips abroad came to an end in 1993 when his U.S. passport expired. His inclusion on the OFAC watch list prevented him from getting a new one. Since he wasn't technically a Cuban citizen, he didn't have a Cuban passport either. He was a man without a country, effectively imprisoned on the island.

ONE DAY IN 1996, Dooley received a phone call from an old friend, a hard-drinking, overweight American diver named Elliott Jones, from whom he hadn't heard in years.

"Roger, we're here in Marina Hemingway," said Jones.

"We" was Jones and his friend Stephen Ziskind, a self-described "all-time slicer-dicer infomercial direct-response guy and half-assed inventor" from Delray Beach, Florida, who had made a fortune from the marketing of Ginsu knives on American TV. Since coming into money, Ziskind, a plump and ruddy man in his midforties with a trim, salt-flecked red beard, had become enamored with sailing, diving, and the ocean. He had attempted to retrace Columbus's first crossing of the Atlantic on his sailboat. Having read that the explorer initially mistook Cuba for Japan, Ziskind was determined to cruise around the forbidden island. He could find no sailing guide to the country's shores, however, so he endeavored to write one. For that he would need someone who knew the coasts well and could introduce him to government officials. Jones had told him he knew just the guy, and the two sailed to Havana to meet Dooley, without warning him of their visit.

Dooley, whose blond hair had by then gone mostly gray, arrived at the marina and stepped aboard a magnificent sailboat called the *Z*, for

Ziskind. Over the course of the day, Ziskind grew fascinated with Dooley, with his rambling stories and seemingly inexhaustible knowledge of Cuba's seas. He was especially touched when Dooley insisted on having him over to his home for coffee, which Ziskind knew to be strictly rationed.

Dooley was as useful as Jones had promised. Despite having rejected the Communist Party two decades earlier, despite having quit Carisub, despite his brother's fall from grace, Dooley had maintained strong connections to the government through his work in tourism. He made the right introductions, and three days later Ziskind was meeting top cabinet officials to discuss permissions for his book project.

"Roger, I want you to come to my house" to work on the guide, Ziskind said.

Dooley was devastated. Here was the opportunity he had been desperate for, a way out of Cuba and an offer of honest, lucrative work. And he had to turn it down. "Steve, I can't go to the United States," said Dooley, who explained his passport predicament. And there was another problem. "It's this stupid thing, but I'm on a list," he said. Dooley related the circumstances that had landed him on the OFAC watch list in the early '80s, when he had worked for American Airways Charter. "If I set foot in the U.S. I'll be arrested and sent to jail for a long time."

For Ziskind, who was used to getting his way, Dooley's situation posed no obstacle. He was friends with a high-powered lawyer named Jonathan Goldstein, a former U.S. Attorney from New Jersey who had helped break up the Mafia in the state and could surely find a solution to Dooley's legal troubles.

Ziskind never published the guide he'd planned to write. That year, the Cuban air force shot down two planes flown by the U.S.-based activist organization Brothers to the Rescue, which had been dropping leaflets encouraging Cubans to defect. The incident had erased all hope of further collaboration with the government. Nevertheless, Ziskind was so grateful to Dooley that he vowed to follow through on his offer to help him leave.

Working their contacts, Goldstein and Ziskind got Dooley a temporary passport and arranged to have him fly on a tourist visa to Nassau, where Ziskind had a house. The plan was for Dooley to fly from there to a small airport in Palm Beach, where they hoped his name would not set off any alarms at U.S. Customs. Ziskind would then charter a plane to send Dooley from Palm Beach to New York—where the law would likely be more lenient toward him than in Florida—so he could turn himself in to the U.S. Attorney's office.

"I remember spending a week in the Bahamas with him going over and over and over again what his response should be to the immigration officers should he be stopped," said Ziskind. In photos taken at Ziskind's house during these discussions, Dooley's expression is pained, his brow furrowed in anxiety. As soon as he landed on U.S. soil, he would face the possibility of a long jail sentence. He had only a few days to decide if it was worth the risk.

If he stayed in Cuba, Dooley feared he would fade into irrelevance and poverty. This, he concluded, was the more daunting risk. Ziskind and Dooley flew into Palm Beach a few days later. Lawyers from Goldstein's firm were standing by at the airport in case Dooley was arrested, as were bail bondsmen. Everything appeared to be going smoothly, but as he waited to board the chartered plane to New York with Dooley, Ziskind got nervous. With an active warrant out for Dooley, every second he spent in Florida increased the likelihood that he would be arrested. But Dooley refused to get on the plane before he could enjoy the ultimate taste of freedom in America: a Double Whopper from Burger King and a slice of cheesecake.

Dooley flew commercial the next day and spent his first night in Manhattan at the Plaza hotel on Ziskind's dime. As he waited to be summoned to a meeting with an assistant district attorney to discuss his case, Dooley spent his days under the high, ornate ceiling of the New York Public Library's reading room, absorbing maps, manuscripts, and books as if he had been dying of thirst.

The call came about three weeks later. He met with the assistant DA at the offices of Goldstein's white-shoe firm, on a high floor of a New

York skyscraper. Goldstein had prepped Dooley for the interrogation. "Don't say any more than you have to," he'd said several times, in Dooley's recollection. "If the guy asks you what you did today, don't tell him what you did yesterday."

Avoiding self-incrimination was a tall order for Dooley, who once he started speaking had trouble stopping. "I don't lie," he told me. "I'm an open book. Maybe I talk too much."

In the end, he admitted to a single, minor infraction fifteen years before, when he had flown from Cuba to Miami and back in a day to buy a replacement for a faulty scuba compressor, technically violating the trade embargo. The confession allowed all parties to walk away satisfied, and Dooley to avoid a trial. His name was removed from the OFAC watch list and was thus no longer associated with some of the world's most notorious criminals and agents of enemy states.

The deal required Dooley to remain in the United States for at least ten months and to check in regularly with an officer of the court. He would have to find work. It would never be simple to start a new life in a country that he had once called home but whose language he now spoke with difficulty. Yet with his skills as a researcher and historian he would surely have qualified for a job related to his expertise, especially in South Florida, where the language barrier would have been less of a hindrance.

Ziskind, who had covered Dooley's hefty legal bill (many times his yearly income in Cuba), had another arrangement in mind: He would hire Dooley to test his latest infomercial invention, an absorbent cotton cloth called the Dye Magnet that would allow loads of whites and colors to be washed together. Dooley was too grateful to Ziskind to refuse.

Though he was born in America, Dooley was living an archetypal immigrant experience. Like so many taxi drivers with PhDs back home, he was forced to put qualifications and ambitions aside, to slide to the bottom of the ladder and start climbing again. For months, he lived in Ziskind's house and worked out of a storage unit in Delray Beach, Florida, running load after interminable load, remarking on the absurdity of life, and wondering how he had gone from discovering a lost treasure galleon to testing towels that retailed for $4.95. *Wash, rinse, repeat. Wash, rinse, repeat.* He woke up every day wanting to quit. But Ziskind was reluctant to let him go. He had lured Dooley to the United States by appealing to the archaeologist's passions. They were going to work together on nautical projects: the sailing guide to Cuba, and then a book about lighthouses. Neither of those had materialized. But Ziskind had come to enjoy simply having Dooley around, a factotum with a colorful past and a debt to pay.

Dooley remained stuck at Ziskind's company for nearly three years, eventually working as a handyman on all aspects of the Dye Magnet project and helping to build sets for its QVC infomercials. As grateful as Dooley was to his benefactor, it was hard for him to imagine how much lower he could fall. Cuba might have been an open-air prison in his mind, but at least he had been respected and well connected there. The most powerful people in the country were never more than a few phone calls away. In America, he was technically free, but in his mid-fifties he was condemned to poverty and humiliating, menial drudgery with no realistic hope of returning to meaningful employment.

But Dooley had never been given to despair. As a sideline to his work for Ziskind, and a way to keep his toe in the ocean, he published a booklet called *Coral Reefs of the Caribbean, the Bahamas and Florida* (Macmillan Caribbean), a bestiary of the marine life he had lived among for three decades. At just eighty lavishly illustrated pages, the book was hardly academic. But as his first byline in America, it provided him with a chance to establish his oceanographic expertise outside of Cuba.

"Roger E. Dooley is a pioneer of underwater research in Cuba," read a biographical blurb on the back cover. "A scuba diver for more than 30 years, he was founder of the Underwater Archaeology Department of the Academy of Sciences. He has written various books on marine life and also produced and directed several documentary films on the subject." The biography was somewhat embellished: Dooley had not published anything longer than a magazine article or a tourism brochure, but perhaps he figured nobody would be able to check as long as Cuba remained closed to American inquests.

If someone were to ask him at this time what his profession was, he would without hesitation say he was an archaeologist, but in truth he had no prospects in the field. Out of habit and irrepressible interest, he nonetheless continued to follow every development in the world of Caribbean shipwrecks. He saved up to visit maritime conferences in Houston and New Orleans. He had access to Ziskind's mother's car and would often sneak away on weekends to Key West (Ziskind balked when he saw the mileage) to socialize with the circle of fellow ship-wreck obsessives who orbited Mel Fisher's operation. Dooley might have scorned their methods and motives and their rum-swilling ways, but there were few others with whom he could share his passion. In his lowest times, they made him feel like somebody. He had grown close with Duncan Mathewson, Fisher's archaeologist, for whom Dooley gladly researched a report on the colonial-era shipyards of Havana, where the *Atocha* was built. He respected Mathewson and understood the compromises he had made in choosing to work for Fisher. He just wasn't prepared to make them himself.

Fisher and his entourage invited Dooley on several occasions to join them in the treasure-hunting business. He was surely tempted. But as desperate as he was to leave Ziskind's side and search for lost ships once again, Dooley demurred. The same qualms that had led him to resign from Carisub in high dudgeon prevented him from saying yes now. He was happy to share his knowledge with the most unscrupulous of colleagues, but treasure in itself was of no interest to him.

Besides, Fisher's name was by then even more sullied than Carisub's: On November 27, 1998, Dooley opened the business section of *The New York Times* to find a photo of Fisher under the headline "Hunter Admits Sale of Fake Gold Coins." Published a few months after police raided Fisher's Key West office, the report quoted his lawyer, who blamed Fisher's fraudulent practices on his treatment for terminal cancer: "He was taking immense amounts of medicine," the attorney said. "He is very, very vulnerable."

It was a busy news day on the treasure-hunting front. Right above the dispatch on Fisher in the *Times*, Dooley found an article announcing Cuba's partnership with several Canadian companies to find and salvage millions from Spanish treasure ships thought to have wrecked off the island. The report claimed that there were four hundred sunken galleons in Havana Harbor alone, estimated to contain billions in gold and silver. Dooley, who knew Cuba's wrecks as well as anyone alive, had to laugh, and not just because far fewer than four hundred galleons, properly defined, had ever sailed through the Caribbean, let alone sunk in it. Once again, treasure hunters were dangling the possibility of ludicrous sums to get financing and press coverage—the oldest trick of the trade. Though no longer practicing archaeology, Dooley decided to write a long, detailed letter to the editor of the *Times,* in which he identified himself as "an active marine archaeologist in Cuba until 1997." He refuted the article's gross historical blunders and distortions with facts he knew by memory from his many visits to the Seville archive. And he took the paper to task for celebrating what he considered government-sanctioned piracy.

"The[re] are a large number of important historical shipwrecks but very few with the possibility of economic value of the kind described in the article," he wrote. "It would be tragic if wrecks of great historical significance were destroyed by amateurs searching for an elusive El Dorado, as has happened so many times before in so many places."

Dooley's letter was never published. But the act of writing it awakened something in him, reviving his dormant fixation on the *San José.* He began once again to collect any scrap of information he could find related to the construction of the *capitana* and the Battle of Barú, not because he thought it would lead anywhere—how could it?—but because no amount of time in Ziskind's home-shopping purgatory could fully extinguish Dooley's obsession with the galleon.

In 1999, Dooley saved up to buy a plane ticket to Washington, D.C., and visited the Library of Congress. He wasn't sure what he was looking for but assumed that, as one of the richest repositories of knowledge in the world, it might contain some useful clue. Over his decades of research, he had grown deeply comfortable in libraries and archives, undaunted by their vastness and complexity, invigorated by the sheer concentration of data. His insatiable thirst for knowledge related to his area of interest—historical Caribbean shipwrecks and in particular the *San José*—had a way of drawing him to relevant sources no matter how buried, the way a starved rat will sniff out bait in the deepest recesses of a labyrinth. For someone accustomed to navigating the chaotic, largely uncharted Archivo General de Indias, the well-indexed Library of Congress was smooth sailing.

Searching through the catalog in the Geography and Maps Division, Dooley saw that the library had acquired a collection of about four hundred old Spanish maps from a London antiquarian in the 1920s. He looked at one after another until he came upon a long-forgotten chart of the Colombian coastline around Cartagena. Dooley laid the map out on a table and examined it under the reading room's fluorescent lights. It had been drafted in 1729, just twenty-one years after the sinking of the *San José,* when memories of the battle were relatively fresh. It was the work of a twenty-four-year-old Spanish cartography student named Domingo Antonio Pérez, who had spent five years taking measurements of the coast's contours and learning the local names of landmarks.

Dooley began by orienting himself on the map: North was left and south was right. His eyes snaked from landmark to landmark, taking in odd elements like the quaint, red-roofed houses Pérez had drawn to designate settlements, the yellowish tint with which he'd shaded shallow reefs, and the mysterious flourish of the pen in one corner that resembled a red dragon. Then he saw a detail that nearly made him gasp.

Just below the Rosario Islands, against the off-white paper sea, a neat hand had etched four tiny x's. Next to them were the words *Bajo del Almirante*—Shoals of the Admiral.

His heart was suddenly racing. Dooley suspected that the admiral in question was none other than Commodore Charles Wager, the English squadron leader who had taken on the *San José* and whom Spanish sources at the time referred to as "the Admiral." This was the only copy of the map in existence. It was as if the document had found him, rather than the other way around. Pérez's chart had never been published, and Dooley could find the name of "Bajo del Almirante" nowhere else.* Surely there was a connection to the battle, he thought, but *what?* What had inspired the naming of the shoals? He ordered a high-resolution scan and added it to his growing file on the *San José,* which he had been dutifully compiling for a decade and a half for no purpose he could clearly articulate. All he knew was that his destiny and the *San José*'s were tied.

---

* On all other modern maps where they were named, the shoals were known as the Tortuguillas.

Chapter 17

The Ghosts of Rota

At the turn of the millennium, Dooley received a call from his friend Duncan Mathewson, Mel Fisher's archaeologist. It was not the *Atocha* he wanted to discuss, or the *San José,* but another ill-fated galleon, lost half a world away.

The *Santa Margarita** was a ship from the Spanish Empire's Manila fleet, which beginning in the sixteenth century ferried merchandise such as porcelain, silk, spices, cotton, gold, tea, and opium across the Pacific, between East Asia and the Americas. The vessel had sunk in 1602 off the coast of Rota, one of the Northern Mariana Islands, now a U.S. territory. In 1995, a treasure salvage company called IOTA Partners received permits from the U.S. Army Corps of Engineers and other authorities to excavate the wreck. It was a troubled project from the beginning, torn between the IOTA investors' impatience for returns and the government's insistence on

---

* Not to be confused with the ship of the same name that sank off the Florida Keys in the same 1622 hurricane as the *Atocha* and was also discovered by Mel Fisher's crew.

archaeological and environmental diligence. The contract required that a qualified marine archaeologist lead the excavation and submit regular reports to demonstrate that the team was complying with regulations.

Mathewson, who was not available, had recommended Dooley for the position and called his fellow archaeologist to describe the project to him. "This is a commercial salvor," Mathewson recalled telling Dooley. "He's got good ideas, but he needs somebody to direct the work and to figure out where the rest of the wreck is."

It was a lifeline. After years in limbo, Dooley was being given a chance to return to the study of shipwrecks. It was the kind of good fortune that a more religious man might have attributed to divine assistance, but Dooley saw it as reversion to the way things should always have been.

He accepted. He relished the change of scenery and the chance to study Manila galleons, which were not his expertise. "For me it was a challenge," he said. Though he would be working on behalf of a treasure-hunting concern, he would not be an employee, a distinction that helped soothe his conscience. In March 2000, he signed a contract with the company as an independent field archaeologist. He would send reports to a colleague in the United States who had been involved in the project, the archaeologist Daniel Koski-Karell. His obligation was not to IOTA's investors but to archaeology and the government of the Mariana Islands.

Shortly after signing the contract, Dooley flew to Seattle to meet IOTA's director, sixty-eight-year-old Jack Harbeston. To my disbelief, the archaeologist would later insist he "didn't put two and two together" that this was the same Jack Harbeston who, since the mid-'80s, had led Sea Search Armada in its fight against the Colombian government over the treasure of the *San José*. Nor did Dooley see a reason to mention his own longtime obsession with the galleon, he told me. "I can't remember even once discussing it," Dooley claimed. "I don't think I ever mentioned the word *San José* with him." Nor would Harbeston recall the wreck's coming up in their conversation. Casa Alegre's *capitana* would come to divide them, but for now the two men got along.

In Seattle, Harbeston showed off a few artifacts from the *Santa Margarita*—copper ingots, glass beads, porcelain shards—in his garage. Dooley was aghast at the poor conditions in which the items were conserved and wondered what he had gotten himself into: Harbeston, he recalled, "had nails rotting in buckets of water."

Dooley landed on Rota in the late spring of 2000 and found that the tropical island's palm tree–studded white-sand beaches bore a passing resemblance to Cuba's shores. He was in his element, filled with purpose once again. The archaeologist had arrived at the beginning of the short diving season, when typhoons were unlikely to sweep across the region. Such storms were what had doomed the *Santa Margarita* in the first place. The story of the galleon's final voyage is among the most haunting in the history of Spanish seafaring. The ship left the port of Cavite, in the Philippines, on July 13, 1601, with cargo bound for Acapulco. It caught the warm-water current of the North Pacific Gyre, the transoceanic highway that looped northeastward toward America, powering the flourishing trade that enriched both continents, and Spain most of all. The galleon encountered so many violent storms in such quick succession that before it had even passed the eastern tip of Japan it had lost its masts, most of its sails, and its pilot. The *Santa Margarita*'s captain attempted to guide the battered vessel back to Manila for repairs. With little means of harnessing the wind or current, the galleon drifted for months. Provisions and drinking water were soon depleted, and hundreds died on the hellish journey. Recalled one survivor, named Sancho, "There were so many who were then dying of hunger and thirst, with sores in the throat, falling gums, molars and teeth"—the unmistakable signs of scurvy.

In February 1602, the crew caught sight of the Marianas and anchored off Rota, by a jagged reef that contained a turquoise lagoon. To the Chamorro natives who watched from the beach, the *Santa*

Margarita must have looked like a ghost ship, "without a rudder and with a small rag for a sail." Only forty men remained of the three hundred who had embarked. Indigenous islanders sailed out to greet the galleon and found its emaciated crew barely clinging to life. The locals offered food in exchange for iron, a trade the desperate Spaniards gratefully agreed to. "One man went so far as to eat thirty coconuts," Sancho recalled. Once the survivors had regained sufficient strength, most were brought to shore, where they hoped to harvest local wood with which to rebuild the *Santa Margarita's* masts, yards, and rudder. But as soon as they set foot on the beach, tensions flared. The Europeans began making threats, and the Chamorro, fearing that the visitors planned to take their land by force, struck the first blow. In the mêlée that ensued, the natives bludgeoned the Spaniards with clubs, threw stones at them, and set them on fire, killing a dozen on the spot. Chamorro villagers later climbed aboard the abandoned *Santa Margarita,* grabbed several sick crew members who had been left behind to die, sailed them ashore, and slaughtered them. The Spaniards who hadn't been killed were treated kindly so that they might be exchanged with the next Spanish sail to pass for a ransom of iron. This, to the Indigenous population, was the most precious of metals, out of which they forged tools and weapons, fishing hooks and coconut oil lamps.

On the sixth day, the *Santa Margarita's* rotten mooring lines parted and the galleon drifted away. It slammed into the reef and sank in shallow water. Chamorro divers combed the wreck for iron. They recovered plenty of gold and silver items as well, but, finding the metals less practical, used them to decorate their trees and houses, as so many garlands and ornaments. Indigenous and Spanish salvors returned to the wreck for years. By the 1980s, when treasure fever gripped the world and sent fortune seekers to the four corners of what had once been the Spanish Empire, little was left of the *Santa Margarita* but a centuries-old tale, as well as ancient nails and sherds of white-and-blue porcelain that occasionally washed up on Rota's beaches. A company called Pacific Sea Resources surveyed the area in view of salvaging artifacts but concluded in a 1987 report that an excavation would cause too much damage to the reef.

IOTA Partners, under Harbeston, had no such concerns. Its 1990 project proposal to the government of the Mariana Islands stated that its "long term goals are to recover shipwrecks in an exemplary archaeological manner, and for a profit." The emphasis, it would become apparent, was on the latter goal. In 1995, the company claimed to have found the remains of the *Santa Margarita* buried in the sand at a depth of fifty feet. The discovery was momentous enough to tempt the esteemed British archaeologist Margaret Rule to risk her unimpeachable reputation by partnering with treasure hunters. Rule was known for overseeing the excavation and raising of King Henry VIII's ship *Mary Rose* in 1982. Her slow, rigorous approach clashed with the accelerated schedule that Harbeston's profit-hungry investors demanded, and the eminent scholar quit within a year.

One archaeologist whom IOTA approached wrote at the time that he got the "distinct impression" the company's director "wanted an archaeological front man rather than the services of an archaeologist."

For a time, the impatient Harbeston assigned artifact recovery to the diving supervisor, who was not trained in archaeology, in a brazen violation of the rules. IOTA cycled through five more archaeologists over the next seven years, all of whom butted heads with the company's leadership over its immediate expectations for gold and silver. Harbeston reportedly complained that archaeologists were doing "meaningless work, [which was] a total waste of time during a short dive season." Per the account of one alarmed local authority, the company director urged his crew to work "as rapidly as possible, with little attention to archaeological concerns. . . . Those artifacts that IOTA determines have no commercial value are to be left in the water."

IOTA staff, meanwhile, rebelled against Harbeston, complaining about his insistent manner and "micromanaging." The excavation devolved into chaos, and little was accomplished for several years.

When Dooley arrived in the spring of 2000, everything changed. "Everybody was attracted to his antics, and he was very intelligent in the way he spoke about archaeology," recalled Trac Huynh, a former U.S. Fish and Wildlife officer who oversaw security on the project and ran operations for several years. "He had a sense of humor and a very good personality." Dooley held meetings at 6:20 A.M. to announce the day's work, regularly breaking the tension with a joke— which the staff sometimes had trouble understanding. "He has this strange Cuban accent, so everybody had to listen extra hard," said Huynh, "and sometimes they missed the punch line." Unlike one previous archaeologist on the *Santa Margarita,* whom Huynh described as an imperious alcoholic holed up in the conservation lab with a bottle for sole company, Dooley rode his scooter to the beach every afternoon and swam out to the reef. With contagious enthusiasm, he took care to welcome all team members into the fold and make them understand the archaeological stakes.

Dooley's first order of business was to verify that the wreck was indeed where IOTA had claimed. The company's divers, untrained in archaeology, had uncovered numerous artifacts in the sand, several dozen yards off the reef. But having studied the shore and read the narrative of the *Santa Margarita*'s sinking, Dooley suspected that the main wreck lay in shallower water, closer to the rocks. Dooley often compares the fieldwork of an archaeologist to that of a detective at a crime scene. The smallest ceramic sherd could be a vital clue. And just as a homicide detective might follow a trail of blood, Dooley searched for answers in the pattern of ballast rocks, recognizable by their roundness and smoothness.

"Don't throw away the ballast rocks!" he urged his staff. "Each rock is a piece of a puzzle. If you find one, don't touch it. Take a picture and call me immediately." Fifteen years after being denied oversight of the *Mercedes* excavation, Dooley had been given a second chance to conduct the kind of rigorous operation he'd longed to lead, albeit in the ethically dubious context of a treasure hunt. He was not about to let it slip away.

The seabed had changed drastically since it had claimed the *Santa*

Margarita. For four centuries, tides, typhoons, and the relentless crash-ing of waves had eroded the reef and sent boulders rolling down to its base. Dooley feared that the galleon was buried not in sand but under layers of rock and coral. To confirm this hypothesis, he had the crew jackhammer three narrow test pits, each about three meters deep, rela-tively far apart. In the third, he found a single ballast rock. He dug pits all around it, one of which revealed more ballast rocks: A direction had thus been established. Following this method, Dooley found his way to a concentration of ballast rocks. The *Santa Margarita,* he had discov-ered, was fifteen to twenty meters closer to the shore than previously thought.

Dooley's team pulled boulders "half the size of a VW," as Huynh described them, off the wreck and into a specially dug pit, where they provided new substrates for coral growth, as required by law to com-pensate for the sections of reef destroyed in the course of the excava-tion. Whereas Harbeston, suspicious of regulation, had made enemies of local authorities over the years, Dooley smoothed relations by invit-ing representatives of various government agencies to the site and reas-suring them that he was taking his responsibilities seriously and not merely rubber-stamping a treasure hunt.

He continued to lift spirits after hours, particularly at the karaoke bar—the only entertainment available to the team on that corner of the remote island. "He was the man responsible for teaching me how to dance," said Huynh. "Because I saw him dancing and I was just amazed. Like, this guy can *boogie.* He was just swinging girls around." He had come fully back to life.

Under Dooley's supervision, the IOTA crew uncovered numerous artifacts from the *Santa Margarita,* including Ming porcelain, gem-stones, religious items, personal effects from the crew, sword scabbard fittings, and fragments of the ship itself—but not a trace of silver or gold. Dooley concluded that Chamorro and Spanish salvors in the seventeenth century had recovered most or all of the precious metal from the wreck well before it was entombed in the rubble. As disheartened as Harbeston and his investors were by this revelation, Dooley was frustrated not to be able to publish his findings and at last gain the professional recognition he had long sought. For one thing, the site was not technically his: He was expected to send reports to Koski-Karell, IOTA's lead archaeologist (who, in keeping with the secrecy that often surrounds commercial salvage, never published a word). But even if he had led the project, Dooley would have been hard-pressed by that time to find a peer-reviewed academic journal willing to publish observations funded by a treasure-hunting operation, no matter how diligent.

THE AGE OF MCKEE, MARX, AND FISHER was long gone. Treasure hunters had once been hailed as roguish heroes, dreamers, risk-takers, literal venture capitalists who spent years in daring pursuit of unimaginable riches. But more than two decades after their heyday, in the 1960s and '70s, they were now more often compared to pirates and grave robbers plundering cultural heritage for profit. The profession's fall from grace went hand in hand with the taming of the underwater Wild West. Advances in robotics extended the depths that could be explored beyond the physiological limits of the human body. Maritime archaeology had grown into a serious academic discipline, no longer the haphazard, improvisatory undertaking it had been in the early days of scuba. Society in general had become more regulated, more cautious, more cognizant of the costs of adventurism.

"I analogize it to elephant hunting," said attorney James Goold, a specialist in maritime law who had successfully fought American treasure hunters in U.S. courts on behalf of Spain since the late '90s, forcing them to return millions of dollars' worth of salvaged coins. "It used to be something that people thought was really cool and adventurous," he said. "Not so anymore."

The global movement to combat treasure hunting culminated with the drafting in November 2001 of UNESCO's Convention on the

Protection of Underwater Cultural Heritage, which sought to protect what the organization estimated to be three million undiscovered shipwrecks lying on the ocean floor. The agreement, forged as Dooley was excavating the *Santa Margarita* in the Pacific, forbade the sale of artifacts from wrecks older than one hundred years. It urged states to preserve their cultural heritage at all costs, arguing that the least disruptive way to do so was by leaving it *in situ*—where it lay. And it enshrined the principle of sovereign immunity, whereby a sunken warship that once flew a nation's flag remained that country's property forever, no matter where it lay. It was no surprise that Spain, which was thought to have lost hundreds of treasure-laden ships over centuries of imperial rule, was among the convention's first signatories.

The debate over the UNESCO charter brought a long-simmering conflict between purist and pragmatic archaeologists to a boil. Many shipwreck specialists around the world, including Dooley, considered the convention to be as ill-advised as it was well intentioned. The blanket prohibition on selling recovered objects—even coins of which there might be hundreds of thousands of multiples, only the first few of which might be of archaeological interest—would mean many shipwrecks would remain undiscovered, since salvors willing to take on the risk and expense of a search expedition would have less incentive to do so, and most governments and academics could hardly justify the budget. Leaving ancient ships in situ, furthermore, would not protect them, critics feared, but instead condemn them to slowly decompose while depriving the public of the chance to commune with history.

Preservationists who support the UNESCO approach acknowledge that the ocean is destructive but argue that it eventually eases up its assault. "A ship like the *San José* is relatively new and is in no danger of disappearing anytime soon," maritime archaeologist Peter Campbell, who studied shipwrecks of antiquity in the Mediterranean and elsewhere, told me. "There are biological, chemical, and physical issues that break down shipwrecks at sea. However, after around the first hundred years, they reach an equilibrium, where they pretty much stop to degrade. But if you start taking away cannon, and start digging in the sediment, you restart all those processes." Campbell conceded that uncovering the ocean's mysteries made for more exciting stories than leaving them untouched. After all, he admitted, "Mel Fisher and Indiana Jones are what got me into archaeology." But like many others who came to the field out of a youthful hunger for treasure and adventure, he eventually grew up and came to reject those ways as reckless and misguided.

"They're a bunch of hypocrites," said veteran surveyor Garry Kozak, an ocean explorer of the Indiana Jones school who had worked on search and salvage expeditions around the world—including Glocca Morra's hunt for the *San José*—since the 1970s and had helped discover numerous historically important wrecks.* (He had also surveyed the depths of Loch Ness in 1978 in an effort to put the monster myth to rest. He found nothing out of the ordinary except for a World War II aircraft that had been ditched during a training mission.) The in situ argument is "a lot of bull crap," he contended. "The ocean is a corrosive environment and everything that is in it is degrading and will disintegrate and go to the bottom. *Titanic* is a classic example of it."

Throughout the early 2000s, as countries ratified the UNESCO statute one by one, Dooley paid close attention, wary of what the consequences might be for his dream galleon. If Colombia endorsed the document, he could kiss the *San José* goodbye. It would become Spain's to claim, and the country was sure to oppose the disturbance of the wreck, which it considered a war grave. To Dooley's relief, Colombia declined to sign the UNESCO charter (as, it should be said,

---

* Among the shipwrecks Kozak has helped locate is that of the World War II cruiser U.S.S. *Indianapolis,* whose crew was torn apart by sharks in the Pacific, as memorably recounted by Robert Shaw's salty captain in *Jaws.* The wreck was found in 2017, at a depth of more than three miles, in an expedition financed by Microsoft cofounder Paul Allen.

did the United States). The reason, one senior minister at the time told me, was that "there are many treasures in our territory"—none more valuable than the *San José*—and Colombia had no intention of ceding them to its former colonial ruler.

While Colombia's decision kept Dooley's *San José* hopes alive, such remote fantasies would not pay his rent in Miami or put food on his table. The *Santa Margarita* had been a blissful reprieve, restoring Dooley's pride and purpose, but now his island idyll was over, and he was no closer to his goal. He had no intention of returning to the kind of humiliating labor he had done for Ziskind's infomercial business. In order to be taken seriously as a maritime archaeologist and have a shot at finding the *San José,* he would need to stay active in that field, but in this he faced a dilemma. Because of his work in the 1980s for Carisub—which would later be widely condemned for its focus on treasure—he believed he would be blackballed by academia. And because he had no academic affiliation, the only opportunities that came his way were from treasure-hunting outfits that had the money to pay for ambitious excavations but whose goals and methods he objected to.

In late 2001, Dooley was introduced to a Toronto-based company called Visa Gold, one of the Canadian treasure salvors Castro had authorized to excavate shipwrecks around Cuba, which had been the subject of the *New York Times* article that prompted Dooley to write a scathing letter to the editors. Visa Gold, a public company whose shares traded on the Toronto Stock Exchange, had been granted a five-year concession in 1997 to search a 1,500-square-mile area around Havana. By the last year of its contract, Visa Gold had not found a single one. In desperation, the company asked Dooley if, with his unparalleled knowledge of Cuba's wrecks, he knew of any worth exploring. As a matter of fact, he did: the ship he had discovered twenty years earlier and had regretted abandoning ever since, *Nuestra Señora de las Mercedes*—the galleon that got away. He suggested Visa Gold request a permit to excavate the site—or what was left of it after Carisub had gone through it—on the condition that they bring in a professional archaeologist to direct the project. (He was happy to oblige.) Visa Gold's contract expired before the plan could be carried out. In the end, all Dooley did for the company was provide some historical context for a small exhibit of items Visa Gold had recovered from the wreck of a nineteenth-century Spanish brigantine and would later put up for sale, including cutlery, perfume bottles, a handful of musket balls, a diamond-and-ruby brooch, and a figurine of Neptune. The company was shut down shortly after, following a brazen stock manipulation scheme designed to boost its plummeting share price.

BECAUSE OF THE POOR REPUTATION of his employers and associates—from Carisub to IOTA Partners to Visa Gold—Dooley was accused over the years of being a treasure hunter himself. He vehemently rejected the term, but then again, few would embrace it in the new millennium. The maverick adventurers of Dooley's generation, men in the mold of Robert Marx and Burt Webber who had proudly cast themselves as modern buccaneers, had ceded the way to a more presentable class of salvors fluent in the language of archaeological ethics and cultural preservation. What mattered was not what one said but what one did. In my dozens of interviews with Dooley, I attempted to determine the extent to which the prospect of treasure—as opposed to pure curiosity—drove his own fascination with shipwrecks. To that end, I once asked him if I could see copies of his diplomas in oceanology and archaeology from Cuba's Academy of Sciences.

He said he didn't have them. "My ex-wife burned them," he told me. "It's a long story." In the mid-2000s, he said, Dooley had helped both of his daughters, Lili and Betty, escape to the United States via Mexico over Zulema's objections. Betty left first. Lili, who was pregnant at the time, said that it was heart-wrenching to leave her mother on her own but that she "did not want for [her] son the level of social, economic and moral deterioration in which Cuba had sunk." In her fury, Zulema—who had just received a cancer diagnosis—took out belongings Dooley had left behind, piled them in a fountain in the yard, and set them ablaze. She watched as her ex-husband's papers—including his diplomas—vanished in flames. When he visited the following week, Dooley told me, there was "nothing left."

Since Dooley had begun telling me his picaresque life's story, I'd had to wonder how much I could believe. His way of glossing over details, of jumping from one topic to another too quickly to follow, combined with his often-inscrutable diction, left me instinctively skeptical. And yet, in reaching through the fog of time and Cuba's totalitarian past to find witnesses who could corroborate what he'd told me, I learned to my astonishment that all of it turned out to be more or less true, barring the odd embellishment. But what he was claiming now—that Zulema had burned his diplomas—struck me as particularly dubious. If it was not true, if it was something he had made up to conceal his lack of credentials, it would give the lie to everything he'd told me.

I asked him how I could possibly verify his archaeological bona fides. I had been unable to reach anyone from Cuba's Academy of Sciences, let alone anyone from his time there nearly sixty years ago. Communication between the United States and Cuba was challenging in the best of circumstances, but tracking down testimonies of Dooley's academic career in the 1960s and '70s was proving more difficult than finding eyewitness accounts of the Battle of Barú from the 1700s.

For want of a physical diploma, Dooley referred me to Roger Arrazcaeta, one of Cuba's most respected archaeologists, who for twenty-nine years had run the Gabinete de Arqueología in Havana. He too had fled Cuba for the United States. Since 2023 he had worked as a conservator for New York's Metropolitan Museum of Art. I messaged him saying I wanted to talk about Dooley. One gray winter afternoon I met Arrazcaeta near his new home in the Bronx. We sat on a park bench overlooking the Long Island Sound, where I hoped at last to elucidate the mystery of Roger Dooley.

In his mid-sixties with a thick salt-and-pepper beard, Arrazcaeta spoke, to my relief, more slowly and coherently than Dooley, leaving little ambiguity. "I never knew Roger to be a treasure hunter," he said. "My relationship with Roger has always been a frank professional one, always about scientific interests."

Not only did the scholar confirm that Dooley had studied at the Academy of Sciences in Havana, but he clearly looked up to him. Arrazcaeta described Dooley as "a pioneer of subaquatic archaeology in Cuba," perhaps the most important one. "He was the best-equipped to lead the way because he was also a diver."

Arrazcaeta had been an archaeology-obsessed teenager when he first met Dooley in the 1970s and was dazzled by the map of Cuba that Dooley had hung in his office, on which scores of colored pushpins represented the shipwrecks that surrounded the island. Years later, when he had risen to the top of his field, Arrazcaeta would come to rely on Dooley's expertise and his extensive personal library, assembled in defiance of the Castro regime's restrictions.

Asked about Dooley's decision to work for Carisub and its effect on his reputation, Arrazcaeta said Dooley had had little choice. "Roger always sought a way to be in this world of subaquatic archaeology," which in Cuba meant working for Carisub. No other institution could provide access to the necessary boats and equipment. "It was the only opportunity."

Joining Cuba's state-run treasure-hunting operation had been the first of several ethical compromises Dooley made in order to pursue his passion for archaeology. It would cast a shadow on the rest of his career. But a distinction must be drawn between Dooley and the people and organizations he had been compelled to work with over the years. An expert on colonial Spanish shipwrecks, Dooley maintained a modest living as a consultant to various entities interested in sunken treasure, some more nefarious than others. So far as I could determine, however, he had never sold a salvaged artifact or plundered a site for gold or silver. Rather than being paid a share of profits, he had always received a salary or consulting fee for his historical research or archaeological work— when he'd requested payment at all. (His occasional assistance to the *Atocha* gang, for instance, had largely been pro bono.) He claimed to be driven above all by a pure love of shipwrecks and history, and no one who'd heard him talk at exhausting length and in eye-glazing detail about seventeenth-century Spanish naval architecture could doubt that. But for a growing portion of the cultural establishment—call it the UNESCO crowd—whoever assisted in the commercialization of sunken treasure was guilty by association.

In Dooley's case, the accusations would only grow louder as he closed in on the richest shipwreck in the sea, thanks to a serendipitous meeting with a woman whose love for him would rival his for the *San José*.

Chapter 18

Adriana

Adriana Gonzalez's timing couldn't have been worse. The forty-four-year-old had moved from Colombia to Miami with her young son in 2007 with the intention of starting a business to sell Colombian products in the United States. Shortly after they arrived, the global economy collapsed, and her business along with it. She had hoped to escape the hardships and violence of her homeland, which she'd known from a young age, ever since her father had been kidnapped and killed by guerrillas. But now she was left stranded in an unfamiliar country, with no clear plan.

She stayed with her sister, who had emigrated to Miami before her. After a while, a friend told her she had been on her own for too long and urged her to find someone on the Latino dating site amigos .com. After a few days of browsing through profiles of perfectly nice-seeming divorced men with drab job descriptions, Adriana received a message from a silver-bearded marine archaeologist with a full head of hair. They had little in common: He was significantly older and, judging from his bio, far more adventurous. But she'd always loved gazing out at the ocean and imagining what was out there—perhaps that was enough. She summoned the courage to reply and felt a surge of girlish excitement when he wrote back. The feeling persisted as they exchanged flirty messages for several weeks.

Adriana experienced different emotions as their first date approached: fear, anguish, curiosity. Dooley arrived on time to pick her up from her sister's house, looking impeccable, as she recalled. He seemed nervous and was uncharacteristically quiet on the drive to Monty's, a casual waterfront restaurant in Coconut Grove with an island theme. Adriana had picked the spot because it was in a crowded area and allowed for easy escape. She had heard horror stories about people who had met over the internet. She wore sneakers in case she had to make a run for it.

They took seats outside under thatched parasols. Where other men might have broken the ice by mentioning the weather or complimenting her looks, Dooley asked Adriana whether, being Colombian, she had heard of the galleon *San José*. To his delight, she had. But she knew little beyond the legend that a fabulous treasure had sunk somewhere off Cartagena centuries before. Dooley remained on the topic for the duration of the meal. "He began talking too much, and faster than normal," she told me. "I felt embarrassed because I had to make an effort to understand what he was saying." But Adriana didn't mind. On the contrary, she was thrilled both by the story of the galleon itself and by the enthusiasm that made the man sitting across from her seem decades younger.

Dooley told her of his fascination with the shipwreck and his determination to find and excavate it. He had a good sense of where it was, he said. All he needed was the permission, and the technology, and several million dollars. In other words, he had nothing but a wild idea.

From that moment on, his obsession became hers. Dooley could not have known when he clicked on her amigos.com profile how valuable Adriana would become to his quest, offering not just love and support but also access to high circles of power in Colombia. Born to a well-connected family in Pereira—"an intermediate town where everyone knows each other," as she puts it—Adriana worked on the campaigns of several friends who had gone into national politics.

For the previous few years, Dooley had closely followed the debate about a proposed modification to Colombia's existing law regarding underwater cultural heritage. The proposal would have clarified and formalized Colombia's impenetrable official process for compensating discoverers of historical treasure. It would have allowed the Ministry of Culture to contract directly with foreign salvors and pay them a portion of the recovered items that didn't qualify as culturally or archaeologically significant. Dooley feared that the passage of the law would trigger a rush of salvors vying for the *San José* under the guise of archaeology. Even though he had no financial backing, he had contacted several lawmakers as well as officials from the Ministry of Culture in hopes of understanding the law's subtleties and getting a head start in the race to find the galleon. But his entreaties had so far gotten nowhere.

Dooley and Adriana would marry a year later. Thanks to his wife's introductions, Dooley met and corresponded with several congresspeople and senators. In these exchanges, he took pains to distinguish himself from the unscrupulous treasure hunters who would surely be gunning for the *capitana*'s treasure. He talked up his sound archaeological intentions and let it be known that he was working with an unnamed institution that had the money and technological capability to conduct a proper deepwater search and excavation. In fact, he had nothing concrete lined up. "It was not exactly a bluff," Dooley later told me. "I knew I could have gotten the financing if I'd wanted."

EVEN AS HE CLAIMED TO already have the funding, Dooley was exploring every option he could think of to search for the *San José*. It was in this spirit that he emailed Jack Harbeston, the now seventy-nine-year-old director of Sea Search Armada and IOTA Partners, on March 8, 2011.

SSA was at that time locked in an intractable legal battle with the Colombian government. As Harbeston approached his ninth decade, fighting for his cut of the galleon's riches had become his life's mission, his last battle. It had been nearly thirty years since Glocca Morra claimed to have found the *San José,* but the resentment was still raw. The company had long demanded 50 percent of whatever treasure was found "in the vicinity" of the coordinates at which SSA had reported finding the galleon in 1982. That claim had been upheld by the Tenth Civil Court of Barranquilla in 1995 and would eventually be upheld by the Colombian Supreme Court in 2007. But since there was no treasure to divvy up, the issue had remained unresolved. SSA sent word to the government in 2010 that it would send an expedition to verify the coordinates and received a threatening reply warning that such an unauthorized attempt would be met with force. Seeing no other solution, Harbeston took the case to the United States, suing the Colombian government in Federal District Court, in Washington, D.C.

Dooley wasn't sure what he expected to come of his outreach to Harbeston; after all, he was convinced that Sea Search Armada had not found the galleon. But the two had gotten along decently well during the excavation of the *Santa Margarita* in the Pacific, and the archaeologist figured it couldn't hurt to stay on Harbeston's good side, just in case.

"Even though we haven't talked recently, I've been following your situation with the Government of Colombia regarding the San Jose," Dooley wrote. "I hope you win the case, you deserve it. . . . I don't know how at this moment—but I'm sure that I could help you."

Dooley told Harbeston of his recent experience with the latest in underwater search technology on a secret private salvage project in the Atlantic, and of his exhaustive archival research on the *San José.* His studies had recently driven him to a startling conclusion: "Let me just say, based on my findings, the San Jose did not sink by a great explosion as the English contend."

Once again boasting of the resources at his disposal, Dooley confessed his deep desire to go after the galleon: "I have always wanted to locate, excavate and conserve the San Jose. I have the personnel, equipment and the investors that would jump in right away if weI *[sic]* had the permission. . . .

"I'm very busy Jack, but I'm very interested in helping you so you can win this case. . . . P.S.: I got married with a beautiful and wonderful woman, she is! *[sic]* Colombian!"

Harbeston's reply, one week later, was dry and businesslike, returning none of Dooley's warmth and not even acknowledging the news of his marriage. He explained that SSA had changed its principal aims. He expected the company to make its investment back not in treasure but in court. "The GOC [Government of Colombia] has convinced us it will never allow anybody but a Colombian insider to recover the San Jose," he wrote. "To put it plainly, <u>we are no longer interested in wasting time and money in an effort to recover the San Jose</u>. That is behind us." Harbeston went on to suggest there could in fact be no treasure left to recover. "The San Jose site might well be looted by this time, since the GOC has circulated the location of our finds to third parties, with no constraints on their broadcasting the information. . . .

"At this time we are focused solely on litigation in US court," Harbeston continued. "If the GOC wishes to settle on reasonable terms for our targets we would consider its offer, but our future expenditures are dedicated to legal fees, not the recovery of the San Jose. If you can structure a settlement within those constraints, I look forward to hearing from you."

Dooley was confused. Who was he to negotiate a settlement with a foreign government on Harbeston's behalf? If nothing else, the correspondence had made clear that any alliance with Harbeston was pointless. But by then, a new player had entered the drama, one with the power to grant Dooley access to what he most desired.

Chapter 19

"A Long Shot"

Since the mid–1980s, each successive Colombian president had vowed to reveal the secrets of the *San José*. In 2010, the country elected a man for whom that goal was especially personal, the centrist political savant Juan Manuel Santos. Born to one of Colombia's most influential families in 1951, Santos left the house at sixteen to become a naval cadet in Cartagena, where he first became enamored with the legend of the *San José.* He went to college at the University of Kansas, became an award-winning reporter and a Nieman fellow at Harvard, and took over as director of Colombia's paper of record, *El Tiempo,* which his family owned. From there he launched his political career. As President Álvaro Uribe's defense minister in the 2000s, he had taken a hard line against the Revolutionary Armed Forces of Colombia—known as the FARC—the Marxist guerrilla army that had terrorized the countryside since the 1960s in a brutal campaign of killings and kidnappings. Santos had run for president on the promise of crushing the FARC. Once elected, however, he abruptly reversed Uribe's policies by seeking to make peace with the militants.

Putting an end to the decades-long war was one of Santos's primary aims as president; after years of tortuous negotiations, his administration would reach an accord with the FARC, earning him a Nobel Peace Prize in 2016. His other key objective would prove in some ways more elusive: at long last to find and excavate the *San José*.

For more than thirty years, Sea Search Armada's crusade to establish its rights to the galleon's treasure had stalled all further attempts to establish the location of the *capitana*. The proposed law allowing private salvage—the one that Dooley had been closely following—failed to pass under Uribe's term. Santos refused to let that be the end of the story. Early in his first term, Santos revived efforts to pass a new law pertaining to the recovery of Colombia's underwater heritage, in hopes that it would encourage private salvage companies to make a bid for the *San José*. Public-private collaborations, he thought, could also relieve the perennially cash-strapped Colombian state of the enormous cost of financing an ambitious expedition.

As drafts of the law wound their way through Congress in the early 2010s, Dooley went back to meeting with lawmakers to stay abreast of its progress so he could be ready to strike. This time he wasn't alone. Among other shipwreck obsessives insinuating themselves into the process was treasure hunter Burt Webber. News that Colombia might officially open up its waters to foreign salvors and lay out a clear pathway for them to be paid a portion of the sunken treasures they found had prompted Webber to join forces with a well-connected mining engineer and naval historian named Daniel De Narváez McAllister, who had long been fascinated not just with the *San José* but also with the so-called Córdoba treasure fleet that had disappeared off New Granada in a 1605 hurricane.

De Narváez, an upper-class Bogotano with a courtly bearing who can trace his Colombian ancestry to 1601 and suspects he is descended from the sixteenth-century Spanish conquistador Pánfilo de Narváez ("I'm very sure we will confirm this with some genetic testing"), claims to have identified about fifty wrecks. He attended all hearings and debates on the proposed law, often accompanied by Webber. In his communications with government officials, he impressed upon them the foolishness of the UNESCO policy of leaving historical wrecks untouched when part of their treasure could be spent on the people of Colombia without a significant archaeological downside. " 'In situ' is dubious when people are starving," he told me. On behalf of an organization of maritime professionals he cofounded, De Narváez wrote directly to President Santos—with whom he used to ride in the school bus—warning him of "a minoritarian group of high-profile fundamentalist archaeologists pursuing their own interests (and who profess an exclusive, almost fanatical ideology of in situ preservation and oppose any sort of commercialization of recovered objects)."

Santos and a majority of lawmakers were receptive to the arguments. On July 30, 2013, Colombia's congress passed Law 1675, which allowed the Ministry of Culture to partner with private contractors to salvage historical shipwrecks. For prospective investors in such projects, Article 15 contained the all-important clause: "The contractor shall be remunerated with up to 50 percent of the value of those objects that do not constitute the Cultural Patrimony of the Nation." The precise percentage would be determined by a special commission on a case-by-case basis. According to the law, artifacts of which there were multiple interchangeable examples—such as uncut gemstones or coins of the same denomination from the same year and the same mint—wouldn't count as patrimony beyond the first few specimens. The rest would qualify as treasure, and the contractor could keep up to half of it.

WITH THE PASSAGE OF LAW 1675, Dooley rushed to secure financing before more established competitors could swoop in with a bid to search for the galleon. He needed an investor who had millions to spare but who could also pass the Colombian government's vetting process. He was reluctant to rely on the disreputable cast that typically backed treasure-hunting operations, not least because they didn't have enough money to fund a deepwater search and the type of rigorous excavation Dooley had in mind, which he believed could easily run to

more than $50 million. He asked Adriana if she could think of a re-
spectable Colombian financier who might be willing to fund the project in the name of cultural preservation. Without hesitation, she
suggested Alejandro Santo Domingo, the thirty-six-year-old billionaire scion of the country's most famous business dynasty, who sat on
the board of the Metropolitan Museum of Art and the British Museum. Dooley cold-emailed Santo Domingo and caught his attention
but failed in the end to strike a deal. Unable to think of another Colombian of similar means and interests, Dooley considered the Mexican telecom tycoon Carlos Slim, the richest man in Latin America,
but nothing came of it. He then thought of the British billionaire
Richard Branson and tried, unsuccessfully, to reach him through his
son. None was willing to take the risk, either on the *San José* or on
Dooley.

Time was running out. In the immediate term, the archaeologist
began to fear that he would be beaten to the punch and that his thirty-
year quest would come to an inglorious end if he couldn't find an investor. But the urgency was existential as well: At sixty-nine, he
suspected that this might be his last shot to accomplish something
great after so many decades in the wilderness.

Having failed to tempt a well-known philanthropist, he changed
tack and sought out a more obscure enthusiast who might instead be
enticed by the galleon's fabled treasure. Two months after the passage
of the new law, he thought of Anthony Clake, a secretive young British financier known—within Dooley's very small circle—for his interest in potentially lucrative shipwrecks. Clake was a star executive of
the London hedge fund Marshall Wace who had pioneered a successful computer-driven investment strategy for the firm a few years after
graduating from Oxford in 2001. He had virtually no online presence.
In a web article listing the City's 25 top fund managers, his entry was
the only one with a question mark in lieu of a photograph. He was
reported to have discreetly invested in numerous shipwreck hunts
around the world, establishing a slew of special-purpose companies,
several of them in tax shelters like the Isle of Man. With an estimated

Boston ship captain William Phips, who discovered an extraordinary treasure off the coast of Hispaniola in 1687.

Art McKee, "the grandfather of treasure hunting," in his Miller Dunn diving helmet on Plantation Key, Florida, 1936.

Kip Wagner poses with a cannon salvaged from the 1715 fleet off Florida's central coast, 1961.
Courtesy of the 1715 Fleet Society

Burt Webber (right) and a Dominican diver storing bags of silver pieces of eight recovered from the shipwrecked Spanish galleon *Nuestra Señora de la Concepción*, late 1970s. *Courtesy of Burt Webber*

Treasure hunter Robert Marx in Jamaica, 1960s. *Courtesy of Allen Exploration*

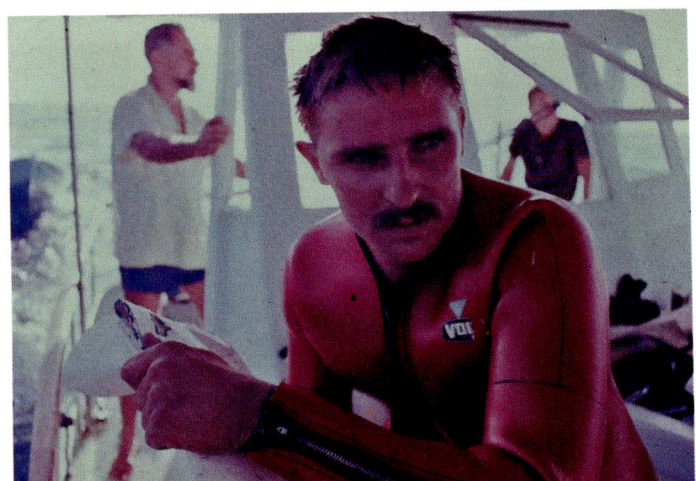

Treasure hunter Mel Fisher displaying gold chains salvaged from the wreck of the *Atocha* off the Florida Keys. *Courtesy of Mel Fisher's Treasures*

Glocca Morra cofounder Jim Banigan (left) with a fellow treasure-hunting investor on board a salvage expedition in the mid 1970s.
Courtesy of Burt Webber

The Swiss mesoscaphe *Auguste Piccard*, later used in the search for the *San José*, exits its shipyard of origin on Lake Geneva, 1964.
Gérard Gery/Paris Match

Warren Stearns, Vice Admiral Francisco Rivera Caminero, and Burt Webber examining a navigation cross-staff salvaged from the wreck of the *Concepción*, 1977.
Courtesy of Burt Webber

Dooley and future antagonist Jack Harbeston brandishing a Ming dynasty porcelain cup from the *Santa Margarita* on Rota, one of the Northern Mariana Islands, in 2002.

Roger Dooley collection

Steve Ziskind at the helm of his sailboat, the *Z*, in the late 1990s, around the time he met Roger Dooley and helped him leave Cuba for America.

Courtesy of Steve Ziskind

Dooley, with friends in Nassau, agonizes over his decision to escape to the United States, 1997.

Courtesy of Steve Ziskind

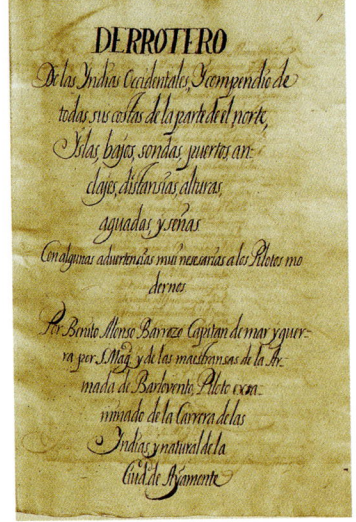

The title page of *Derrotero de las Yndias Occidentales, 1689,* the sailing manual written by Benito Alonso Barroso, a master pilot of Spain's Caribbean treasure fleet. The document provided Dooley with key clues to the location of the *San José*.

Roger Dooley collection

Colombian president Juan Manuel Santos (left) greeting Dooley at the New York residence of the Colombian ambassador to the United Nations on September 24, 2014.

Courtesy of the office of Juan Manuel Santos

Dooley and Adriana Gonzalez, his future wife, in 2008.

Roger Dooley collection

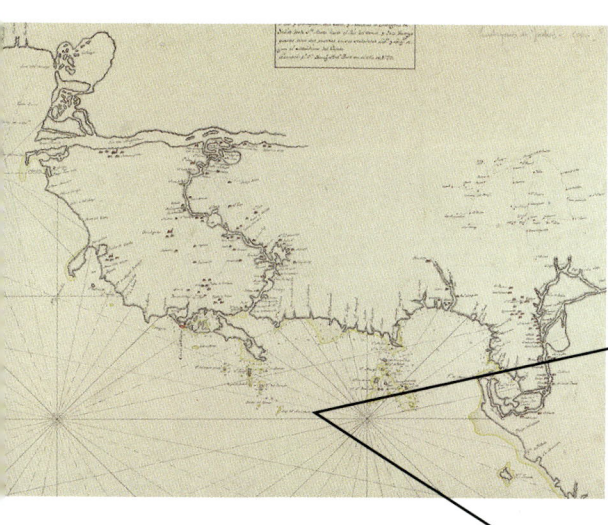

When Dooley discovered this 1729 map of the coastline around Cartagena de Indias in the bowels of the Library of Congress, he was convinced that the reef described as *Bajo del Almirante*—"Shoals of the Admiral"—was a reference to the battle of June 8, 1708.

Roger Dooley collection

The REMUS 6000 autonomous underwater vehicle, critical to Dooley's search for the *San José*, being launched from the dock of the Woods Hole Oceanographic Institution in Falmouth, Massachusetts.

Ken Kostel/© Woods Hole Oceanographic Institution

Dooley (center) planning the search for the *San José* in Cartagena in spring 2015, flanked by Woods Hole's Mike Purcell (in yellow shirt) and subsea data analyst Garry Kozak (with glasses).

Roger Dooley collection

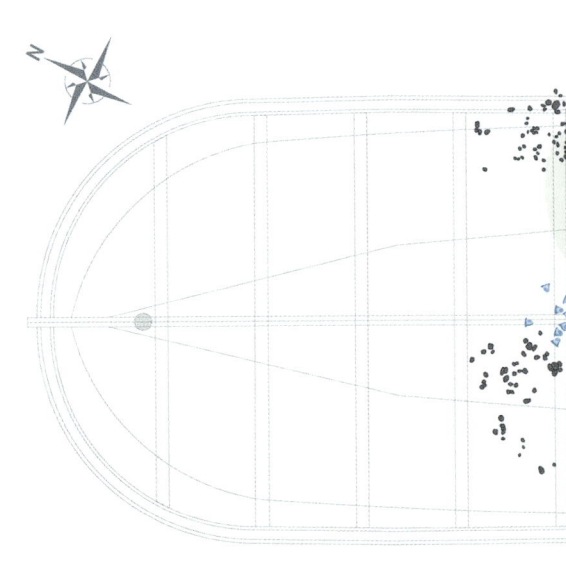

"Uh-oh…" Dooley realizing upon viewing the REMUS 6000's data in a Cartagena apartment that the *San José* had been located. Herman León (with cap), Ernesto Montenegro (in orange shirt), Purcell (seated, in dark shirt), and Jeff Kaeli (far right) look on, November 26, 2015.

Roger Dooley collection

President Santos and Dooley aboard the *Seabed Prince* as it floated above the wreck of the *San José*, May 19, 2016.

Roger Dooley collection

Celebrating the discovery of the *San José* at the Cartagena residence of President Santos: (from left) culture minister Marian Garcés, Santos, Dooley, and Ernesto Montenegro, December 4, 2015.

Roger Dooley collection

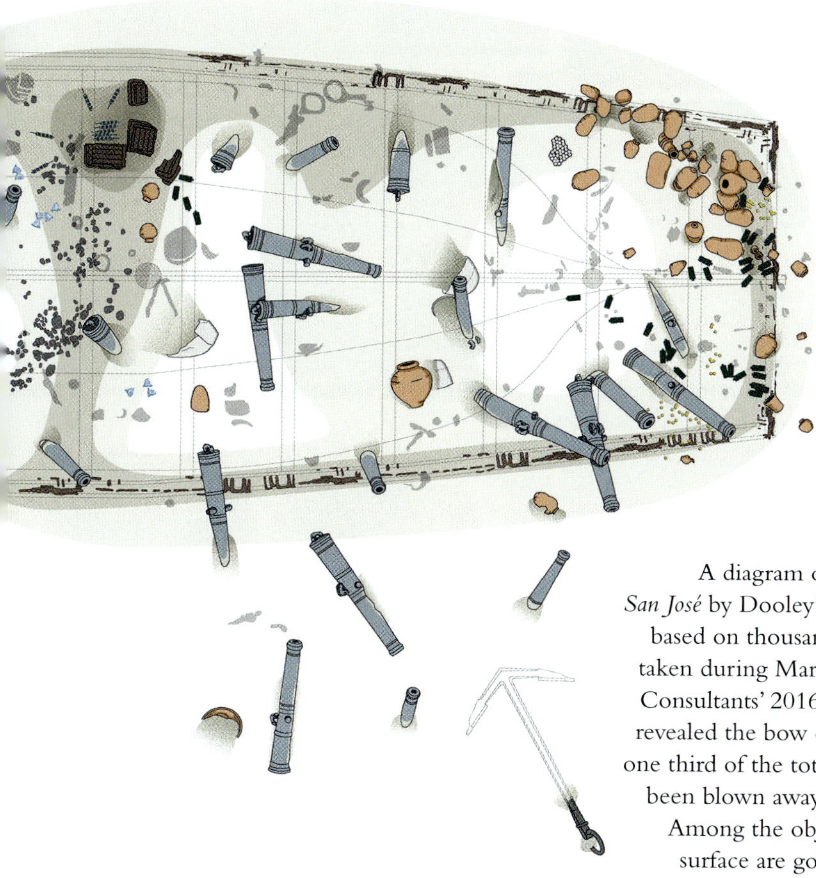

A diagram of the wreck of the *San José* by Dooley's daughter, Liliam, based on thousands of photographs taken during Maritime Archaeology Consultants' 2016 survey. The study revealed the bow of the ship—about one third of the total length—to have been blown away during the battle. Among the objects visible on the surface are gold coins and green gin bottles (toward the stern), ceramic jars, cannons, enema syringes, and dozens of Chinese porcelain cups (represented here in light blue).

Liliam Dooley

Artifacts on the wreck of the galleon *San José* (clockwise, from top left): the three bronze cannons that first indicated to Dooley that he had found the shipwreck; the cannons' dolphin-shaped cascabels on the breech proved the tell-tale details; earthenware vessels known as *tinajas*; eight-escudos gold coins, visible on the seabed; Chinese porcelain cups.

Armada de Colombia/Dimar

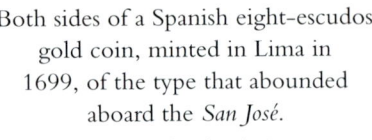

Both sides of a Spanish eight-escudos gold coin, minted in Lima in 1699, of the type that abounded aboard the *San José*.

Courtesy of Sedwick Coins

Dooley visiting Mapil, Spain, the Basque-country birthplace of the *San José*.

Roger Dooley collection

net worth in the nine figures, he didn't need the money. He knew well that treasure hunting is rarely profitable, and that was partly the point: Through clever accounting, he could legally write off the cost of an unsuccessful search to reduce his significant tax burden.

In the fall of 2013, Dooley sent Clake an offer to be the principal backer in his search for the *San José*. It was a gamble. Colombian officials, after all, might not approve of Clake's treasure-hunting past, nor would they relish the irony of seeing the bounty coveted by Commodore Wager revert to English hands after all three centuries later. But Dooley's options were quickly narrowing.

"I going *[sic]* to tell you a story that I haven't told you before because it was a long shot. But now my dream may have finally come true," his email began. Writing in shaky English, Dooley related the story of the *San José*, which he called "the *Titanic* of Colombia," and explained how the passage of Law 1675 had created an opening for foreign salvage companies to make a run at the galleon.

"There've been many publication *[sic]* about this battle but the story that most stand *[sic]* out is the fabulous treasure that was onboard the *San Jose* when she sank," he wrote. "Every treasure company in world would like to have a permit to locate and recover her treasure. The exact amount of her treasure is not known but certainly every expert will agree, based on the manifests that were sent to Panama and her unquestionably *[sic]* contraband, that in today's market her treasure should be worth over 5 billion of dollars. . . .

"Not only will [the study of the *San José* wreck] contribute to the knowledge of shipbuilding and naval history but we will finally come to know what really did happen during the battle of June 8, 1708 and it will shed new light on what was exchanged in the commercial Fair of Cartagena in the summer 1708 which is absolutely not known, finally and not the least of which, his *[sic]* hull will reveal the biggest treasure ever recovered from a shipwreck in all of the world."

As long as I'd known him, Dooley had expressed strong misgivings about the focus on the *San José*'s treasure rather than its historical importance, which was what truly interested him. But now he was tailoring the message to the recipient, well aware of what was most likely to excite Clake.

Dooley told the hedge funder about the origin of his *San José* obsession, when he had encountered the trove of letters in Seville in the summer of 1984. He laid out his general plan for the search, excavation, and conservation of the wreck and talked up his contacts in the Colombian government. Then he went for the kill: "Anthony, I truly believe that you are the right investor for this project, you have the capital, you love this type of research and most important you will not only receive an enormous profit (I'm sure at least 100 million US) but you will be known as the person who [achieved] a unique historical/cultural goal, that is, who locate, excavate and conserve the richest and most well known shipwreck in the world."

The archaeologist ended his plea with an apology for his English and asked for Clake's immediate response. He did not have to wait long:

Dear Roger

No problem at all. This sounds very interesting. Yes _ I would certainly be interested in working with you as an investor.

Good luck!

Chapter 20

The Treasure of the *San José*

After agreeing to fund Dooley's project, Anthony Clake founded a company called Maritime Archaeology Consultants (MAC) for the sole purpose of going after the *San José*. The intensely private investor did this through an intermediary to keep his name out of it. Dooley was listed as the company's initial director and began receiving a salary amounting to about $100,000 a year. Since he was not investing his own money—only his time and expertise and sweat and tears—he did not stand to earn a percentage of any treasure recovered. Nor, he said, would he have accepted it. "I don't want to be rich," he would later tell me. "I'm never going to be rich. I just want to lead a nice normal life. . . . With my salary it's enough." He paused. "Of course, they might give me a bonus, give me a gift, I don't know. What am I gonna do, throw it away?"

The $5 billion Dooley teased in his pitch to Clake was well above what Dooley would later tell me he believed the galleon's treasure could in fact be worth. But it was far lower than the $17 to $20 billion Sea Search Armada cited in its various lawsuits against the Colombian government. It was hard to take SSA's estimate seriously, given that the company had every incentive to inflate the value of the treasure it claimed to have been robbed of. And yet those figures would be repeated in headlines around the world for years.

Such exorbitant dollar amounts were ultimately meaningless. They were estimates of the treasure's numismatic value, as determined by what coins would sell for in the open market. They were the result of multiplying the number of coins thought to be contained in the wreck by the price that similar coins had sold for at auction in the past. It would be a straightforward calculation—if anyone had a clear idea how much gold and silver went down with the galleon. All that was known for sure was what had been registered for the king: about 580,000 pesos in the hold of the *San José,* and the same amount in the *San Joaquín.* But no complete manifest existed of the much greater private treasure loaded onto the sister galleons during the fairs of Cartagena and Portobelo. In fact, Dooley said, none was ever written. Smuggling in the second half of the seventeenth century was so rampant that it was assumed every returning ship contained significant contraband. In response the Crown decreed that it would no longer inspect private cargo and instead imposed a flat fee on passengers arriving from the New World.* (The policy, of course, gave travelers little reason *not* to smuggle.)

Without a manifest to specify the *San José's* cargo, the size of the galleon's treasure was a mystery even to those aboard the ship, including

---

* The measure was enacted by royal decree after divers salvaging the wreck of the *Maravillas* in the late 1650s recovered more silver and gold from the seabed than was ever registered aboard the galleon. The discovery infuriated King Felipe IV, who realized then how much treasure was being hidden from him. He didn't know the half of it. For the past 320 years, the *Maravillas* has been the shipwreck that keeps on giving, a seemingly inexhaustible underwater silver mine that has rewarded treasure hunters from William Phips in the 1680s to Robert Marx in the 1970s, hotelier Herbo Humphreys in the 1990s, and plastics scion Carl Allen today.

Casa Alegre, who surely packed his own cabin with undeclared riches. Historians seeking to assess the treasure had to rely on a handful of quotes from primary sources, citing wildly varying amounts. Among the more credible were those of Don Miguel de Villanueva, the admiral of the fleet, who wrote in one letter that 9 to 10 million pesos had likely sunk with the *San José*. Add the typical amount of unregistered gold and silver stuffed into every crevice of returning galleons—in the form of coins, bullion, bars, disks, jewelry, or even dust—and it was conceivable the vessel contained closer to 11 or 12 million pesos, and maybe more. But it was just as possible that Villanueva overestimated the haul.

Dooley conservatively estimated that the *San José* carried at least 7 million pesos to the seafloor, and at most 12 million—a range more or less in line with the estimate of the scholar Carla Rahn Phillips. The bulk of the coins that made up the treasure would be of the largest denominations in wide circulation: silver pieces of eight, worth one peso each; and eight-escudos gold coins, worth sixteen pesos. Both were about an inch and a half in diameter, the size of a modern silver dollar.* Spanish coins of that era were known as *macuquinas* in Spanish, or cobs in English, a derivation of *cabo de barra,* meaning "end of a bar." Each coin was cut from a bar of gold or silver and hammered with a bas-relief design featuring a prominent Jerusalem cross with lions and castles on the reverse, and the pillars of Hercules emerging from ocean waves on the obverse, along with the date and the mark of the mint that issued them. (Most silver coins on the *San José* were minted in Potosí, and most gold coins in Lima.) As a result of the hammering, cobs were not perfectly round, their shape mattering less than their weight—exactly one troy ounce for both a silver piece of

---

* The piece of eight, which would evolve into the modern American dollar, amounted to eight reales, each of which would thus be the equivalent of 12.5 cents. A vestige of this system remains when we refer to a quarter as "two bits"—the proverbial price of a shave and a haircut.

eight and a gold eight-escudos coin*—as guaranteed by an assayer who left his initials on each coin.

To modern collectors, a Spanish coin from that era is a slice of history worth far more than its weight in gold or silver. And as with every collectible—as with every object—its price depends on its scarcity and quality. Each coin tells a story, even if that story can never be fully traced. Collectors of Spanish cobs might like to imagine that the silver pieces of eight or gold escudos they hold in their hands have gone through those of literal pirates of the Caribbean or otherwise seen action. Coins from the *San José* would leave no doubt about it.

Those coins would be worth whatever collectors were willing to pay for them. The logic that leads to estimates in the billions of dollars for the galleon's precious cargo is circular: It is a legendary ship in part because its treasure is estimated to be worth billions, and the treasure is estimated to be worth billions because it comes from a legendary ship. But it is not exempt from the laws of supply and demand. A single gold coin from the *San José* might sell for thousands or tens of thousands of dollars at auction. Yet if all 7 million to 12 million pesos were to hit the market at once, the price of the cobs would quickly approach the raw value of the gold and silver.

This, of course, is another way to assess the worth of the *San José*'s treasure: to estimate what the gold and silver aboard would go for if it were melted down and sold at current rates for those commodities. Dooley, who said he was against the idea of liquefying cultural heritage, nonetheless calculated what this value would be if the *San José* contained 7 million pesos—the low end of his estimate for the size of the galleon's treasure. He presumed, on the basis of detailed accounting from the mints of Potosí and Lima, that 3 million would be in silver (amounting to about one hundred tons) and 4 million in gold (just over eight tons). Per market prices in 2025, the silver aboard would be

---

* The coins were not pure silver or gold but were alloyed with a small percentage of less valuable but more solid metals like copper.

worth approximately $100 million in today's dollars, and the gold about $1 billion. On the high end of Dooley's estimate, the meltdown value of the precious metals aboard the shipwreck would be closer to two billion dollars—and this was not counting jewelry, cases of pearls, or the innumerable emeralds of New Granada, both rough cut and inlaid into crucifixes that the wealthy passengers of the *San José* believed would protect them.

Chapter 21

The Search Box

With Clake on board, Dooley rushed to complete his research on the Battle of Barú so he could gain a more detailed understanding of the conflict and eventually establish a search area. He was already familiar with the Spanish testimony but had yet to review the English accounts. Dooley traveled to London to consult the logs of the *Expedition, Portland, Kingston,* and *Vulture*—the four ships in Wager's squadron—at the National Archives. He made a separate trip to the National Maritime Museum in Greenwich to find the journal of the commodore himself.

At the British Library, while waiting in the manuscript room for a librarian to bring him the materials he'd requested, Dooley ambled to an old-fashioned card catalog and, as he had a habit of doing, opened the first drawer. He began flipping through the cards with a pianistic dexterity honed by his many years of archival research. He opened drawer after drawer, looking through the A's, the B's, the C's. Under D, he landed on a card titled *Derrotero de las Yndias Occidentales, 1689,* by B. Barrozo. He felt a spasm of excitement. *Derrotero* was the Spanish term for a mariner's handbook, a detailed description of sailing routes that pilots would rely on to aid their navigation. This one appeared to be a guide to the West Indies, from just two decades before the sinking of the *San José*.

Dooley's eye hooked on the author's surname and wondered if, by some barely believable stroke of luck, the B. Barrozo in question was Benito Alonso Barroso, a master pilot of Spain's Caribbean treasure fleet who helmed the *San José* on its voyage to the Americas but died before the battle at which it met its end. The volume buried in the British Library's stacks appeared to be his *derrotero,* indicating the winds and currents to follow and reefs to avoid. If so, it might contain critical clues to the galleon's whereabouts when it encountered Wager's squadron.

Dooley hurried to the librarian's desk and requested the item. Soon after, he had his hands on its worn leather binding. He opened the large, colorful covers and examined the manuscript written in Barroso's elegant hand, gingerly turning the pages until he arrived at the sections he'd been looking for: "Route from Portobelo to Cartagena" and "Route from Cartagena to Portobelo." How this document had made its way to London, Dooley had no idea. He doubted that any other scholar of the *San José* (or aspirant to its treasure) had ever come across it. The text was written in the second person, addressing future pilots. It was as if Barroso were speaking directly to Dooley: "You will go in demand of the Barú Islands and passing them, you will go southeast to look for Bocachica, which is the port of Cartagena." He advised on the safe distance to keep from the coast and warned of the treacherous shifting sand bars. The *derrotero* didn't indicate the resting place of the galleon—it couldn't have—but it was nonetheless essential. Combined with everything else Dooley had already found, it would allow him to begin drawing the boundaries of his search box.

BACK HOME IN FLORIDA, he set out to establish where the *San José* could have been when it sank by ruling out where it couldn't have been. Although much of the archaeological profession had gone digital, Dooley still worked with pencil and paper. He rolled maps onto his dining room table and brought out files containing copies of hundreds of archival records. He gathered his life's work: notes from three decades of research; reports from Spanish and English officials; testimonies from witnesses on other ships; the letters he had discovered in Seville in 1984; Domingo Antonio Pérez's map from 1729 indicating the "Shoals of the Admiral"; and Benito Barroso's *derrotero,* specifying the route likely taken by the *San José* on the last leg of its journey to Cartagena.

Dooley consulted an astronomical database to determine the precise time the sun rose (5:40 A.M.) and set (6:22 P.M.) on June 8, 1708, since by all accounts the fleet left shortly after daybreak and the *San José* squared off with Wager's *Expedition* at sunset. From modern nautical charts, he gleaned information on winds and currents in that area at that season.

It was not common practice for officers on Spanish ships at that time to keep a log. England's more fastidious Royal Navy kept daily records of weather, bearing, latitude, wind speed and direction, and coastal landmarks in logbooks that were then entrusted to the Admiralty archives, where Dooley viewed them three hundred years later. But as the English were strangers to those waters, he chose to lend more credence to Spanish reports.

Dooley sought to delineate three areas: (A) corresponding to the *San José*'s starting point when it set sail that morning, (B) marking where it could have been when the wind turned and Casa Alegre tacked to the northwest, and (C) covering the range of the *San José*'s possible positions when it confronted Wager's *Expedition,* caught fire, and sank.

Information about the fleet's location that morning was frustratingly vague. Spanish sources mentioned only that the ships spent the drizzly night from June 7 to June 8 off the San Bernardo Islands, about a day's sail from Cartagena. How far off, it was impossible to know. Dooley's Area A would have to remain loosely defined. Rather than a starting point, it would be a heading: northeast toward Rosario Island, known then as Ciruelo, aided by a light wind from the south-southeast.

Determining the limits of Area B—everywhere the *San José* could have been between 3:00 and 4:30 P.M. when it veered to the northwest—was critical. First, Dooley had to establish the northern border of the box, the farthest progress the galleon could have made on its northeastern course before changing tack. The well-established route called for the fleet to round Isla del Tesoro, the northernmost of the cluster of islands off the coastline, before heading east toward Boca Chica, the "little mouth" that was the only entrance to Cartagena Harbor. Several witnesses mentioned that the fleet had been unable to pass Tesoro before the wind turned, leading most historians to assume that the *San José* had been around the latitude of that island when it veered to fight Wager. But Dooley was convinced they were wrong. Two important witnesses—including the Count of Vega Florida, who had fought so valiantly at the helm of the *Santa Cruz*—reported that the fleet had not even passed Rosario Island, farther to the south. Dooley thus drew a straight line at the level of Rosario Island, perpendicular to the ships' northeastern bearing. The line would define the northern border of Area B, which he believed the *San José* could not have gone beyond.

To mark the southern limit of Area B, Dooley drew a line eight nautical miles away, accounting for the possibility that the ship was sailing more slowly than usual. That line was at the level of the Tortuguillas, the reef referred to in the 1729 map as the Shoals of the Admiral, based on Dooley's strong intuition that this name had something to do with the battle.

Dooley then had to decide how wide to make the rectangle delimiting Area B. Several witnesses reported that their ships had remained close to the islands. Any farther than five nautical miles, Dooley reasoned, would not have been considered close. And since there were no charts during that period to indicate depths in the region, no pilot would have dared sail closer than two nautical miles from the reefs. Basic arithmetic dictated that the width of Area B—the armada's likely location between 3:00 and 4:30 P.M.—should be three nautical miles.

On the basis of Area B, Dooley could now begin mapping Area C, his ultimate goal, encompassing all the points at which the *San José* could have gone under. All accounts confirmed that the wind dropped around 3 P.M., then began blowing lightly from the north-northeast in the late afternoon. "The Spanish fleet had no other choice than to change its heading toward the northwest," Dooley told me.* "What we don't know is how far the *San José* sailed in that direction." That would depend on its speed. With a moderate ocean breeze propelling it from behind—known as a broad reach—a galleon of that period could typically sail at five knots (roughly equivalent to four or five miles per hour on land). But traveling at a beam reach—nearly perpendicular to the breeze, as the *San José* was—a galleon's speed would be limited to three to four knots. Combining speed, time, and bearing, and factoring in a margin of error for each to account for discrepancies and imprecisions in testimonies, Dooley at last outlined Area C.

To check his work, he went back to the archival discovery that had set him on this path in the first place: the letters that Cartagena's governor, José de Zúñiga, had sent the Spanish king to inform him of the tragedy. In separate missives from this file, Zúñiga had written that the battle took place "six leagues [about twenty miles] at sea from this port" and that "explosions had been heard at sea eight leagues [about twenty-seven miles] from the San Bernardo Islands." Dooley traced lines corresponding to those distances and found they intersected smack in the middle of his 120-square-mile search box. His job was done.

In calculating the area, Dooley had made two big bets that put him at odds with other researchers: that the fleet never sailed beyond Rosario Island and that the "Shoals of the Admiral" were somehow related to the battle. Both assumptions dragged his search box

---

* Galleons in that period, he explained, could not sail any closer than a sixty-degree angle off the wind, as opposed to the forty-five degrees that most modern sailing vessels can achieve, almost facing the wind head-on.

significantly to the west of previous estimates of the *San José*'s location, including the area delineated in the exhibit on the *San José* at the Cartagena Naval Museum—which placed the galleon off Isla del Tesoro, about ten miles away. Robert Marx had also proposed a search box closer to so-called Treasure Island, perhaps overly influenced by its tempting name.*

A few years earlier, the respected American historian Carla Rahn Phillips and U.S. Navy captain Thomas R. Beale—a professor at the Naval War College—had copublished a journal article that included their own best guess about the *San José*'s location. Rahn transcribed the logs from Wager's squadron, which Beale then analyzed to determine the most likely position of each of the four ships—the *Expedition*, the *Portland*, the *Kingston*, and the *Vulture*—at various stages in the battle. From this information, combined with English eyewitness accounts, Rahn and Beale drew a box of the *San José*'s probable resting place.

There was hardly any overlap between Dooley's area and Rahn's, which was well to the northeast. But Dooley was confident in his superior understanding of the ocean, drawn from a youth spent largely at sea rather than in study halls. He also believed that Rahn was mistaken in her reliance on English sources rather than on the Spanish, who had a better knowledge of the area.

The only way to prove her wrong, of course, would be to find the galleon. But although he could now count on financing, for the moment he was armed only with maps, papers, and a hunch. Unless he could wrangle the search technology and the permission of the Colombian government—the most daunting challenges yet—none of that would matter.

---

* Sea Search Armada's coordinates remained classified, so Dooley did not have access to them. Even if he had seen them, he would have had every reason to dismiss them after Tommy Thompson's 1994 expedition failed to find the galleon at the spot SSA had reported.

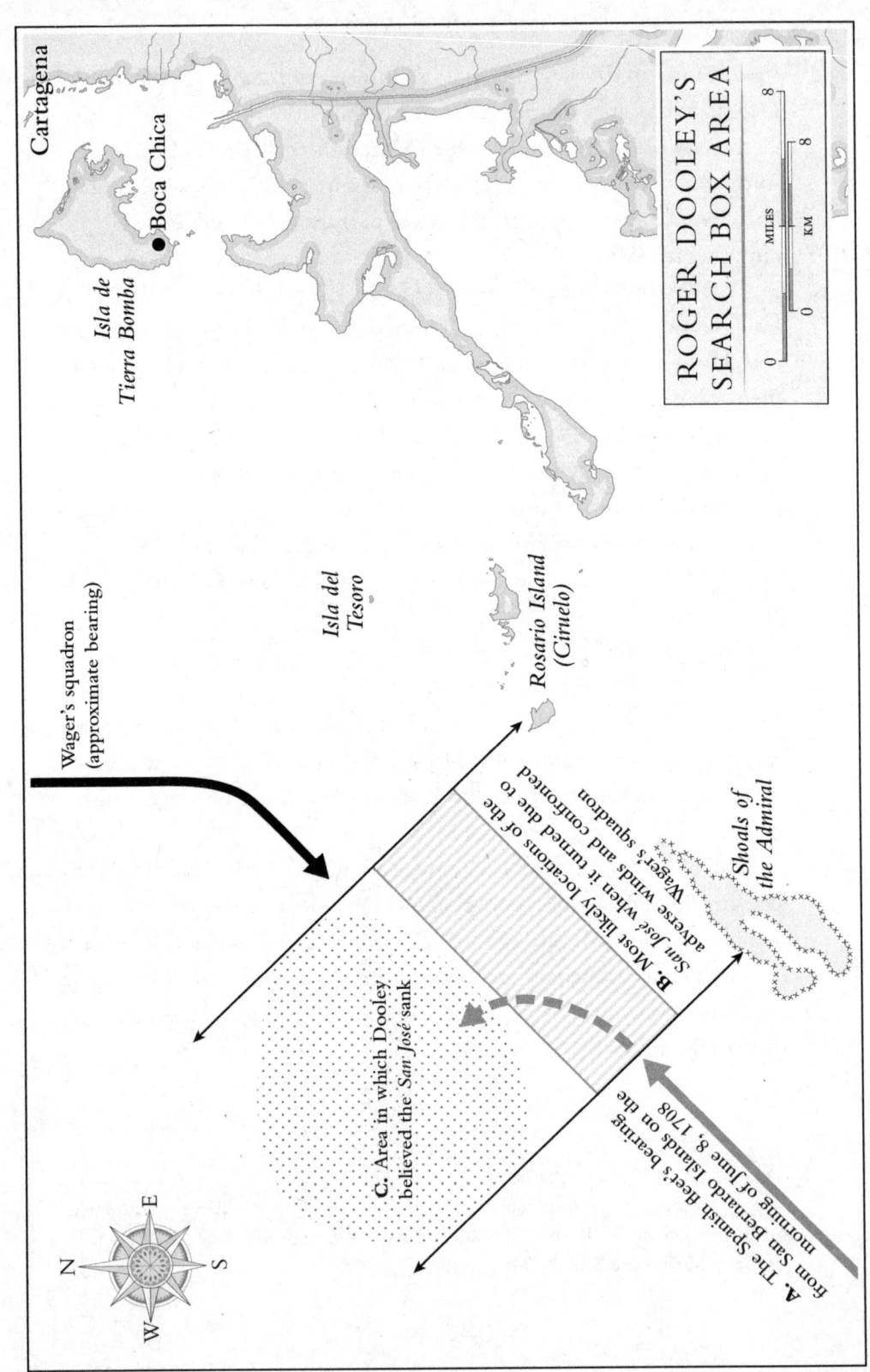

ROGER DOOLEY'S
SEARCH BOX AREA

Cartagena

Boca Chica

Isla de
Tierra Bomba

Isla del
Tesoro

Rosario Island
(Ciruelo)

Wager's squadron
(approximate bearing)

Most likely locations of the
San José when it turned and confronted
Wager's squadron due to
adverse winds and

Shoals of
the Admiral

C. Area in which Dooley
believed the San José sank.

A. The Spanish fleet's bearing
from San Bernardo Islands on the
morning of June 8, 1708

MILES

KM

Chapter 22

"Let's Find the *San José*"

In early 2014, having secured Clake's investment and defined his search area, Dooley was ready to make his pitch to the Colombian government. Thanks to an incessant barrage of emails and phone calls, he succeeded in scheduling a half-hour meeting in Bogotá with Dr. Ernesto Montenegro, the deputy director of the Colombian Institute of Anthropology and History (ICANH), the government entity overseeing all archaeological activity in the country.

They met at ICANH's offices in the Candelaria neighborhood, the capital's picturesque colonial old city at the foot of a jungle-covered mountainside. Bald, round-faced, with laughing eyes and an easy smile, Montenegro had a doctorate in social anthropology from the Sorbonne, in Paris, and had studied maritime archaeology at the University of Barcelona but was by no means an expert on the *San José*. Dooley presented Montenegro with a large, framed copy of Pérez's map from 1729, showing the "Shoals of the Admiral" that he believed to be related to the site of the battle. After decades of currying favor with officials in Cuba, he had learned never to introduce himself to powerful people without a gift. And perhaps his years in the film industry had taught him about the importance of props and stagecraft. For maximum effect, Dooley had recruited his daughter Lili, a skilled graphic designer, to digitally clean up and beautify the map.

Montenegro found Dooley "very formal, very cordial . . . and very agreeable," but the first thing he noticed was the archaeologist's distinctive cadence. "He has a strange way of speaking," Montenegro said. "Well, all Cubans speak strangely, but Roger more so."

The scheduled thirty minutes turned into three hours, as Dooley detailed his plan for the search and excavation of the galleon. He was ready to begin immediately. Montenegro was in no rush. "Roger was saying, 'Let's do this tomorrow, let's go,'" Montenegro recalled with a laugh, "and my role was to tell him no: We can't go." Though Law 1675 had passed in Congress, it had not yet been fully structured, and Montenegro told Dooley that they needed to let the process play out.

The two men had a different sense of urgency. Montenegro was forty; Dooley was nearly seventy. Having dreamed of this moment for three decades, and having lost his prime years to Cuba's dysfunction and the struggles of starting a new life in the United States, he was not inclined to patience. As the months passed without a response from Montenegro, it became clear that Dooley had hit a dead end. By proceeding through regular channels, Dooley feared, he would become ensnared in Colombia's notoriously sluggish bureaucracy. He concluded that there was only one person he needed to convince: Juan Manuel Santos. But scoring a meeting with Montenegro had been difficult enough. How would he ever cross paths with a president?

Adriana tapped her network and informed him that, as it happened, Santos was scheduled to attend a luncheon hosted by the Colombian American Chamber of Commerce at the Four Seasons Miami, on Brickell Avenue, in July of 2014. This was it. There would never be a better opportunity. Dooley bought a ticket and arrived at the sixth floor of the high-rise hotel just before noon. The archaeologist stuck out among the crowd of polished Colombian American community leaders and business owners, and not just because he was carrying an oversized framed copy of Pérez's map under his arm. He was visibly nervous. His life was building to this moment, and he could not afford to waste his chance to speak with the only man who, he believed, stood between him and the *San José*.

Dooley took his seat in the carpeted Grand Ballroom, ate his mediocre meal, and listened impatiently as Santos, who had just been reelected to a second term, gave a speech about his commitment to make peace with the FARC. Dooley looked at his watch. He was interested in Colombian politics only inasmuch as they applied to shipwrecks.

When his speech was over, Santos was swarmed with glad-handers. Lingering awkwardly in the outer orbit of the cluster that had formed around the president, Dooley looked for an opening to break in. He sidled along a wall in an attempt to squeeze past the scrum. He got to within six feet of the president, just close enough to get his attention. Dooley was about to call out when Santos thanked the gathering and abruptly disappeared through a door that his security team had been ushering him toward. Dooley's pulse quickened. His opportunity was slipping away. He bolted to the stairwell and raced down six flights, framed map in arms, to catch up with Santos before he left the building. He pushed open the door to the ground-floor lobby only to see the president exit the building, get into a car, and drive off.

His heart straining, sweat beading on his brow, Dooley watched the specter of the *San José* sail away. It was unlikely he'd ever get a better chance to make his case to the only man who could grant him access to the galleon. But far from making him realize how naive he had been to assume he could cold-pitch a head of state, the humiliating experience doubled his resolve. Next time, he would not fail.

Once more, Adriana came to his aid. She again turned to her network to find someone who could arrange an encounter while Santos was in the United States. He would next head to New York, where the Colombian consul, Elsa Gladys Cifuentes, happened to be an old friend of Adriana's. (The two were from the same city in Colombia and had worked together on a political campaign years before.) Adriana told her about Dooley's quest for the *San José*. Fascinated by the story of the galleon, Cifuentes vowed to help.

"Tell your husband to come to New York," she said. "I'll find a way."

Dooley booked a flight immediately. He had been in Manhattan for two days when Cifuentes called to invite him as her plus-one to a reception Santos was expected to attend on September 24, at the Upper East Side residence of the Colombian ambassador to the United Nations.

The cocktail party lasted several hours. As Santos held court with dignitaries, diplomats, and journalists, Dooley bided his time, wandering around the opulent town house before settling into a chair by the front door. Little by little the crowd began to thin out. By midnight, almost nobody was left. Cifuentes had long since gone home. As the last few guests were saying their goodbyes, Santos descended the stairs.

"President Santos," Dooley called out in his sea-soaked rasp. The president, a short man whose confident demeanor and impeccably tailored clothes made him seem taller, turned and found himself face to face with a white-bearded old man who had appeared—as Santos would later tell me—"out of nowhere."

Who is this hippie? he wondered.

"I just need three minutes with you," said Dooley. "I want to give you this gift. This is a map. A map of Colombia that nobody has seen. And I want to be the first one to give it to you, because it has a relation with the galleon *San José*." Santos listened politely as Dooley pointed out the Shoals of the Admiral and explained why he believed it was the key to locating the galleon. "I am sure that I can find it," Dooley said. "And I have the funding to pay for it."

Santos shook Dooley's hand, thanked him, and took the map. The archaeologist watched the president disappear back into Manhattan, satisfied that he had done all he could. Realistically, this should have been the end of it.

But Santos couldn't shake the memory of the bearded stranger.

The encounter had brought back fond recollections of the president's days as a young navy cadet in Cartagena. Santos did not understand exactly how the map would help Dooley find the galleon. There was no prominent X, no drawing of a ship, no direct reference to the battle. But as a piece of theater, it had worked to perfection.

Behind the map, Dooley had scotch-taped a letter for Santos, which the president now unfolded and read. The note began by congratulating Santos on his recent reelection and wished him success in his peace negotiations with the FARC. Then came Dooley's meticulously constructed pitch. First, he talked up his qualifications as a maritime archaeologist and a leading expert on the *San José*.

> *At the beginning of the 80's I located some unpublished and extremely important documents about the Battle of Cartagena and especially about the* San José. *Due to the historical/archaeological importance of this fact, I have continued researching this shipwreck to the present.*

Dooley went on to argue that the Colombian government had long been misled on the subject of the *San José* and presented himself as the only reliable source of information about the galleon.

> *I can tell you that there is a lot of misinformation in the national and international press and on the part of professionals, officials and institutions of your government. Based on extensive historical research over many years, carried out mainly in the General Archive of the Indies, on cartographic and oceanographic studies, as well as the reconstruction of the last voyage of the Count of Casa Alegre's fleet on June 6 [sic], 1708, I can assure you that the* San José *did not sink where the North American company Sea Search Armada indicated. Nor was the* San José *shipwrecked in the area indicated in the Naval Museum of Cartagena.*

Anticipating that Santos might question his motives, Dooley sought to assure the president of his honorable intentions:

*Every time the San José is mentioned, only the fabulous treasure it
carried comes to light, and although it is true that the funds that were
lost in its sinking were large, they were not the only important thing
about this shipwreck. I can assure you that San José has other
"treasures" that are equally important. Once it is located, excavated,
preserved and studied it will be known.*

Finally, he got to the point:

*I am currently the founder and director of the English company
Maritime Archeology Consultants, Ltd. and my deepest desire is to
be able to help Colombia recover and preserve its Underwater Cultural
Heritage. I created this entity with the sole purpose of executing the
San José Project. I have the necessary capital not only to locate and
archaeologically excavate this galleon but to guarantee that Cartagena
de Indias has a Conservation laboratory capable of preserving all the
evidence that is recovered. We will have the most high-tech equipment
on the market and a multidisciplinary team of international experts in
collaboration with its specialists.*

*Mr. President, I would very much like to be able to explain to
you personally and in more detail the information presented above,
but I understand that due to your responsibility at the head of the
government it would be very difficult to do so, so I ask you, with all
due respect, to give me the possibility of being received by the Minister
of Culture to transmit all the information to her.*

Santos was transfixed. In his four years as president, he had encountered his share of cranks and con men pushing sunken-treasure
schemes.* He admitted he was inclined at first to dismiss Dooley as

---

* Santos had good reason to be wary of such ventures. In 2011 he had personally attended a session of Colombia's Shipwrecked Antiquities Commission
that had examined the claims of an American entrepreneur and diver named

"another treasure hunter," but was "struck by his conviction, his passion." And if Dooley was right that Sea Search Armada had not found the galleon, then perhaps this mysterious old man might at last provide a way out of the legal morass into which the American treasure hunters had dragged the Colombian government more than two decades earlier and would put an end to their claim once and for all.

Santos was moved a few weeks later to write a response:

Dear Mr. Dooley,

> . . .

> *I would like to send you an affectionate message of thanks for the map of Cartagena de Indias that records the geographical and historical facts that reflect the importance of this submerged heritage as a part of our national cultural patrimony.*

> *Likewise, I wish you success in your mission through Maritime Archeology Consultants, Ltd., a project that seeks the preservation and conservation of specialized finds in the field of archaeology.*

> *Cordially,*
> *Juan Manuel Santos*

Before long, Dooley was summoned back to Bogotá to meet with the country's assertive, no-nonsense culture minister, Mariana Garcés

---

Jay Miscovich, who said he had found thousands of uncut Colombian emeralds from a Spanish shipwreck on the seabed off of Key West, Florida, a discovery potentially worth millions of dollars. Miscovich's eye-watering find attracted numerous investors—as well as a lawsuit by the descendants of Mel Fisher, who claimed that the emeralds almost certainly came from the *Atocha,* to which they had the rights. Further investigation by experts including Daniel De Narváez revealed that they had been coated with epoxy—which was not invented until the twentieth century—and that some in fact came from a gem store in Jupiter, Florida. After the hoax was uncovered, Miscovich blew his head off with a 12-gauge shotgun.

Córdoba. Under the newly promulgated law, Garcés had the authority to contract with private companies to find and salvage historical shipwrecks. When he arrived at Garcés's office, Dooley found that Ernesto Montenegro, the subdirector of ICANH who had rebuffed him months earlier, would join the meeting. Dooley laid out all his cards. "Roger was very technical," Montenegro recalled. "He put the historical map on the table and applied his knowledge of navigation and meteorology." Dooley shared his research indicating that the fleet had most likely turned to the northwest before even passing Rosario Island, and nowhere near Tesoro, which most other researchers had fixated on. "They never reached Tesoro, which is on the tenth parallel," Montenegro recalled of Dooley's presentation.

Following the meeting, Santos asked Garcés and Montenegro for a report.

"Do you believe in him? Do you believe in Roger?" the president asked.

Montenegro and Garcés said they did.

"Well, then," Santos said, "let's find the *San José.*"

Chapter 23

Woods Hole

To have an informed hunch about the galleon's location was one thing. Actually finding it, at the depths where Dooley believed it lay, would require the kind of cutting-edge equipment out of reach even for most militaries at that time, and certainly for Colombia's. Dooley assured Garcés and Montenegro he knew just where to get it: from the same people who had helped find the *Titanic.*

Established in 1930 in Falmouth, Massachusetts, a short ferry ride from Martha's Vineyard, the prestigious Woods Hole Oceanographic Institute (WHOI)—affectionately pronounced "hooey"—was dedicated to marine science and engineering, drawing the brightest minds in the field like a Bell Labs of the deep. It was a nonprofit research institution whose mission, as stated on its web page, was "to understand the ocean and its interaction with Earth as a whole, and to communicate a basic understanding of the ocean's role in changing the global environment." Since the Second World War, much of the advanced survey technology developed at WHOI had been commissioned by the U.S. Navy. A large portion of its work remained classified, but its manned submersibles and autonomous underwater vehicles had also been used in a number of high-profile expeditions, including the discovery of the *Titanic,* in 1985, in partnership with its French counterpart, IFREMER, and, in 2011, the finding of the wreckage of Air France 447, an Airbus 330 that had plummeted into the Atlantic Ocean en route from Rio de Janeiro to Paris two years earlier, killing all passengers and crew.

Both of those targets had lain more than three thousand meters deep. In the search area that Dooley had delineated for the *San José,* the depth of the seabed didn't exceed one thousand meters. If he was right, and the galleon lay in that area, WHOI's technology would surely find it, Dooley thought. The cost would be in the millions, but his investor, Anthony Clake, made clear that he was good for it. The more pressing question was whether WHOI would take the job, given the loftiness of its mission. If its directors got the impression that it was a profit-driven treasure hunt, they would certainly turn it down. Having pumped up the importance and estimated value of the *San José*'s treasure to Clake, Dooley would now have to downplay it in pitching Woods Hole and instead sell the organization on the historical importance of the wreck—and on himself. For that, he would need to meet its vice president of marine operations, Rob Munier, who oversaw WHOI's survey projects. Dooley had a plan, and it involved crashing another cocktail party.

This one wouldn't be so far from home. In late 2014, Dooley found his way to an event in Key Largo for the National Academy of Sciences' Sea-Space Symposium, a gathering of top executives from the undersea and aerospace industries, which he was told Munier would attend. Dooley buttonholed Munier as he had Santos, and— like Coleridge's Ancient Mariner, condemned to forever tell and retell his harrowing story to unsuspecting revelers—recounted his decades-long quest to find the *San José.* Soft-spoken and personable, Munier was fascinated by the prospect of finding the famous ship but maintained what he calls a "healthy skepticism" about the man laying out that vision. "A person like Roger, with this just amazing personality, you don't know," said Munier. "And at Woods Hole Oceanographic, we get a fair number of people who want to affiliate with us in some fashion, and we have to be able to suss that out. We have to be careful."

Munier was intrigued enough to invite Dooley to WHOI's Falmouth headquarters to make a formal presentation. The archaeologist prepared his pitch materials with his daughter Lili and arrived a few weeks later with a small delegation that included the perpetually sunny Ernesto Montenegro, of Colombia's ICANH, and the gloomy side-scan sonar specialist Garry Kozak, on whom Dooley would rely to interpret the survey data—an especially delicate task given that the target was a wooden ship that had been decomposing for three hundred years. With more than forty years' experience, Kozak was almost dolphin-like in his ability to read the ocean by echolocation. If the data showed a smudge on the seabed, he could usually tell at a glance whether it was man-made or geological. Yet he had been hesitant to go after the *San José* when Dooley first approached him, and not just because he had been down that road before when he helped to set up Glocca Morra's sonar system in that company's own search for the galleon in the early 1980s. Kozak said he had doubts about Dooley himself.

"Honestly, I gotta tell you, when I first met Roger, I thought he was a little bit of a crackpot," said Kozak. "I thought he was a loose cannon. He just was so great at telling stories. You had to question: Were they made up?"

When Dooley tapped him to join the *San José* search, Kozak saw the old near-pathological optimism at play. "I sort of smirked and laughed and said, 'Yeah, sure, that's going to be doable.' [I thought that] with the problems with the Colombian government, and the politics, there's no way anybody is going to get a permit to actually go do it." Dooley surprised him by securing the government's authorization and the meeting with WHOI. Kozak was in.

As time went on, Kozak came to better appreciate Dooley's oddness. "He's very flamboyant and overly optimistic," said Kozak, "and those things can resemble somebody who's bullshitting you. But he wasn't. He was dead serious. He had historical knowledge and facts. And it was because of his flamboyance and his optimism that he never got discouraged by any roadblocks that were thrown up in front. He would wake up with a smile, and he would always be happy. And he would just pound forward to find another path to make stuff work."

In January 2015, Dooley, Montenegro, and Kozak met Munier at his office on the second floor of a cedar-shingled, weather-beaten old Cape Cod house, above a quaint coffee shop where the world's brightest marine engineers got their breakfast burritos. Joining Munier at the conference room table was WHOI's principal engineer, the athletically built Mike Purcell, who looked and acted well younger than his nearly seventy years. Dooley, as usual, brought armfuls of materials: maps, charts, copies of archival documents. As he laid out his plan, he toned down his usual exuberance, striking a professional, matter-of-fact tone he hoped would reassure the WHOI team. "I think he was reserved because he's sort of judging us," said Purcell, "and we're sort of judging him as to whether we're going to be good partners." But Dooley could contain himself for only so long. "As we became more familiar," Purcell said, "the true Roger came out, with the excitement level that he has, and trying to solve every problem in the next hour."

The presence of Montenegro, representing the Colombian government, and Kozak, whose expertise was well established, bolstered Dooley's credibility. Following the meeting, Munier and Purcell traveled to Cartagena "to validate what we were hearing," said Munier. At the end of the three-day visit, "Mike and I were pretty convinced that this would fit nicely within our mission, that we'd be advancing our understanding of the ocean, and we'd have a chance to deploy some technology and be involved in something that was interesting."

Munier adds, "But, of course, we didn't know just to what extent Roger's ideas were going to be accurate."

IF THE SEARCH WAS GOING TO HAPPEN, it had to begin by the spring of 2015, just a few months later. Woods Hole was available for only a brief window before its services were required in the Pacific. Dooley feared that both Clake and Santos—the two powerful men he had somehow convinced to buy into his fantasy—would lose faith in him if the expedition were postponed. Having advanced at a geological pace for nearly thirty years, his pursuit of the *San José* was now hurtling forward at full speed. Several obstacles still stood in the way. The Colombian government and Clake's Maritime Archaeology Consultants had yet to settle on terms, most importantly the amount of treasure MAC could claim as remuneration. Culture Minister Mariana Garcés at first offered 10 percent. The secretive Clake, who was referred to in official documents only by the mysterious moniker of "the Originator," entrusted the haggling to a trusted collaborator named Ross Kevin Hyett, a British treasure-hunting investor and former professional race car driver. Noting that Colombia's new law on submerged cultural patrimony allowed salvors to keep "up to 50 percent" of recovered treasure, Hyett asked for a 40 percent cut. As a negotiation tactic, he suggested that the total amount of gold and silver aboard the galleon was far less than the public had been led to believe. The mere 10 percent initially proposed, he argued, was overly influenced by "the general opinion that the riches of the Galleon of San José are extremely substantial. However, while that may be true, there are innumerable speculations and exaggerations regarding its true value." In a particularly brazen flourish, given his own treasure-hunting investments, Hyett added that " 'treasure hunters' have multiplied its real value to exuberant figures." The estimated value of the treasure—the ultimate unknown in the *San José* saga—rose and fell according to the needs of the moment.

Ultimately, Colombia agreed to grant MAC 20 percent of whatever treasure was recovered from the *San José*. In addition, the contract required that the operation be run from a Colombian navy ship and that at least 50 percent of the personnel involved in the search be Colombian, "in order to guarantee the transfer of knowledge."

When the authorization was signed, on May 26, Dooley messaged his daughter Lili, with whom he had shared every triumph and frustration in his pursuit of the galleon. While Adriana provided un-flagging emotional support (and invaluable connections), Lili was Dooley's closest collaborator, his secret weapon. It was she who had designed all of the materials for his presentations to Woods Hole and the Colombian government, giving his rough sketches and charts a professional sheen that had helped win over the people in those rooms. She had touched up the copy of Pérez's 1729 map that had caught the interest of Santos. Dooley's success belonged to her as well. His message reached her in Havana, where she was visiting Zulema. She had just left the hospital. On the same day that her father offi-cially launched his dream project, her mother had died.

Chapter 24

On the Trail of Casa Alegre

Dooley was about to embark on the mission he had fantasized about for nearly half his life, at an age by which most men settle into retirement and abandon their ambitions of youth. He stood less straight than he once had and his rail-thinness was a distant memory, but his energy was undiminished.

From the outset, however, Dooley was at a disadvantage. Shortly after the contract with MAC was finalized, Colombia's maritime authority, Dimar, granted the group a permit to search an area that, at approximately eight by six miles, covered only about two-thirds of Dooley's total proposed search area—four of his six subdivisions. The reason, several people told me, was that the longitude at which Sea Search Armada claimed to have found the galleon in 1981 cut through the remaining third of Dooley's box (albeit miles away); if Woods Hole were to encounter the shipwreck in the same general area, SSA's unrelenting complaints of having been robbed of their right to half the treasure would suddenly become even more problematic. For the Santos administration, that headache was best avoided.

Dooley traveled to Cartagena with Adriana and rented a sprawling eighth-floor apartment in a luxurious waterfront building along one of the city's tonier stretches. The balcony overlooked the bay in which the *San José* had been expected to arrive on June 8, 1708. It was to serve as a base of operations, where Dooley and Kozak would analyze sonar data together after each day's mission. WHOI's six-man team, led by Mike Purcell, landed on June 11, 2015. Because of a miscommunication with Colombia's customs authority, their equipment didn't arrive with them. It was an inauspicious start. The delay would cut into the precious little time MAC had been granted to find the galleon before Woods Hole had to leave for the other job. With Clake's millions and a president's hope on the line, to say nothing of his own credibility, Dooley began to worry.

The most valuable member of the Woods Hole team—an autonomous underwater vehicle (AUV) called the REMUS 6000—wouldn't arrive for another five days. Developed for the U.S. Navy by WHOI engineers beginning in the 1990s, REMUS (Remote Environmental Monitoring Units) machines were designed initially to survey underwater minefields. A REMUS AUV could be programmed to swim in tight rows across a defined area of the seabed, then loyally return to its surface support vessel. It could be equipped with any number of survey tools and could perform tasks either too tedious or too risky for human divers. "If it's dull, dirty, or dangerous," said the young MIT-trained engineer Jeff Kaeli, who helped operate the REMUS 6000 during the *San José* search, "it's a good job for robots."

The "6000" in this particular AUV's name referred to the maximum depth, in meters, at which it could safely operate. The yellow, torpedo-shaped robot was about twelve feet long, weighed two thousand pounds, and was powered by a lithium-ion battery that allowed it to swim for twenty hours or so before it had to be recharged. It was one of two that had been commissioned in the mid-aughts by billionaire Ted Waitt, founder of Gateway computers, in order to search for the wreck of the twin-engine monoplane that Amelia Earhart crashed into the Pacific in 1937.* The search was unsuccessful. Waitt ended up selling the twin AUVs to fellow American billionaire Ray Dalio, the ocean-obsessed manager of Bridgewater Associates, one of the world's most profitable hedge funds. Dalio loaned the REMUS 6000s back to Woods Hole, which used them to run searches and hydrographic surveys across the planet. Before arriving fashionably late to Cartagena, the REMUS had located the black box of Air France Flight 447 and had visited the *Titanic.* "She's no trailer queen," boasted Kaeli of the dinged-up device. "Never trust a robot that doesn't have some scars."

The modified shipping container—called the "van"—that housed the REMUS was brought aboard an aging Colombian navy research vessel called the A.R.C. *Malpelo* (which happened to be the same ship that treasure hunter Tommy Thompson had used twenty years earlier when he discovered that there was nothing on the seabed at the coordinates where Sea Search Armada had reported finding the galleon). For the following week, the *Malpelo*—with its cramped staterooms and, as Kaeli recalled, "showers that made you feel about as clean as when you walked in"—would be home to the Woods Hole crew, as well as a contingent from the Colombian navy.

A strong sense of camaraderie prevailed, but communication between the two groups was difficult, since only one senior officer aboard spoke decent English, Capt. Julio César Monroy, the executive officer of the *Malpelo.* A jovial presence, the thirty-one-year-old was in disbelief at the assignment before him. The *San José* was part of his family lore: His father, a prominent lawyer and former journalist, shared a lifelong passion for the story of the galleon with his childhood playmate and future newsroom colleague Gabriel García Márquez, who would later incorporate the shipwreck and its treasure into his novel *Love in the Time of Cholera.* Now Monroy was part of an effort to bring

---

* Waitt was a producer of the 2009 biopic *Amelia,* starring Hilary Swank, and surely figured that finding the missing aircraft would be good publicity.

the wreck out of the realm of legend. In his eighties and in frail health, Monroy's father peppered his son with questions about the classified mission that the captain was not allowed to answer. If it succeeded, Monroy said, "I knew I would be fulfilling his dream."

From day 1, the expedition put Dooley's preternatural optimism to the test. On June 21, the *Malpelo* set off for the edge of his search box, about thirty miles from the Bay of Cartagena. The sea was unusually choppy. Braving the spray and the bucking of the deck, the WHOI team lowered the REMUS into ten-foot waves, having programmed it to "mow the lawn" across an area of the seabed that would take it approximately fifteen hours to cover. The mission was aborted after just forty minutes. Shortly after being released, the robot sent a distress signal and was ordered back up to the surface, where WHOI heaved it aboard with the aid of a grappling hook attached to an A-frame bolted to the deck. Inspecting the AUV back in its van, the engineers detected a leak in the housing of its camera. Another day had been lost.

The problem was quickly fixed, and for the next week, the REMUS performed every task it was given. It swam relatively slowly, at an average speed of three knots, maintaining a constant height above the seabed—typically forty meters—as it emitted high-frequency sonar pulses that spanned four hundred meters to each side. Without GPS to guide it underwater, the REMUS was forced to rely on its own devices. A former Boy Scout, WHOI's Jeff Kaeli compared those internal navigational instruments to the way a Scout might orient himself in the woods by using a compass and counting his steps. The compass, in this analogy, was a fiber-optic gyroscope, which measures the time it takes a pulse of light to snake around a coil in the AUV's hull; from infinitesimal variations with the speed of light in a vacuum, the device could calculate the direction of the rotation of the earth, which can very slightly shorten or lengthen the light's journey. From that result, the REMUS could deduce where north was. The equivalent of a Boy Scout counting steps to figure out how far he's traveled, Kaeli said, was a Doppler sensor that measured the compression and expansion of sound waves from returning pings—much like the distortion in the siren wail of a passing ambulance—in order to precisely establish the AUV's velocity. This figure, when multiplied by the amount of time elapsed, revealed the distance traveled. As ingenious and well calibrated as they were, these dead-reckoning systems developed small errors over time. To correct them and establish its position with absolute precision, the REMUS sent pings every eighteen seconds to transponders that had been dropped to the seafloor and triangulated their returning signals.

Woods Hole's advanced systems guaranteed a level of accuracy that had been unavailable to Glocca Morra's systems in the 1980s and would leave no doubt about the coordinates of the wreck, should Dooley's calculations prove correct. With every passing day, however, that prospect became more uncertain.

After each outing of the REMUS, Woods Hole engineers would rush to transfer its data to a hard drive in a navy speedboat that ferried it back to Cartagena so that Dooley and Kozak could go over it at the operation's headquarters. For hours each evening, the two hunched over a computer screen scrolling through image after image of nothing. Even if the *San José* was in the area, Kozak warned Dooley, "There's always that possibility that you won't see it."

Sonar readings of the largely flat seafloor resembled yellowish static with a thick black band down the middle, corresponding to the area directly below the REMUS that the side-scan sonar's beams couldn't reach, known as the nadir. *Scroll. Scroll. Scroll.* Tedium, rather than the whip-cracking action of the movies, is often the reality of archaeology. Dooley didn't expect the remains of the *San José* to look anything like a ship in the sonar readout—the brine-soaked timbers had surely crumbled, and sediment likely blanketed the site—but neither did they expect the debris field to be as wide as that of vessels that had wrecked in shallower, more storm-tossed waters.

Every so often, a small asperity would cast an acoustic shadow and break the monotony. To the eager untrained eye, some such forms might even have resembled a ship, but the sardonic Kozak was quick to deflate any hopes. "Geology," he would say flatly, and keep scrolling.

As always prone to positive thinking, Dooley reminded himself that, in a rigorous search, *not* finding what you're looking for is a measure of progress, as it reduces the area in which that object must be. While the logic was undeniable, it was not intuitive. It went against a natural human tendency to assume that the probability of success dwindled the longer one came up empty. And it didn't do much to alleviate Dooley's fear, nagging behind his confident facade, that he might have somehow miscalculated, or overlooked a key piece of evidence, in establishing his search box—or that the wreck might indeed be in the part of his search box that Dimar had not allowed him to explore.

On its sixth dive, the REMUS completed its coverage of the authorized search area having found a truck tire and a shipping container but no significant targets. With just three days to spare before they had to pack up their equipment and head to the Pacific, Woods Hole's engineers decided to revisit the southern part of the search area, where the seabed was particularly craggy, to make sure they hadn't missed anything. The AUV flew at lower altitude, with higher-resolution sonar. Increasingly nervous as he awaited its return, Dooley visualized it swimming among the peaks, valleys, and canyons, and wondered what it "saw"—or didn't see.

The REMUS detected nothing but rock formations. Both time and unexplored space were in short supply. An internal report by Woods Hole reveals the sense of defeatism that had fallen upon the team by day 7: "This mission looked at two potential targets, perhaps grasping at straws, and then completed a large area survey south of the original search area." As the likelihood of failure became more distinct, blame started going around: "Moving south was not the preferred new search area, but it is what was approved by Colombia."

Dooley had made it clear that his own preferred new search area was to the west, where the remaining third of the archaeologist's box lay. But it seemed Colombian authorities were more comfortable searching for the galleon where Dooley said it wasn't than risking finding it closer to the coordinates where Sea Search Armada had long said it was. The Colombians seemed at first to be vindicated when the survey in the unpromising southern search area revealed an anomaly that Kozak deemed likely to be the remains of a ship. The elation quickly dissipated, however, when the anomaly was measured and found to be of a size inconsistent with the *San José*.

The expedition ended on June 28, and Woods Hole left Cartagena without a prize to show for its efforts. The REMUS and its minders headed to Hawaii to survey fields of deep-sea mineral deposits. Meanwhile, Dooley, Adriana, and Montenegro shared a depressing postmortem dinner at a Cartagena pizzeria. "We spoke with pessimism," recalled Montenegro. "We felt regret, like, maybe we didn't do everything right. We felt something like guilt, at least that was my sentiment." Dooley, for his part, was inconsolable. Yet his own crushing disappointment at the dying of his dream was unaccompanied by any kind of guilt. He believed he had done everything right. Above all, he felt seething anger toward the too-timid authorities who had refused to listen to him. "I was disgusted, because I wanted a broader search area. We had argued about it, but they decided to cut off a piece of it." By limiting the permit, he felt, Colombia had set him up to fail.

Dooley broke the bad news to Clake, who, to the archaeologist's surprise, considered it good news. Speaking of the half-explored search area, he said, "The remaining 50 percent is 100 percent," a cryptic pronouncement that revealed the wunderkind financier's unconventional, hyperanalytical way of thinking. With this statement—another way of formulating the idea that failing to find something brings you closer to finding it by ruling out where it is *not*—Clake was expressing his full faith in Dooley and his eagerness to search the entirety of the area the archaeologist had mapped out.

With Clake's vote of confidence and his assurance that he would continue to finance the search, Dooley pepped back up and got into action. He and Montenegro met with the culture minister, Garcés, to beg her to authorize an expansion of the search zone to cover the remainder of Dooley's area—the last two of his six subdivisions. Dooley assured her that Sea Search Armada was nothing to worry about: They had not found the *San José*. He would.

The tough-talking minister was hesitant to grant the request.

"Are you sure it's there?" she asked Dooley.

"I am sure," he said. "And if I don't find it, I'll cut my own head off."

Garcés smiled at the unflinching will of the man sitting before her. It was he, after all, who had conjured the project into existence, trudged through Colombia's notorious bureaucratic quagmire, gathered the financing and formidable resources. Anyone less stubborn, or more realistic, than Dooley, would have given up long before. Such an opportunity was unlikely to occur again, she thought. Was it not foolish to come so close only to demobilize?

Garcés relented and began the process to expand the authorized search zone. Woods Hole and the REMUS would not be available again until November. It took nearly that long for the new permit to be sorted out. Issued on October 20, 2015, it would end up covering 583 square miles—far more than Dooley needed or asked for. But who was he to refuse? Out of caution, Garcés and Dimar, the maritime authority, had carved a tiny parcel out of the new permitted zone, a box inside the box: Any survey data from within a half mile of Sea Search Armada's coordinates was to be entrusted to the Colombian state, for its exclusive use.

From that moment on, Dooley's threat of self-decapitation, should he fail to find the galleon, would become a running joke between him and Garcés. As a reminder of the mission's daunting stakes—especially for Dooley, who had devoted so much of his life to the search—they would draw their fingers across their throats like a blade.

Chapter 25

The Telltale Dolphin

The weary *Malpelo* cruised back out to the search area on November 23. Half a year since leaving the Caribbean, the Woods Hole team, including Purcell and Kaeli and the REMUS 6000, returned to the same waters and picked up where it had left off. If this was life and death for Dooley, for WHOI it was a job. On its first day, the AUV was sent to the apparent shipwreck spotted back in the spring on the previous expedition's last day to take pictures and test that all systems functioned properly this time. The new expedition was off to a much smoother start: no problems at customs, no damaged equipment, no unexpected delays.

Because the AUV's data had to be transferred to shore, there was a two-day lag before Dooley and Kozak could review it and, if a target was found, ask the REMUS to examine the site more closely. By that point, the device was already off to the next section of the search area.

On the search's second day, Tuesday, November 24, Dooley and Kozak—back at the same waterfront apartment Dooley had rented to serve as the operation's headquarters—were examining the sonar readings and photos taken on the earlier mission, of the unknown shipwreck. It appeared to be a modern fishing vessel, and no effort was made to identify it further. Dooley's mind was not on that boat but on whatever the REMUS might have been flying over at that very moment. It had been programmed that day to cover an especially important forty-three-square-mile patch of the seabed just west of the zone explored in May, and which had been part of Dooley's original search box. The area was extended at the last minute to include the most delicate of coordinates, at which Sea Search Armada had reported finding the wreck of the *San José* in 1981. Even accounting for the wide positional error that Sea Search Armada had long claimed, if there was a large target in the vicinity, the sonar would likely register it. If such a target were to be identified as the long-lost galleon, it would represent the ultimate humiliation for Dooley: His entire effort would have served only to confirm that Glocca Morra had already found the *San José,* three decades earlier.

On board the *Malpelo,* Purcell and his crew also fretted over what the REMUS was seeing—or rather hearing. "We were joking: 'Don't find it here!'" Purcell recalled.

Had the *Auguste Piccard* in fact located the galleon? Had Tommy Thompson lied about *not* finding it when verifying those coordinates years later? The REMUS would be the first to know the truth.

Twenty-five meters above the seabed, in near-absolute darkness, the yellow robot hummed along, emitting regular squeaks far above the range of human hearing. Obeying its programming, it traveled east to west, then west to east, back and forth like a shuttle in a loom, weaving a sonar tapestry that would eventually stretch from south to north. The process would take the REMUS exactly seventeen hours. As it swam over the spot SSA had pinpointed decades earlier, its sonar pulses bounced against a craggy seafloor, several hundred meters deeper than the area SSA had reported. It would be two days before Dooley could view the readings that indicated what he had long since claimed, as Tommy Thompson had before him: that the *San José* was not there.

■   ■   ■

THE REMUS CONTINUED ON ITS STEADY PATH, cruising above a subaquatic wasteland. Several hours later, around three miles to the north in waters six hundred meters deep—back within Dooley's original search box and well outside the problematic area surrounding SSA's coordinates—its sensors came across an oasis in the desert.

Later that week, an officer from the *Malpelo* shuttled to shore, crossed the street from a small pier to the building that housed the operation's headquarters, and took the elevator to the eighth floor. He unlocked a waterproof yellow box, opened it, and handed Dooley a hard drive containing the data from the REMUS. Kozak and Dooley took their usual seats side by side at a desktop computer on a long, chart-strewn table in the waterfront apartment. They plugged in the drive and began reviewing the data. Kozak clicked through thousands of nearly identical grainy sonar readings. The emptiness before him did nothing to dispel his doubts about Dooley, who was sitting to his right, watching anxiously. Then Kozak saw something different.

"Okay, whoa," Kozak said, nodding. "We've got something there that is not geological."

Dooley put on his reading glasses and leaned closer. "This really looks . . . Mm-hmm."

Kozak pointed to a few light specks on the screen that looked like breadcrumbs on a rust-colored yellow placemat. To an average observer, even to Dooley, who had viewed countless such images in his career, these tiny anomalies might have seemed like mere noise. But to Kozak, they jumped out. They were too bright, too well defined, their acoustic shadows too large.

"A spread of debris on the bottom," he said. "Scatter pattern." It was the most promising image the two had yet seen, but it had been taken from nearly eighty feet above at a relatively low frequency. "We can't really come to any conclusion," Kozak said. "We need that high-frequency side scan and photos." Dooley agreed. He immediately sent word to the *Malpelo,* instructing Purcell and his men to take a closer look at the target.

The REMUS was midway through a mission when engineers

redirected it to the new target site. This time the device traveled just thirty feet above the ocean floor. Leaving the AUV to do its job, the Woods Hole crew, the *Malpelo's* captain, and Captain Monroy, the executive officer, tucked into a Colombian approximation of Thanksgiving dinner that Adriana Dooley had ordered and had asked the patrol boat to deliver to the *Malpelo,* to give the Americans a taste of home. The gesture was well appreciated. "Good day all around considering the meal and vehicle was collecting data" over the target, Woods Hole would later report.

As the WHOI gang reveled, Dooley paced anxiously in the apartment. The lag between dispatching the AUV and receiving results had never seemed so long.

When the REMUS's scans finally came in, they confirmed that the anomaly was a shipwreck. And this time it was of approximately the right dimensions to be a 140-foot vessel or at least a significant part of it. Dooley had known enough disappointment not to get too excited. There was good reason to think it might not be the *San José.* Cartagena had been a major port for nearly half a millennium, and it was impossible to know how many ships could have foundered in the surrounding waters in that time. Only photographs, taken from even closer, could determine the nature of the newly found wreck.

Presuming that any part of the *San José* was still visible, Dooley had long wondered how he would identify it. Its name would not be written on the bow or the stern or a ship's bell, and the carving of Saint Joseph would not have survived. Finding a concentration of rounded, volcanic ballast stones would provide supporting evidence, as would locating the five large anchors known to have been aboard the *San José.* But the "irrefutable proof," Dooley said, would lie in the cannons. As on all *almirantas* and *capitanas,* they would be made of bronze rather than iron. For months, he had been telling his colleagues that the telltale detail would be the cascabel, the decorative loop of metal on the tail end of the gun. Each one would be shaped like a splendid, if somewhat unrealistic, dolphin. Cannons from other countries included dolphins on the handles but not the cascabel. Such had been the stylistic signature of Spanish cannons from the late 1500s to 1683, the year Seville's master cannon maker Enrique Habet died. When the craftsman's son inherited the trade, he replaced the cascabel dolphin with a more functional, less magical knob of bronze. Dooley's research indicated that all of the *San José*'s sixty-two guns had been made by Habet. If the archaeologist saw a cannon with a dolphin on its cascabel, he would know that he had accomplished his mission. If he didn't, he would be back where he started.

THE WOODS HOLE TEAM SWAPPED OUT one of the REMUS's payload sensors with a Prosilica GT3400C camera and sent it back to the site, programming it once again to swim thirty feet above. Flashes went off every two seconds, startling sea life accustomed to perfect blackness. For hours, the AUV followed tight track lines over the general target area.

The REMUS surfaced in the late morning, when the sea was typically calm, and signaled its location to its masters. A panel on the device's bow popped open and paid out line that enabled the Woods Hole crew to snag it with a grappling hook shot from aboard the *Malpelo* and haul it in. Unlike after previous missions, when the engineers would take a cursory look at the data to make sure all was in order before sending it back to Dooley and Kozak on shore, the team proceeded with especial discretion and care in downloading and reviewing the results of the latest survey.

"Go to your bunk and close the door," Purcell told the young engineer Jeff Kaeli as he handed him the hard drive. "Have a look and tell me what you find."

Retiring to his ten-by-twelve-foot stateroom, Kaeli began clicking through the photos on his laptop. He was soon lulled by the sameness of tens of thousands of images of sand. "The ocean bottom is incredibly boring until it's not," he said. At one point, he saw a tubelike form sticking straight out of the seabed. The object did not wake him from his torpor. He could see that it was man-made—no straight lines in nature—but assumed it to be some kind of industrial pipe that had perhaps fallen from one of countless freighters that sail into Cartagena Harbor every year.

Then he clicked to the next image.

Kaeli was looking at three more tubular, man-made forms. Even his untrained eye could recognize them as cannons.

He clicked back to the "pipe" in the previous image and magnified it. Now he could see that it, too, was a cannon. A white crab was sprawled over its muzzle.

Suddenly fully alert, leaning toward to his computer screen, Kaeli clicked forward through the photographs that followed. More cannons. Wreckage.

He felt a rush of elation: *I'm pretty damn sure we found what we came for.* He sat for a moment, savoring the thought that he was the only person on earth to know.

THE NEXT DAY, THURSDAY, NOVEMBER 26, Purcell and his team came ashore and hand-delivered the hard drive to Dooley and Kozak at the Cartagena apartment. Purcell did not let on that he had seen the data, and told Dooley that he and his men were there only because the *Malpelo* had to return to port for urgent repairs—which was also true. Much as William Phips's second-in-command, Francis Rogers, had initially played coy about finding the treasure of the *Concepción* in 1686, Purcell did his best to keep a straight face.

But such was the feeling that something significant was about to happen that nearly everyone involved in the search at the top level crowded around the desktop computer. Among them were Montenegro and Capt. Herman León, Dimar's chief observer. The project's videographer, Adam Geiger, made sure the cameras were rolling.

Dooley took a seat beside Kozak and put his glasses on. Kozak opened the file of images Kaeli had reviewed and found that the engineer had cheekily spared them the trouble of clicking through all the images: The first photo was that of the three cannons, lying in a bed of seashells.

"Uh-oh . . ." said Dooley. "Oh my God."

The archaeologist would later describe the shock he felt. "In that instant, as my eyes remained fixed on the image, I disconnected from reality. My body was literally paralyzed, but my mind was racing at the speed of light, flipping through the pages of my life."

The images that followed revealed a large concentration of artifacts nested in the mud. Olive jars. Green glass bottles that had contained medicinal gin. The hilt of a sword that looked as if it had been thrust into the sand. Cannon after cannon.

Montenegro applauded. Kozak nodded in acknowledgment—whatever remaining skepticism he'd had about Dooley vanished right then. The men around Dooley reached out a hand to touch him, pat him on the back, tousle his hair. He began to laugh.

It was a large shipwreck, from more or less the right period, but was it *the* shipwreck? The key, Dooley reminded the men around him, would be the cannons. The guns in the photographs were ornate, of a style commonly used in Spanish ships of the colonial era, yet they looked too new, too clean to be iron, which would have severely corroded over the centuries and amassed layers of concretion. They were thus necessarily made of bronze. So far, so good. Dooley then zoomed in on the cascabel of one of the cannons. There, staring him in the eye, was the figure of a bounding dolphin.

Roger Dooley knew then that he had found the galleon *San José*.

He was overwhelmed. The wreck site was even more beautiful than he'd imagined. He hadn't expected so much of it to remain uncovered after all this time. Montenegro, who was looking over Dooley's shoulder, recalled that the event felt more like a revelation than a discovery: "We didn't just find it—it appeared to us like the Virgin."

The wreck was well within Dooley's original search area. In the ultimate vindication, the Shoals of the Admiral shown on the 1729 map of Cartagena, which Dooley believed held the key to finding the

San José, turned out to be the bit of land closest to the wreck. What wasn't so clear was whether the shipwreck lay in Colombia's territorial waters. Dooley read out the coordinates of the target at the level of what would have been the mainmast—76°00'20"W 10°13'33"N—to Captain León, who scrawled them on a piece of yellow paper, then plotted them on a map. He blanched: From his quick calculations, the site appeared to lie just at the edge of Colombia's territorial waters, the twelve-nautical-mile band surrounding the coastline, within which there was little ambiguity over the ownership of any object on the seabed. If indeed the wreck lay just outside the limits, it would still be in Colombia's contiguous zone (within twenty-four nautical miles from shore) as well as its Exclusive Economic Zone (within two hundred nautical miles from shore), which, according to the country's law on underwater cultural heritage, would still allow Colombia to claim the remains of the ship. But defending such a claim in an international court would be less straightforward.

Dooley was not so preoccupied by questions of borders and sovereignty. They did nothing to dent his glory. As he rattled off numbers, Adriana, sensing the commotion, hurried across the apartment and stood behind her husband. When she saw the cannons on the screen, her jaw fell. She put an arm around Dooley and kissed him on the head. He turned to her and said "*Veintitres años,*" then repeated the words in English for the others in the room. "Twenty-three years I've been waiting for this." (As he would later explain, he had miscalculated in the thrill of the moment: It had been more than thirty years since he'd caught the scent of the *San José.*)

As if releasing the emotion Dooley could not articulate, Adriana put a hand to her mouth and wept, waving off the cameras.

Dooley was about to turn seventy-one, the same age the Count of Casa Alegre had been when he went down with the galleon.

"I'm still thinking I'm dreaming," he told Geiger, the cameraman, who zoomed in on Dooley's face shortly after the discovery was confirmed.

Drinks were poured in celebration.

"*Palabras?*" asked Montenegro. A few words?

Dooley, a talker but not a speaker, seemed caught off guard. He raised a glass of whiskey and thanked everyone who had helped find "the best shipwreck in the world." In his excitement, he spilled some whiskey on the floor. "And this is only the beginning, of a new history with Colombia."

"*Por Colombia!*" toasted Adriana, shooting her glass skyward in tribute to her homeland.

Captain León, in uniform, tempered the exuberance with solemnity, sparing a thought for his fellow seamen: "For the sailors, the old sailors," he said in hesitant English, "the six hundred lives that are in the bottom of the sea, and also in heaven."

Dooley raised his glass. In his decades of research, he had come to know the names of several of the men who'd died aboard the galleon. Yet the vast majority remained anonymous. He vowed to identify as many as possible by tracking down the claims of their widows in the years that followed the disaster. But to him, the most important character in this story was the *San José* itself. He had found it at last. He took the sweetest sip of his life.

Chapter 26

"Hemingway"

The only people who knew that the galleon had been found were in that apartment. It was now critical to inform President Santos of the discovery immediately, before he left for a scheduled state visit to Spain. Should the news break while he was in Madrid, Spain would be sure to press its claim to its lost ships around the world, and Santos—taken by surprise—would be forced to reject that claim without preparation, while standing side by side with the Spanish prime minister during a joint press conference. A poorly timed revelation had the potential to reignite long-dormant postcolonial enmities and cause a diplomatic embarrassment.

Santos was still in Cartagena, at a presidential residence on the bay that could be seen in the distance from Dooley's rented apartment. It was determined that only Garcés, the culture minister, could tell Santos of the discovery. But that night, of all nights, for the first time since the search for the galleon began, the minister was unreachable. Through a series of frantic phone calls to people in her orbit, Captain León learned that she was vacationing on the idyllic Colombian island of Providencia, off Nicaragua. When the receptionist at her hotel told León that

Garcés had asked not to be disturbed, the captain told her it was a matter of national importance. Within minutes, Garcés called back.

"*Verdad?*" she asked when told the news. Really?

"We are 90 percent sure," said Montenegro, with a scientist's aversion to absolutes.

"Well, are you sure, or aren't you?" responded Garcés, who may have been peeved that her vacation had been disrupted for something less than certain.

Montenegro was cowed into certitude.

"Yes, ma'am, I'm sure."

Montenegro was still on the phone, standing on the balcony of the apartment, when he saw a helicopter take off at the far end of the bay, by Santos's residence. The president had left for Spain. Garcés hung up immediately and tried to call him, without success.

To avoid a contretemps while the president was abroad, the operation was put on lockdown. Purcell and his team went back aboard the *Malpelo* and proceeded with the survey as if nothing had happened. Gossip can spread on ships as easily as disease. But since the search area was outside cellphone range, those on the *Malpelo* were effectively sequestered, prevented from leaking the news in an overeager call to a friend or relative. "We were not worried about Woods Hole," said Montenegro, "but about the whole crew."

On the *Malpelo*, executive officer Julio Monroy, whose elderly father had long been singularly fascinated by the *San José*, could sense that something had happened. "I stepped into the officers' room and Mike [Purcell] was there alone," Monroy recalled. "He was thinking, excited, and he couldn't suppress his smile." Purcell was forced to confess: "I think we found it." Monroy and the ship's captain were then asked to sign forms ensuring their silence.

Over the next week, while Santos was in Spain, the REMUS returned to the site of the galleon to take more photos from close range. It also investigated another wreck that its sonar had identified, probably Spanish, about as old as the *San José,* but not believed to have contained any gold or silver.* ("Does anyone give a shit about *that* wreck?" Kozak asked wryly, noting the supposed hypocrisy of purist archaeologists who express dismay over the focus on the *San José*'s treasure.)

In that time, Monroy struggled to keep the secret about the *San José*. He resisted the urge to tell his father and dodged increasingly insistent questions from his crew. At dinnertime on December 4, the *Malpelo* was back at anchor in the Bay of Cartagena. A server in the officer's mess brought Monroy his plate and whispered, "Sir, we found the *San José*."

Monroy did not know how to respond. Was the server trying to trick him into breaking his silence?

Far from it. As the server had just seen on the TV in the kitchen, President Santos—safely back from Europe—had tweeted it:

> *Great news: We found the Galleon San José! Tomorrow I will give*
> *the details at a press conference from Cartagena.*

To prepare for the next morning's presentation to the press, Santos invited Dooley, Garcés, Montenegro, and several naval officers and dignitaries to an informal get-together at the sprawling presidential estate at the tip of a peninsula jutting out into the Bay of Cartagena. The official agenda of the gathering was to brief Santos about the search. The evening would double as a celebration of Dooley, the guest of honor.

Attendees arrived at Santos's fortress-like estate by boat, after nightfall. Dooley entered the sparsely furnished, brightly lit, echoey main hall, a large black poster tube slung over his shoulder. With his dark blazer and blue boat shoes, his longish white-blond hair and his full white beard, the archaeologist stuck out among the paunchy guests and neatly groomed officers. He was unquestionably the man of the hour.

As the gathering waited for Santos, Dooley got to work. He

---

* It is thought to have been named the *Santa Teresa*.

unscrewed the poster tube and pulled out large-format copies of his final search chart and of Pérez's map from 1729 and placed them on easels on opposite sides of the room. He then took a seat against the wall, pulled out a crumpled printout on which he'd written notes for remarks, and nervously rehearsed his speech, his lips moving silently as he read. He would be sure to thank the president, the minister, and all those who had allowed him to search Colombian waters. He would then say that finding the galleon had been only the first step in the unprecedented archaeological project he planned to lead, and possibly the simplest: No one had yet undertaken a proper excavation at such depths. Already he was thinking of the next thing.

Santos finally strode in, wearing a blue oxford, khakis, and white espadrilles. He greeted Garcés, the officers, and Montenegro, then embraced Dooley with genuine warmth, gripping the archaeologist's right arm as he shook his hand.

"How marvelous," Santos said. "This is truly a historical thing."

The president had gambled on a strange old man he'd met at a cocktail party just over a year before and was now hailing him as something like a national hero. Drinking the moment in, with a smile that flashed his gleaming dentures, Dooley reminded Santos of that evening in New York and of the significance of the 1729 map he had gifted the president. He ushered Santos to the copy of the map that was sitting on an easel. "The closest point" to where the *San José* was found, Dooley gloated, "is the *Bajo del Almirante*."

The congregation huddled around Dooley as he related the story of Wager and Casa Alegre and explained how he had established his search box and found the *San José*. He had never known such glory.

Santos pointed on the map: "It's more or less here?" he asked.

"Yes, more or less there," said Roger.

"So it belongs to the president!" Santos said, his hand on his chest, as the room erupted in laughter.

Dooley took his seat in the place of honor, on an armchair next to Santos, who sipped red wine while Ernesto Montenegro, mic in hand, recounted the details of the expedition. Though he fully credited Dooley,

Kozak, and Woods Hole—the "dream team," Santos interjected— Montenegro was making it clear with this short presentation that he, and not Dooley, was now in control of the *San José* operation.

"It's very important that, based on an archaeological and scientific conversation, we don't focus on economic questions"—a euphemism for how the project was being paid for—"but rather on how we should explore, how we should intervene, how we should move forward with the process of conservation that we established . . . with Dr. Dooley."

Even as he was thanked and honored, Dooley was subtly being sidelined. He had done his part: He had found the *San José*. Though there would still be a role for him, it would no longer be as central. As Montenegro went on, describing vague plans for the future of the galleon, Dooley looked off into the middle distance, beginning to worry that his triumph would be short-lived.

HIS FEARS WERE CONFIRMED THE FOLLOWING DAY. Dooley had hoped to give his speech during the following press conference at the naval base in Cartagena. He'd planned to attend alongside Kozak and the Woods Hole team on the *Malpelo,* which was docked at the base. But by the morning he'd yet to receive details on the time and place of the conference. As the hours passed by without an update, he came to a brutal realization: He had not been invited.

He would watch the event only later, on YouTube. At Santos's side, where he believed he should have been, were Garcés and Montenegro.

To the crowd of journalists and naval officers, Santos presented the finding of the *San José* as "the most important discovery of underwater cultural heritage . . . in the history of humanity" and announced that "a great museum" would be built in that city to tell the galleon's story and display its contents. He gave credit to Garcés and Montenegro, to ICANH and Dimar and "our beloved navy." He thanked the members of the shipwreck commission and named numerous government officials who had little, if anything, to do with the project. He said

nothing of the men who had actually found the galleon, except to allude to a collaboration with "international scientists of the highest
level," which he referred to only as a "dream team." But he named no
names. Garcés touted the effort as the "most important public-private
partnership in the history of the Colombian state" but did not hint at
the source of the money—the "Originator," Anthony Clake. Nor,
most glaringly, did anyone utter the name of the man who had conceived this project in the first place.

Santos then played a video montage of the search, cut together
from Geiger's footage. The edit showed the REMUS but not the
Woods Hole logo on its side. Viewers could overhear Dooley's unmistakable voice but would not see his face or his name, only the back of
his head. In depicting that glorious, emotional evening in Dooley's
apartment when the photographs of the cannons confirmed the discovery of the *San José*, the video showed neither Dooley, nor Kozak,
nor Purcell, nor the crying Adriana. It included only Montenegro,
calling the moment a "major triumph" and thereby becoming the face
of the operation. "There is no other Colombian who knows more
about these subjects than Dr. Montenegro," Santos said after the video,
rattling off Montenegro's academic credentials. The message was clear:
This was a Colombian mission, aboard a Colombian ship, overseen by
Colombian officials. Certainly that was an easier sell than the full
picture—that the storied galleon had been found by a Cuban American archaeologist, with American surveyors, bankrolled by an English
hedge-funder who was after its treasure.

As he watched the video, Dooley was not merely upset. He was
heartbroken. The omission of his efforts from the public record tainted
the joy he'd felt at realizing his ambition. And it was clearly deliberate.
Santos knew well who deserved credit for the achievement, as he had
shown during the reception at the presidential residence the night before with his effusive praise of Dooley. But that had been behind closed
doors.

A few days after the press conference, perhaps feeling a measure of
remorse, Santos acknowledged that there was one key person he had

not mentioned. In an interview with Colombia's W Radio on December 17, he was asked about the project's origins.

"I will tell you this tale," said Santos, "which is a small part of a marvelous story that will remain in the history books." During a consular event outside the country, the president recalled, he had been accosted by "a man who looked like Hemingway . . . with white hair and a white beard." The man, Santos recalled, asked him for two minutes of his time and offered him a framed copy of a large antique map he'd found at the Library of Congress. "He told me, 'This map is not known to anyone,'" said the president. "'This site'—he showed me the site—'does not appear on any other map and that site almost guarantees that I know where the galleon is.'" As if to establish the stranger's bona fides, Santos specified that "Hemingway" was married to a Colombian woman.

The head of state clearly relished the fable-like quality of the story. But when the interviewer pressed for more details, Santos allowed only that the mystery man "is not a treasure hunter. He's not after money and he genuinely has an anthropological, historical, and cultural vocation."

Santos would later tell me he had chosen not to name Dooley in order to protect him from the scrutiny that he believed would inevitably target the *San José* project. In those early days, he said, "everything was not formalized. I saw that putting him on the spot would be more negative than positive. As a matter of experience, [I've found that] with such an important event, when you work without keeping everything closed, they would simply try to derail the process and go after whoever is involved" ("they" being the project's critics). "Roger organized a dream team . . . but I think we said it's better not to say who they were and keep things sort of low profile until we have everything under control."

DOOLEY MAY HAVE FELT BETRAYED, but Santos's instincts were right: Everything that followed the discovery would be a fight. As

Montenegro put it, "From that moment on, the *San José* left the world of myth and entered the world of politics."

The announcement that the billion-dollar galleon had been found triggered a vociferous outcry from several fronts. The swiftest response came from Spain. Two days after Santos's announcement, the country's minister of culture, Iñigo Méndez de Vigo, told the press that "Spain has a right to ownership" of its sunken warship no matter how much time had passed, citing the principle of sovereign immunity enshrined in the UNESCO Convention on the Protection of Underwater Cultural Heritage. As a conciliatory gesture, Méndez de Vigo offered his nation's cooperation in salvaging the wreck. When the Santos administration failed to respond, the Spanish foreign minister, José Manuel García-Margallo, issued a blunter warning: "If this cannot be resolved on friendly terms," he told the press, Colombia "must understand that we will claim it and defend our rights."

Recent events had shown that this was not mere bluster. In 2007, the Spanish government targeted the American treasure-hunting company Odyssey Marine Exploration after its founder, Greg Stemm, announced the recovery of seventeen tons of silver coins—an estimated $500 million worth—from a wreck in international waters off the Portuguese coast. Stemm, a college dropout who began his career as a press agent for Bob Hope, never publicly identified the wreck, but authorities in Madrid knew it to be *Nuestra Señora de las Mercedes,* a thirty-six-gun Spanish frigate sunk by British ships during the Napoleonic Wars in 1804 and believed to have transported a million silver dollars.* After the bounty was shipped to Florida, Spain sued Odyssey in U.S. courts, citing the principle of sovereign immunity. The case

---

* It bore the same name—Our Lady of the Mercies—as the galleon Dooley discovered off the Cuban coast in the mid-1980s. The Spanish Crown christened thousands of ships in the colonial era, and there were only so many patron saints and incarnations of the Virgin Mary to go around. Indeed, there were numerous other *San Josés*.

culminated in a victory for Spain after the Eleventh Circuit Court of Appeals ruled in 2012 that the *Mercedes* was Spain's property and so, therefore, was everything it contained. The Supreme Court declined to take up the appeal, and Odyssey was ordered to return all the coins to Spain.* Buoyed by this precedent, the Spanish government felt confident in pressing its rights to the *San José*.

It was far from alone. Spain might have been where the *San José's* treasure was heading in 1708, but the lands from which it came could also make a case that it belonged to them. The Peruvian government had advanced that argument in 2012 when it appealed to the U.S. Supreme Court to block the transfer of the *Mercedes's* coins to Spain on the grounds that much of the silver and gold was mined and minted in its territory, even if that territory was then part of the Spanish Empire. The Supreme Court rejected that motion as well, but what was to stop Peru from trying again, in another court, with the *San José*? Some contended, meanwhile, that Panama had a more credible claim to the treasure than Colombia, since the fleet left from Portobelo and never reached Cartagena on that final journey. Several Indigenous groups— most prominently the Quechua-speaking Qhara Qhara nation in Bolivia, from the mountains around the mines of Potosí that supplied the bulk of the fleet's riches—would likewise stake a claim to the galleon's silver, as the descendants of those who had toiled and died in slavery-like conditions to extract it from their own ancestral lands on behalf of their Spanish conquerors.

And then there were the treasure hunters who said they'd already found the *San José*. Sea Search Armada's cases against the Colombian

---

* Odyssey has said that the fix was in: Stemm pointed to classified diplomatic cables obtained by Wikileaks in which the American ambassador to Spain appears to offer help in reclaiming the treasure of the *Mercedes* in exchange for the restitution of an 1897 Pissarro painting to a California family that claimed it had been illegally taken by the Nazis before ending up in a Madrid museum. The connection could never be confirmed, and the Pissarro remains in Spain.

government were still unsettled in the spring of 2015, when Colombia finally offered to negotiate on the condition that SSA drop all litigation. The American company's decision makers, who could not have known that Dooley's search for the galleon was already under way, did as told.

The company's leadership, including director Jack Harbeston, felt blindsided and betrayed by Santos's announcement. "While the [Government of Colombia] was ostensibly progressing in good faith toward an agreement with SSA and an expedition to the San Jose," read an internal chronology Harbeston shared with me, "it in fact covertly planned and executed a search for the San Jose using third party contractors."

After Santos announced the discovery of the *San José* in December 2015, he shared a few of the high-resolution photos of the wreck with the press. They corresponded in no way to the murky evidence Sea Search Armada had presented in 1982. They showed a wreck with still visible sides, strewn with artifacts and cannons—far more compelling and convincing than the mound of coral SSA identified, which may or may not have concealed a 140-foot-long man-made object. But this did not stop Harbeston and his allies from protesting that the supposed discovery was merely a rediscovery of the same wreck site, which—for all anyone knew—could have extended over a large area given that the *San José* was said by some witnesses to have exploded. And since Santos had declared the coordinates of Dooley's wreck to be a state secret, he could not prove what Woods Hole's survey had established: that it was not in the "immediate vicinity" of SSA's target.

None of these arguments swayed Santos. "There are a lot of owners who are now popping up," he said at the time. "No sir, this is the Colombian people's cultural heritage."

Of the foreign countries staking a claim, Spain posed the most credible threat. But Santos stood his ground. Poking the specter of the Spanish Empire had long been a winning political strategy in Latin America, so there was little incentive for Santos to give in.

"At the heart of this debate is the inability of Spain to come to terms with the reality of its lost empire," the mining engineer and naval historian Daniel De Narváez told me. "The *San José,* like many other wrecks, is not some floating embassy of Madrid at the bottom of the sea—it is an artifact of shared, often painful, history. Spain's insistence on ownership is not about preserving history but about preserving the illusion of a past that no longer exists."

History, geography, and international law were on Santos's side. First, his administration cited Colombia's constitution of 1821, following Simón Bolívar's ousting of the Spanish, which stipulated that anything the Spanish Crown left behind became the property of the new nation of Colombia. Second, the galleon was thought to lie at the cusp of Colombia's territorial waters; even if it lay slightly outside, it would still be within the country's Exclusive Economic Zone, and thus arguably beyond Spain's reach. Finally, Colombia was not bound by the UNESCO charter, which would have given Spain rights to the galleon.

Santos confidently fended off all foreign claims to the galleon's treasure. Little did he suspect that the biggest threat to the *San José* project would come from within Colombia itself.

A WEEK AFTER THE PRESIDENT'S ANNOUNCEMENT, Colombian academics and scientists expressed their fears that the government would allow treasure hunters to pillage the site. Several of them would sign an open letter to the Santos administration, published in the right-wing Spanish newspaper *Diario ABC.*

"Since the announcement made by the Colombian president, Juan Manuel Santos," read the letter, "there has been speculation about the possibility that, as allowed by recent Colombian legislation, the objects that have remained on the seabed in Colombian waters for 307 years . . . might end up being the object of massive commercialization. That is not a worthy end for such historically valuable cultural heritage."

The letter, which was signed by 118 experts, including the pioneering maritime archaeologist George Bass of Texas A&M and the

San José historian Carla Rahn Phillips, denounced the secrecy that surrounded the project and its private backers. Its author was the Spanish journalist Jesús García Calero, who argued that prioritizing the extraction of the *San José*'s treasure over the rigorous scientific study of its full range of artifacts would forever compromise the richness of the tales the wreck had to tell.

"These galleons were microcosms of Spanish society at the time," Calero later told me. "Their wrecks are like beautifully illuminated books that tell the story of the Spanish Empire. But those books would lose their meaning if someone were to rip up their pages to take out the golden letters."

Dooley might have agreed with the sentiment, but none of the signatory experts knew of his involvement, if they'd heard of him at all.

Calero would end up being one of the *San José* project's most tenacious detractors, and the open letter he published a foundational document for a sustained opposition to the effort. The most vocal of the Colombian signatories, archaeologist Juan Guillermo Martín of the Universidad del Norte, began writing articles in the national press in which he dismissed the *San José* operation and the new law that permitted it as fundamentally corrupt. He insisted that the project be halted and handed over to an international team of specialists who could establish a clear plan of study, financed through transparent sources uninterested in profit. Above all, he endorsed UNESCO's view that underwater cultural heritage was best left undisturbed, in situ.

"The best would be to leave the galleon where it is," Martín would tell me. "It's been there three hundred years, well conserved, and can surely last for centuries more until we acquire the technology, the experience, and the resources to do a suitable job."

DOOLEY WAS ON A TIGHTER SCHEDULE. Finding the galleon had been just the first step in his plan. The next and most important phase was to extract its stories in the form of artifacts and treasure. The intervention Dooley had in mind was unprecedented, the deepest proper archaeological excavation ever conducted.* MAC's agreement with the government covered just the exploratory stage. There was no guarantee that MAC would be authorized to lead the excavation, but both Dooley and Clake were banking on it—Clake for the fortune, Dooley for the glory.

The archaeologist eventually resigned himself to the reality that, because the project was shrouded in secrecy, his glory in discovering the *San José* would have to remain private, known only to his closest collaborators, friends, and family. And given the uproar the announcement had caused, perhaps that was for the best, he thought. His first call—after telling Clake of the discovery—had been to his daughter Lili. Once again, the good news came at a distressing period for her; this time it was she who was at the hospital, in intensive care following complications from an appendectomy. The news filled her with a healing joy. "I am the happiest person in the world," she said, "because I know that his name will remain in history, as the archaeologist who found it."

The other person he would have wanted to tell of his greatest achievement was his older brother, who had been such an imposing figure in his life. But having died in Havana in 2005, Michael would never know. He had fallen so far out of favor with the government that, despite his military accomplishments, there had been no funeral. "By the time I found out," Dooley recalled, "he was already buried."

---

* The *Central America* and the frigate *Mercedes* (1804) were deeper, but in both cases the sole focus was the extraction of treasure, not archaeological study.

Chapter 27

"The Perfect Shipwreck"

The contract for the excavation was, by law, open to bidding. Any contractor in the world could in theory submit a proposal. It was thus conceivable that, having found the *San José,* Dooley would lose it to a rival outfit. MAC had a leg up on the competition since it had already been vetted by the Colombian government and had proven its merits by discovering the galleon. The company had undergone a series of changes since its founding. Although still financed by Clake, it had moved its corporate base from the U.K. to Switzerland. This was done as a precaution. Should MAC come into possession of artifacts from the *San José,* Spain—which imposed strict restrictions on the ownership and sale of Spanish cultural heritage—would likely seek to reclaim them. Yet by moving its assets to Switzerland, MAC would be beyond the reach of any European Union extradition warrant. Dooley, meanwhile, had ceded the directorship of MAC to trusted associates of Clake's—first to the former race car driver Ross Kevin Hyett and later to Oliver Plunkett—in order to focus on the daunting archaeological tasks at hand.

The wreck had to be properly studied before anything could be brought to the surface. To put together a viable proposal to excavate the *San José,* Dooley would have to create a hyperdetailed three-dimensional model of the site and a scientific survey of its immediate surroundings, the composition of the ocean floor, and the variety of sea life. Losing no time, he applied for a new permit from Dimar and convinced Clake to fund another expedition. With just two years left in his mandate, President Santos helped fast-track the approval so that he might see the excavation begin before the end of his second and last term, in mid-2018.

At a meeting between MAC and the Colombian government to finalize the new contract, several proposed conditions were discussed. One was that MAC would fund the establishment of a new museum. Another was that the company would also finance the construction and maintenance of a life-size replica of the *San José,* to exact specifications, using only the technologies of the time. When a representative for MAC objected to the requirement and asked to drop it from the contract, citing the enormous cost and questioning the point of building a wooden ship on late seventeenth-century designs, Culture Minister Garcés was flummoxed.

"But it was your idea," she told the MAC team.

At that moment, recalled one participant in the meeting, "the penny dropped, as everyone in the entire room, twenty-five people, all turned and looked at Roger. Roger had literally invented this. He'd sold this vision to the president that they would be standing on the quayside in Cartagena, all dressed in white shirts . . . and as the sun was setting over the horizon, the white square sails of the *San José* [would appear] as it comes into port, following its transatlantic journey from Spain." The attendee added, "He's a lovely guy but he drives you mad."

Dooley's second expedition was more sophisticated and expensive than the first, but also more constrained. Whereas the 2015 search mission had called for an autonomous vehicle to cover an area several hundred square kilometers wide, the new operation would involve a manually controlled robot, which would be tethered to a support vessel and remain within a few hundred meters of the site. The work would require a ship equipped with a state-of-the-art control room and a dynamic positioning system that would compensate for currents, winds, and waves to keep the vessel from moving, since the slightest tug on the robot's leash could distort the data it recorded. No Colombian ship, let alone the tired old *Malpelo,* was suited to the job. MAC turned instead to the Norwegian subsea survey company Swire Seabed, which specialized in oil and gas exploration. The pride of its fleet, the 280-foot *Seabed Prince,* traveled from its home port of Bergen, Norway, and arrived above the wreck on May 18, 2016. It would barely move an inch for another nine days.

This time, Dooley was on board to direct the international team of experts he had gathered, whose range of specialties reflected the ambitiousness of the project. Among them were the gruff, hulking Spanish naval historian Cruz Apestegui, one of the world's top experts on seventeenth-century ship architecture and construction; the ponytailed Spanish archaeologist Claudio Lozano; the mustachioed Cuban chemical engineer Manuel Almeida, a specialist in marine conservation; the goateed Colombian archaeologist Carlos Del Cairo; and the balding English surveyor Peter Holt. To lend cohesion to this motley assemblage, Dooley asked his daughter Lili to design official shirts for the expedition: sky blue, printed with the name SAN JOSE and the date 1708 beneath a drawing of the crouching lion thought to have adorned the galleon's prow.

The bulk of the work was to be carried out by two large, heavy-duty ROVs from Schilling Robotics. A crane lowered the first over into the dark sea on the night of May 18, under a nearly full moon. Beneath the surface, the vehicle's bright lights gave it an extraterrestrial glow as it descended toward the seafloor, soon disappearing from view.

On the second day, a helicopter landed on the helipad of the *Seabed Prince.* Out climbed President Santos, wearing khaki pants, a white shirt open at the collar to reveal a gold chain, and a blue ballcap emblazed with a dove. (Peace negotiations with the FARC were ongoing.) He strutted across the deck and up the stairs to the bridge, where he saluted the captain, then embraced Dooley.

Sitting with the research team around a large table, Santos emphasized the magnitude of the mission, then asked for a show of hands:

"*¿Cuantos Colombianos?*" How many Colombians?

Only about half the room raised a hand. In addition to the archae-ologist Carlos Del Cairo were a trio of biologists from Colombia's Marine and Coastal Research Institute (INVEMAR) and three Co-lombian officials who'd participated in Dooley's last expedition: Capt. Herman León, Capt. Julio Monroy, and the man who had made him-self the public face of the *San José* project, Ernesto Montenegro.

Santos was curious about the technical aspects of the wreck. Sitting between Dooley and Montenegro, he asked how, precisely, the galleon had sunk. Dooley said the ballast in the hull and the keel seemed to have kept it more or less upright for the two minutes it took to reach the bottom and that it may have spiraled downward. Unfastened objects would have spilled off with each turn and rained down alongside it.

"There was no explosion," Montenegro interjected. "The ship is whole."

Having not yet surveyed the site in detail, Dooley was less certain that the ship was intact, but he acknowledged that the archival record left some ambiguity about the force of the explosion, or whether it had happened at all. Days after the battle, for instance, Pedro de Asarta, the captain of sea and war aboard the vice-flagship *San Joaquín,* reported that although the *San José* did catch fire, there had not been "the blast or thunder caused by the blowing up of a pow-der magazine." The galleon had cracked open and sunk, Asarta de-clared, because it had been poorly repaired after having briefly run aground weeks earlier. There was good reason to discount Asarta's testimony, since he was on a different galleon far away from the ac-tion. Nevertheless, Dooley believed the study of the site would likely confirm that English reports of a massive explosion were inaccurate and that the fiery blast shown in the eighteenth-century English painter Samuel Scott's famous depiction of the battle and other con-temporary renditions—showing sailors flying into the air—had little to do with reality. "It never happened," he told Santos. The dominant theory, as it had been among the Spanish at the time of sinking, was that the galleon's hull had been in dire need of caulking, leaking in several areas, and that the vibrations from the cannon fire had caused it to break apart.

Santos returned to shore that afternoon. For the following week, the team spent nearly every waking hour in the control room dominated by a panel of large screens showing what the ROVs were seeing in real time from various angles. Black-T-shirted, tattooed Norwegian technicians who looked like they could be roadies for a metal band sat before the screens in large, egg-shaped swivel chairs, gripping joysticks to control the robots' various cameras, sensors, and appendages on the ROV hovering over the wreck six hundred meters directly below. The sweat on every forehead attested to the stifling atmosphere in the room.

On the third day, an unpredictable event nearly derailed the expedition, as if Neptune himself were protecting his prize from invaders. As the ROV descended slowly to the seafloor, its cameras recorded a green-black void. Suddenly, a large creature appeared on the screen, causing even the coolheaded Scandinavians to jump in their swivel chairs. It was a massive swordfish, who had taken a quixotic stab at the robotic intruder and gotten its spear-like bill stuck in the machinery. The fish was now thrashing wildly, posing a serious threat to the multimillion-dollar device upon which Dooley's expedition depended.

"I need to pull him out," said one of the Norwegians. "He can cut down the wire. We need to save the ROV." Wielding his joystick, the operator attempted to grab the creature's tail with a robotic claw and had about as much luck as a kid with a carnival crane. After several more frantic seconds, however, the fish managed to dislodge its sword and swim away.

In assessing the damage, the ROV operator discovered the swordfish had actually helped. "The camera is better now," he laughed. "He may have fixed it."

THROUGH THE ROV'S EYES, Dooley could vicariously swim over the shipwreck he had coveted for most of his adult life. The delight he felt could be compared only to the thrill of breathing underwater and flying over the coral reefs off Havana the first time he'd strapped on an air tank. He directed the technicians to move the camera left, right, up, down, forward, back. The lens hovered among the fish and crustaceans, tantalizingly close to objects that had last seen the light of day at sunset on June 8, 1708. It paced the length and breadth of the ship as Casa Alegre once had. Exploring a deepwater site by ROV was a different kind of thrill from that of diving on a wreck, but it was no less breathtaking. The site's depth was precisely what had kept it so pristine, beyond the reach of currents, storms, and pirates. The sides of the ship could be easily traced along the seafloor, suggesting that the wood beneath had not totally disintegrated. Dooley at last saw up close and in full color artifacts that had been indistinct in the grayscale photos Woods Hole had taken from a greater distance. He soon grew familiar with the various regions of the wreck. Greenish copper cauldrons, crushed under a cannon at the level of the missing mainmast, which had once stood thirty-five meters tall, indicated where the galley would have been. Hundreds of blue-and-white Chinese porcelain cups, most of them unbroken, were concentrated at one end of the wreck. Dooley concluded that they were contraband since foreign-made items were barred from trade within the viceroyalty of Peru. To the east of the field of china was an abundance of pewter clysters, large syringes designed to be filled with water and inserted rectally to administer enemas, a procedure that was all the rage in France in the late seventeenth century because of King Louis XIV's fondness for it. The tools were likely French in origin—yet more evidence of widespread smuggling.

At the stern of the wreck, where Casa Alegre's quarters would have been, were numerous gold escudos and finger-sized gold bars, still scintillating after three centuries on the seabed. Several large clusters of tarnished silver coins lay nearby. That so many riches remained visible on the seafloor, free of sediment as if they had just fallen, hinted at the vastness of the treasure buried below and gave reason to believe the most extravagant estimates of the galleon's wealth. The amount of precious metal scattered across the site conformed almost too well to the popular notion of a treasure-filled shipwreck. This was not what actual ancient wooden wrecks were supposed to look like. After centuries in seawater, ships typically dissolved to nothing, leaving little but a widespread scattering of artifacts and ballast rocks that over time could be buried under sediment and coral. The *San José,* by contrast, was too compact, too well delineated, too naked, too much like a ship.

The researchers were forbidden from taking any artifacts from the wreck. They did, however, use the ROV to bring up samples of soil and rock from nearby (as well as a piece of coral that latched on to the vehicle). The environmental data collected during the *Seabed Prince* survey explained why the site remained so coherent. The soil around it was flat, barren silt. The current at that depth was virtually nonexistent, and the wreck was distant enough from shore that it remained largely untouched by the sediment spewed out by the Magdalena River. A pass over the wreck with a sub-bottom profiler (a device emitting low-frequency sonar pulses that can penetrate the ocean floor) allowed Dooley and his team to see that, far from having rotted away, the galleon remained largely intact, nestled about six meters deep in the mud. Dooley and his colleagues deduced that the keel of the *capitana* had struck the bottom with such force as to wedge open its own grave. There was a good chance that the artifacts within—even organic materials like wood and leather—would be perfectly conserved in this anoxic tomb. The *San José* appeared to be, in Dooley's words, "the perfect shipwreck."

Cruz Apestegui, the Spanish naval architecture expert, echoed the thought: "The treasure of the *San José* is the *San José.*"

Dooley and Apestegui were inseparable on board the *Seabed Prince.* They were a pair of archaeological detectives, analyzing images of the site to determine what had happened to the *San José* after it crashed into the seafloor. Once again, the bronze cannons were critical clues. Twenty-two of them were strewn about like pick-up sticks. Forty of them were unaccounted for. Several had spilled over the port side of the galleon, suggesting that the entire port flank—everything above the waterline—had toppled in that direction, taking much of the deck, several cannons, and the galleon's largest anchor with it. The surface of the wreck, it seemed, corresponded to one of the lower decks.

The thousands of photographs taken of the wreck were digitally stitched together, using specialty software, into a single high-resolution photo mosaic that resembled an aerial shot of the site. For Dooley and Apestegui, this composite image was the most revelatory of all. By mapping the known dimensions of the *San José* onto the photo mosaic, the two could now see that the entire bow—the front third of the ship—was missing. Where it should have been was instead a dip in the seafloor. This absence told a story of horrific violence, at last elucidating the mystery of the ship's rapid sinking. There appeared to be a clean break roughly between where the mainmast and the foremast had once been planted. The break was at the level of the powder magazine, where munitions were stored. Examining this evidence, Dooley reasoned that his initial hypothesis had been wrong: It appeared likely that there had indeed been an explosion—perhaps not the hellish fireball that Wager had described, let alone the fanciful depictions of English paintings and maps that showed human figures being projected high into the sky, but powerful enough to split the galleon in two and blow away the foremast, to which the few survivors had been clinging. Its exact cause could be determined only by a thorough excavation, if it could be determined at all. Until the missing bow was found, it would remain a mystery.

To Dooley's trained eye, this subtle decline in the level of the seabed brought the last moments of the *San José* to life as only archaeology can, attesting to the horrors much as the pyroclastic flow of Mt. Vesuvius forever preserved the final agony of Pompeii's citizens. Dooley mentally placed himself within the *San José* at the moment of the detonation he now believed had taken place. Those closest to the explosion would have had the quickest and most merciful deaths. The blast cracked the hull apart and immediately the sea invaded the ship, rushing into every space, climbing from deck to deck, bursting into every room as if animated by murderous rage. Soon the *San José* was no more seaworthy than a sideways bucket. The hundreds trapped inside scurried alongside the rats to what few pockets of air remained, many of which would have been unbreathable, saturated with smoke from the fire that had spread throughout the ship. Within seconds, the water extinguished all the flames and lanterns, and in their final seconds the men and boys within the sinking carcass of the *San José* would have heard screams, coughs, gasps, and gurgles in total darkness. Once the water submerged them, they would have experienced nothing but the panic of death, and an unendurable pain in their ears from the crushing pressure as they dropped, weighted with tons of silver and gold, to the ocean floor hundreds of meters below.

Dooley didn't believe that any human remains would be found on the site. "The ship opened up completely," he said. "Everyone drowned and remained floating. The people weren't encased inside like in a submarine." Whatever bodies did fall within the galleon or plummet alongside it were probably on decks that remained above the seafloor and have since collapsed or disappeared. They would thus likely have been devoured long ago by the organisms large and small that lived on the wreck. If he was right, then Spain's designation of the site as a war grave would have no merit, since it would be an empty tomb. But that was far from certain. Dooley and his fellow archaeologist Montenegro frequently debated the question.

"The chances are very low," Montenegro said, "But what if a body is buried in the mud?" The conditions below the seabed, he added, were conducive to the preservation of organic matter. "We have a pH that is alkaline but not incompatible with bones. We have a very good temperature, and we have biological activity that is not drilling down."

The truth of what happened to the men of the *San José* perhaps lay right on the surface of the wreck. Biologists on the expedition found it odd that thousands of white seashells lay within the outline of the ship, and virtually none beyond. One Colombian scientist, who was unaffiliated with MAC but had reviewed the images, stated that the bivalves would have had to draw the calcium carbonate they needed to form their shells from a nearby deposit. The most abundant source of the stuff in the immediate surroundings, he posited, would have been the skeletons of the galleon's passengers and crew. If the theory is correct, each shell is the fragment of a ghost.

Chapter 28

"I Was Not Meant to Die That Day"

Dooley's two expeditions cost MAC a combined $7 million, pocket change compared to what Anthony Clake hoped to gain from his share of the *San José*'s treasure. The data collected in 2015 and 2016 formed the basis of MAC's official proposal to excavate the galleon. Dooley's plan involved working around the clock for several months, alternating eight-hour shifts with two world-renowned maritime specialists: the Falkland Islands–born, Oxford-trained archaeologist Mensun Bound, whose storied career included fieldwork on Henry VIII's *Mary Rose,* an ancient Etruscan vessel, a sixteenth-century cargo ship in the South China Sea, and a Nazi battleship off Montevideo; and the Norwegian marine technology specialist Fredrik Søreide, who had conducted the only purely archaeological deepwater excavation in history, on an eighteenth-century wreck about 170 meters deep in the Norwegian Sea in the mid-2000s. Dooley designed a plan that was, if anything, overzealous in its archaeological diligence, as if to deflect accusations that he was a treasure hunter. It called for the construction of a giant metal framework around the wreck, to anchor the remotely operated robots in place and ensure that they didn't accidentally disturb the site. Dooley estimated that the cost of such an operation would be about $70 million, which would make it the most expensive underwater excavation ever.

MAC submitted Dooley's plan to the Santos government in September 2016. It was considered the only official bid, though the state did receive letters of interest from parties in France, the United States, and Colombia. None was more than a few pages long. They could not compete with the vast amount of data Dooley had gathered in his two surveys of the galleon, with the knowledge he had accumulated over the course of his thirty-year obsession, or with his seemingly inexhaustible financing.

As far as Dooley was concerned, the approval of MAC's proposal was a fait accompli. It would just be a matter of time before he would be allowed back to properly interrogate the wreck of the *San José* and caress its artifacts with his own hands. But he had not counted on the determination of his enemies.

As MAC's proposal worked its way through various state agencies and lawyers, which demanded revision after revision, opponents of the government's galleon project endeavored to block it, or at least slow it down so that no contract could be signed by the end of Santos's final term. The self-appointed leader of this opposition was a pugnacious Cartagena historian named Francisco Muñoz, a member of the local historical academy whose name adorned plaques on landmarks throughout the city. In September 2017, Muñoz formed a one-man watchdog agency he called, grandly, the National Oversight Office for the Social Control of the Submerged Cultural Heritage of Colombia (VNPCS per its initials in Spanish). Through this entity, Muñoz overwhelmed the government with letters, petitions, and requests for information about the *San José* project, throwing sand in the gears of the political machine and casting Dooley's hopes back into limbo.

Critics like the Spanish journalist Jesús García Calero and the Colombian archaeologist Juan Guillermo Martín rallied to his banner, as did a number of independent lawyers and journalists. Their efforts lifted the veil of secrecy that had so far concealed the involvement of MAC from the public. Though Clake's anonymity was preserved, the revelation that the money behind the project originated in England, the homeland of Commodore Wager, only inflamed the opposition's ire.

It was obvious to Muñoz that MAC and the Santos administration were conspiring to steal the treasure that belonged to the Colombian people. "The robbers are going to flee the bank, escorted by police," he told me.

For all his righteous indignation at the idea of commercializing the San José's patrimonial riches, Muñoz found common cause with the unabashed treasure hunters at Sea Search Armada. He echoed SSA's argument that MAC had simply "rediscovered" the same debris field that Sea Search Armada had supposedly identified in 1982. The surprising alignment of Muñoz and SSA gave rise to widespread suspicions—shared with me by Colombian officials—that the latter was funding the former. Muñoz denied this, and it seemed just as likely that the two joined forces on the principle that the enemy of an enemy is a friend.

Muñoz found an ally within the government as well. Leandro Ramos, a young deputy attorney at the Office of the Inspector General of Colombia—which held other state institutions to account—issued a report in March 2018 identifying perceived irregularities in the bidding process. The document accused the Santos administration of favoritism for allowing MAC to make numerous revisions to its proposal over more than a year. Ramos was more forceful with his condemnation in a subsequent interview, describing MAC as "these pirates from England," and President Santos as the "boss" of a "criminal plot" to make off with the San José's treasure.

In a country prone to conspiracy theorizing, this spy-thriller notion of a sordid alliance between Santos and English elites took hold. From his perch at the right-wing Spanish paper Diario ABC, Calero fanned the flames by evoking a persistent rumor. "Is Tony Blair also in the operation, as has been said?" he asked in a 2018 column. "The former Labor prime minister manages investments in Colombian mining concessions due to his friendship with Santos. There are no more

indications." Calero indeed offered no evidence to support the impu-
tation, which a spokesperson for Blair vociferously denied.

Sea Search Armada, for its part, fully endorsed the notion of an
international conspiracy. "This scheme to steal at least SSA's share of
the San Jose," the company's director, Jack Harbeston, believed, "had
to involve political figures in Colombia, the U.S. and Great Britain."

When Santos was asked about these allegations, he laughed them
off. "Some of them insinuated that I had an economic motive," he said
of his detractors. "And I said, 'I wish I did!'"

IN UNCOVERING THE PAPER TRAIL of the government's dealings
with MAC, Muñoz, Calero, Ramos, and their allies at last discovered
the name that Santos had been so careful to keep concealed: Roger
Dooley. Opposition sleuths dug up what little biographical information
could be found on him. It was no simple task, since Dooley had spent
most of his life behind Cuba's totalitarian wall, had later worked mostly
on hush-hush operations, and had a virtually nonexistent public profile.
But diligent googling revealed that Dooley had been on the U.S. Treasury's OFAC watch list, colloquially referred to in Latin America as the
"Clinton list." It soon also emerged that he had also worked for Carisub, among outfits that were notorious among maritime scholars for
their unprincipled ways. Since Dooley had been urged by Montenegro
and other government officials not to speak publicly or engage with
the opposition, he could not defend himself. He had no chance to explain that complex and relatively innocuous circumstances had landed
him on the list, that he had been removed from the list, or that he had
resigned from Carisub over its archaeologically unethical practices. The
critics had all the evidence they needed to conclude that, as one of
them told me, Dooley was "a criminal guy, involved in many salvages
in the Caribbean Sea, maybe involved in drug trafficking and illegal
trafficking of persons between Cuba and the United States."

▪ ▪ ▪

THE CRITICISM DID NOTHING to diminish Santos's personal affection for Dooley or his belief in the project. His administration successfully fought off every challenge to its partnership with MAC, and the two parties signed a contract for the excavation of the wreck on March 23, 2018. In the final version, the government agreed to give MAC a share of up to 45 percent of the *San José*'s nonpatrimonial gold and silver. MAC further agreed to contribute to the construction of a major new museum in Cartagena to conserve and display the galleon's artifacts. UNESCO promptly issued a letter of condemnation, but Colombia had made it clear that the international organization had no say in its undersea affairs.

It seemed Santos and MAC had won. Yet the opposition's delay tactics had succeeded in running out the clock. With elections set for the spring of 2018, Santos had just a few weeks left in his term, and the president had every reason to expect his successor would work to undo his proudest achievements, following the pendulum effect that held sway in Latin American politics. He had been bested.

On July 23 of that year, the day he was supposed to announce the public-private partnership to excavate the wreck, Santos returned to the national airwaves to make a different, more regretful declaration: He was suspending the process.

This was a far cry from Santos's triumphant first press conference three years before. The swagger was gone. Here was a man defeated but defiant. The outgoing president attributed the decision to sustained activism by "concerned citizens," to which he affixed a disdainful pair of air quotes. With nothing left to lose—or perhaps in the hope that his successor, the right-wing Iván Duque, would restart the partnership—he at last introduced the nation to the true discoverers of the *San José*. Though he still didn't identify MAC's principal financier, whom he referred to simply as "the Originator," Santos namechecked the search expedition's main participants, including Woods Hole and Garry Kozak, describing them once again as a "dream team."

And at long last, he spoke the name of the man who had cracked the mystery of the *San José*. The driving force behind the effort, he said, had been an archaeologist named Roger Dooley: "Thanks to the studies of Dr. Dooley"—the honorific "doctor" reflecting not a PhD but rather a peculiarly Colombian expression of respect—"it was possible to establish an effective search area." Santos then played a longer video documenting the search effort in 2015. The moment Dooley appeared on camera, it was clear: white hair, white beard. Here was "Hemingway." The video even showed Adriana crying.

FOR DOOLEY, SANTOS'S PARTING GIFT came too late. Dooley's dream had come to an end, and the recognition he had long craved had by then curdled into opprobrium.

The most troubling of the accusations against him came from Jack Harbeston, his onetime collaborator turned nemesis. Upon hearing that Roger Dooley was behind the discovery of the *San José*, the director of Sea Search Armada flew into a rage. He told the press that he believed it highly likely Dooley had stolen the coordinates of the galleon while working for him on the excavation of the *Santa Margarita* in the Pacific.

Sea Search Armada would later suggest that this had been Dooley's intention all along. Harbeston's daughter Kathleen Harbeston-Regn, who would largely take over from her elderly father in SSA's fight against the Colombian government, implied as much in describing the circumstances that led Dooley to get hired on that project as a field archaeologist under Dan Koski-Karell. "He just happened to come off the Clinton list, then happened to be at the same conference as Sea Search Armada's lead archaeologist," Regn told me. "Things magically happen occasionally, but it seems like there's a tremendous amount of coincidences in that timeline. And he's known for being obsessed [with the *San José*] long before he became an employee" of Harbeston's. "So there's motive there."

As supposed evidence of this convoluted plot, Harbeston leaked to the press the email that Dooley had written him in 2010, asking about the possibility of a partnership. He also told journalists that he had found files related to the galleon on Dooley's desktop after he left the island of Rota. "When we were routinely cleaning out the computers at the end of the work season," he said, "I found on his computer notes about the *San José* and they were in Spanish. . . . He just didn't do a good job of cleaning it off his hard disk. So this worried me." Harbeston shared these jottings with me. They consisted of emails to family and to fellow researchers, inquiring mostly about other shipwrecks. They did contain one page of notes on the *San José,* including reference numbers of *legajos* at the Seville archives, as well as the possible coordinates of the shipwreck. But, inconveniently for Harbeston's theory, this suggested position was many miles away from that reported by SSA in 1982. (In fact, it was on land, in Venezuela.) Altogether, this would-be smoking gun confirmed only Dooley's long-standing fixation on the galleon, which was no secret.

For Dooley, Harbeston's accusation was not only preposterous and insulting but fundamentally illogical. "If I had found the *San José* by stealing their coordinates," he said, "I would have found it at those coordinates," rather than three miles away.

Those coordinates, moreover, were widely acknowledged—including by Sea Search Armada—to have been inaccurate. Many believed that Warren Stearns, SSA's chief backer in the early '80s, intentionally reported incorrect coordinates, either to strengthen his negotiating position with the government or perhaps to buy time in order to properly find the galleon. SSA had described the site around the target as a rugged, coral-covered slope about two hundred meters deep. No such terrain existed anywhere near the reported coordinates, according to topographical charts.

What, then, was the vaguely ship-like form picked up in 1981 by the side-scan sonar mounted to the *Auguste Piccard,* Glocca Morra's submarine? This sonar reading was, after all, the central element supporting Sea Search Armada's claim to the galleon. Since it had been established that the bow of the *San José* broke off, likely as the result of an explosion, could that section of the ship have drifted and landed miles away from the stern? Could both objects not have been two different parts of the *San José*?

Rodrigo Pacheco-Ruiz, a marine archaeologist at the University of Southampton who has aligned himself with the UNESCO camp, was doubtful. "If this was a shipwreck and not a natural rocky outcrop, I would say that it could be more a metal-hulled ship," he told me after analyzing SSA's sonar image.

SSA nevertheless insisted on the possibility that the object they had found was the missing bow of the ship. Yet they also claimed that it was about 140 feet long, approximately the same length as the entire vessel. Both things could not be true. As for the single cannon SSA had caught on video, even a lay observer could see that it was unlike the bronze cannons that littered the wreck—it was stubbier, more rugged, almost certainly made of iron and thus likely not from a *capitana* or an *almiranta*. There was no dolphin on the breech. What's more, former members of the Glocca Morra crew admitted they could never find their way back to the gun. (Dooley conceded that the *San José* had at one point carried dozens of iron cannons in its hull as ballast but said the guns had been left behind in Portobelo in 1708 and replaced with river rocks.)

There was strong evidence to suggest that whatever Glocca Morra found in 1981 was not the *San José,* and that the remains of the galleon were discovered by Roger Dooley in 2015. But it didn't matter. While the details of Dooley's expeditions remained a state secret, Harbeston's allegations had been picked up by news outlets across the Spanish-speaking world. A few weeks earlier, Dooley had no public reputation. Now SSA had succeeded in vilifying him and undermining what little renown he'd acquired.

In the wake of Harbeston's accusations, even MAC distanced itself from the archaeologist. A representative for the company Dooley had helped create told the Colombian press that MAC executives "did not know Mr. Roger Dooley before 2013," or know that Dooley had had any contact with Sea Search Armada, until he disclosed that information in May 2018. Faced with the threat of litigation over the alleged theft of information, MAC downgraded Dooley—the man who had single-handedly defined the search area and wrangled the resources and technology behind the discovery—to merely "one of the researchers who provided information and worked jointly with the company." The message was clear: Dooley was on his own again.

IN THE END, BOTH MAC AND SSA would be cut out of the action. As Santos predicted, his successor in Bogotá's presidential palace, the hardliner Iván Duque, rolled back nearly all of his signature achievements, including the contract with MAC. Rather than take sides in the controversy, the new administration punted. Vice president Marta Lucía Ramírez, tasked with managing the issue, declared in 2020 that the *San José* shipwreck and all of its contents were "assets of cultural interest." As a consequence, no artifact could be sold or even leave Colombia. SSA had claimed 50 percent of the treasure, and MAC only slightly less. But after Ramírez's ruling—which the UNESCO camp applauded, as it would leave the galleon in situ—neither could claim a single peso.

Dooley had never stood to profit from the treasure itself, but Ramírez's decision deflated any hope he'd had of excavating the wreck, at least until another president came to power.

The removal of the galleon from his life left Dooley with a profound sense of grief. The ship had been the first and last thing Dooley had thought about most days for decades. After all this time, he could not simply stop thinking about it. Since the wreck itself was off-limits, Dooley set about learning everything he did not yet know about the *capitana*. He returned to the General Archive of the Indies in Seville and consulted with a variety of experts in shipbuilding, iconography, artillery, and other fields.

In time, he tracked down an all-important *legajo* that he believed would chronicle in detail all the modifications made to the galleon before it left for the Americas from Cádiz, Spain. Dooley thought the *legajo* would be the keystone to the archival edifice he was meticulously constructing. But when he requested it, he was told it was among the few bundles that had been affected by the fire that tore through the archive in the 1920s. Whatever was left of them was too delicate to handle. The revelation would torture Dooley from then on: There would always be something about the *San José* he would not know.

His bottomless obsession left him feeling alone, resentful of the people he believed to be sabotaging his project. "I'm the only one who cares about the damn ship," he told me. The archaeologist still believed he would excavate the *capitana* one day, no matter how distant. His resolve remained unaffected. His body, however, was not so resilient.

The last thing Dooley remembered from the afternoon of May 25, 2021, was walking up to his building in Miami with a bag of groceries. Witnesses would recall what happened next, how he collapsed in the lobby and the items he'd been carrying spilled across the ground. A neighbor rushed to his side and performed CPR. Adriana had been waiting for him to return from the supermarket when the head of security arrived at the door of their apartment to tell her that Dooley had been taken to the hospital. When Adriana got there, doctors informed her that her husband had had three more cardiac arrests in the ambulance. They gave him a 10 percent chance of survival.

Adriana entered Dooley's room and saw him lying unconscious, hooked to machines, seemingly lifeless. She remembered reading in a book that, at the moment of death, the soul stays close for a while before leaving the body. Through the sobs, she spoke to him to keep his soul from fleeing.

"Don't leave me," she pleaded. "I need you." She then appealed to his deepest desire: "You must fulfill your dream of seeing the *San José* galleon."

Dooley wouldn't open his eyes for another three days. His chest was open for much of that time as surgeons performed multiple operations on him, during the course of which his heart stopped again. Dooley survived thanks in part to a valve from a pig's heart. By the time I met him, several weeks later, he had made a total recovery, speaking and gesticulating at his usual clip, and eating *ropa vieja* and ice cream with abandon. He lifted his shirt to reveal a large scar across his torso.

"I was not meant to die that day," he told me. "I was meant to excavate the *San José*."

BY THE TAIL END OF DUQUE'S TERM IN 2022, MAC had taken down its website and gone dormant. Anthony Clake had essentially written off the *San José* project as a $7 million loss. While he had failed to secure the greatest treasure in history, the experience had supercharged his passion for ocean exploration. In 2017, Clake founded his own marine robotics company called Ocean Infinity, which grew to be one of the leading surveyors in the world, deploying a fleet of highly advanced AUVs and ROVs to search for natural resources and wrecks. At its head, he placed former MAC director Oliver Plunkett, who promptly made a splashy announcement that the company would search for the fuselage of Malaysia Airlines Flight MH370, which was thought to have crashed in the Indian Ocean in 2014. The aircraft would remain undiscovered, but Ocean Infinity scored a coup in 2018 by finding the wreck of another elusive vessel, the Argentinian navy submarine A.R.A. *San Juan,* which had gone missing in the southern Atlantic a year before with forty-four sailors aboard.

Clake was also behind the discovery in early 2022 of one of the only other shipwrecks that could rival the *San José*'s legendary status: the *Endurance,* Antarctic explorer Ernest Shackleton's three-masted barquentine that was crushed in the ice of the Weddell Sea in 1915. The archaeologist who found it was Mensun Bound, whom Clake and Dooley had selected to help excavate the *San José*. Bound vowed that the *Endurance*—perfectly preserved in frigid Antarctic waters—would remain untouched.

The same could not be said of many other wrecks that Clake had gone after, several of which had been filled with treasure. The hedge fund titan's relentless pursuit of undersea riches would lead *Bloomberg Businessweek* to name him the "Lord of the Deep" in an article that shattered his jealously guarded anonymity and revealed him to be the mysterious "Originator" of the *San José* search. Dooley was shocked to read the *Businessweek* exposé, which reported, among other things, that Clake had a 25 percent stake in a search and salvage effort that sent robots 4,500 meters down to extract fifty tons of silver coins from a Scottish freighter that sank off the coast of West Africa in 1942; after being melted down, the silver was sold. "I don't know what to say," Dooley told me.

With MAC seemingly out of the picture, the question of how to finance the excavation became ever more uncertain. The last year of President Duque's term was roiled by sweeping nationwide protests against proposed new taxes and government corruption, which led to several deaths in clashes with police. Amid such furor over basic standards of living, it was hardly conceivable that the government would fund an ambitious deepwater excavation—likely costing more than the entire annual budget of the Ministry of Culture—with public money. Let alone a new museum.

Dooley believed Ramírez's decision to declare the wreck and its contents objects of cultural interest, and thus off-limits, made it less likely that the galleon's artifacts would ever break the surface of the sea. The math just didn't work. By outlawing the sale of objects of which there are many nearly identical specimens, the government would be saddled with the cost of conserving more artifacts than any museum could possibly display. "What are you gonna do with a million coins?" he asked.

Dooley had long claimed to be unconcerned by the *San José*'s treasure. "The gold and silver are the least interesting part of the wreck," he told me. But he acknowledged that they were the sources of the global fascination with the galleon. And he continued to see in them a means of financing the excavation. Refusing to accept defeat, he devised a new plan. He imagined that the gold and silver could be entrusted to the Bank of Colombia, to do what it pleased with the precious metals. The coins that were not displayed could be used to bolster the country's reserves of gold and silver and justify the payment of private contractors to salvage the wreck. To propose the plan, however, he would have to await the results of Colombia's presidential elections, a contest that in its final round pitted the populist businessman Rodolfo Hernández against the leftist former guerrilla Gustavo Petro. It was unclear which would be more amenable to Dooley's idea.

DUQUE'S ADMINISTRATION HAD RESOLVED not to touch the archaeological site of the *San José*, but this did not mean that his government would do nothing. In the spring of 2022, the country's navy embarked on its own nonintrusive survey of the shipwreck and its surroundings, using a newly acquired remotely operated vehicle mounted with a camera. The Swedish-made Saab Lynx was smaller, cheaper, and generally less capable than the advanced machine Dooley had relied on in 2016. (Dooley would spitefully call it a "Mickey Mouse ROV" good for "inspecting pipes" and not much else.) But it had the benefit of belonging to the nation. It would allow the state to no longer depend on outsiders, who had their own intentions—noble or not—concerning the galleon. This would be a Colombian mission, aboard a new Colombian research vessel, employing Colombian equipment and Colombian personnel.

When the navy's ship A.R.C. *Caribe* arrived at the coordinates of the *San José*, on May 7, 2022, the research team brought out a flower arrangement that had been made by a *palenquera*—one of the many traditionally dressed descendants of African slaves that roam the streets of Old Cartagena with bowls of tropical fruit balanced on their heads, a fixture of tourists' Instagram feeds. The team threw the arrangement in the water above the resting place of the galleon and its men.

"We made a ceremony in order to say thanks to those souls and to request their permission and ensure them that we didn't have any intention to disturb them," recalled Capt. Alexandra Chadid, the scientific director of the expedition.

Technical problems plagued the expedition on the first day. One of the researchers had thought to bring a vial of holy water, blessed by a priest in Cartagena. Rosary in hand, he sprinkled the water on the malfunctioning ROV, which, by Chadid's account, miraculously began working. By the time it descended to the site, it was the wee hours of May 8. Chadid and her team saw this as an auspicious sign, as the number 8 seemed to appear everywhere in this story. The battle, for example, had taken place on June 8, 1708. And among the first objects caught on the ROV's video camera was an eight-escudo gold coin.

The naval officer in charge of the entire *San José* project going forward would be Herman León, a military oceanographer who had been an observer on Dooley's two expeditions and had since risen to the rank of vice admiral. For León, the galleon was not just the most valuable shipwreck in history but a powerful emblem of Colombian sovereignty. By developing its subsea capabilities, however modest at first, and tending to its own underwater cultural heritage, Colombia would be taking a step toward realizing its full geopolitical potential. As the state strove to extricate itself from a century of conflict with armed dissidents and drug cartels, the *San José* could provide the chance to tell a more positive, flourishing story about what Colombia might become.

"Some countries live in ice, some countries live in desert," he told me. "We have the Caribbean, which is much bigger than the Mediterranean. And we have the Pacific also. Our nature is to be a great ocean nation. This national symbol can identify, as Gabriel García Márquez said, an opportunity for a life beyond the war." This triumphant narrative, he said, would find its fullest expression in a new museum built in Cartagena to showcase the galleon's history, its artifacts, and its heaps of gold and silver. "This is our goal," León said. "That's why we need to do it by ourselves."

▪   ▪   ▪

ON JUNE 19, 2022, GUSTAVO PETRO was elected president, becoming Colombia's first leftist leader. He would take up residence at the Casa de Nariño, the presidential palace in Central Bogotá, just steps away from the Palace of Justice that his rebel movement, the M-19, had besieged in 1985 in a deadly assault. Petro, who at the time went by the pseudonym of Aureliano—after the revolutionary protagonist of García Márquez's *One Hundred Years of Solitude*—denied participating in the siege, citing a solid alibi: He had been in jail.

Given his radical past, and the fact that he had campaigned as a champion of the poor, there was reason to doubt the new president's willingness to devote millions of dollars to excavating the gold-filled galleon. Yet there was equally good reason to suspect that he would support anything his predecessor, Duque, had been against.

As always, Dooley put his faith in the more optimistic possibility. He was confident that he could bring the president over to his way of thinking as long as he could be in the room with him.

Santos was hopeful as well, having succumbed to Dooley's strange magnetism himself. The centrist former president did not publicly agree with Petro on much, but they enjoyed a cordial relationship behind the scenes, at least at first. Santos, who remained fixated on the galleon and regularly met with Dooley, helped arrange a meeting between him and Petro a few months into the president's new term.

Dooley arrived at the Casa de Nariño on the afternoon of November 3, nearly an hour early. Once again, he had brought large-format visual aids to help him tell the story of the galleon, including the copy of the 1729 "Shoals of the Admiral" map and four large posters designed by his daughter Lili.

Dooley, whose hair had grown long during the COVID pandemic, was still setting up in a conference room adjacent to Petro's office when the president poked his head in. When he saw the energetic seventy-eight-year-old propping posters up on stands, he apologized.

"Oh, okay, I'll come back," said Petro, smiling beneath his thick-framed rectangular glasses.

The Dooley show was about to begin. The archaeologist was told he had just thirty minutes with the Colombian leader, but he appeared to be in no rush. He introduced himself and relished the expression on Petro's face when he tried to reconcile Dooley's Cuban accent with his Irish surname and complexion. This had long been a reliable ice-breaker for Dooley, a way into his life's story. He recounted his childhood in Havana, his formative run-ins with Castro and the *barbudos,* his years in the militia and the 116th Battalion, and his exploration of Cuba's shipwrecks. Petro was hooked. As a committed leftist and one-time rebel, he was not reflexively turned off by Castro: He appreciated the romance of his revolutionary movement and its ideals. Dooley's Cuban journey, and the compromises that it had forced him to make, had long been a source of suspicion and had caused him to become a pariah among purist archaeologists. But in the president's eyes, that backstory became Dooley's greatest selling point.

Transitioning masterfully to the *San José,* Dooley told Petro about his fateful discovery of Governor Zúñiga's letters at Seville's Archive of the Indies in 1984. He recounted the history of the galleon, listed the factors that made its wreck unique, and explained why its excavation would shed light on the foundation of the modern world and present an unparalleled opportunity for Colombia.

"You don't know how lucky you are," Dooley said. "It is the only *capitana* that ever sank. Second, it sank in deep water, so nobody touched it. Third, the hull was buried in soft sediment, so the cargo is likely in perfect condition. It is the perfect wreck. Excavating it in deep water will be very expensive, sure, but if it had been in shallower water, it would have been destroyed and pillaged."

Petro had not expected much to come of the meeting, which he'd agreed to out of respect for a predecessor. He had not mentioned the galleon in his presidential campaign and had every incentive to avoid the political pitfalls associated with it. But whatever his first impressions had been when he walked in to find the strange archaeologist in the conference room, he had by now been converted to Dooley's cause.

He asked his trusted personal aide Laura Sarabia to cancel his afternoon meetings. For the next few hours, he and Dooley would plan the future of the *San José*. The president was especially excited about the prospect of building a new maritime museum in Cartagena. He even had an idea for who could run it.

"Roger, you're married to a Colombian?" the president asked.

"Yes."

"Why don't you retire in Cartagena and become the director of the *San José* museum?"

Dooley could hardly believe what Petro was suggesting. Seconds before, he would never have dared to dream of such a scenario, and yet he could think of no better way to spend his final years. He heartily agreed.

While they were talking, a package had arrived at the presidential palace. It had come in the nick of time from the framer to whom Dooley had entrusted a copy of a painting he had commissioned, depicting the *San José* at sea in exacting detail, according to his meticulous research. Dooley opened the package and gifted the framed artwork to Petro. He would have given the president the original, but it hung over Anthony Clake's mantelpiece in London.

That evening, Dooley called me from the airport.

"I can't talk much over the phone," he said, "but I just met with the big guy." Dooley sounded ecstatic but tired. "This changes everything."

Following Petro's meeting with Dooley, Sarabia scheduled meetings for Dooley with the head of the Colombian navy, the new minister of culture, the new head of ICANH (the national institute for anthropology and archaeology), and the minister of finance, to whom Dooley would lay out his idea for how Colombia could fund the excavation without relinquishing a single coin.

Petro expressed his desire to see the excavation of the galleon happen by the end of his four-year term, in 2026. The picture that the archaeologist had gifted him was displayed prominently on his office wall, where all visitors and TV cameras could see it. In an interview with Colombian radio, he credited Dooley with the discovery of the ship and argued that his contribution should be recognized.

"He is a Cuban-gringo gentleman who became a *miliciano,* then became an expert on Spanish ships, and is also the most knowledge-able authority on the history of the galleon *San José,*" Petro said. "It was he who made a calculation, based on history, of where it could be, and located it along with the national navy."

Dooley's work, he continued, "must be rewarded because in the end the goal is to salvage [the *San José*'s contents]. . . . The Galleon no longer exists, but the treasure remains."

Long an advocate of Indigenous causes, Petro also acknowledged the Qhara Qhara nation's claims to that treasure, much of which had been pried from the group's ancestral lands in Potosí. He proposed a way to right the wrongs of history by giving its members a share of profits from the yet-to-be-built museum. Such an initiative was in line with a broader effort of his left-wing government to, as Petro put it, "decolonize culture."

NEWS OF PETRO'S DETERMINATION to salvage the galleon, as well as his full-throated appreciation of Dooley, reinvigorated the enemies of the project. Their de facto leader, historian Francisco Muñoz—who had since moved to Sweden—renewed his calls for the government to investigate what he called "the alleged looting of the wreck of the galleon *San José.*"

Muñoz and his acolytes had long pointed to small discrepancies on the surface of the wreck in comparing survey photos from 2015 to those from 2016—ceramic pots that became slightly more exposed, different arrangements of seashells, shifting mounds of silt—as proof that MAC and the Santos government had illegally extracted objects from the site. At a depth of six hundred meters, such changes are likely not due to the current, which is almost nonexistent, as Dooley's 2016 survey confirmed.

Dooley asserted that no artifact had been touched on his watch, and he attributed changes at the site to natural phenomena. "Our wreck lies in an area that is almost flat, compose[d] 95% of silt and clay (like mud)," Dooley wrote in an email. "Therefore, once our wreck arrived it create[d] like an oasis, in the desert, like a small reef, with plenty of wood, hiding and protecting places, holes, etc., therefore it was invaded by many marine organisms." The most likely culprits, he said, were larger fish in search of food, who flapped their fins to move the sand around.

Navy sources who examined the site in 2022 confirmed that it had not been disturbed and seconded Dooley's explanation. Muñoz's crusade to charge the Santos government with piracy seemed obviously doomed until March 18, 2024, when Colombia's congress announced that it would investigate Juan Manuel Santos himself for the crime of looting. No one seemed more surprised than Muñoz, who tweeted, "Miracle! Miracle!"

In an interview that took place days later, Vice Admiral León, the officer in charge of the *San José* project, had no patience for Muñoz and his stunts. "This is speculation," he said of the accusations against Santos. "I think that in the future [Muñoz and his allies] will receive what they deserve because they are destroying the life of a lot of people that are involved in the project. Not only Roger [Dooley], but the minister [of culture], the president. . . ." León was particularly outraged by the international embarrassment caused by the investigation of a former president for the theft of a national treasure. "It is like someone in Colombia hearing the news that President Obama went to the Library of Congress in Washington and stole the Declaration of Independence."

Meanwhile, Muñoz's strange bedfellows at Sea Search Armada pursued their case against the Colombian government. Now in his early nineties, Jack Harbeston was not going anywhere. Having received a series of unfavorable or inconclusive judgments in Colombian and U.S. courts, he and his associates took their forty-year-old claims of expropriation to the International Court of Arbitration in the Hague in December 2022. By declaring the *San José* and its contents to be assets of cultural interest, the complaint argued, Colombia had robbed SSA of its 50 percent share of the galleon's gold and silver, or $10 billion, according to the company's new back-of-the-napkin math estimating the *San José*'s treasure at $20 billion.

In the course of the case, the Colombian government sought to put SSA's claim to rest once and for all. To prove beyond a doubt that what the treasure hunters had claimed to have found was not the *San José,* the nation's lawyers turned in late 2024 to the same internationally respected organization Dooley had called upon to survey his search area: the Woods Hole Oceanographic Institute, which charged $1.4 million for the job. Once again, the REMUS 6000 roamed the waters off Cartagena. Once again, WHOI found nothing remotely resembling a shipwreck at the coordinates reported by SSA in 1982, about three nautical miles from the site Dooley found in 2015. They did, however, locate an anomaly that seemed to match the sonar reading identified by Sea Search Armada as "Target A," that is, the *San José.* It was more than five miles away from Dooley's wreck. Their suspicions were confirmed when they found what appeared to be the metal basket left behind by the *Auguste Piccard.*

On May 22, 2024, during an unseasonal downpour that was flooding the streets of Cartagena, journalists, sailors, and government officials massed beneath a tarp on the deck of the military research ship A.R.C. *Simón Bolívar,* docked at the naval base along the bay. The Ministry of Culture had gathered everyone for a press conference to announce the launch of a new exploration of the wreck site, which would—it was hoped—at last pave the way for an excavation.

Officials were in a celebratory mood. Presiding over the event was Petro's culture minister, Juan David Correa, a thin, balding, bespectacled, heavily tattooed forty-something in a short-sleeved cow-print shirt, who would look more at home behind the counter of a record store than behind a podium. The gathering included many longtime participants in the *San José* saga, such as Montenegro, León, Monroy, and Chadid; representatives of Bolivia's Qhara Qhara nation and Colombia's Kogui people, dressed in colorful traditional garb and chewing coca leaves; and two young musicians representing the local Afro-Colombian community, whose brief performance served as a reminder of Cartagena's central role in the slave trade of the Americas during the Spanish Empire.

Correa shared few concrete details about the plans for the expedition, which would depart that week aboard the A.R.C. *Caribe,* save that this first phase would be a nonintrusive data-gathering operation. The true purpose of the meeting, culture ministry officials made clear, was to "change the narrative" around the *San José,* to shift the emphasis from its legendary gold and silver to the plight of the human beings whose lives and lands had been sacrificed to extract it.

"There are particular interests that continue to haunt this story with the greed and avarice of those who want to continue seeing this as the possibility of a treasure and not as what it really is," Correa said, in a veiled condemnation of all those who had sought to profit off the wreck over the years, from the Originator to Sea Search Armada. "The treasure," he said, "is history."

The history that mattered, in this case, was that which had too long been overlooked. There was an air of penance to the proceedings, a seeking of forgiveness and permission. One after the other, Indigenous leaders described the galleon as a vessel for telling their peoples' stories and confronting the atrocities committed against them. As they chanted in their native tongues, the event became something like an exorcism.

The day culminated in a speech by the Qhara Qhara elder Cenobio Fernández, alternating between Spanish and Quechua. "If we allow those resources"—the contents of the *San José*—"to once again fall into other hands, such as treasure hunters, or the Kingdom of Spain," Fernández said, "that would be violating once again the memory of our ancestors, who have suffered precisely so that those resources could be in the galleon *San José*. What was in there was the fruit of genocide." It was crucial, Fernández concluded, to honor the galleon's "spiritual value."

Conspicuously absent from the gathering—because he had once

again not been invited—was Roger Dooley, the man without whom there would have been no galleon to honor, no sins to expiate or ghosts to exorcise. After the conference, I sat with Correa in the bridge of the *Bolívar* and asked him whether he could foresee a role for Dooley in the future of the *San José,* given all he could contribute. After all, I reminded Correa, Dooley was sitting on terabytes of data about the site from his 2016 survey—likely far more than the navy could collect with its humbler ROV—which the government could have access to if it agreed to reimburse MAC's costs.

"We've spoken with Roger, and have a conversation pending," Correa said in an almost inaudibly soft voice, a large wad of coca leaves conspicuously stuffed into his cheek. "But this is not a moment for anyone outside our institutions to participate."

The minister quickly lapsed back to the spiritual agenda he had set for the day: "This is a moment of comprehension. The doors have never been closed, neither for him nor for anyone. Because we are setting out to tell the story in a different way and not act in the same way that the world has acted traditionally."

For all of this lofty talk of the galleon's world-changing potential, the government had set aside just $4 million for the project, and it was unclear how much more it could afford to spend.

The navy's expedition left Cartagena the day after the press conference and returned ten days after that. Correa spun the mission as a success, announcing that it had found previously undocumented artifacts. The minister hinted at another expedition within the following months to "conduct a small extraction" of artifacts on the surface of the wreck, perhaps "some crockery," to understand what might happen to these objects "upon contact with the atmosphere." Such an operation never took place.

That was as far ahead as the government was willing to look. At that pace, it was unlikely to find the funds for an ambitious excavation—the kind Dooley was once poised to lead—in the foreseeable future, let alone by the end of Petro's term. The president's priorities hadn't changed—he still believed in Dooley and his vision—but the forces both human and natural that had long kept the *San José* in Neptune's grip were too powerful to overcome.

MAC and Clake, for their part, expected the Colombian government to pay them back for their investment in Dooley's two expeditions, which, with interest, amounted to about $10 million by their count. In early 2025, the company sued Colombia for nonreimbursement and for reneging on the excavation contract signed with the government in 2018, citing damages of $50 million.

The cultural, legal, and political quagmire that followed the discovery validated Robert Marx's estimation that "treasure is trouble, and the more treasure, the more trouble."

A MAC official likewise reached the conclusion that the treasure of the *San José* was, in a manner of speaking, cursed. "It's one of those things that's really interesting to reflect on," he said, "whether, actually, everyone's lives would have been better off if it had never been found. The mystery was interesting enough, and finding it has only caused years of problems for more people."

Like many others involved in the saga, the official feared that plans for a thorough excavation would "never quite get there."

In the meantime, all those whose hopes were pinned on the revelation of the galleon's treasure and artifacts, on a discovery of the true cause of its sinking, and on the construction of a long-promised museum would continue to wait.

So would the galleon. It would sit patiently, quietly, at the same spot it had occupied for more than three centuries, a site of mass death but also of teeming life. It would transform and evolve, an organism in itself, ever so slowly digesting the traces of humanity it contained.

Epilogue

There's a Colombian saying: *La cara del santo hace el milagro.* The
face of the saint performs the miracle. In order to make something happen, best to show up in person. No one knows this better
than Roger Dooley, whose infectious passion for the *San José* has won
over two heads of state despite his unorthodox background. But a year
after his meeting with Petro, in which the president had embraced him
and vowed he would have a central role in the excavation, nothing had
come of it. Correa, Petro's culture minister, had kept him at arm's
length, and Ernesto Montenegro had taken the archaeological lead on
the project. If nothing changed, if he remained in Miami waiting for
his phone to ring, Dooley feared that he would be cast aside entirely.
He would have to be closer to the rooms in which the decisions were
being made.

He and Adriana decided to move to Colombia. When I visited
Dooley in Miami in January 2024, his possessions—his books, maps,
and endless files on the *San José*—were packed into boxes labeled
"Cartagena."

For the first time since I'd met him, he wasn't wearing his Rolex
Sea-Dweller, having just sold it for $10,000 to a dealer who surely had

no idea what it had represented. He didn't make a big deal of it, but I knew how sad he must have been to part with it. The watch had been his most cherished possession, and an object of animated discussion every time we'd met. It had reminded him of his late brother, who by giving him a Rolex, the ultimate status symbol in Castro's Cuba, had told him he loved him—something the Dooleys could never say in words. The timepiece had been on his wrist throughout his many adventures, had seen shipwrecks and presidents and billionaires. But it was also the most valuable thing he owned, and he needed the money. This was another reason to move to Colombia: His salary from MAC had long since run dry, and he could no longer afford to live in Miami as he waited to see what might happen with the *San José*. It was not in Dooley's nature to lament his fate, but I was heartbroken for him. Perhaps I had fallen under his peculiar spell as well. The impression I had formed of him, after three years of reporting on the race for the lost *capitana,* was fundamentally at odds with his public image as a modern pirate. I believed in the sincerity of his obsession with the ship itself. I believed that he cared about its treasure only inasmuch as it could get other, more powerful people as excited as he was about excavating the galleon.

Just two weeks before, Juan Guillermo Martín, one of the leaders of the *San José* opposition, characterized Dooley in an editorial as "a looter of wrecks who has made his fortune working for different companies that traffic in submerged cultural heritage around the world." Seeing Dooley surrounded by cardboard boxes, I noted the irony in that description. Not only had he not made a fortune, but he had gone broke in pursuit of a sunken dream. Rather than wallow in resentment and self-pity, however, Dooley continued to believe he could bring even his most ardent critics—including Martín—to his side. He just needed to get in a room with them.

As he took in the ocean view from his twenty-first-floor balcony for one last time, he recited another proverb, which he attributed to Spanish sailors: *Después de la tormenta siempre viene la calma.* After the storm always comes the calm.

When I had interviewed Juan Manuel Santos over coffee at his office, the former president compared Dooley to the protagonist of Hemingway's *The Old Man and the Sea*. It was an apt analogy: The novella tells the story of a perennially unlucky elderly Cuban fisherman who one day hooks a marlin of biblical proportions and refuses to let go even as sharks circle his skiff and attack his catch. The old man returns to shore with nothing to show for his struggle but the marlin's bones, collapses in his shack, and drifts off to sleep. Like the old man, Dooley caught the prey of his life in his autumn years and was immediately attacked by other predators. Like the old man, he was left with nothing but dreams. Yet his were not rueful reveries. They were plans. He did not ask himself *what if* but *what now*.

Dooley believed that the Petro administration's ambitions exceeded its means, and assumed that the government would eventually recognize this and either abandon the project or seek outside help. This would provide an opening for him. He devised a new plan to work his way back into the center of the galleon's story. As he had so many times before, he tacked across the headwinds, approaching his destination at an angle: He planned to create a nonprofit foundation dedicated to the study of the *San José*, built around his life's work—his unmatched archives, his terabytes of data, his unparalleled knowledge of the ship—and raise private funds that would dwarf Colombia's tiny research budget and allow for an excavation worthy of the site's importance, which he would direct. Since history's greatest treasure was no longer up for grabs, the philanthropists Dooley approached would stand to gain nothing but pride. Santos, who had become a close friend and was still deeply influential in Colombia's highest circles, was committed to making introductions. It was a long shot, but so was finding the *San José* in the first place. "I'm never going to give up, as long as I'm alive," he said.

Dooley was so fixated on this objective that he couldn't appreciate that he had already accomplished the ambition of his life when he discovered the wreck. As soon as he did, he set a new goal. As every sailor knows, the horizon never gets any closer.

"For me, he is the example of a great man," said Vice Admiral León, the leader of the navy's *San José* project, who witnessed the moment in 2015 when Dooley and Kozak realized they had found the galleon. "Somebody that made his dream true at the age of seventy—I'm not talking about his history, his past." León was careful to specify that he was speaking "as a person," rather than as a representative of the navy or the government, "because if I say in Colombia that I admire Roger Dooley, they'll say, 'Ah, you're another treasure hunter.'" But he couldn't lie: Dooley had profoundly affected him as "a man that made a dream possible by working all his life," he said. "And that, for me, is maybe the best example of the kind of life that we should all try to live, as long as we have air in our lungs."

IN MAY 2024, the week of the press conference in which Correa announced the launching of the latest phase of the galleon project, Dooley was just a mile or so away, meeting with one of Cartagena's wealthiest men to sell him on the idea of his *San José* foundation. Other meetings would follow, with other rich men, including the esteemed naval historian Rodolfo Segovia, who had served on the Commission of Shipwrecked Antiquities and had made a fortune as head of the Colombian oil company Ecopetrol. Segovia was won over, and within the year, he and Dooley would officially create the Fundación *San José*.

La cara del santo hace el milagro.

The foundation, Dooley had explained in his pitch, would provide the financing and the content for the world-class museum that the government had teased but could never deliver. Cartagena had long contented itself with being one of the most beautiful cities in the world. Its cultural institutions, by most accounts, failed to reflect the richness of its history. A museum of the kind Dooley envisioned—involving both centuries-old artifacts and the latest narrative technology, including virtual reality—would be a boon to Cartagena, giving visitors a reason to stay an extra day for an experience of wonder that did justice to the time-scrambling imagination of the city's most famous writer,

Gabriel García Márquez. Dooley became giddy when he described his vision for the institution. It would display fairy-tale riches alongside objects that could properly tell the story of the *San José*, of the Indies fleet, of the Spanish Empire, of the origins of the global economy, of the conquerors and the conquered, of their descendants who thrive and suffer today. President Petro had offhandedly told Dooley he would be that future museum's director, and Dooley—forever straddling the line between optimism and naivete—believed him. He could already see the museum, with a restaurant on its top floor serving modern riffs on galleon food, with waiters in period costume. He even had a spot picked out for the building, on an empty lot just beyond the sixteenth-century fortifications that had withstood so many attacks and that still stand today as reminders that the struggles of the past dictate those of the present.

The overlap of the centuries was apparent on a boat trip I took with Dooley that rainy week in May 2024, tracing in reverse the final leg of the journey that the *San José* was meant to make on June 8, 1708, before Commodore Wager intercepted it. From the Bay of Cartagena, near where the galleons were meant to anchor, we motored out of Boca Chica, between the twin forts that had once guarded the harbor. The skipper on the flybridge above our heads pushed the throttle forward and we jetted off in open waters toward Isla del Tesoro, the all-important turning point that the *capitana* never reached. I looked over my shoulder at the same shoreline that both Wager and Casa Alegre had gazed upon more than three hundred years before. Beneath La Popa, the monastery-topped hill that served as the principal landmark for the English and the Spanish, skyscrapers now coexisted with the ramparts and turrets that those men had spied.

Past and present merged in Dooley as well. Back on the water, as the boat sped against the current of time, he became young again, refreshed by the sea air. At nearly eighty, imbued with new vigor, his long hair flying, the archaeologist stepped on the rain-slicked gunwale and swung around to the side of the boat. Rung by rung he climbed the ladder to the flybridge, the vessel going so fast it was practically bouncing across the water. His foot slipped on the top rung and he barely caught himself. Those watching from the lower deck—including his wife, Ernesto Montenegro, and a small documentary crew—clutched their chests and shouted at him to come back down, but he either didn't hear them over the sound of the motor or didn't care. He wanted to be at the helm beside the captain, and he wanted a better view of the horizon.

Acknowledgments

From the first attempts to locate the *San José,* in the late 1970s, the saga of the lost *capitana* has been clouded in secrecy. Once President Juan Manuel Santos declared the matter to be classified, the veil enshrouding the galleon became even more opaque. Neither the Colombian government nor the Woods Hole Oceanographic Institute nor Maritime Archaeology Consultants would speak about the issue. My deepest thanks go to the man who broke the silence, and without whom the golden galleon would never have been found. Throughout our innumerable conversations over four years, Roger Dooley answered every question I had, albeit in his roundabout, befuddling way. He made no attempt to steer the narrative, even as I'd made it clear that my characterization of him would be warts-and-all. I am honored that he trusted me to tell his full story. "Write whatever you want about me," he told me, insisting only that I get the technical and historical details of the *San José* right. "I know where you live," he added. He was joking. I think. His passion, tenacity, and resilience are models for us all, as is his pathological optimism. And I have been touched by the warmth extended to me by his family, including his wife, Adriana, and daughters, Lili and Betty.

Journalism has a momentum of its own. Once Dooley started talking to me, other knowledgeable sources emerged, some with Dooley's encouragement, some to make sure their opposing perspectives were represented. I'm grateful to all of them, including former president Juan Manuel Santos; Ernesto Montenegro; Mike Purcell, Rob Munier, and Jeff Kaeli of Woods Hole; Daniel De Narváez; Alejandro Mirabal; Carlos and Jorge Andrade; Steve Ziskind; Carla Rahn Phillips; Burt Webber, Mensun Bound; Jim Sinclair; Carl Allen; Sean Kingsley; Jim Delgado; and the ever-gracious *San José* expert Rodolfo Segovia, whom I'm thankful to have had the privilege to meet before his death in the summer of 2025.

I'm also grateful for my earliest conversations with critics of the MAC project, a loose alliance that included the journalist Jesús García Calero, the veterans of Glocca Morra and Sea Search Armada, the archaeologist Juan Guillermo Martín Rincón, and the historian and watchdog Francisco Muñoz.

Gathering the material from archives around the world required the help of several people, including Isaac Muk, Willem Marx, Laure Bjawi-Levine, and Javier de Solis, the eleventh count of Casa Alegre. I'm also indebted to the research and fact-checking prowess of CB Owens, whose commitment to leaving no sentence unverified—combined with his immense curiosity—led him to entertainingly esoteric lengths. Along the way, I benefited greatly from the help of friends and colleagues, among them Scott Anderson, Juan Camilo Agudelo, Ash Barhamand, Brett Berk, and Donna Barnett. Toward the end of my reporting, I had the pleasure of joining forces with the team at Explora Films—notably Mariana Lloreda and Mauricio Velez—whose immense generosity has extended beyond our professional partnership.

When I first became interested enough in a publishing career to read the acknowledgments, I often wondered how so many people could have meaningfully contributed to a work signed by only one name. As I struggle to keep my thanks to these few pages, I understand how foolish I was. My closest and most valued collaborator throughout the five years it took me to write *Neptune's Fortune* was, once again, my devoted editor, Kevin Doughten, who over the course of two books has taught me the hidden mechanics of story and pushed me to always probe deeper into character. From a common love of *Indiana Jones* and classic Blue Note records, a deep literary bond was born; whatever I will write until my final word will bear his influence. My thanks extend to the whole Crown team, particularly Gillian Blake, Gwyneth Stansfield, Chantelle Walker, Julie Cepler, and the indefatigable Jess Scott. I owe this book—hell, my career—to the unwavering support and sage guidance of my friend and agent, Todd Shuster, as well as his Aevitas colleagues Allison Warren, Erin Files, Jack Haug, Anna Shumway, and Mags Chmielarczyk. There's no harder-working group of representatives out there. I also thank my colleagues at *The Hollywood Reporter*—including Dave Katz, Nekesa Moody, and Maer Roshan—for giving me the freedom to indulge my fascination with a three-hundred-year-old shipwreck.

There would have been no book to speak of had my dear former colleague and current editor at *Vanity Fair* Claire Howorth not assigned (and masterfully edited) my initial feature on the topic, which was published in early 2022.

Going back further, I would likely not be a writer today had my father and grandfather, both authors and journalists named Thomas Sancton, not blazed the path before me. My mother, Sylvaine, meanwhile, showed me by example the importance of reading extensively and critically, and greatly improved the manuscript with her suggestions. Finally, my greatest support system, my beating heart, has been my family: my partner, Jessica; our daughters, Maya and Leila; and our dogs, Suki and Violet. Everything I do is for them.

A Note on Sources

After publishing my first book, about a madness-plagued Antarctic expedition, in 2021, I told myself I would not write another harrowing sea story. But the thought of the *San José* would not leave me alone since I'd first read about it in the news. Out of curiosity, I looked up what happened with the shipwreck. It had been more than five years since the announcement of the find; surely the ship and its fabled treasure had been excavated by then, I thought. I soon learned that the gold and silver were still firmly in Neptune's clutches and that the disputes that had kept it out of reach showed no sign of abating. Suggestions that the treasure was cursed didn't sound so wild.

In reporting on the saga, beginning with a feature article for *Vanity Fair,* I interviewed characters from every side of the story, including Colombian and Spanish politicians, maritime law specialists, treasure hunters, historians, archaeologists, the Sea Search Armada team, and, of course, Roger Dooley, whose story struck me as by far the most poignant. Realizing that I'd only skimmed the surface with the magazine article, I relented: I would have to write another boat book. It was simply too good a tale.

As a reporter, I was wary of putting too much faith in Dooley, whose eccentricity and outlandish backstory raised a panoply of red flags. In addition to his odd and disorienting manner of speaking, he was nearly eighty years old, and though he displayed the energy and mental acuity of a much younger man, memories that old are never fully reliable. (Example: He insisted that two important speeches Fidel Castro gave a year apart took place on the same day. While Dooley did evidently attend both, he seemed to have conflated them in his memory.) What little archival trace he might have left in Cuba remained largely inaccessible—or had gone up in flames when, as he claimed, his ex-wife had burned his papers in a fit of rage.

My strategy to uncover the truth, and the story-enriching details, was that of the most successful treasure hunters: patience. I would have him tell his story over and over again and confront him with any discrepancies and contradictions that emerged. Over four years and more than two hundred hours of interviews, these became ever rarer. The more we spoke, the more I believed him. I also consulted Dooley's essays about diving and archaeology, notably for *Mar y Pesca* magazine and for a 1978 compendium titled *Cuba arqueológica*.

Unsatisfied with relying so heavily on one man's account, however, I sought corroboration from a wide range of sources. I was able to check his story against the recollections of friends, family, colleagues, and contemporaries. His influential role as a pioneer of diving and maritime archaeology in Cuba was widely confirmed, including by Metropolitan Museum of Art conservator Roger Arrazcaeta; Carisub veterans, such as Alejandro Mirabal and Carlos Alberto Hernandez; and the Office of the Historian of Havana.

My portrait of Dooley was informed in its nuances by the published and unpublished writings of journalist and political scientist Richard Fagen, who dove with him several times in Cuba and kept detailed and amusing notes of their encounters, archived among his papers at Stanford University. To fill out the texture and historical context of Cuba at the time, I relied on several in-depth secondary accounts, notably the magisterial *Che Guevara,* by Jon Lee Anderson; *Fidel Castro,* by Robert F. Quirk; and *Havana Nocturne,* T. J. English's wonderful chronicle of the decadent gangsterism of the Batista regime's final years.

Some of the dialogue from Dooley's life—such as his recalled conversations with his brother, Michael, or his Carisub boss Vicente La Guardia, both of whom are dead—is taken from my interviews with him, amalgamations of every version he has told me. Aside from those, everything between quotes throughout the book is transferred verbatim from a primary source or an interview.

While looking into Dooley's stint as a field archaeologist on the *Santa Margarita* site in Rota in the early 2000s, I spoke with crew from the IOTA partners team and drew from maritime archaeologist Aleck Danielle Tan's thoroughly researched master's thesis about the project, submitted at East Carolina University in 2000 and titled, "Manila Galleons in the Commonwealth of the Northern Mariana Islands: An Analysis of the Cultural Impacts on *Santa Margarita* and *Nuestra Señora de la Concepción.*"

When Dooley embarked on the 2015 search for the wreck of the *San José* off Cartagena, he was so convinced of its imminent success that he hired filmmaker Adam Geiger to document the process. Geiger was also on hand to film the 2016 survey of the site aboard the *Seabed Prince.* The hours of unedited footage he shared with me were a nonfiction writer's godsend, yielding a bounty of quotes and details and effectively making me a fly on the wall.

Nearly every major figure involved in those expeditions agreed to speak with me, including the team from the Woods Hole Oceanographic Institute, representatives from the Colombian Navy, ICANH, and Dimar, and former president Juan Manuel Santos, who met me in his office in Bogotá, underneath a painting of himself, with a bust of himself in the corner. I also spoke with members of the two administrations that succeeded his, under presidents Iván Duque and Gustavo Petro.

For all the breathless reporting in major global outlets immediately following the discovery, only a handful of assiduous journalists— mainly in Colombia and Spain—stayed on the story in the months and years that followed. I owe them all a debt, in particular the Spanish investigative reporter Jesús García Calero of *Diario ABC*. I'm also grateful for the relentless efforts of Francisco Muñoz, Colombia's self-appointed national overseer of underwater heritage, to bring government documents to light. He did all *San José* obsessives a great service by publishing many of these files in his two-volume study of the saga, *Galeón Señor San José* and *La Emboscada*.

For the chapters on Glocca Morra/Sea Search Armada, I spoke with director Jack Harbeston and several of his associates, as well as the surviving crew of their various search expeditions, including aboard the mesoscaphe *Auguste Piccard*. Since the initiation of Sea Search Armada's case against the Colombian government before the Permanent Court of Arbitration at the Hague, however, the SSA team has gone silent and has declined to answer queries by both me and my dogged fact-checker on this book, CB Owens.

I made multiple requests, to various members of the team, to see the supposed video evidence of the anomaly SSA claimed to be the wreck of the *San José* but was told that the tapes had gone astray. Yet select clips appear in a friendly YouTube interview with Francisco Muñoz. One shows an iron cannon, another reveals what appears to be a woodpile, but none of what I've seen shows clear evidence of a wreck or a large man-made object beneath the coral.

I approached this book as both a journalist and a historian, with one foot planted in the twenty-first century and the other in colonial times. At the General Archive of the Indies, in Seville, I consulted many of the same three-hundred-year-old documents that guided Dooley's quest for the *San José*. (To my disappointment, the reading room is no longer in the grand vaulted edifice where Dooley did so much of his research but in a far less picturesque building across the street. An intimidatingly burly security guard watched on suspiciously, ready to prevent me from absconding with archival material, as one treasure hunter supposedly did years ago.)

It was not the practice of the Spanish fleet in the early eighteenth century to keep detailed logs of every journey the way it was for the

English. But following the disastrous loss of the San José, the governor in Cartagena summoned testimonies from more than a dozen witnesses, which today are filed at the archive in perhaps the most important *legajo* for those seeking to learn about the last days of the *San José:* INDIFERENTE, 2609. Among those testifying were Miguel Agustín de Villanueva, captain of the galleon *San Joaquín,* Nicolás de la Rosa, Count of Vega Florida and captain of the *gobierno;* José Canis, captain of the hulk known as the "urca de Nieto"; Esteban de Trave, his second in command; José de Zúñiga, governor of Cartagena; Pedro de Medranda, general of the South Sea Armada; Judge Francisco de Medina; and several passengers bound for Cartagena.

Once I learned to decipher the handwriting, the puzzling contractions, and the strange run-on syntax, these detailed and dramatic accounts allowed me to re-create the battle in all its chaos. Their stories did not always match and were occasionally in outright contradiction. It's worth noting that each declarant was keen to avoid or deflect blame for the tragedy that occurred. I accorded more weight to witnesses closer to the action, such as Judge Medina, who saw the galleon burn from a few ships' lengths away, than to, say, Admiral Villanueva of the *San Joaquín,* who was nowhere to be seen when the *capitana* and the *gobierno* were under attack.

The man whose impressions of the battle I most wished to relate— Don José Fernández de Santillán, the Count of Casa Alegre—never got a chance to record them. My portrait of him was drawn from letters preserved in the Indies archive, as well as the family papers of Javier de Solis, the eleventh Count of Casa Alegre, who kindly shared them with me.

I would have been at a loss to find my way through the byzantine Spanish archives had trails not been blazed by diligent researchers like Dooley, Rodolfo Segovia, and Carla Rahn Phillips, whose 2007 book *The Treasure of the San José* is the basis for much of the current scholarship on the galleon. English accounts of the battle were simpler to track down. The logs of the *Expedition, Portland, Kingston,* and *Vulture*—as well as the records of the court martial of the captains of the *Portland*

and *Kingston* for having let the *San Joaquín* escape to Cartagena—are easily accessible at the National Archives in London's Kew Gardens. Commodore Wager's diary is held at the National Maritime Museum in Greenwich. Details about Wager's early life are harder to come by, and even harder to fully believe, and the perhaps apocryphal story I cite about his teenage derring-do comes from the anonymously written nineteenth-century compendium *Thrilling Narratives of Mutiny, Murder and Piracy: A Weird Series of Tales of Shipwreck and Disaster.* (It may yield another book idea or two.)

My disquisition on galleons and their evolution owes much to the late Spanish historian Fernando Serrano Mangas. As much as I depended on such secondary sources, I turned whenever possible to primary accounts from the age of galleons. Many of these make for delicious reading still today. Eugenio Salazar's humorous description of shipboard life achieves the rare feat of provoking genuine laughter across centuries. Jorge Juan and Antonio de Ulloa's *A Voyage to South America* (published in Spain in 1748), from which I extracted several key details in my description of the Portobelo fair, is rightly considered among the best travelogues ever written. And Bartolomé Arzáns de Orsúa y Vela's harrowing *History of Potosí* remains an invaluable document of the exploitation and suffering that fed Spain's hunger for silver.

Any study of colonial Spanish coinage in the New World must recognize the work of historian Glenn Murray, who has dedicated much of his career to cataloguing the output of the empire's major mints on the Spanish main. For a more metaphysical inquest into the lure of the noble metals, *The Magic of Gold,* by Jenifer Marx, proved a useful and delightfully written secondary source, though the author shares some of the sensationalist tendencies of her husband, Robert Marx.

Marx and his treasure-hunting colleagues left a voluminous record of books and interviews. I drew from these to shape my characterization of the men Dooley refers to as the Big Five, supplementing their often self-mythologizing accounts with contemporary news reports and interviews with former collaborators.

To get into the mindset of a shipwreck obsessive, I got certified in scuba diving. (I took a course at a pool in Yonkers, New York, a far cry from the warm and limpid Caribbean waters that enchanted the Big Five and Roger Dooley.) The experience helped deepen my understanding of the discipline, but I don't think I'll be discovering treasure anytime soon. I had hoped to dive on the wreck of the *Cristobal Colón,* the nineteenth-century Spanish cruiser that Dooley discovered in Cuba's Oriente province in the 1970s. But it was made clear to me that the site was too challenging for a novice. I also thought seeing the *San José* with my own eyes would have made a terrific scene in this book, but nobody, not even Dooley, has had that privilege, since at 600-plus meters it is too deep to reach on air tanks. Yet Dooley is not letting that keep him from his beloved *capitana.* For several years, he has been endeavoring to marshal a small submarine to take him to the wreck site. He now has the equipment lined up, and all he needs is the permission. I would not be surprised if it happens. But even if it does, there will surely be another dream to replace that one, and deeper to dive into the story of the *San José.*

Bibliography

ARCHIVAL COLLECTIONS

Archivo General de Indias. Seville, Spain
The National Archives. London, UK
The British Library. London, UK
The Library of Congress. Washington, DC
Roger Dooley collection. Pereira, Colombia
National Maritime Museum. Greenwich, UK
Archival Collections at Stanford University. Stanford, California

BOOKS AND ARTICLES

Acosta, José de. *Historia natural y moral de las Indias.* Valencia: Valencia Cultural, 1977.

Aiton, Arthur S., and J. Lloyd Mecham. "The Archivo General de Indias." *The Hispanic American Historical Review,* vol. 4, no. 3 (1921), pp. 553–67. Baltimore: Williams and Wilkins Company, 1921.

Alsedo y Herrera, Dionisio de. *Aviso histórico, político y geográfico con las noticias más particulares del Perú, Tierra Firme, Chile y Nuevo Reyno de Granada.* Madrid: D. M. Peraltade, 1740.

———. *Memorial informativo, que pusieron en las reales manos del Rey . . . el Tribunal del Consulado de la Ciudad de los Reyes, y la Junta General del Comercio de las provincias del Perú.* Lima, 1725.

Anderson, Jon Lee. *Che Guevara: A Revolutionary Life.* New York: Grove Press, 1997.

Anonymous. *Thrilling Narratives of Mutiny, Murder and Piracy.* New York: Hurst & Co. [date unknown].

Apestegui Cardenal, Cruz. *Los ladrones del mar: Piratas en el Caribe—corsarios, filibusteros y bucaneros, 1493–1700.* Barcelona: Lunwerg, 2000.

Arana Salazar, Mario. "El rescate de un patrimonio económico y cultural, el Galeón San José." Bogotá: Facultad de Estudios a Distancia, 2014.

Ariza, Daniela Vargas, et al. "The Cobs in the Archaeological Context of the San José Galleon Shipwreck." *Antiquity,* published online by Cambridge University Press, June 10, 2025.

Armstrong, T. L. *A Master on the Spanish Main.* Independently published, 2019.

Bass, George F., ed. *Beneath the Seven Seas: Adventures with the Institute of Nautical Archaeology.* London: Thames & Hudson, 2005.

Bendeck Olivella, Jorge. *El galeón perdido.* Bogotá: Villegas, 2003.

Bethell, Leslie, ed. *The Cambridge History of Latin America.* Cambridge: Cambridge University Press, 1984.

Bonifacio, Claudio. *Galleons and Sunken Treasure.* CreateSpace, 2010.

Bound, Mensun. *The Ship Beneath the Ice: The Discovery of Shackleton's "Endurance."* New York: Mariner, 2022.

Burchett, Josiah. *A Complete History of the Most Remarkable Transactions of Sea, from the Earliest Accounts of Time to the Conclusion of the Last War with France.* London: W.B., 1720.

Burgess, Robert Forrest. *Sunken Treasure: Six Who Found Fortunes.* New York: Dodd, Mead & Co., 1988.

Casey, Susan. *The Underworld: Journeys to the Depths of the Ocean.* New York: Doubleday, 2023.

Castillo Mathieu, Nicolás del. *La llave de las Indias.* Bogotá: Ediciones del Tiempo, 1981.

Chellel, Kit. "Lord of the Deep." *Bloomberg Businessweek,* Nov. 16, 2023.

Clowes, W. Laird. *The Royal Navy: A History from the Earliest Times to the Present.* London: Chatham, 1996.

Coxe, William. *Memoirs of the Life and Administration of Sir Robert Walpole, Earl of Orford.* London, 1798.

Cuartel, General de la Armada, ed. *Historia de la Armada: Páginas de la historia de España escritas en la mar.* Madrid: Ministerio de Defensa, 2023.

Cullen, Vicky. *Down to the Sea for Science: 75 Years of Ocean Research, Education, and Exploration at the Woods Hole Oceanographic Institution.* Woods Hole, Mass.: Woods Hole Oceanographic Institution, 2005.

Defoe, Daniel. *An Essay Upon Projects.* New York: Cassell & Company, 1888.

Diamond, Jared. *Guns, Germs, and Steel: The Fates of Human Societies.* New York: W. W. Norton, 1997.

Dooley, Roger E. "Desarrollo de la arqueología subacuática en la provincia de Oriente." *Cuba arqueológica.* Santiago de Cuba: Editorial Oriente, 1979.

———. "El blacao: Un serio peligro durante el buceo." *Mar y pesca,* Havana.

————. "Tras las huellas del hombre en el mar . . ." *Mar y pesca,* June 1974, Havana.

————. "Vivendas submarinas." *Mar y pesca,* Havana.

Dooley, Roger E., and Alfonso Silva Lee. *Coral Reefs of the Caribbean, the Bahamas, and Florida.* London: Macmillan Caribbean, 2007.

Driver, Marjorie G. *The Account of Fray Juan Pobre's Residence in the Marianas, 1602.* Guam: Micronesian Area Research Center, University of Guam, 1989.

Earle, Peter. *Treasure Hunt: Shipwreck, Diving, and the Quest for Treasure in an Age of Heroes.* New York: Thomas Dunne/St. Martin's Press, 2008.

————. *The Treasure of the Concepción: The Wreck of the Almiranta.* New York: Viking Press, 1980.

English, T. J. *Havana Nocturne: How the Mob Owned Cuba . . . and Then Lost It to the Revolution.* New York: William Morrow, 2008.

Escobar Sierra, Hugo. *Misterios en el rescate del Galeón "San José": Graves denuncias en el Senado de la República.* Bogotá: Corporación Renovar, 1988.

Exquemelin, A. O. *The Pirates of Panama.* New York: Frederick A. Stokes, 1928.

Fernández Duro, Cesáreo. *Disquisiciones nauticas: Por el capitan de navio Cesáreo Fernandez Duro.* Madrid: Impr. de Aribau y c.a., 1876.

Fontaine Ortiz, Elvin. *Fidel y la guerra desconocida.* Havana: Editora Política, 2014.

Gage, Thomas. *Thomas Gage's Travels in the New World.* Westport, Conn.: Greenwood Press, 1981.

García del Pino, César, and Francisco Escobar Guio. "Almiranta 'Nuestra Señora de las Mercedes': Naufragio," *Revista de arqueología,* vol. 24, no. 262, (2003), pp. 54–59.

Grissim, John. *The Lost Treasure of the Concepción: The Story of One of the World's Greatest Treasure Finds and Burt Webber—the Man Who Never Gave Up.* New York: Morrow, 1980.

Hanke, Lewis. *Bartolomé Arzáns de Orsúa y Vela's History of Potosí.* Providence: Brown University Press, 1965.

Haring, Clarence Henry. *The Spanish Empire in America.* San Diego: Harcourt Brace Jovanovich, 1947.

————. *Trade and Navigation Between Spain and the Indies in the Time of the Hapsburgs.* Cambridge, Mass.: Harvard University Press, 1918.

Hastings, Max. *The Abyss: Nuclear Crisis Cuba 1962.* New York: Harper, 2022.

Hernandez-Díaz, Concepción. "Asistencia espiritual en las flotas de Indias." *Actas de las IX Jornadas de Andalucía y América: Andalucía, América y el mar.* Seville: University of Seville, 1989.

Hernández Oliva, Carlos. *Naufragios: Barcos españoles en aguas de Cuba.* Seville: Renacimiento, 2009.

Hormaechea, Cayetano, Isidro Rivera, and Manuel Derqui. *Los galeones españoles del siglo XVII* (2 volumes). Barcelona: Associació d'Amics del Museu Marítim de Barcelona, 2012.

Horner, David. *The Treasure Galleons: Clues to Millions in Sunken Gold and Silver.* New York: Dodd Mead, 1971.

Kamen, Henry. *The War of Succession in Spain, 1700–15.* London: Weidenfeld & Nicolson, 1969.

Kinder, Gary. *Ship of Gold in the Deep Blue Sea*. New York: Atlantic Monthly Press, 1998.

La aventura del Guadalupe: Su viaje a La Española y su hundimiento en la Bahía de Samaná. Barcelona: Lunwerg, 1997.

La Guardia, Ileana de. *Au nom de mon père*. Paris: Denoël, 2001.

Lane, Kris E. *Potosí: The Silver City That Changed the World*. Oakland: University of California Press, 2019.

López de Gómara, Francisco. *Cortés, The Life of the Conqueror*. Translated and edited by Lesley Byrd Simpson. Berkeley and Los Angeles: University of California Press, 1966.

Lyon, Eugene. *The Search for the Atocha*. New York: Harper & Row, 1979.

Marx, Jenifer. *The Magic of Gold*. Garden City, N.Y.: Doubleday, 1978.

Marx, Robert F. *Quest for Treasure: The True Story of Robert Marx's Unrelenting Struggle Against Storms, Sharks, Political Intrigue, and Modern-Day Pirates in His Effort to Recover This Lost 1656 King's Treasure*. Dallas: Ram Books, 1982.

———. *Shipwrecks of the Western Hemisphere: 1492–1825*. New York: World Pub Co., 1971.

Mather, Cotton. The Life of Sir William Phips. New York: Covici-Friede, 1929.

Mathewson, R. Duncan, III. *Archaeological Treasure: The Search for Nuestra Señora de Atocha*. Woodstock, Conn.: Seafarers Heritage Library, 1983.

———. *Treasure of the Atocha*. New York: Pisces, 1986.

Meisel Roca, Adolfo, and María Teresa Ramírez, eds. *La economía colonial de la Nueva Granada*. Bogotá: Banco de la República, 2015.

Mirabal, Alejandro. *"Reporte arqueológico sobre el pecio CDH-004 (Identificado como Nuestra Señora de las Mercedes, 1698)."* Unpublished.

Muckleroy, Keith. *Maritime Archaeology*. Cambridge: Cambridge University Press, 1978.

Muñoz Atuesta, Francisco Hernando. *Galeón Señor San José*. Bogotá: independently published, 2019.

———. *Galeón Señor San José, Tomo II: La Emboscada*. Bogotá: independently published, 2023.

Muñoz y Rivero, Jesús. *Manual de paleografía diplomática española de los siglos XII al XVII*. Madrid: Impr. de Moreno y Rojas, 1880.

Murray, Stephen Murray. *Guía de las cantidades acuñadas cecas de Potosí y Lima*. Segovia: Amigos de la casa de la moneda de Segovia, 2016.

Notario López, Ignacio, and Iván Notario López. *The Spanish Tercios, 1536–1704*. Oxford, UK: Osprey, 2012.

Obregón, Mauricio. *De cóndores y sirenas: Memorias de un aventurero ilustrado*. Bogotá: Villegas, 2004.

Olaya, Vicente G. *La costurera que encontró un tesoro cuando fue a hacer pis: Y otras historias de la arqueología en españa*. Barcelona: Espasa, 2021.

Oppenheimer, Andres. *Castro's Final Hour*. New York: Simon & Schuster, 1993.

Padilla, Nelson Freddy. *El galeón San José y otros tesoros*. Bogotá: Penguin Random House Grupo Editorial, 2016.

Pepys, Samuel. *Memoirs of Samuel Pepys*. London: H. Colburn, 1825.

Pérez Galdós, Benito. *Trafalgar: A Tale.* New York: W. S. Gottsberger, 1884.

Perrottet, Tony. *Cuba Libre!: Che, Fidel, and the Improbable Revolution That Changed World History.* New York: Blue Rider Press, 2019.

Phillips, Carla Rahn. "The Galleon San Jose, Treasure Ship of the Spanish Indies." *Mariner's Mirror,* vol. 77, no 4. (November 1991), pp. 353–63.

———. "The Sinking of the Galleon *San José* on 8 June 1708: An Exercise in Historical Detective Work." *Mariner's Mirror,* vol. 94, no. 2. (May 2008), pp. 175–86.

———. *Six Galleons for the King of Spain.* Baltimore: Johns Hopkins University Press, 1986.

———. *The Treasure of the San José: Death at Sea in the War of Spanish Succession.* Baltimore: Johns Hopkins University Press, 2007.

Pointis, Jean-Bernard-Louis Desjean, Baron de. *Relation de l'expédition de Carthagène faite par les François en 1697.* Amsterdam: Chez les Héritiers d'Antoine Schelte, 1698.

Polo, Marco. *The Travels of Marco Polo.* New York: Barnes & Noble, 2005.

Pope, Frank. *Dragon Sea: A True Tale of Treasure, Archeology, and Greed off the Coast of Vietnam.* Orlando, Fla.: Harcourt, 2007.

Potter, John S. *The Treasure Diver's Guide.* Garden City, N.Y.: Doubleday; 1960, 1972.

Prieto, Carlos. *La minería en el Nuevo Mundo.* Madrid: Revista de Occidente, 1968.

Prott, Lyndel V., and Ieng Srong, eds. *Background Materials on the Protection of the Underwater Cultural Heritage.* Paris and Bournemouth, UK: UNESCO/Nautical Archaeology Society, 1990, pp. 179–83.

Quesada, Alejandro de. *The Bay of Pigs: Cuba 1961.* Oxford, UK: Osprey, 2009.

Quirk, Robert E. *Fidel Castro.* New York: Norton, 1993.

Ratcliffe, John E. "Bells, Barrels and Bullion: Diving and Salvage in the Atlantic World, 1500 to 1800." *Nautical Research Journal,* vol. 56, no. 1 (Spring 2011), pp. 34–56.

Ribot García, Luis Antonia, and Luigi de Rosa, eds. *Naves, puertos e itinerarios marítimos en la época moderna.* Madrid: Actas, 2003.

Rieseberg, Harry E. *I Dive for Treasure.* New York, National Travel Club, 1942.

Romans, Bernard. *Concise Natural History of East and West Florida.* New York, 1775.

Salazar, Eugenio de. *Seafaring in the Sixteenth Century: The Letter of Eugenio de Salazar, 1573.* San Francisco: Mellen Research University Press, 1991.

Segovia Salas, Rodolfo. *Del galeón San José y otras historias.* Bogotá: El Áncora Editores, 2019.

Serrano Mangas, Fernando. *Función y evolución del galeón en la Carrera de Indias.* Madrid: MAPFRE, 1992.

———. *Los galeones de la carrera de Indias, 1650–1700.* Seville: Escuela de Estudios Hispano-Americanos de Sevilla, Consejo Superior de Investigaciones Científicas, 1985.

Shrieberg, David, and Cecilia Rodríguez. "Three Centuries of Greed." *San Jose Mercury News West Magazine,* January 29, 1989.

Søreide, Fredrik. *Ships from the Deep: Deepwater Archaeology.* College Station, Tex.: Texas A&M University Press, 2011.

Soule, Emily Berquist. *The Bishop's Utopia: Envisioning Improvement in Colonial Peru.* Philadelphia: University of Pennsylvania Press, 2014.

Tan, Aleck Danielle. "Manila Galleons in the Commonwealth of the Northern Mariana Islands: An Analysis of the Cultural Impacts on *Santa Margarita* and *Nuestra Señora de la Concepción.*" Master's thesis submitted at East Carolina University, 2020.

Thacher, John Boyd. *Christopher Columbus: His Life, His Work, His Remains as Revealed by Original Printed and Manuscript Records.* New York: G. P. Putnam's Sons, 1903.

Thomas, David A. *Battles and Honours of the Royal Navy.* Barnsley, UK: Leo Cooper, 1998.

Throckmorton, Peter. "The World's Worst Investment: The Economics of Treasure Hunting with Real Life Comparisons." In *Underwater Archaeology Proceedings from the Society for Historical Archaeology,* edited by Toni L. Carrell. Pleasant Hill, Calif.: Society for Historical Archaeology, 1990, pp. 6–10.

Tippin, G. Lee, and Herbert Humphreys, Jr. *In Search of the Golden Madonna: The Treasure Finders of the RV Beacon.* Canton, Ohio: Daring Pub. Group, 1989.

Tucker, Wendy. *Today's the Day! The Mel Fisher Story.* New York: Brick Tower Press, 2022.

Ulloa, Antonio de. *Voyage to South America.* London: L. Davis and C. Reymer, 1758.

UNESCO. *Underwater Archaeology: A Nascent Discipline.* Paris: UNESCO, 1972.

Vicente Maroto, M. I. *Diálogo entre un vizcayno y un montañés sobre la fábrica de navíos.* Salamanca: Ediciones Universidad de Salamanca, 1998.

Vila Vilar, Enriqueta. "Las ferias de Portobelo: Apariencia y realidad del comercio con Indias." *Anuario de Estudios Americanos,* vol. 39 (1982), pp. 275–340.

Volker, Roy, and Dick Richmond. *In the Wake of the Golden Galleons.* St. Louis: OroQuest Press, 1976.

Wagner, Kip, and L. B. Taylor, Jr. *Pieces of Eight: Recovering the Riches of a Lost Spanish Treasure Fleet.* New York: Dutton, 1966.

Weller, Robert. *Galleon Hunt.* West Palm Beach, Fla.: Treasure Brokers, 1992.

Index

ABOUT THE AUTHOR

■ ■ ■

JULIAN SANCTON is a writer and editor whose work has appeared in *Vanity Fair, Esquire, GQ, The New Yorker, Departures,* and *Playboy,* among other publications. He has reported from every continent, including Antarctica, which he first visited while researching his previous book *Madhouse at the End of the Earth.* He lives in Larchmont, New York, with his partner, Jessica, and their two daughters.